AF870620

Urban Development in the Margins of a World Heritage Site

International Institute for Asian Studies

Publications

The International Institute for Asian Studies (IIAS) is a research and exchange platform based in Leiden, the Netherlands. Its objective is to encourage the interdisciplinary and comparative study of Asia and to promote (inter)national cooperation. IIAS focuses on the humanities and social sciences and on their interaction with other sciences. It stimulates scholarship on Asia and is instrumental in forging research networks among Asia Scholars. Its main research interests are reflected in the three book series published with Amsterdam University Press: Global Asia, Asian Heritages and Asian Cities.

IIAS acts as an international mediator, bringing together various parties in Asia and other parts of the world. The Institute works as a clearinghouse of knowledge and information. This entails activities such as providing information services, the construction and support of international networks and cooperative projects, and the organization of seminars and conferences. In this way, IIAS functions as a window on Europe for non-European scholars and contributes to the cultural rapprochement between Europe and Asia.

IIAS Publications Officer: Paul van der Velde
IIAS Assistant Publications Officer: Mary Lynn van Dijk

Asian Cities

The Asian Cities Series explores urban cultures, societies and developments from the ancient to the contemporary city, from West Asia and the Near East to East Asia and the Pacific. The series focuses on three avenues of inquiry: evolving and competing ideas of the city across time and space; urban residents and their interactions in the production, shaping and contestation of the city; and urban challenges of the future as they relate to human well-being, the environment, heritage and public life.

Series Editor
Paul Rabé, Urban Knowledge Network Asia (UKNA) at International Institute for Asian Studies, Leiden, The Netherlands

Editorial Board
Henco Bekkering, Delft University of Technology, The Netherlands
Charles Goldblum, University of Paris 8, France
Xiaoxi Hui, Beijing University of Technology, China
Stephen Lau, University of Hong Kong, Hong Kong
Rita Padawangi, University of Social Sciences, Singapore
Parthasarathy Rengarajan, Gujarat Institute of Development Research, Gujarat, India
Neha Sami, Indian Institute of Human Settlements, Bangalore, India

Urban Development in the Margins of a World Heritage Site

In the Shadows of Angkor

Adèle Esposito

Amsterdam University Press

International Institute for Asian Studies Publications

Asian Cities 6

Cover illustration: Vat Enkosei in Siem Reap
Photo: Adèle Esposito, December 2015

Cover design: Coördesign, Leiden
Lay-out: Crius Group, Hulshout

ISBN	978 94 6298 368 7
e-ISBN	978 90 4853 405 0 (pdf)
DOI	10.5117/9789462983687
NUR	740

© Adèle Esposito / Amsterdam University Press B.V., Amsterdam 2018

All rights reserved. Without limiting the rights under copyright reserved above, no part of this book may be reproduced, stored in or introduced into a retrieval system, or transmitted, in any form or by any means (electronic, mechanical, photocopying, recording or otherwise) without the written permission of both the copyright owner and the author of the book.

Every effort has been made to obtain permission to use all copyrighted illustrations reproduced in this book. Nonetheless, whosoever believes to have rights to this material is advised to contact the publisher.

Printed by CPI Group (UK) Ltd, Croydon CR0 4YY

For Nathalie and Charles

Contents

List of figures

Abbreviations

ADHOC	Cambodian Human Rights and Development Association
AFD	Agence Française de Développement
AHA	Angkor Handicraft Association
AIMF	Association Internationale des Maires Francophones
APSARA	Authority for the Protection and Management of Angkor and the Region of Siem Reap
APUR	Atelier Parisien d'Urbanisme
ARTE	Architecture Recherche Technique Environnement
ASEAN	Association of Southeast Asian Nations
BCEOM	Bureau Central d'Etudes pour les Equipements d'Outre-Mer
CDC	Council for the Development of Cambodia
CPP	Cambodian People's Party
CSCNC	Cambodian Superior Council of National Culture
DED	Deutscher Entwicklungsdienst
EFEO	École Française d'Extrême Orient
EHESS	École des Hautes Etudes en Sciences Sociales
EIC	Economic Institute of Cambodia
ENSAPB	École Nationale Supérieure d'Architecture de Paris-Belleville
FDI	Foreign Direct Investment
FUNCIPEC	Front Uni National pour un Cambodge Indépendant, Neutre, Pacifique et Coopératif
GDP	Gross Domestic Product
GIE	Groupement d'Intérêt Economique
GIZ	Deutsche Gesellschaft für Internationale Zusammenarbeit
GTZ	Deutsche Gesellschaft für Technische Zusammenarbeit
ICC-Angkor	International Coordinating Committee for the Safeguarding and Development of the Historic Site of Angkor
ICEA	Ingénieurs Conseil & Economistes Associés
ICOMOS	International Council on Monuments and Sites
IFLA	International Federation of Landscape Architects
INALCO	Institut National des Langues et Civilisations Orientales
IPRAUS	Institut Parisien de Recherche Architecture Urbanistique Société
IUCN	International Union for the Conservation of Nature
JICA	Japanese International Cooperation Agency
KOICA	Korean International Cooperation Agency
LEAP	Livelihood Enhancement and Association of the Poor
LICADHO	Cambodian League for the Promotion and Defense of Human Rights

MDG	Millennium Development Goals
MGC	Mekong Ganga Corporation
MLMUPC	Ministry of Land Management, Urban Planning, and Construction
MoU	Memorandum of Understanding
NGO	Non-Governmental Organization
OECD	Organization for Economic Co-operation and Development
RED	Regional Economic Development Program
RUFA	Royal University of Fine Arts
SDC	Swiss Agency for Development and Cooperation
SEATO	Southeast Asia Treaty Organization
SMDP	Shoemart Development Corporation
SOCHOT	Société Cambodgienne de l'Hôtellerie et du Tourisme
UNDP	United Nations Development Program
UNESCO	United Nations Educational, Scientific, and Cultural Organization
UNTAC	United Nations Transitional Authority in Cambodia
YTL	Yeoh Tiong Lay
ZEMP	Zoning and Environmental Management Plan for the Angkor Region

Glossary of Khmer terms

Baray បារាយណ៍
Headley (1977) gives the following definitions of the term *baray/baaraay*: 1) 'a light'; 2) 'a wide or open country, a wide plain'; 3) 'a place, region, country, open spot'. More specifically, he defines the *baaraay* tik *tlaa* as an 'ancient Khmer reservoir in Siem Reap province'. However, De Bernon (1977) views this translation as problematic:

> [T]he word baray is, by the way, unknown in the epigraphic vocabulary. None of the first lexicographers [...] makes use of this term to designate a hydraulic structure. In the title block of the general map in his guide to the Angkor monuments, written in Khmer, Huot Tāt uses the transliteration *pārāy* to designate the large bodies of water enclosed by dikes that we are familiar with, but does not give any other information about them.

De Bernon goes on to explain that other authors agree on the Sanskrit origin of the term *pārāyana*. This term appears in the expression *pārāyana dik thlā* 'to designate a type of large reservoir in the Siem Reap region'. In their view, a Sanskrit word unknown in the inscriptions may have served to form a term in the regional vocabulary of Siem Reap. This might have been introduced during the period between the fall of the Angkor Kingdom in the fourteenth century and the establishment of the French protectorate (*époque moyenne*) or possibly in more recent times.

Boeung បឹង
Lake. More precisely, this word designates a trough that gives shape to a lake or a large pond fed by natural or artificial channels during the rainy season and used to store water for agricultural use during the dry season (Starkman and Blancot, 1997).

Borey បុរី
Sanskrit toponymic affix designating cities and other urban spaces. It has become a separate word in Khmer, but there is no consensus on its origins and exact meaning. For many Cambodians, the term designates the ancient Khmer capitals. For others, it is a bounded, rectangular inhabited space, sometimes surrounded by walls. A third definition associates the *borey* with ancient toponyms no longer used in Khmer. In postcolonial Cambodia the

term was used to designate residential areas or groups of public facilities. During the Vietnamese occupation, it signified public administrations and their residential estates, where public officials used to live. Since the end of the 1990s, the term has come to be used of residential developments which may include a dozen to several hundred shophouses (Fauveaud, 2014).

Chas ចាស់
Old. Term used of both objects and people.

Kaet ខេត្ត
Province, region, territory.

Kandal កណ្ដាល
Central.

Khum ឃុំ
Commune. Administrative unit established by the French protectorate in 1908, grouping several villages (*phum*) together (Delvert, 1961).

Kompong កំពង់
Harbour, port.

Kraom ក្រោម
Low, below, lower than.

Krong ក្រុង
City, town.

Leu លើ
On, above, towards.

Neak ta អ្នក តា
Divinity, expression of energy, spirit associated with a specific village community; it maintains the link between the villagers and their land, water, and ancestors.

Okhna ឧកញ៉ា / ឧក្ញា
Honorific title once granted to important Khmer dignitaries. A sub-decree resurrected it in 1994, specifying that the title would be given to those individuals who make a US$100,000 donation to the Cambodian government

and show 'an ostensible commitment to direct some of their wealth towards the greater good' (Sek and Henderson, 2014).

Phnom ភ្នំ
Mountain, hill, height.

Phsar ផ្សារ
Market place, fair.

Prasat ប្រាសាទ
Ancient temple, tower, monument, beautiful building, palace.

Prek ព្រែក
Natural or excavated channel, stream, tributary of a river, enclosed watercourses that receive water from a river; artificial breaches that link a river or a water-wheel with a source of stored water (Starkman and Blancot, 1997).

Phum ភូមិ
Village. Delvert (1961) says that this word generally designates any temporary or permanent inhabited place. According to the administrative system established by the French protectorate in 1908, a *phum* is a group of families living in houses built close to each other and recognizing the authority of a village leader.

Pteah ផ្ទះ
House.

Sala សាលា
House, building, room, school. The term is often used to designate semi-open buildings built by the roadside for travellers who want to stop and rest. With the addition of suffixes, several other terms are created: for instance, *sala kdei* (tribunal), *sala kaet* (provincial headquarters).

Sangkat សង្កាត់
Part, quarter, district, section. The term *sangkat krong* សង្កាត់ ក្រុង designates a district within a city.

Srok ស្រុក
State, region, country, royal court, nation, territorial subdivision of a province. The term is also used to designate a village or home town.

Stung ស្ទឹង
Small river, river tributary.

Teukdey ទឹកដី
Territory (from *teuk* ទឹក, water and *dey* ដី, land).

Thmey ថ្មី
New.

Tonlé ទន្លេ
This word means river (Antelme and Bru-Nut, 2001), but it is also used to refer to lakes and to the sea. In the geography of Cambodia, *Tonlé Sap* specifically indicates 1) the confluent that flows into the Mekong in Phnom Penh; 2) the Cambodian lake which is the largest freshwater resource in Southeast Asia.

Trapeang ត្រពាំង
Pond, marsh. This term is often used to designate the ponds used for water storage, which are laid out along the four points of the compass in line with Angkor cosmology (Starkman and Blancot, 1997).

Wat វត្ត
Buddhist monastery, more precisely 'the plot of land on which a monastery is located' (Headley, 1977, p. 970). This word can also designate tradition, discipline, practice, and respect.

Note on transliteration
Different transliterations of Khmer terms are available in British and American English. This book follows those that I have found most frequently in academic sources and tries to maximize the likelihood of a non-Khmer speaker's attempt to read Khmer words.

Acknowledgements

First, my thanks go to those people in Cambodia and France who have contributed their time to answer my questions, provide me with valuable documents, and guide me during my fieldwork. In particular, I would like to thank Pen Sophal, Beng Hong Socheat Khemro, and Keo Sar for being so generous with their time and attention.

The research for this book during 2006-2009 was supported by a fellowship from the French Ministère de l'Enseignement Supérieur, de la Recherche et de l'Innovation. Further fieldwork between 2010 and 2015 was made possible through funds provided by the Center for Khmer Studies, the research unit UMR-AUSser, and the Architecture School of Paris-Belleville (ENSAPB). Parts of this book were written while I was based at the International Institute for Asian Studies (IIAS, Leiden, Netherlands) as a postdoctoral fellow. My thanks go to Philippe Peycam and Willem Vogelsang for hosting me and for their faith in my competence.

I would like to thank my research department, AUSser, for the supportive academic environment it has provided for more than ten years. I believe that I have developed both as a person and as a researcher through the productive exchanges – including the conflicts – with my colleagues during this lengthy period. Particular appreciation goes to Pierre Clément for his guidance, trust, and encouragement to move beyond my limits. I will always be grateful to Nathalie Lancret for her intellectual guidance, affection, and constant presence. Another person who deserves special mention is Charles Goldblum, a wise and benevolent guide. I am also indebted to Adeline Carrier for her perceptive suggestions, to Victor T. King and Michael Herzfeld for their encouragement, to my Khmer teachers Michel Antelme and Deth Joseph Thach, and to Tim Winter as a source of inspiration. Special thanks also go Olivier Coutard for his perceptive comments on parts of this book. Thanks to Virginie Morellec, Dato Tarielashvili, and Sebastien Preuil for allowing me to use some of their photographs, and to Clément Musil for drawing the maps that illustrate this book. Thanks also to my copyeditor, Linda Gardiner, who went through several drafts of this work and enabled me to complete the book in good time. Thanks to Paul Rabé, the Asian Cities Series Editor; to Paul van de Velde and Mary Lynn van Dijk of the IIAS publications team, and to Saskia Gieling and Jaap Wagenaar at Amsterdam University Press. I also extend my appreciation to the three anonymous referees for their comments, which helped me to improve the work.

Without my parents I would not be the person and the researcher that I am now: my mother taught me to love drawings and books, and my father, who is sorely missed, trusted my intelligence. Both of them encouraged me to use my mind to search for freedom and happiness.

Finally, I would like to thank Patrick, for being the loving anchor of my life.

Author's Preface

Since colonial times, Angkor has captured the attention of the international heritage community and has been seen as one of the most important archaeological sites in the world. It has also become a major international tourist destination, especially after being listed as a UNESCO World Heritage Site in 1992. Today, it is visited by more than two million tourists every year. Tourism plays a significant role in the reconstruction of the national economy. Cambodia has gone through twenty years of turmoil: the dictatorial regime of the Khmer Rouge, the civil war, and the Vietnamese occupation destroyed social organizations, economic growth, and the transmission of culture and traditions. When Cambodia eventually regained its status as an independent and sovereign country in 1991, its political, social, and economic systems had to be rebuilt from scratch with the assistance of the United Nations. Reconstruction efforts coincided with the recognition of Angkor as the heritage of humanity, only one year later. International fame bolstered hope for economic development, while at the same time it aroused concern for the reconstruction of the national identity based on Cambodia's archaeological heritage. Angkor has come under the spotlight of post-war development. It has monopolized the institutional concern for heritage, preventing other forms of legacy from being recognized as valuable. The focus of cultural policy in Angkor has gone hand in hand with the convergence of wealth and investment in Siem Reap. In 2007, this town, located six kilometres away from the main temples, was still surrounded by one of the poorest rural areas in the country.

The sharp contrasts between celebration and indifference, wealth and poverty, caught my attention when I first visited Cambodia as a postgraduate student in 2005. Developers and speculators have invested large amounts of capital in Siem Reap during the last twenty years. However, the town has lacked any kind of cultural policy or programmes for urban conservation and planning. While the focus of scholarship has mainly been directed to the magnificent remains of Angkor, I became interested in its urban surroundings, which embodied an intriguing contradiction between cultural marginality and economic centrality.

In my own early life in Turin, a secondary city in northwest Italy, my first experiences of the urban environment generated a sense of marginality. I lived in the southern suburb of Mirafiori, which had mostly been built after the Second World War to house the rising industrial proletariat employed by the Fiat car factory. Blocks of residential buildings had mushroomed in the rural landscape and pushed out the farms. The post-war history of the urbanization of Mirafiori was 'transparent' in public consciousness and policy. As children, we learnt little about how and when our neighbourhood was built. Moreover, collective perceptions of this disadvantaged suburb tended to be negative, at a time when heroin addicts were intimidating the other residents. I had the impression that the environment where I lived had no history, and that only my personal memories could make it pleasant and valuable. As a teenager, I discovered the centre of Turin: when I travelled from the dull, urban periphery to the exciting centre every Saturday afternoon, I had the feeling that being a suburbanite made it impossible for me to experience beauty on a daily basis. Later, as an architecture student, I started looking at the suburbs of my childhood with fresh eyes. I remember taking dozens of pictures of roads and spaces, which my newly acquired knowledge enabled me to situate in their historical context. I discovered hidden features of the city from the early 1920s and the remains of a sixteenth-century castle. History, I saw, had always been present, though beauty was less visible in the industrial suburbs than in the historic centre. This awareness prefigured the municipal policies that introduced conservation and redevelopment projects for Turin's industrial heritage and Mirafiori only a few years later. In my personal experience, the wide gap that separated the town of my childhood from my first fieldwork site was bridged by the desire to uncover the meaning and beauty of an urban landscape widely perceived as insignificant. My early experience as an urban citizen nourished my research, impelling me to look at the political and social structures that cause meanings, knowledge, and alternative aesthetics to be concealed and overlooked. Siem Reap has been a crucial case study, because it has allowed me to investigate the dualistic opposition of a significant archaeological park and a more recent urban development largely perceived as having no meaning. By acknowledging the artificial nature of this opposition and, at the same time, its rootedness in society, I hope to have suggested some possibilities of overcoming it.

At Siem Reap-Angkor, power alliances between government institutions and private developers have become entrenched during Cambodia's recent history, and have intersected with the global politics of international heritage. They are kept alive and even reinforced by the present political situation. The reconstruction of Cambodian institutions has established a neopatrimonial political system in which personal interests prevail through the use of socially constructed tactics, confirming and strengthening the legitimacy of those who own and perform power. This system generates extreme inequality and authoritarian behaviour. It mirrors the unscrupulous drive for prestige and social recognition, which wealthy Cambodians associate with the power to act in space, often to the disadvantage of those who cannot secure sufficient resources or connections with powerful individuals. A number of scholarly works have condemned the misuses of power and short-sighted strategies of some Cambodians. They have identified the patronage system as one of the main obstacles to the establishment of the rule of law, and constructed an image of Cambodia as a country that must be educated in the values of heritage, sustainable development, and institutional accountability. Without denying the quality and usefulness of these works in fostering political and social change, as I read them I felt uneasy, since I had the impression that they were imposing an external, overarching gaze and claiming the right to say what was 'good' and 'bad' for Cambodia. I sensed the influence of that gaze on my own early perception of disruptive urban dynamics, and I realized how powerful it was, weaving a web of concepts and beliefs that distanced me from direct experience of my own fieldwork.

My own approach has emerged from that discomfort. It consists of analysing rationales, structures, and mechanisms. Within these broad categories, I have paid special attention to urban planning, policies, and legislation in the field of land management and urban development, and political discourse, as well as strategies and tactics shaped by those involved in the processes of territorial and urban transformation. Large amounts of development assistance from outside the country function to convey the donors' preferred development models. Foreign consultants perform their authority as experts in a country still reconstructing its intellectual and professional elite. The inextricable connections between the private and the public sector dictate the directions of urban development, to the detriment of the disadvantaged segments of the population. The academic literature expresses severe criticism of the Cambodian state and the country's political economy. In line with this, sections of this book develop a critical analysis of the failure of urban planning, the consequences of land speculation, and intense construction activity in the Siem Reap region. However, during my fieldwork, I maintained a distance from this critical framework of analysis. When I interviewed some of those who have been responsible for negative urban transformations, I tried to focus on the individual expression of meanings, aspirations, and self-interested calculations, which construct these people as subjects. My efforts to present an understanding of individual and collective systems of meanings and objectives reflect my positionality as a researcher and my philosophy as a human being. I do believe that genuine understanding of the real nature of a situation, a person, or a society makes transformation more likely. Such an understanding might even be more effective – and certainly more respectful of the capacity for individual and collective self-determination – than a proactive but directive approach to defining desirable directions for change. This approach to the understanding of contemporary Cambodian politics and its roots in national trauma and insecurity thus constitutes, for me, a form of political engagement.

A Map of Southeast Asia and Cambodia

CAMBODIA - SOUTHEAST ASIA

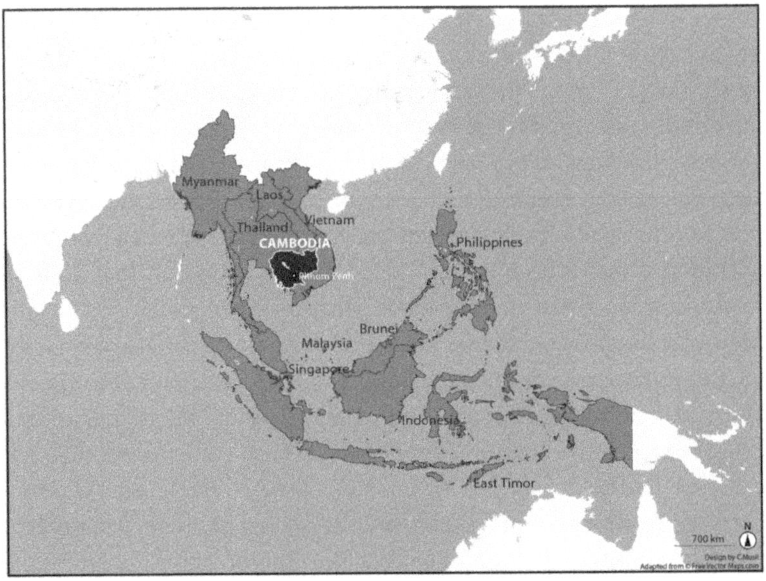

SIEM REAP - CAMBODIA

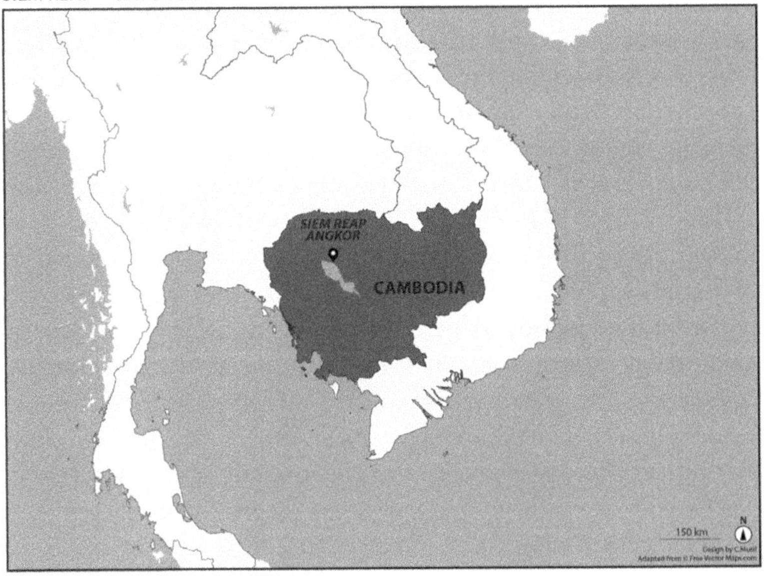

© Esposito 2017

Introduction

The archaeological park of Angkor includes the major monuments of the ancient Khmer capitals, built between the ninth and fifteenth centuries, with ruins and monuments dotting a landscape of tropical forest, cultivated land, and rural communities (Winter, 2008). UNESCO established this park as a consequence of the listing of Angkor as a World Heritage Site in 1992. Aiming to preserve the monuments' physical authenticity and visual integrity, international experts proposed that only projects for heritage conservation and tourism management should be allowed within the precincts of the park. Its boundaries are marked by small, red pillars displaying the symbol of the UNESCO World Heritage Convention. Beneath the symbol, a double arrow indicates the perimeter of the archaeological park. These pillars are sometimes found in the countryside, where they arbitrarily distinguish an 'inside' and 'outside' of the park in rural and village environments where neither monuments, nor tourists are in sight (Figure B). A hierarchy was thus established in which a different status was assigned to spaces that often had similar physical and social characteristics, but which arbitrarily fell inside or outside the perimeter of the archaeological park, depending on their distance from the major monuments.

The establishment of the park led to the formation of a 'heritage territoriality', that is to say a territory composed of different spaces separated by boundaries, subject to specific sets of regulations, and infused with diverse social and cultural meanings. In particular, the creation of the park has generated what I call a 'non-heritage space'. I use this neologism to designate an area excluded from heritage recognition, but within the orbit of the heritage site. This space undergoes intense transformation because of its proximity to and concomitant exclusion from heritage status. Here, a politically and socially constructed distinction allows for the implementation of tourism-related developments that would be forbidden within the archaeological park. The non-heritage space therefore absorbs the carry-over effects of tourism growth, but is excluded from the recognition of values that its own legacy and traditions may possess. By the same token, it is also 'freed from' the constraints and regulations that are likely to accompany heritage recognition. It can thus be used as a space of development, where aspirations for social change, economic growth, and modernization find their way through new plans and projects.

Pressure for the development of this non-heritage space has been particularly strong in the vicinity of Angkor. Only recently emerging from the dictatorial regime of the Khmer Rouge (1975-1979), war, and foreign occupation, Cambodia (Figure A) began to embrace economic liberalization in the 1980s under the Vietnamese administration. The Paris Accords signed in 1991 inaugurated peacekeeping and national reconstruction, and accelerated the liberalization process. Extremely permissive legislation on investment[1] has gradually opened the country up to foreign capital and projects. Tourism has been viewed as a profitable 'light industry', which can provide quick returns on investment while requiring modest initial capital (Hall and Page, 2000). For this reason, tourism has played a role of paramount importance in the restructuring of the Cambodian economy, accounting for 29.9 per cent of GDP in 2015 (Table C). The World Heritage Site of Angkor has catalysed and concentrated a remarkable development in tourism, with a 10,000 per cent increase in international tourism between 1998 and 2008 (Winter, 2008).

Villages, agricultural areas, and open fields form the non-heritage space of Angkor. At the heart of this space, six kilometres from the main temples, lies Siem Reap. In precolonial times, the town was simply a conglomeration of villages strung out along the river of the same name. The French Protectorate established Siem Reap as a provincial capital and a tourist resort when the first archaeological park of Angkor was created in 1925. After Cambodian independence in 1953, Siem Reap maintained these functions, although tourism development was in its infancy. The UNESCO World Heritage listing confirmed the town's focus on tourism; today, it accommodates more than two million tourists a year (Sor, 2016b).[2] International experts attempted to re-list the Siem Reap-Angkor region as a cultural landscape under the UNESCO World Heritage system in subsequent years. The cultural landscape would have covered a surface approximately equal to the area of Siem Reap Province (10,000 km^2), and would have included minor archaeological outposts, villages, and natural areas, as well as Siem Reap town, in an all-encompassing system of special conservation regulations. However, these attempts failed. As available sources do not elucidate the reasons for this failure, it is only possible to make assumptions. The re-listing of Angkor as a cultural landscape would have extended a binding regulatory system to the entire Siem Reap province. The enforcement of this system would have restrained development pressures in the region. Developers would have been obliged to conform to specific land use and construction rules. In Chapter 2, we will see how reluctant developers were to comply with planning measures

1 See Cambodia Law on Investment (5 August 1994) and Amendment to the Law on Investment of the Kingdom of Cambodia (24 March 2003).

2 http://siemreaptourism.gov.kh (accessed 13 May 2016).

that foreign consultants tried to implement in Siem Reap town. For its part, the Cambodian government supported the developers' claims for the deregulation of construction activity in the expanding urban area, in line with its intention to use Angkor as a major catalyst for investment and economic growth. In this context, the listing of Angkor as a cultural landscape would have put a brake on the process of growth as imagined by the political and economic elites. In contrast, the separation between a heritage and a non-heritage space accommodates the government's combined strategy of heritage conservation and tourism-related development.

Consequently, Siem Reap's urban space is subject only to ordinary regulations in the areas of construction and land transactions, as is the rural territory which surrounds the urban core. Approximately 150 hotels, an equivalent number of guesthouses, several golf courses, museums, and commercial activities were built in the town between 1992 and 2008. The town and its surroundings have been highly exposed to development projects directly or indirectly related to the tourism economy. The borders of the non-heritage space have been pushed further and further out as property developments have been implemented. Intense urban transformation has restructured the area, reshaped architectural and urban forms, and triggered extensive reconfigurations of the social and political relations among those active in the fields of conservation, tourism, and urban development.

In the eyes of developers, the non-heritage space has appeared as a promised land of unbridled individual freedom. The divide between the heritage and non-heritage spaces has become increasingly sharp as the international celebrity of the ancient Khmer capitals has encouraged intense development on the margins. National and foreign investors have acquired an unconditional trust in the open-ended process of tourism development. This unshakeable faith has encouraged volatile investment, property development, and numerous small-scale architectural projects. While investors have expanded their power over ever larger areas of urban land, ordinary families, residents, and other users of local facilities have seen their capacity to own, shape, and occupy the urban space weakened. Siem Reap's urban community of citizens has been 'deprived of leadership and stewardship by the actions and attitudes of people both present in and absent from these environments' (Markusen, 2004, p. 2303). Significantly, Siem Reap province was still the third poorest in the country in 2007, with an estimated 52 per cent of the population living below the national poverty line.[3] The rural

3 The poverty line is established at 2,000 Riels or US$0.50 per day (GTZ, 2007; Hauser-Schäublin, 2012). Within the province, differences exist between the districts. The northern ones, such

surroundings of the World Heritage Site, now partially included in the perimeters of Siem Reap municipality, are forgotten places on the periphery of 'a place of hyper-growth' (Ong, 2006, quoted by Winter, 2008).

It is my aim here to examine the conditions that led to the formation of this forgotten place in the vicinity of the World Heritage Site. The origins of these conditions, I argue, can be found in the World Heritage system and, more particularly, in the theoretical and methodological foundations that have determined how heritage has been perceived and managed in Cambodia since colonial times. I examine the dialectic between the peripheral position of Siem Reap in the politics of heritage and its concomitant centrality to economic dynamics. I view this as a particular manifestation of the deeply rooted discursive dualism that tries to reconcile 'conservation' and 'development' in heritage policies, especially in developing countries. On the one hand, heritage must be conserved and therefore protected from the threats represented by modernization and tourism-related transformations. On the other hand, it is seen as a source of economic growth that can be exploited to develop domestic and international tourism and also help to generate images of places and cities that enhance their uniqueness and resulting comparative advantage on the competitive global market (Harrison and Hitchcock, 2005; Prigent, 2013). The consequences of this dialectic have concerned both planning and development, and the conflicts and disconnections between these two raise questions about how the power to determine urban transformation has been distributed, exerted, contested, and subverted in Siem Reap. International donors and consultants have positioned themselves as 'cultural brokers' (Lewis and Mosse, 2006) in the field of planning – that is to say, as mediators between different cultural and professional systems who ought to be able to import international knowledge in the field of heritage and urban planning into the local context of Siem Reap-Angkor, while also managing the reconstruction of the Cambodian political and economic system. In the specific context of Cambodia, where urban knowledge was destroyed with the mass killing of intellectuals and professionals during the Khmer Rouge period, they have maintained a stranglehold on urban planning. This has, however, had little impact on the urban fabric; the politics of urban planning has only marginally contributed to the transfer of knowledge and capacities that foreign sponsors look for. For their part, developers have benefited from underhand agreements with

as Srei Suam, Angkor Chum, Varin, and Svay Len, are the poorest, because they are far away from the main hub of development in Siem Reap, their soil is not very fertile, and there is little agricultural diversification (Hauser-Schäublin, 2012).

officials and members of the political elite, which have left them undisturbed in the material production of the city.

The history of urban governance in Siem Reap disproves the belief that the state is the main regulator of development for the public good. Rather, a neopatrimonial system has been established in Cambodian politics, which 'features a combination of a modern bureaucracy and personalized patron-client relationships within a traditional system of patrimonialism, with no clear distinction between the public and the private realms' (Un and So, 2011, p. 294). Patrimonialism can be traced back to pre-Angkorian times, when Hindu values favoured the emergence of a trend towards personalized power. Kings were viewed as demi-gods (*devaraja*) and granted absolute power (Sahai, 1970, quoted by Rabé, 2009). As early as the ninth to twelfth centuries, statues representing 'persons of distinction' as Buddhist and Hindu divinities bore witness to the existence of a 'cult of big men' (Coedès, 1947, quoted by Rabé, 2009). Buddhists believe that their social position is the result of merit gained during previous lives. For this reason, they rarely contest social hierarchies, but respect the leaders' moral authority and expect them to assist the lower strata of the population (Pak, Horng, Eng et al., 2007). These leaders often act as benefactors (*saborashon*) by making donations to pagodas and disadvantaged local people in exchange for their loyalty and political support (Formoso and Stock, 2016).

At different periods, patron-client relations determined the distribution of political power. During the French Protectorate, Cambodian civil servants were in charge of tax collection. This prestigious role allowed them to accumulate personal power through direct connection with French administrators. In postcolonial times, Norodom Sihanouk presented himself as the father of the nation. He relied on personalized, absolute power, which enabled him to annihilate his political enemies. He described the Cambodian poor as the 'little people', for whom he showed paternal affection (Jeldres, 2005; Chandler, 2003, quoted by Rabé, 2009). Even the Khmer Rouge, who claimed to have collective leadership, gave Pol Pot a leading role at the head of the party and the state (Pak, Horng, Eng et al., 2007).

Patrimonial structures have changed in the context of contemporary economic liberalization (Rabé, 2009). Through family alliances established by marriage and the accumulation of economic resources and opportunities, a power elite of tycoons has centralized power (Formoso and Stock, 2016). In this situation, low-income people with limited social capital often have no other option than to co-operate 'with dominant classes in order to maximize their own security' (Rabé, 2009, p. 282). The state has endorsed the leading role of the economic and political elite. It has been enmeshed in networks of diplomatic and tactical alliances, which have diverted international development assistance to the advantage of particular interests. The internationally driven efforts to direct the establishment of the rule of law in Cambodia led to the formation of an 'unconsolidated democracy' (Linz and Stepan, 1996) in which elements identified with democratic government can coexist with authoritarian practices (Keang Un, 2006). This system benefits the elites in power who resist undertaking reforms. Civil society and social movements are discouraged, as major threats to the stability of the system. This understanding of the political and economic context helps me to reflect more broadly on the role of contemporary Cambodian cities in the context of national economic liberalization, the emergence of Cambodian political and economic urban elites, and the shortcomings of international development doctrines which often appear disconnected from local politics.

I approach the non-heritage space as a political and social arena. I draw here on the metaphor of the arena as it has developed in the field of political anthropology (Dartigues, 2001), where it has been interpreted in several ways: as the place of political activity, the structural centre of social order (Geertz, 1983), a critical point of intersection between social systems (Long, 1989), the meeting place for heterogeneous and strategic groups (Olivier de Sardan and Bierschenk, 1993), and the encounter between allies who exchange various kinds of resources (Darré, 1996). In the arena of Siem Reap, alliances and enmities are constantly being played out. However, the use of urban space is not confined to the role of a backdrop for the performance of politics and economics: 'Buildings serve as a reminder of the practices of the past and the starting point for both the performance of unfinished fantasies and the desire to overcome troubling memories and remake oneself within, as well as beyond, one's particular time and place' (Kusno, 2010, p. 3). Following Kusno, I see architecture and urban design as semiotic activities that strive to combine two apparently competing objectives. Architectural forms are used as reminders of history, tradition, and heritage; at the same time, they make it possible to envision urban modernity.

Since colonial times, urban space in Cambodia, and in particular in the capital Phnom Penh, has been conceived as a 'semantic production': that is to say, it was used to give material form to political and ideological strategies and contributed to the construction of national identity (Fauveaud, 2011). In colonial times, architectural and urban projects enhanced exoticized representations of local traditions. Tradition was imagined as a fragile construct, opposed to modernity, which Western influences

Figure B UNESCO signpost indicating the boundaries of the Angkor archaeological park

Photo by the author, 2015

would irremediably compromise. After Cambodian independence, the architectural style developed by a group of Cambodian architects (including Vann Molyvann, Lu Ban Hap, Chhim Sun Fong, Seng Suntheng, and Mam

Figure C Total contribution made by tourism and travel to Cambodia's GDP

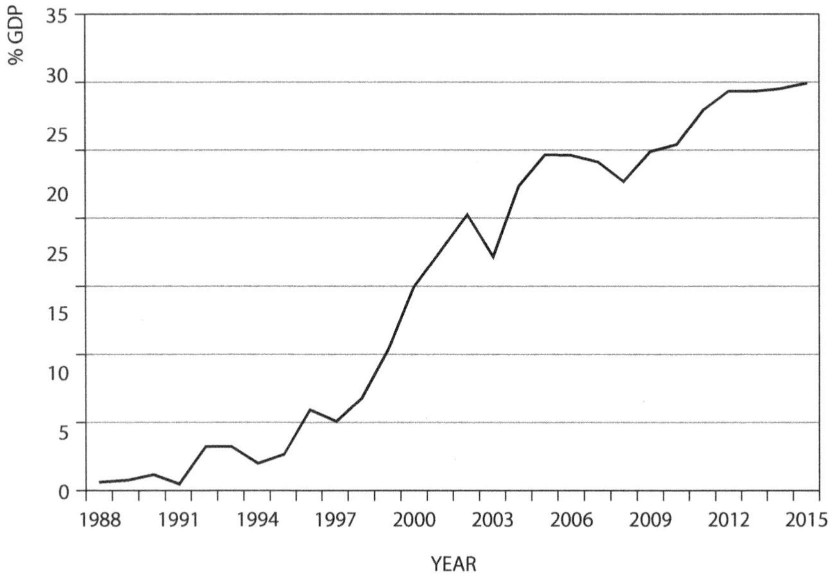

Source: World Travel and Tourism Council, 2016; table: http://knoema.fr/atlas/Cambodge/topics/Tourisme/Contribution-totale-du-tourisme-et-voyage-au-PIB/Contribution-totale-au-PIB-percent-proportion; accessed 21 July 2016

Sophana) created original architectural assemblages combining national tradition with the International Movement. Their style was later named 'New Khmer Architecture' (Collins and Ross, 2006).

In contemporary Cambodia, the dual quest for tradition and modernity is a source of contradiction: images and ideas of urban modernity are so distanced from inherited forms that they arouse the fear that Cambodia's cultural roots will be forgotten. At the same time, ideas of tradition shaped in colonial times still exert a strong influence on contemporary imaginings of the past, and offer a selective understanding of national heritage that Cambodians have largely appropriated. My analysis of contemporary architectural and urban projects unpacks the assemblages of built forms, which combine representations of tradition and modernity. I pay special attention to 'tourist enclaves', those spaces that 'are carefully staged and designed so that [the touristic] performance is somewhat prescriptive' (Edensor, 1998, p. 62). In doing so, I reflect on how tourist architecture negotiates the notion of authenticity, responding to the twofold tourist demand for a taste of heritage and locality, but without foregoing modern standards of comfort. Based on the analysis of colonial and postcolonial images of heritage and tradition, I propose the notion of 'emotional authenticity' as an analytical framework, which helps us to understand how this negotiation is played out in architectural and urban projects. Emotional authenticity pays less attention to the originality and accuracy of cultural references. Rather, it relies on the ability of an object or space to provoke intense feelings and provide dramatic experiences through selective, strategic evocations of the past and tradition. The analysis of tourism-related projects in Siem Reap brings me to question more broadly the directions of contemporary architectural and urban production. In doing so, I address the complex and convoluted logic that underlies the construction of Siem Reap on the periphery of the World Heritage Site.

Ordinary diversity? A secondary tourist city in Southeast Asia

Robinson (2006) has argued that 'ordinary cities', once on the margins of the world economy, take specific and diverse paths towards urban modernity. So far, she points out, the study of world cities has dominated the directions and paradigms of urban studies. World cities have been viewed as models and winners in a global hierarchy based on economic parameters that subsequently determine the rank of other cities. Bunnell and Maringanti (2010) have called the focus of academic research on such primate cities 'metrocentricity' and argued for a methodological and conceptual reorientation of urban studies, which would place more emphasis on secondary cities. Such cities are broadly defined as those that play a secondary and sometimes marginal role in the world economy. Focusing the spotlight of academic attention on them helps to call into question the knowledge paradigms that have influenced the understanding of contemporary urban phenomena. Following this principle, Chen and Kanna (2012, p. 1) focus on secondary cities from a global perspective in order to 'bring better to light global processes that have been marginalized or neglected in the literature on global cities'. These processes, they write, 'include the emergence of alternative and new cartographies of globalization [...] the role of local, regional, and "deep" (economic, colonial, national) histories in shaping contemporary urban globalization; and the multifarious, complex role of cultural and symbolic structures in urban experience and the construction of global urban circuits'. Franck, Goldblum, and Taillard (2012) have investigated the specific trajectories of secondary cities in Southeast Asia. They argue that Southeast Asian secondary cities share some features with metropolises; however, they do not fully embody the metropolitan model, nor are they on the way to forming new metropolises. Rather, they experience *métropolisation en mode mineur* ('metropolization in a minor mode'). 'Metropolization', a term rarely used in Anglophone literature (with a few exceptions, e.g. Krätke, 2007), designates processes that were once typical of metropolises, but may affect only specific parts or aspects of a developing city (Leroy, 2000). The term thus encapsulates the possibility that alternative urban models can be developed and leaves the way open to researchers who may want to explore the unique characteristics of such urban trajectories.

The recent development of Siem Reap as an international tourism hub raises questions about the integration of secondary cities into international heritage diplomacy and the global tourism economy through processes of metropolization. Today, Siem Reap is the second largest Cambodian city after Phnom Penh, with approximately 250,000 inhabitants living in the urbanized area of the municipality established in 2008 (Fauveaud, 2015a) (Figure C). Only 30,000 people lived there at the beginning of the 1990s, when a scarred population of refugees was authorized to return to the cities after fifteen years of political turmoil. Until 2008, Siem Reap was a province and a district composed of twelve urban and rural communes. It was only in 2008 that it became a municipality encompassing three additional rural communes.[4] Through this reform, Siem Reap was aligned with Phnom Penh, the national capital, and other Southeast Asian metropolises (e.g. Hanoi and Ho Chi Minh City), which have also recently experienced the extension of their administrative areas.[5] These reforms have all absorbed rural areas into the perimeter

4 Siem Reap is a province, a district, and, since 2008, a municipality. The province comprises twelve districts, 100 communes, and 921 villages. It covers a surface of approximately 10,549 km^2 and had a population of 896,309 inhabitants in 2008. Siem Reap district covers a surface of 446 km^2, of which 340 km^2 is land area and the other 106 km^2 belongs to Tonlé Sap lake, the largest source of fresh water in southeast Asia. Siem Reap district had a population of 146,379 in 2006 and has had an average population growth of five per cent since 1998 (DED, 2007). Siem Reap municipality was created in 2008. It comprises 108 villages and eleven communes, which previously formed part of the district, and two additional rural communes.

5 Phnom Penh's master plan, designed in 2003 by the Office of Urban Affairs, integrated twelve additional communes into the area of the municipality, as well as three new satellite cities – Camko City, Boeung Kak, and Koh Pich (Goldblum, 2012). Ho Chi Minh City's municipal area expanded in 2008 to include provinces in the Southeastern surroundings of the city. Following this reform, the master plan expects that urbanization rates in the whole Ho Chi Minh municipal area will expand from 77 per cent to 90 per cent by 2050. In 2008, Hanoi Municipality included Ha Tay Province and Son Tay City in a conurbation composed of an urban core and several satellites.

of the municipality. These areas are intended for future developments that often involve urbanization. The urbanization pattern is organized around the development of corridors and new centres in the form of neighbourhoods or satellite cities. 'In a minor mode' the establishment of Siem Reap municipality reproduces this strategy, since it aims to expand urbanization on former rural and agricultural land and involves the construction of several urban complexes with both commercial and residential functions. It also reveals the desire of national institutions to extend to a secondary city the processes of economic and urban development typical of metropolises. Even if Siem Reap cannot aspire to metropolitan status, the strategy is aimed at encouraging its economic dynamism and international connections.

However, Siem Reap's municipal perimeter currently encloses hybrid forms combining rural and urban elements. Typically, urban forms have increased in the years following the Angkor World Heritage listing, with the rapid expansion and increased density of the built areas and concomitant decrease in agricultural and uncultivated land. Transportation networks have developed with the construction of new roads, a harbour, and an international airport. Numerous commercial facilities, including shopping malls and residential complexes echoing the model of the gated community, have profoundly changed the urban landscape, once mainly composed of wooden houses on stilts and other small-scale buildings. In addressing the trajectory of Siem Reap from a village to a fast-developing city, I investigate the strategies and means through which a secondary city overcomes its peripheral position and engages in growth and modernization.

The case of Siem Reap casts more light on the dynamics at play throughout Southeast Asia. Previous research has shown that secondary cities such as Melaka and Penang have been marginalized in the restructuring of economic systems and commercial exchanges (Sandhu, Wheatley, and Mat Tom, 1983). Ancient capital cities, such as Luang Prabang, have seen their political role declining. Since the 1980s, heritage and tourism have become major programmatic choices for the revitalization of urban and national economies, and for the integration of these secondary cities into regional and international cooperation networks (Dearborn and Stallmeyer, 2010; Hitchcock, King, and Parnwell, 2009, 2010; Jenkins, 2008). Heritage recognition has functioned as a major driver of urban change, as it has catalysed demographic and economic flows.

At Siem Reap-Angkor, however, institutional heritage is located outside the city, and the disconnection between the heritage site and the

Figure D Siem Reap urban area in 2005

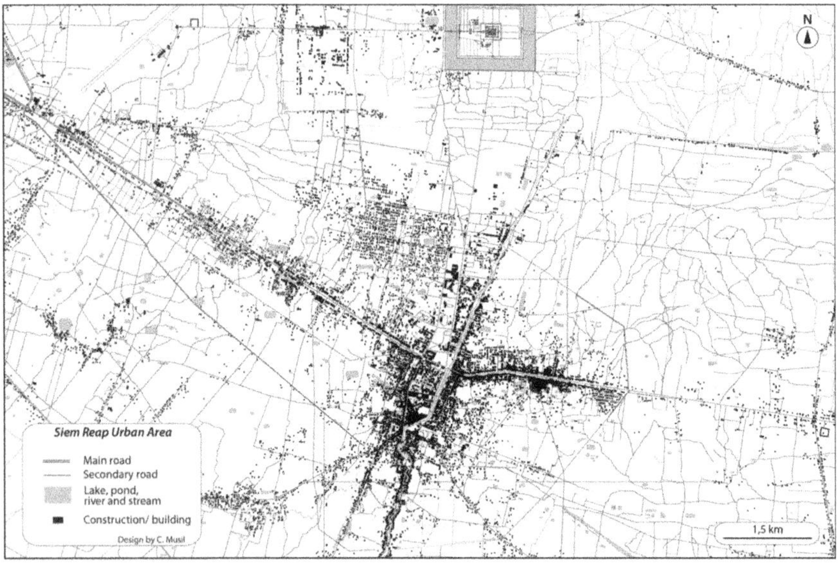

After JICA 2006, © Esposito 2016)

tourism hub determines some specific processes of urban development. These specificities may not lie in the forms produced, but rather in the processes themselves and their social and economic complications, which have often been obscured by the common notion that, in today's economy, the urban landscape is becoming homogenized (Sassen, 2012). My analysis of these processes moves from economic tactics to their built consequences, and from project design to implementation, and conceives of the shaping of the urban fabric as a collective social endeavour. Inhabitants, small-scale developers, and builders do not draw on highly specialized professional knowledge, nor are they going to produce original architectural and urban models. For these reasons, their projects have to be defined as 'ordinary'. However, they appropriate international references, which reach them from multiple sources (their own travel, magazines, projects implemented in Phnom Penh or built in Siem Reap by foreign chains and investors, etc.) and mould them into the existing urban structure and landscape. They are thus the producers of various forms of diversity that concern the processes of architectural production as well as the built results. 'Ordinary diversity' characterizes the evolution of Siem Reap as a secondary city exposed to international influences triggered by tourism.

Building the city after conflict

Cambodia had just emerged from dictatorship, war, and foreign occupation when Angkor was listed as a UNESCO World Heritage Site in 1992. The turmoil started in the late 1960s. Following the country's independence from the French Protectorate in 1953 and Norodom Sihanouk's rise to power as head of state and leader of the Sangkum Reastr Niyum ('the Community of the Common People') in 1955, Cambodia became involved in the Vietnam-US war: North Vietnamese troops were active in the southwest of the country and the American army responded with bombing campaigns (Winter, 2007). During this decade, the Khmer Rouge movement gradually gained influence within the country, first taking root in the jungle in the northeast and gradually spreading across the countryside. Criticizing the military action of the USA and claiming that it would liberate the country from both the Vietnamese and the Americans, the movement established a close relationship with the Chinese Cultural Revolution. The propaganda of the Chinese Cultural Revolution was disseminated around the country by various groups, including 'the Overseas Chinese, the Chinese Embassy, the Khmer-Chinese Friendship Association (KCFA), the five Chinese language newspapers, and Chinese instructors working with the Cambodian army' (Armstrong, 1977, p. 204). In 1967, a peasant revolt in Battambang region, probably triggered by a land dispute, was violently repressed by the government. It sowed doubt about the consensus enjoyed by Sihanouk among the rural population and fear of a possible move towards revolutionary communism under the double influence of Vietnam and China (Forest, 2008). Sihanouk reacted by intensifying the repression of those suspected of subversive activities. However, his personal power and ascendancy eroded over time. The stability of his political regime was further threatened by economic difficulties, political rivalries, and lack of consistency in his national and foreign policies. This situation created favourable conditions for a military coup, which may have benefited from US complicity (Clymer, 2013). The Khmer Republic was subsequently established, headed by General Lon Nol. Martial law was introduced in order to fight the rise of communism in the country. Its expansion was a response to the penetration of Vietnamese communists into Cambodia and the turmoil caused by repeated American and South Vietnamese bombing and exactions. The 1973 Paris 'Agreement on Ending the War and Restoring Peace in Vietnam' only increased American military intervention in Cambodia and massively pushed the population to embrace communism. The Khmer Rouge rode the wave of popular indignation. They took over in Cambodia and marched into Phnom Penh in 1975 (Chandler, 2008). They emptied the city of more than three million people, who were forced to relocate to cooperatives and work camps established in the countryside. Siem Reap was evacuated on 17-18 April 1975. A local informant interviewed by Vigers (2005) explained that 'the town was completely destroyed, especially the wooden houses. Only the brick and concrete buildings remained. They pulled down the wooden houses to get firewood, to have some heat [...] to heat up their meals, to prepare their food' (pp. 97-98).

Drawing on Mao Zedong's policy of the 'Great Leap Forward', the Khmer Rouge were ready to provoke a profound and rapid transformation of Cambodian society. Villages, towns, and cities were seen as barriers to the revolution and had to be annihilated. The totalitarian collectivization of economic resources aimed to recreate Cambodian society and reconstruct national identity on the basis of an idealization of the rural past and the peasantry. Nevertheless, Angkor remained an icon during this period; it 'was simply too *Cambodian* to be disregarded' (Chandler, 1996, p. 246, quoted by Winter, 2007, p. 45). Chandler's (1996) analysis of a collection of speeches by the Communist Party of Kampuchea shows that Angkor was cited for its power to mobilize labour and as an example of national grandeur. Furthermore, Angkor was proudly represented on Democratic Kampuchea's flag and was shown to Chinese delegates during a visit in 1977 (Kiernan, 1996, quoted by Winter, 2007).

The Khmer Rouge destroyed urban life, and the pluralism and diversity that it represented, and promoted the idea of a homogeneous population all wearing the same clothes and with similar haircuts. The uniformity of this rural peasantry would eradicate the old society, perceived as corrupted and rotten (McIntyre, 1996). Several hypotheses have been advanced to explain why the Khmer Rouge evacuated the cities (Rabé, 2009): some historians believe that the urban population was moved closer to food resources in the countryside (Hildebrand and Porter, 1976; Vickers, 1999, quoted by Rabé, 2009). Others believe that deportation was part of a strategy to control the urban population, which was generally less supportive of the Khmer Rouge revolution than rural villagers (Kiernan, 1996, quoted by Rabé, 2009). Also, massive evacuations enabled the Khmer Rouge to expel and kill minority groups such as the ethnic Chinese and Vietnamese and hence to better control political dissidents (Ibid.). However, their ideology and strategies did not prevent the Khmer Rouge from implementing a limited programme of urban repopulation in Phnom Penh, which was necessary to achieve their economic objectives. For this reason, some hospitals, factories, and government offices were put into operation again, and local and imported goods were exchanged among foreign countries, Cambodian cities, and the countryside. The Khmer Rouge regime, in short, did not completely abandon the Cambodian capital; rather, it 'reconfigured the city to meet its political and economic needs' (Tyner, Henkin, and Sirik, 2014, p. 1889).

The purges by the Khmer Rouge regime killed approximately one and a half million people in only four years. Vietnamese troops put an end to these massive killings in 1979, when they invaded the country and established a new government. The People's Republic of Kampuchea lasted until 1989, as a satellite country of the socialist regime in Vietnam (Forest, 2008). The foreign administration helped with the reconstruction of state institutions and social cohesion, although Khmer Rouge guerrillas established an enduring and destabilizing presence in the north. During those years, economic negotiations with Thailand were begun, and diplomat Chatichai Choonhavan spoke of transforming Indochina 'from a battlefield to a trading market' (Becker, 1986). In 1989, the first political and economic reforms in this direction were undertaken: the National Assembly revised the Constitution, the market economy was reintroduced, foreign investment became legal, and private ownership of land reinstated. Cambodia became a neutral and non-aligned country. These reforms led to the 1991 Paris Peace Accords, which declared the independence and sovereignty of the country and condemned the Khmer Rouge regime. The United National Transitional Authority for Cambodia, composed of 22,000 foreigners who lived in the country for a year and a half, accompanied the re-establishment of a constitutional monarchy and administrative, institutional, and political system. It also catalysed the manna of foreign assistance and a first wave of foreign investment.

Cambodia experienced a sudden wave of internationalization after years of stagnation and isolation. Its process of rapid economic development has been mainly driven by the garment and tourism industries. Phnom Penh and Siem Reap respectively have been the centres of growth of these sectors. The new law on investment (1994) and the land laws (1992 and 2001) encouraged the development and exploitation of land for economic purposes and offered a permissive regulatory framework to foreign entities. At the same time, Cambodia's situation as a country under reconstruction has attracted massive flows of international development assistance.[6]

6 International development assistance amounted to approximately 10-20 per cent of GDP between 1991 and 1995 and 10-13 per cent subsequently (De Vienne, 2008). Between 2013 and 2015 alone, Cambodia received 2.03 billion dollars in aid from international donors, 3.8 billion if we include loans; one billion of this was granted by China. Turton, Shaun and Nass, Daniel, 2016, 'Analysis: Foreign donors taken for granted?' *Phnom Penh Post*, 17 June. http://m.phnompenhpost.com/national/analysis-foreign-donors-taken-granted (accessed 20 June 2016).

The weak but developing institutional system, the substantial weight of the tourism economy in the politics of national reconstruction, and the extensive intervention of foreign entities in several fields including heritage, development assistance, and investment, have been major determinants of the politics of urban development in Siem Reap. Volatility, dependence, and haste have characterized the processes of urban expansion and transformation. The existing literature on Siem Reap has criticized these recent dynamics: it has focused on urban sprawl, the destruction of the historical fabric, environmental dangers, poverty, and social justice, and has proposed sometimes pessimistic evaluations of current urban trends. For instance, Hetreau-Pottier (2011) asks whether undergoing processes of urban transformation corresponds to a 'first phase of "deculturalization"' in which Siem Reap is simply perceived as a 'consumer item' (p. 15). The dangers and risks associated with the overexploitation of natural resources have been identified (Hauser-Schaüblin, 2011), and the unequal participation of the population in development processes has been seen as a major shortcoming of the development pattern (Baromey Neth, 2011). Lack of updated planning and failed implementation of urban plans are among the city's main contemporary problems: 'Taken as a whole, it is difficult to convey adequately the dizzying array of tourist-related developments that are sprouting up in seemingly random fashion throughout Siem Reap. Not only are master plans often out of date due to the fast pace of development, but they are often difficult to access, and their enforcement can be problematic' (Heikkila and Peycam, 2010, p. 298). This literature has generally been fascinated by urgent problems in need of quick solutions. For this reason, it has failed to understand the whole picture of urban politics over longer time frames. My objective is to consider the recent development of Siem Reap across a wider spectrum, investigating the ideas, role, and evolution of Cambodian urbanism and predicting future developments in the fields of planning and architecture.

To do this, I draw on an emerging subfield of urban studies that looks at Cambodian cities. Research on Cambodia has mainly focused on rural environments. Colonial narratives have certainly contributed to directing scholarly attention to rural areas, as they depict Cambodian villages as idyllic expressions of an archaic tradition, while describing human settlements as chaotic and crowded and attributing the foundation and planning of the 'modern city' (Rabinow, 1995) to the French Protectorate. In addition, years of turmoil have caused the cities to stagnate. For this reason, urbanization rates are still low (21 per cent between 2011 and 2015) compared to other countries in the region.[7] However, the urban economies generate approximately 50 per cent of the national GDP.[8] The discrepancy between urbanization rates and the cities' economic weight raises questions about the future of the cities, which are undergoing dramatic urban transition.

Some research into this transition has already been conducted, but has almost exclusively focused on Phnom Penh. As Percival and Waley (2012) observe, 'urban issues in Cambodia have been under-researched compared with cities in other South-east Asian countries' (p. 2875). Two major avenues of investigation can be identified. The first looks at the urban consequences of neopatrimonialism and economic liberalization (Fauveaud, 2011, 2014, 2015, 2016; Springer, 2010, 2011, 2013). The politics of urban land is central to this avenue of research, which examines the evolution of the Cambodian land system since colonial times (Carrier, 2007; Un and So, 2011).

Neopatrimonialism is characterized by pervasive patron-client relationships, operating along clan and family lines, which shape the distribution of power and processes of decision-making in every field of social life. Associated with forms of authoritarianism based on the ascendancy of top-level patrons and political leaders, neopatrimonialism reorders the city in a way that maintains the privileges of the political elites on the level of the nation state and secures the interests of capital on the global level (Springer, 2010). This system enables the accumulation of land in the hands of a few people (Springer, 2011, 2013). As urban land is seen as a source of enormous profit, they exercise coercive power and symbolic violence to ensure their stranglehold on this valuable good. They also capture inflows of regional and international capital and are able to direct programmes of urban redevelopment (Fauveaud, 2015a).

Far from increasing social justice, the reconstruction of the Cambodian legislation and state apparatus has been instrumentalized to the advantage of the elites. Violence in the urban environment is normalized through various forms of institutionalization (Springer, 2011). These authorize operations of eviction and urban cleansing (Blot, 2013), which erase informality from central urban areas (Clerc, 2010), promote modernized urban images in central urban locations, and produce urban spaces that are showcases of internationalization processes (Fauveaud, 2014b).

7 During the same years, Thailand had an urbanization rate of 47 per cent, Indonesia of 53 per cent, and Laos of 36 per cent (data.worldbank.org).

8 Sidgwick, Erik and Hiroshi Izaki, 2013, 'Urbanization and Growth', *Phnom Penh Post*, 27 November. http://www.phnompenhpost.com/analysis-and-op-ed/urbanisation-and-growth (accessed 5 May 2016).

Another avenue of investigation, closely intertwined with the first one, focuses on the processes, people, and types of project that reshape Phnom Penh as a metropolis. Apart from the most powerful patrons and wealthy investors, a multitude of smaller-scale developers, owners, and families participate in the development of the Cambodian capital. Fauveaud (2014a, 2015a) has investigated their modus operandi and relations with the institutional environment from a socio-geographical perspective. His research shows that individuals and groups shape strategies that enable them to benefit from the specific situation of Cambodia, where an under-regulated institutional environment is opening up numerous opportunities for personal profit. Looking closely at processes of metropolization, Goldblum (2012) shows the complexities of the spatial and physical production of the Cambodian capital. New Cambodian institutions are challenged by the double objective of reconstructing the modern nation state and mastering the physical restructuring of the city.

The transformation and extension of Phnom Penh are marked by several types of project that are profoundly altering its organization and landscapes: mega-projects (Paling, 2012) such as satellite cities (Goldblum, 2012; Percival and Waley, 2012), and residential developments called *borey* (Fauveaud, 2015b, see Chapter 3). These projects, in many cases sponsored by foreign direct investment (FDI) from other Asian countries (China and South Korea are predominant), introduce global urban references (Percival and Waley, 2012). This 'inter-referenced' urbanism (Ibid.), which echoes 'an eclectic array of cities throughout the region and the world' (Paling, 2012, p. 2895), reflects the desire of private developers to fill the gap that separates Phnom Penh from other Asian metropolises, although projects constructed in Cambodia are often smaller and less ambitious. This 'modesty' indicates the still uncertain regional and international status of the Cambodian capital, mainly due to its unstable and volatile economic and political situation.

My research draws substantially on this body of work. The urban transition of Siem Reap presents similar challenges for Cambodian institutions, which have to deal with potentially disruptive processes of urban transformation. Through the double analytical framework of neopatrimonialism and neoliberalism, it is possible to grasp the complex array of networks of power and influence that determine land allocation and the success (or failure) of planning. My analysis of agents of development addresses the collective tactics that negotiate the law and make urban development a 'secretive affair' (Springer, 2011). It does so by investigating the specificities of these tactics in the context of a resurgent urban economy monopolized by the presence of a major tourist and heritage site. One of the original features of my approach is its interdisciplinary character (drawing on history, discourse analysis, architecture and urban studies, anthropology of development, political economy, and sociology) and the diversity of the entwined perspectives from which I look at urban politics. The vast majority of urban research on Cambodia has been focused on Phnom Penh; it is thus timely to explore the urban transition of a secondary Cambodian city in which expectations and resources are being catalysed to create exponential economic and urban development.

Understanding the politics of heritage from the margins

Siem Reap has a marginal position in the politics of heritage due to a complex set of reasons and decisions taken ever since colonial times. The grandiose heritage of Angkor has dazzled decision makers at the national and international level, who have formulated an 'authorized heritage discourse' (Smith, 2006) celebrating the role of historic monuments in the construction of Cambodian national identity. The academic field of critical heritage studies has deconstructed discourses produced and disseminated by international organizations and nation states. It has cast more light on the political nature of heritage and called for a pluralistic attitude to the assessment of heritage and identity values (inter alia Harrison, 2013; Winter, 2012; Waterton and Watson, 2013). In the case of Asia, scholars of critical heritage studies have examined the consequences of World Heritage listing on places, societies, and cultures, and have questioned the local relevance of international heritage systems (Chapagain and Silva, 2013; Winter and Daly, 2012; King, 2016). Knowledge and arguments developed in this field are highly relevant to my work on Siem Reap-Angkor, where the authorized heritage discourse has overlooked minor forms of heritage and the ordinary built legacy.

By 2010, Angkor housed approximately 100,000 people in some 30 villages scattered around the archaeological park. However, the heritage policies that followed the listing of Angkor as a UNESCO World Heritage Site paid no attention to the 'living dimension' of the site (Miura, 2004) and focused on the high culture of monumental remains and material architecture. In contrast, several researchers have looked at these villages and communities (Miura, 2004, 2011; Gillespie, 2009, 2012; Luco, 2008, 2016). They have showed that a narrow definition of heritage has dispossessed villagers of the capacity to engage in a thoughtful relationship with their past, and has neglected the value that local dwellings, landscapes, traditions, and crafts may have for them. Researchers have also examined the tensions between the villagers' aspiration to benefit from the economic development of Cambodia and the restrictions on their daily life imposed by the regulations for the World Heritage Site.[9] In particular, Miura calls for an anthropological approach to the understanding of heritage, which would include ownership claims by the local people. In a similar vein, Lloyd Rivera (2009) has assessed Cambodian legislation and suggested that it should further encourage the involvement of local communities, and take into consideration local customary systems in the shaping of localized approaches to the 'living traditions'.

Winter (2007, 2008) adopts an overall approach to the Angkor region. He has looked at the emergence of Angkor as a global heritage site in the context of post-conflict reconstruction, nation-building, and the socio-economic rehabilitation of Cambodia, inquiring into the conflicts underlying the competing agendas of heritage conservation and tourism development. His contribution is particularly valuable, as he has examined the multi-scalar connections among programmes and interested parties, which have contributed to shaping the heritage agenda and have had significant consequences for heritage management, spatial transformation, tourist practices, and daily life. Dealing with the spatial aspect of the site, Butland (2009) has examined the meanings and representations of space, which several categories of local entity communicate through their discourse. She focuses her analysis on texts and oral communications with the goal of challenging the perception of Angkor as an archaeological park and positing the notion of cultural landscape as an inclusive framework to assess the value of heritage.

Despite the prolific output of research on Angkor and the critiques of the shortcomings of the heritage management system, only a few reports and scholarly papers have examined the consequences of World Heritage listing on the surrounding urban environment. Gaulis (2007) discusses the establishment of a planning and management system for the Angkor region, sponsored by international development assistance, following the listing of the archaeological park as a UNESCO World Heritage Site. Hetreau-Pottier has studied urban history (2008) and criticized the destruction of Siem

9 This research has taken root in the interest in indigenous societies and their practices, expressed by a small number of researchers since colonial times (Peycam, 2010): Etienne Aymonier (1844-1929), Adhémard Leclère (1855-1917), and Evelyne Porée-Maspéro (1906-1992) were the main figures of this interdisciplinary and human-centred approach to research on Angkor. Later, Georges Condominas (1957), Jean Delevert (1961), and Solange Thierry-Bernard (1964) pursued this research path with their work on contemporary Cambodian society, popular knowledge, and practices. Since the 1990s, this 'humanist' research approach has re-emerged in the newly founded field of 'Khmer studies', which looks at ancient, modern, and contemporary Cambodia from a variety of perspectives in the human and social sciences.

Reap's built heritage as a result of tourism and land speculation (2008b). In a report that presented the town to a group of experts attending an international roundtable,[10] Esposito and Nam (2008) examined the politics of urban development from a variety of perspectives, including tourism, environmental issues, the conservation of the built heritage, planning, and urban service provision. Hauser-Schäublin (2011) has analysed the problems related to the tourism economy, land use, and consumption, as well as their impact on the inefficient distribution of economic benefits in Siem Reap province. Vigers (2005) observes that Angkor and Siem Reap are two distinct entities that have interacted since colonial times. Through the testimony of older Siem Reap residents, he unpacks the memories concealed in the built landscape, which unintentionally haunt the urban environment[11] without being a cause for conscious celebration. Heikkila and Peycam (2010) argue that the economic development of Siem Reap depends on the exogenous meanings given to the archaeological site since colonial times, based on 'use', 'exchange', 'symbol', and 'myth'. They claim that a new economic strategy would re-contextualize Angkor within the broader region where it is located.

No research work has hitherto covered the town of Siem Reap in any significant detail. This lack is symptomatic of a deeply ingrained approach to the study of heritage recognition that has looked at its consequences 'from within' the heritage sites themselves. That focus might seem obvious and legitimate. However, the case of Siem Reap-Angkor shows that the World Heritage listing has engendered new forms of geographical connectivity, multi-scalar power games, and influence peddling among international, national, and local entities, which can only be fully assessed by including the space developing in the orbit of the World Heritage Site, where most of these relations are played out. This is especially true in the case of Cambodia and other developing countries of Southeast Asia where the tourism economy represents a large share of GDP[12] and investment converges on the periphery of the heritage sites. I see the archaeological park as a 'generator of conditions' that have triggered the development of the non-heritage space. Far from being a passive recipient, the non-heritage space creates a relation

10 The PRCUD (Pacific Rim Council on Urban Development) annual roundtable, which took place in Siem Reap in 2008, in collaboration with the Getty Foundation, the APSARA Authority, and the Center for Khmer Studies.

11 Vigers developed this argument following De Certeau, who claimed that 'On n'habite que des lieux hantés' ('We only live in haunted places') (De Certeau, 1990, p. 162).

12 Southeast Asia is the second region of the world for the direct and total contribution of tourism to national GDP (respectively 4.8 and 12 per cent) preceded by North Africa for the direct contribution (5.2 per cent) and the Caribbean for the total contribution (14.6 per cent).

of complementarity and mutual dependence vis-à-vis the heritage space. The latter could not exist as a tourism site without the infrastructures and facilities offered by the former; conversely, tourism is the main driver of the development of the non-heritage space and exerts a strong attractive power on capital, population, expertise, and various other types of resource that converge in the non-heritage space. I look at the multifaceted political, economic, and social interactions between the heritage and non-heritage spaces as a way to understand the politics of urban development on the margins of the heritage site. By doing so, I aim to lay the foundation for a research approach that strives to reintegrate the marginal spaces of heritage recognition into the map of knowledge.

Designing a research trajectory

When I first arrived in Cambodia in 2005, property speculation in Siem Reap had only just started. I could observe the first consequences for the urban landscape: large hotels mushroomed along the main roads, groups of precarious wooden houses disappeared overnight, and fenced but undeveloped land plots were waiting for projects.

I conducted two fieldwork projects of one month each in 2005 and 2006, before settling down in the town in December 2007 for a full year. During the first months, I used to stand in front of the massive hotels for long hours, with cars and motorbikes whizzing by at great speed, in order to draw and then analyse their architectural types and styles. I also used to inventory all the tourism infrastructures built in the city, for the purpose of understanding how rapidly and profoundly they were changing the urban face of Siem Reap. I realized quite quickly that the majority of the new buildings were lacking real architectural quality. Also, they were replacing older houses which, in my view, possessed both historical and aesthetic value. Tourism infrastructures and facilities consumed large amounts of energy and overexploited natural resources with swimming pools and golf courses, which needed to be irrigated on a regular basis. Unregulated urbanization caused traffic problems and land use conflicts, with the city's edges expanding and agricultural space being gradually pushed further and further away.

I was looking at the city through the lenses of the architect and urban planner with a specialization in heritage conservation. As such, I was used to observing, describing, and diagnosing malfunctions in the built space, and I used the tools of design and planning to develop solutions that would help improve it. Adopting this perspective in Siem Reap, I could not but be highly critical of the disruptive urban transformation taking place. However, I also realized that this approach would confine my work to a normative and prescriptive account of how urban forms and management could be improved if only the structural problems of Cambodian politics could be solved. The direct and unwanted consequence would be a judgemental criticism of institutional weakness and corruption. While researchers working on contemporary Cambodia have often taken a stand against these, I was aware that my individual position as a researcher was different, and that my analytical capacities were directed rather towards the investigation of functioning, processes, collective and individual motivation, and the deconstruction of paradigms. In spite of this internal awareness of my identity as a researcher, I faced the inadequacy of my analytical and methodological tools. I experienced a moment of intense disorientation, which compelled me to retrace my steps and look for alternative approaches.

The result of this inductive exploration has been a substantial shift in the focus of my work, which has moved from the analysis of built forms to the analysis of the social, cultural, economic, and political processes leading to their production. Throughout the year that I spent in Siem Reap and subsequent one-month fieldwork projects undertaken in 2009, 2013, and 2015, I directed my attention to several categories of people actively involved in those processes: planners, public officers, architects, constructors, investors, and small-scale promoters such as expatriates and Khmer families. I deliberately narrowed down my research focus to the 'producers', leaving aside other approaches that could have addressed the inhabitants' own perception of urban transformation, or tourists' practices and understanding of the city (Winter 2007). The reason I focused on producers is that I saw Siem Reap as a fascinating city 'in the making'. I was offered the opportunity to give an account of the intense and frenetic processes of urban transformation between 2005 and 2015.

I analysed the political and professional strategies and the collective tactics of investment in the urban environment. This analysis was rooted in the knowledge of Cambodia's political economy, institutional framework, legislation, and investment statistics, which I compiled on the basis of data provided by government institutions. It developed through a series of semi-directive interviews and questionnaires[13] and the examination of policies

13 107 semi-directive interviews were conducted between 2007 and 2015 with the following categories: international experts, Cambodian public officials, international lawyers working in Cambodia, representatives of professional associations, developers and investors, architects and constructors, NGO managers, owners and managers of tourist facilities, and travel agents

and political discourse. While I did not get much data from interviews with high-ranking Cambodian officials, those meetings encouraged me to analyse political discourse and strategies. I realized how important the silences and omissions, hesitations, and embarrassed smiles were for understanding the complex, conflicting, and sometimes shameful implications of Siem Reap's recent urbanization. I closely associated discourse and tactics with the analysis of proposed or actual processes of spatial transformation. To do this, I used tools that were more familiar to me: drawing and mapping on various scales (the building, the neighbourhood, the urbanized area), the analysis of planning and building permits,[14] and the exhaustive inventory of the approximately 300 hotels and guesthouses built between 1992 and 2008.

I also explored how the making and transformation of the built space is permeated with meanings. The producers of the city appropriate the images, ideas, and agendas of heritage for their own ends, and use them to give form to the urban fabric. The analysis of a sample of tourism-related projects has revealed that producers draw on several 'universes of reference' for architecture, borrowing from different cultural systems and historical backgrounds. To identify the threads of architectural references and borrowings that contribute to contemporary architectural design, I retraced the colonial and postcolonial history of representations of Cambodian heritage, as well as the architectural history of the main types of global tourism facility, such as hotels, museums, and theme parks, arguing that contemporary tourism architecture in Siem Reap assembles inherited colonial representations of places and traditions with models, styles, and a decorative repertoire derived from internationally circulating models.

In the small town of Siem Reap, the Western expatriate community has dominated a large segment of the tourism market, and a small number of influential individuals (both Cambodian and foreign) compose the economic and political elite. I ended up becoming closely acquainted with some of my informants, and in my fieldwork I learnt more through informal conversations in restaurants and bars than from carefully prepared interview guidelines. Moreover, as a PhD student, I was based at the IPRAUS research institute,[15]

and tour operators. Also, 78 questionnaires were submitted to developers, owners and managers of tourist facilities, and real estate agents.

14 Four hundred building permit applications were examined at the Cadastral Office of Siem Reap Province and at the national headquarters of the Ministry of Land Management, Urban Planning, and Construction (MLMUP). This survey was conducted in 2008 at the MLMUP and in 2009 at the Cadastral Office.

15 IPRAUS is the *Institut Parisien de Recherche Architecture Urbanistique Sociétés* ('Paris Research Institute Architecture Urbanism Societies').

which had formerly been directed by Pierre Clément, one of the main figures of urban and overall planning for Siem Reap-Angkor during the 1990s. Thanks to my position as an 'insider' at the institute, I could easily access a collection of planning documents and maps produced by his architecture office. I also had the opportunity to be involved in the activities organized by the research department in Siem Reap: these included a student workshop in planning and architecture (2004-2005), then the establishment of the Observatoire urbain de Siem Reap/Angkor. Architecture-Patrimoine-Développement ('Observatory of Siem Reap/Angkor: Architecture-Heritage-Development'), which aimed at monitoring the general and urban transformation of the heritage site and the city. In order to avoid introducing a bias in the research process due to my acquaintance with urban planners working as consultants in Siem Reap, I had to create some distance from the professional culture and expert knowledge that was also my own. This was made possible through deep immersion in fieldwork for long periods of time, which enabled me to appreciate the gaps between planning ideas and the realities of the situation that I aimed to examine. Moreover, the expansion of the theoretical framework of the research to the anthropology of development helped me to construct productive critiques of expert knowledge.

I reframed the interdisciplinary contributions derived from analysis of processes and urban forms in terms of an analysis of the heritage system that 'makes them possible' on the margins of the archaeological park. Angkor's nomination files, regular reports by UNESCO, transcriptions and minutes of the meetings of the ICC-Angkor,[16] colonial archives and secondary sources, heritage legislation, and UNESCO conventions and charters helped me identify the knowledge paradigms and structural organization of the World Heritage system as a generator of the conditions for unbridled urban development. By producing a critique of the World Heritage system and its colonial background, I hope the results of my research may be relevant to other heritage sites in developing countries, where intense development pressures have magnified the structural shortcomings of the World Heritage system.

16 The International Coordination Committee for the Safeguarding and Development of the Historic Site of Angkor (ICC-Angkor) was established during the Tokyo Conference which took place in October 1993 in order to present and discuss all projects to be implemented in the World Heritage Site and its surroundings. The committee brings together various categories of participant including representatives of Cambodian institutions, international organizations, donors, consultants, and experts. The ICC Committee's meetings take place twice a year (one Plenary Session and one Technical Session).

The content and structure of the book

Each chapter presents a specific perspective from which to view the formation and development of the non-heritage space on the periphery of the World Heritage Site of Angkor.

Chapter 1 lays the groundwork for understanding how the non-heritage space was established historically. It examines how the institutional practice of heritage took root in Cambodia in the late nineteenth century and the beginning of the twentieth, under the influence of the French colonial power. An entrenched and stable idea of heritage underpinned this institutional practice. It was grounded in the notion of the 'historic monument' constructed by the European political and cultural elites in modern times. In order to protect the monuments, boundaries marked the limits of the archaeological park of Angkor, first established in 1925. The monuments, the park, and the boundaries constituted the fundamental triad of heritage conservation. However, the implementation of this triad produced a hierarchy of core and marginal spaces in the Angkor region that marginalized other forms of legacy and space; these have ended up on the periphery of the archaeological park – and of heritage recognition. Since colonial times, Siem Reap has been developed as a place for tourists, with little concern for its built forms and landscapes. The World Heritage listing confirmed and even expanded this heritage management system: today, the archaeological park covers a surface of 401 square kilometres and Siem Reap has become a tourist hub accommodating more than two million visitors a year. Analysing the internal inconsistencies and the drawbacks of this system within the Cambodian context, I show that its recent reinforcement has resulted in functional segregation and spatial fragmentation, which exacerbates the social tensions underlying the urban development of Siem Reap.

Chapter 2 analyses the politics of urban planning on the doorstep of the archaeological site. As Cambodia has only recently emerged from war and foreign occupation, international donors have offered substantial technical and financial aid for urban planning. The marginal space of Siem Reap has become central to at least a dozen consulting firms since the 1990s; they have provided ideas, models, and patterns for developing a tourism hub and a sustainable city in close proximity to a major heritage site. In order to do so, they have used planning tools, including zoning and inventories, whose international dissemination is ensured by international consultants working in developing countries. The chapter looks at how planners connect these tools and models with their understandings of local architectural and urban forms, tropical environments, and landscapes. On the one hand, planners are seen as 'cultural brokers', who transfer knowledge and technical skills in a country seriously lacking trained architects as a result of the massacres by the Khmer Rouge. On the other hand, these planners learn lessons from Siem Reap-Angkor and develop planning models and layouts that draw on local characteristics and traditions. This two-way flow of knowledge helps us to understand aid as an intercultural encounter. It also helps us to address the social entanglements of international assistance in Cambodia. However, social, political, and economic struggles have led to the abandonment of all the urban plans designed for Siem Reap, while projects sponsored by international assistance, including a tourism district and a tourist and commercial harbour on Tonlé Sap lake, are diverted from their original purpose and manipulated for the sake of private profit. Moving beyond the frequent critiques of the inefficacy of international assistance, the chapter views foreign-sponsored planning as a powerful disseminator of ideas, which may penetrate Cambodia's political and professional milieu in the long term.

Chapter 3 investigates the tactics that property developers use to gain the power to act in the urban space, thus defeating planning strategies. These tactics include the diversion of land law, the concealing of information on the origin of investment capital, and the negotiation and gradual diluting of urban regulations. The chapter argues that Cambodian law and administrative procedures contain 'grey zones' that facilitate such tactics. Far from acting as regulators of urban development, state authorities implicitly endorse these tactics through undercover alliances between the political elites and the developers, made possible by the aforementioned structural grey zones in the Cambodian institutional system. First, the chapter discusses the complex power games that govern the shaping of Siem Reap. Next, it shifts from the social, economic, and political dimensions of urban development to its material effects. It analyses the processes of urban transformation in the most strategic sectors of Siem Reap, where a great number of projects have been built in the last twenty years. It also draws attention to the role of the inhabitants in shaping urban space. In Cambodia, the inhabitants have traditionally played an important part in the development of towns and cities and in the transformation of buildings, spaces, and landscapes. While this role seems to be undermined by the rise of an aggressive private sector, the chapter shows how small family-based businesses and Western expatriates maintain a fusion of rural and urban forms in Siem Reap's urban villages. The chapter ends with an analysis of the transition of Siem Reap from a village to an urban area, expanding without constraints towards the east and west. It investigates the hybrid and complex nature of the urban landscape, which is evolving towards a modernized urban, dispersed environment, while at the same time preserving the legacies of the rural substrate from which it originated.

Chapter 4 looks at another aspect of Siem Reap's position of marginality: the fact that the urban space evades the regulatory power of the state and the international organizations, which impose an official idea of the past and a centralized heritage management system. This marginality enables alternative visions of Cambodia's past and heritage to emerge, expressed through contemporary architectural design. The chapter argues that this design appropriates and synthesizes three sources of architectural ideas: images and narratives, inherited from colonialism, about the Khmer heritage and traditions; models and types of tourist architecture; and motifs, types, and techniques expressing ideas of urban modernity. It asks how these three sources provide inspiration for architectural projects, and how thinking about contemporary Khmer architecture has evolved in the last twenty years, gradually incorporating environmental concerns through the adaptation of the buildings to the climate as well as allusions to local dwelling types, colonial legacies, and Neo-Khmer architecture from the 1960s. Influences from nearby countries are also discussed as important incubators of ideas of urban modernity, which architecture encapsulates as major visual evidence of the economic progress of Cambodian society.

Finally, the Conclusion moves outwards from the case of Siem Reap to the comparative exploration of several case studies from Southeast Asia in which national and local authorities have chosen heritage and tourism as major programmatic domains. I reframe thinking about the consequences of heritage recognition, as well as the dialectical relation of conservation and development and of heritage and contemporary design, within a broader question: how are the multiple forms of the built heritage celebrated, manipulated, reproduced – or forgotten and destroyed – in the making of Southeast Asia's cities today?

1 'Before you build a wall, think of what you are leaving outside it'[1]

The construction of core and marginal spaces in the Angkor region

In the ancient Khmer language, the word 'Angkor' means 'capital city'. Seven Khmer capitals, built between the ninth and fifteenth centuries, extended their power over a broad territory covered by rice fields, interspersed with sanctuaries and villages, and connected by roads and open-air water infrastructures. However, Angkor, as it has come to be understood today, bears no resemblance to this original usage. Instead, it conjures up either an exotic colonial past or a nation's ancient legacy and its vision for the future. When we say 'Angkor', we no longer mean a capital city but a social construct – a collective and selective symbol of a multi-layered historical, cultural, and social reality. And while it might appear that this construct has naturally blossomed from the passing of the centuries, it has only recently been developed in the official discourse of Cambodian and international institutions.

A well-entrenched and stable idea of heritage underpins this social construction. It is grounded in the notion of the 'historic monument', as European political and cultural elites have shaped this in modern times (Gillman, 2010), and assigns the highest importance to the historical, scientific, and artistic value of archaeological remains. In Cambodia, colonial and postcolonial institutions have, at times, adhered to this notion of heritage, while the international community represented by UNESCO has helped them to build a heritage management framework for the World Heritage site of Angkor that assigns the greatest importance to the remains dating from the ancient Khmer civilization.

In this chapter, I examine how the institutional practice of heritage took root in Cambodia in the late nineteenth century and beginning of the twentieth, under the influence of the French colonial power. I show how international organizations and donors involved in the conservation of

1 'Se alzi un muro pensa a cosa lasci fuori'. Calvino, 1993, p. 387 (translated from Italian by the author).

Angkor have confirmed the validity of this heritage system[2] for its conservation since the 1990s. This has produced a geographical hierarchy of core and marginal spaces in the Angkor region. The monuments and their immediate surroundings have been put at the core of the heritage management system, and the creation of archaeological parks has crystallized the idea of Angkor as an identifiable and delimited heritage space. However, this process has led to the marginalization of other types of legacy and space, which have ended up on the periphery of the archaeological parks and of heritage recognition.

Based on the analysis of heritage policies, official documents and discourses, legislation, and management plans, this chapter examines the cultural ties and political rationale that underpin the formation of a dualistic geographical system formed by a heritage space – the archaeological park of Angkor – and the non-heritage space. The non-heritage space is under-regulated and viewed as the backdrop of the World Heritage Site. All the developments that would not be permitted within the heritage space can find their place there. This space is thus particularly fragile given the consequences of the fame of the World Heritage Site: these include increasing numbers of tourists, intense construction activity, destruction of vernacular architecture, and overexploitation of natural resources. This dialectic of inclusion and exclusion, generated by the heritage management system, is crucial for identifying the initial conditions that determine how Siem Reap, the modern town located six kilometres from the main temples, has been developed into an international tourism hub.

My thinking about the creation of a global heritage site at Angkor is based in a rich academic literature that looks at the politics of the UNESCO World Heritage list from various perspectives. This literature contributes to developing one of the main theoretical positions of critical heritage studies (see Introduction), according to which heritage does not exist per se, but is constructed through a social, political, and economic process (Kirshenblatt-Gimblett, 2002; Smith, 2006; Smith and Waterton, 2009; Harrison, 2013). Following this line of thought, it is argued that the selection of World Heritage sites depends on Western cultural particularism (Raj Isar, 2011) disguised by claims to universality. UNESCO principles have long focused on the conservation of monumental remains and the built heritage, in line with nationalistic constructions of identity and collective memory directed by states, which, even in non-Western locales, have willingly imported exogenous theoretical frameworks for heritage recognition and

2 By heritage management system I mean the interconnected notions, values, measures, regulations, and practices that determine how a heritage site will be managed.

management (Peleggi, 2002). The academic literature has investigated the influence of the powerful West and the regimes of dependence, appropriation, and reinterpretation that come into force in postcolonial countries. The World Heritage List has been seen as an 'indisputable global-level instrument which mobilizes resources, reproduces dominant arguments and rationales, establishes programs, agendas, and policies, and dispenses status surrounding the conservation and preservation of the thing called heritage' (Askew, 2010, p. 19). It produces iconic sites and imposes 'a common stamp on cultures across the world and their policies creating a logic of global cultural uniformity' (Logan, 2001, p. 52).

Substantial empirical research has provided insight into the consequences of UNESCO World Heritage listing on spaces, places, and societies. In many cases, the production of 'heritagescapes' (Di Giovine, 2009) results in tourism pressure that endangers heritage integrity. Often, tourism development pushes resident populations out. Heritage sites are deserted by locals and converted into commercial centres for tourism consumption (Berliner, 2010), affected by increasing property prices, restrictive urban regulation, and profit opportunities from the rental or sale of buildings located in the listed areas. This heritage literature has looked at the commodification of World Heritage sites for tourism, identifying the negative consequences of a World Heritage listing. In their attention to the exclusion of local population from heritage management (inter alia Smith and Waterton, 2009), heritage studies have joined with broader debates on the role of communities and their empowerment in places where the dominance of the nation state has tended to marginalize grassroots movements and local particularism in favour of overarching discourses on national identity and societies (Hoggett, 1997). Literature on the politics of UNESCO heritage has thus focused on the conflicts and disputes that arise when different perceptions of value, agendas, and interests converge on highly symbolically significant sites.

UNESCO has not been deaf to criticism. At the end of the 1980s, it initiated an evaluation of its principles that has aimed at overcoming the unbalanced and non-representative nature of the World Heritage List (Frey, Pamini, and Steiner, 2013) and the focus on high-culture and monumental heritage (Esposito and Gaulis, 2010). In order to remedy these limitations, new notions of value and new heritage paradigms, such as cultural landscape, intangible heritage, and cultural diversity, have been introduced through operational guidelines and conventions. Some writers have suggested that this 'anthropological turn' ('l'anthropologisation progressive' of UNESCO, Brumann and Joseph, 2013) has succeeded in integrating claims and cultural insights from the peripheries of the World Heritage system (inter alia Logan,

2001). Others have argued that the reform of the World Heritage system has only led to new forms of cultural globalization based on a 'global system of common difference' (Wilk, 1995, quoted by Berliner and Bortolotto, 2013).

One of the main arguments in support of this critique is that UNESCO cannot override nation-state power structures, since the World Heritage Committee (WHC) is formed of 21 representatives of its member states. The WHC generates iconic symbols, and in so doing creates an arena of competition for status among the states (Hevia, 2002). The WHC thus inevitably establishes a global hierarchy of places and cultural expressions, which, despite reform at the theoretical level, will endlessly engender new forms of domination and under-representation. This competition between states has been said to value the 'transactional potentials' of heritage sites over their conservation value (Meskell, 2015, p. 3). Putting sites on the World Heritage List is a way to consolidate 'relationships, strategic partnerships and worldviews that are determined by economic, ethnic, religious, and geographical imperatives' (Meskell, 2015, p. 4). Forming consistent national identities that use heritage sites as icons to increase visibility on the international scene and secure access to cooperation networks, funding, and assistance, ends up being more important than actual conservation. Contemporary heritage studies go beyond the focus on conflict and dissension in order to address 'power relations of collaboration in terms of mutual gain *and* self-interest' (Winter, 2015, p. 998). Rather than exclusively focusing on nation states as the main producers of the politics of the past, they look in more depth at the circulations of individuals and concepts and the establishment of new forms of transnational governance (De Cesari, 2010; De Cesari and Rigney, 2014). They deconstruct the widespread and limiting vision of UNESCO as a monolithic structure, by choosing it as an object of ethnological inquiry (Nielsen and Illouz, 2013) or by analysing the role that it plays in broader geopolitical strategies at the regional or continent-wide level (Winter, 2015, 2016).

The first chapter of this book offers an analytical perspective on the politics of UNESCO World Heritage, which has been largely overlooked in previous research. Meskell quotes a Brazilian delegate who 'rebuked the technical priorities of the Advisory Bodies back in 2012, saying that the Committee "evaluates sites, not management plans"' (p. 12). He adds that 'many politicians and diplomats are not interested in the presentation of properties: site borders, buffer zones and management plans do little to inspire' (p. 12). These tools do not interest the delegates who are directly involved in the World Heritage List, nor have they aroused much academic interest in the field of heritage studies. They have been made the object of research into the professional practice of planning and management; but the research in question asks whether these tools are efficiently used, not whether they are valid ones.

My aim is to approach these tools as objects of critical inquiry. In choosing Angkor, one of the most important of international heritage icons, I suggest that heritage inventories, borders, and zoning are not purely technical tools, but are embedded in the political process of heritage making. They have enormous consequences for the politics of heritage, because they establish decisions about selection and exclusion in durable, physical form. They thus facilitate segregation and spatial fragmentation of the heritage and the non-heritage space. I argue that conservation tools are more resistant to change than notions of heritage. While the history of heritage values at Angkor has mirrored the evolution from historical monument to cultural landscape, which can also be observed in UNESCO's principles, conservation measures have not followed. In practice, only the archaeological park containing the major ruins, not the broader cultural landscape, has been assisted by international conservation programmes and funding. This disconnection of theory from practice, and of discourse from management, reveals a shadow zone in UNESCO politics. Behind its claim to transparency, fuelled by immense quantities of published reports and minutes of meetings, the simple act of setting boundaries reproduces inherited systems of power and crystallizes a politics of territorial representation. My objective is to bring to the surface the mechanisms and the political and historical factors that make this reproduction possible, and explore their impact on the region of Siem Reap.

1.1 The triad of heritage conservation

Angkor is the site of the ancient Khmer capitals, built between the ninth and fifteenth centuries. King Jayavarman II is widely considered to be the founder of the Khmer kingdom and the first of the great Khmer builders. He initially established his capital at Kulen, north of Angkor. In 802 CE, he founded the city of Hariharâlaya at Rolûos,[3] some ten kilometres east of Siem Reap. All his successors, with the exception of Jayavarman VI, who moved the capital to Koh Ker, 96 kilometres from the main complex of Angkor (Chapman, 2013), settled on this territory and founded several capitals. Yaçovarman I built the first capital on the site nowadays called Angkor. This city grew up

3 The capital city at Rolûos was organized around temples and a hydraulic network composed of canals and an artificial lake (the Lolei).

around Phnom Bakheng, one of the hills of the Angkor plain, on which he built a 'mountain-temple'.[4] During the same period, temples were also built on the two other hills, Phnom Kraom and Phnom Bok. A *baray* bordered the city. In the ancient Khmer civilization, the term *baray* designated an artificial lake created by embankments. The two largest of these are the Eastern *baray*, built in the tenth century, which has now dried up, and the Western *baray*, eight kilometres long and two kilometres wide, built in the eleventh century. Archaeologists are unclear about their function, which may have been linked to the practice of agriculture and also to religious cults (Penny, Pottier, Kummu, et al., 2005). One of the best-known kings, Suryavarman II, built Angkor Wat during the eleventh century. Jayavarman VII, who is seen as the greatest Khmer builder, founded Angkor Thom, the royal capital surrounded by a wall three kilometres long, and many temples including Preah Khan and the Bayon.

Successive urban foundations have left traces that have marked the Angkor region down to the present. Impressive stone temples and large-scale water infrastructures were built on broad areas with scattered villages deep in lush vegetation. The population lived in perishable wooden houses on stilts. Orchards and rice fields surrounded the villages. It is not easy to establish where Angkor ends, because its remains are scattered over vast areas. We do not know with certainty why the Khmer kings founded various capitals. Several hypotheses have been made, including the desire of each king to legitimize his power through a new urban settlement, or possibly problems relating to water management. Because of the gradual silting of the canals and artificial lakes due to the land's slight slope and frequent flooding, the kings may have been obliged to abandon previous locations, build up new infrastructure and capitals, and eventually abandon Angkor as a capital site altogether. Frequent Siamese attacks from Ayutthaya, starting around 1351, are also among the most credible explanations of the displacement of the capital. In the most violent of these, the city was apparently sacked in 1431 (Forest, 2008, p. 21; Chapman, 2013). Nevertheless, villages were maintained for centuries, and the ruins of the magnificent temples were used as places of worship and regularly maintained by villagers using simple techniques (Edwards, 2007). European explorers, archaeologists, and artists started to travel around Cambodia in the second half of the nineteenth century; only when seen by Western eyes would these remains come to be considered valuable works of art and made known to the European

4 A mountain temple is a stepped pyramid representing Mount Meru, the centre of the universe and residence of the gods in Hindu mythology.

public through travel narratives, press articles, and colonial exhibitions (Dagens, 1995; see Chapter 4).

In 1907, as soon as the French Protectorate was established in Siem Reap province,[5] home to the remains of Angkor, the École Française d'Extrême Orient (EFEO),[6] a research institute aiming at the production of knowledge on Asian civilizations, established its headquarters in Siem Reap (1908) and regularly appointed a *conservateur d'Angkor* ('Monuments Conservator') to direct restoration work on the main temples (Peycam, 2010). Archaeologists and conservationists seized ownership of the site from the *sangha* (the Buddhist community), which had previously been the sole controller of the temples (Baille, 2007). Angkor soon became the main investigation site for the EFEO, since the ancient Khmer civilization had played a major role in the history of Indochina and the archaeological remains were particularly notable in their number, scope, and value (Mangin, 2006). The EFEO became the sole institution in charge of the site's conservation in Cambodia, with the endorsement of the king.

EFEO's conservation approach was centred on the notion of the historic monument. This notion had gained momentum among the European and political cultural elites since the nineteenth century; recognition of the historical and artistic value of monuments contributed to constructing national identity in modern European states (Choay, 1992; Harrison, 2013). The original meaning of the word 'monument' derives from the Latin verb *monere*, which designates the act of remembering and warning by means of an object, the *monumentum*. According to Choay (1992), this meaning is universal, as every continent and society has manufactured some objects with the aim of remembering – or helping future generations of people to remember – key events or local beliefs. Since the seventeenth century, however, this meaning has been gradually abandoned in Western societies, to be superseded by new definitions related to aesthetic beauty, prestige,

5 The French Protectorate of Cambodia, established in Siem Reap in 1863, acquired Siem Reap only in 1907. The Cambodian provinces of Siem Reap, Battambang, and Sisophon had fallen under the control of the Siamese in 1794, probably in exchange for the permission accorded to Eng, the Cambodian king, to rule in Udong. In 1867, France signed a treaty with Siam, stating that Bangkok renounced any influence on the Cambodian king, and that in exchange the Siamese would hold onto Battambang principality, which was made up of the three provinces. In 1907, however, following a treaty signed by France and Siam, the three provinces were given back to Cambodia, and therefore fell under French control (Chandler, 2008; Forest, 2008, p. 41).

6 The EFEO was founded by the Académie d'inscriptions et de belles lettres ('Academy of Inscriptions and Literature') and by the Governor General of Indochina. At the time of its creation, in 1898, it was called the Mission archéologique d'Indochine ('Archaeological Mission of Indochina'). In 1900, the name was changed to École Française d'Extrême Orient.

and archaeological value. By the eighteenth century, monuments still served the memory of past generations, but this memory expressed the particular vision of history and beauty shared by the cultural and political elites. Choay (1992) argues that this transformation of meaning and values had two main causes. Firstly, Western societies since the Renaissance assigned increasing importance to the concept of art. Whereas during the Middle Ages art aimed to attain perfection in order to please God, from the Quattrocento onwards its purpose became the expression of beauty. Secondly, thanks to the development and dissemination of 'artificial memories' – objects recording the thing to be remembered, in particular the invention of the printing press – the collective 'memory function' of the monument gradually declined. The definition of the historic monument came to be associated with objects expressing a specific set of values – artistic, historical, archaeological, scientific, and so on – which were associated with the official identities and historical memory of the nation.

In the nineteenth and twentieth centuries, the European powers exported the notion of 'historic monument' to their colonies, claiming that these values were universal and went beyond national frontiers. The colonial government of the Dutch East Indies enacted an Ordinance Regarding Monuments in Indonesia (*Monumentum Ordinantie*, No. 19, 1931) which framed the protection and restoration of the temples of Borobudur and Prambanan (Bloembergen and Eickhoff, 2011). In 1904, the British colonial government implemented the Monuments Preservation Act in India, which institutionalized conservation practices based on European experience and strictly controlled by the state (Sengupta, 2015). France viewed the historic monuments of Indochina as 'goods of public interest', where 'public' referred to an extended idea of the French nation, including its colonial territories.[7] Inventory, classification, and collection were the main tools for protecting

7 This is shown by a letter written by E. Senart (French Indian specialist and founder of the Association Française des amis de l'Orient) to the archaeologist Louis Finot in 1901: 'The task of a civilized power goes beyond the immediate concerns of the present: it is its duty to take care of this truly national heritage of the past, of languages and stories, the traditions and the monuments [of the colonies]. It is not a question of satisfying curiosity; it is a strict duty and a resource of the government. One runs a country better that one knows more intimately: we effectively work for its sake if we awake its respect for and emulation of its past grandeur' (BEFEO, 1901, p. 9; translation from the French by the author). However, according to this official – and, in some way, contradictory – political discourse, France protected the historic architecture of Cambodia for the sake of the Cambodian nation. Edwards (2007) writes that through the conservation of the historic monuments, France contributed to awakening a sense of national belonging in Cambodia, which sustained the first nationalist movements in the 1930s up until national independence in 1953.

the historic monuments in France and in the colonies, based on French laws that led to the production of legislative documents for Indochina (Mangin, 2006). More specifically, the decree of 9 March 1900 'on the conservation of monuments and objects of historic and artistic interest' covered the main points of the French law 'on the conservation of historic monuments and works of art' (*Loi sur la conservation des monuments historiques et les objets d'art*, 1887). In 1923, the French law on historic monuments of 1913 (*Loi du 31 décembre 1913 sur les monuments historiques*) was also enacted in Indochina.

In line with these normative documents, French epigraphists and archaeologists began to inventory the Angkor remains in 1907 and reached a total of 1,070 artefacts by 1973, when the EFEO had to abandon the archaeological site in the face of the advance of the Khmer Rouge. However, the *résident supérieur*, the highest public official representing the French government in the colony, considered that the ordinary measures used for protecting other monuments in Indochina 'would be totally ineffective for preserving a group of monuments which will be visited by an increasing number of tourists, and which is distant from administrative centres'. Angkor deserved special treatment: the *résident supérieur* suggested the establishment of 'a special conservation centre [...] now that the colony may find it advantageous to attract more visitors'.[8] These were the beginnings of the establishment of an ambitious heritage management system for the purpose of conservation and tourism development.

The EFEO's conservators established the first system of boundaries around the main ruins in 1911. These initially only covered the road connecting Siem Reap to Angkor, as well as circular areas within a 200-metre radius around the main monuments.[9] Boundaries were fundamental legal tools for protecting historic monuments as well as the visual qualities of the landscapes surrounding them. Following the Charter of Athens of 1931, protective boundaries were introduced by several European countries into legislation on the preservation of historic monuments since the beginning of the twentieth century; Italy was the first, followed by France.[10] The idea

8 NAC, No. 409, 'Lettre du Résident Supérieur du Cambodge au Gouverneur Général de l'Indochine' (Letter by the *résident supérieur* of Cambodia to the Governor General of Indochina), 1914, signed 'Baudin' (translation from the French by the author).

9 These perimeters were established by a royal order on 31 March 1911: NAC No. 15197, 'Dossier général sur le parc d'Angkor: la gestion du tourisme, horaires, subventions, travaux relatifs aux ruines, 1909-1913' (General dossier on the Angkor Park: tourism management, opening hours, grants, public works, 1909-1913).

10 In Italy, Legge per la tutela delle cose d'interesse artistico o storico, No. 1089, enacted on 1 June 1939; in France, the law of 25 February which modified the law on historic monuments of 1913.

Figure 1.1 The archaeological parks of Angkor, as defined by the EFEO in 1925 and the Khmer Republic in 1970

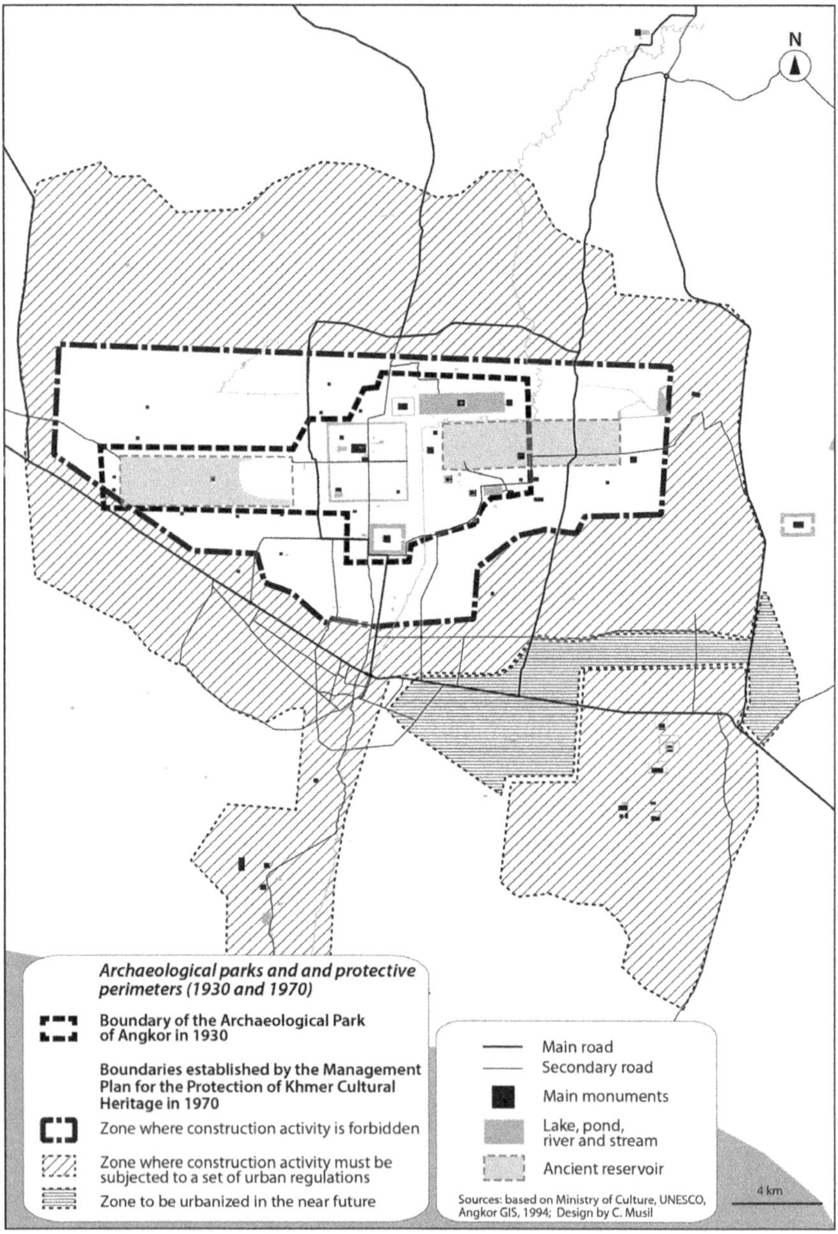

© Esposito 2016

was that a monument 'should be viewed as a midspace object' (Lamprakos, 2014, p. 16) and therefore needed a protected space around it, whose physical transformations had to be controlled in order to preserve its authenticity and integrity. A radius whose point of origin was the monument led to the external perimeter of this unique type of space, which was subject to special regulations concerning new buildings in order to maintain the monument's authenticity and integrity. The space delimited by boundaries also served to create privileged vistas and panoramas from and towards the monuments along roads or through cleared, controlled, or newly planted vegetation.

A few years later, this system based on circular and linear protective zones was abandoned. Applied to a group of monuments, boundaries had to enclose an overall area encompassing the monumental complex. In 1925, the EFEO established an archaeological park composed of a rectangular area of approximately 90 square kilometres (Figure 1.1) including some twenty monuments (Gaulis, 2007), which were also connected through the two main tourism routes called the *petit circuit* and *grand circuit* (Dagens, 1995) (Figure 1.1). The park was an enclosed space subject to control and protection, an area entirely governed by regulations concerning the transformation of space, structures, landscapes, land ownership, transactions, and uses. The tropical vegetation was, in part, cleared away from the park. The movement of farm animals across the park and the activities carried out by the villagers were controlled, with the purpose of offering tourists beautiful, ordered views over and from the monuments. The region, its structures, people, landscapes, and activities, had to conform to the colonizers' aesthetic ideas and values.

The EFEO founded a heritage management system based on three fundamental components: the monument, the boundaries, and the park. This conservation triad lay at the base of a doctrine of conservation that continued even after the independence of Cambodia in 1953, until it was forcibly interrupted by the advance of the Khmer Rouge in 1972-73. The work of the EFEO indelibly marked the culture and practice of conservation at Angkor, as is shown by the subsequent heritage management of national Cambodian institutions directed by the UNESCO international community.

1.2 Angkor, an international icon

The legislation of the kingdom of Cambodia incorporated the notion of historic monuments at the beginning of the 1950s. The Civil Code (1951) mandated a listing of those cultural properties worthy of protection for the common good of the population, to be in the inalienable domain of the state (art. 640). In a reiteration of colonial heritage management, villagers living close to the Angkor monuments were relocated in 1961 (Baille, 2007). In 1970, the Khmer Republic, headed by General Lon Nol, proposed the establishment of a new and bigger archaeological park at Angkor (Figure 1.1), but the project could not be implemented because of the ongoing civil war and subsequent rise of the Khmer Rouge regime.[11] Immediately after the fall of the Khmer Rouge in 1980, the Revolutionary Government of the People of Kampuchea, established under Vietnamese supervision, enacted a decree on the 'protection of historic cultural properties, monuments and natural sites'.[12] Even if no conservation work could be undertaken, since military conflict still threatened the security of the archaeological site, this decree bears witness to the attention paid to archaeological monuments even in times of conflict. The decree includes a section on the 'Angkor Park' and 'Angkor conservation', which draws on the list of protected cultural properties established by the EFEO. Different levels of protection applied to three types of protected zone where construction regulations were introduced to prevent inappropriate land development.

After several decades of regulatory work, the triad formed by the monument, the boundary, and the park has been confirmed as the basis for the social construction of a firmly rooted idea of Angkor. In other postcolonial Southeast Asian countries, 'the construction of national heritage followed transnationally diffused inventories and matrices' (Löfgren, 2001). As Herzfeld and De Cesari explain, 'nationalist successors to colonial powers continue many of the policies of the former occupiers in the name of national redemption' (2015, p. 427). The reasons why postcolonial nation states have appropriated heritage notions and systems are complex: they relate, inter alia, to the direct involvement of foreign agents in heritage conservation, the appropriation of cultural influences from former colonial powers, the exchange of practices and experiences at the transnational and regional scale, and the strategies of international cooperation developed by independent nation states willing to raise funding and be involved in heritage and tourism networks that share a Eurocentric heritage culture.

11 *Plan Directeur pour la protection du patrimoine culture khmer*, prepared by the Ministry of Education, Culture, and Work.

12 Ministère de l'Information de la Culture et de la Presse, République Populaire de Kampuchéa, Décret loi sur la protection des biens culturels historiques, monuments et sites naturels ('Decree-law on the protection of historic cultural properties, monuments, and natural sites'), Conseil Révolutionnaire du Peuple de Kampuchéa No. 227-80-CRP, Archives of the ICOMOS documentation centre, Paris.

With the exception of minor restoration work at Angkor Wat, undertaken by the Archaeological Survey of India and the Polish Ateliers for Conservation of Cultural Property during the 1980s (Chapman, 2013), the monuments were left abandoned for almost twenty years after the EFEO had to flee the country between 1972 and 1973 ahead of the advancing Khmer Rouge. They were overall in a generally poor state of conservation when the 'Agreements on a Comprehensive Political Settlement of the Cambodia Conflict' restored peace to Cambodia on 23 October 1991. The agreements were signed by Cambodia and eighteen other nations in the presence of the United Nations Secretary-General, Javier Pérez de Cuéllar. They confirmed the sovereignty of Cambodia and condemned the Khmer Rouge, who, until then, had been considered the legitimate rulers of Cambodia, even though its seat at the United Nations had remained unfilled since 1990.

As soon as the Paris Peace Accords were signed, the international community of foreign donors, state representatives, and heritage specialists turned their attention to Angkor, which was considered to be 'one of the most important and iconic archaeological sites in Southeast Asia' (UNESCO, 2009). UNESCO launched one of the most ambitious international campaigns in its history for the safeguarding of Angkor. Between 1997 and 2009, the projects sponsored by international cooperation for the safeguarding of Angkor cost more than US$50 million (Ibid.).

Consensus over the moral responsibility of an international community of experts and donors to preserve an outstanding cultural heritage shared by all humanity has inspired campaigns for other symbolically significant heritage sites threatened by various forms of destruction (Turtinen, 2000), such as the Egyptian and Sudanese temples of Abu Simbel threatened by dam construction (1959), the city of Venice (1966), and the Buddhist temple of Borobudur in Indonesia (1972). The principles of collective responsibility in the field of heritage conservation can be found in the work of the jurists of the seventeenth and eighteenth centuries. Hugo Grotius (1583-1645), the Dutch jurist who founded international law, articulated a set of moral rules for military commanders in their handling of cultural properties. Abbé Grégoire (1750-1831), a priest, intellectual, politician, and formative figure of the French Revolution, considered cultural artefacts to be common intellectual and aesthetic assets (Esposito and Gaulis, 2010, p. 33). After the end of the First World War, the League of Nations, an intergovernmental organization founded in 1919 to maintain peace through negotiation, disarmament, and collective security, underlined the need for mechanisms of international cooperation in the heritage sphere that would facilitate the protection of valuable monuments, even in situations of conflict (Hall, 2011).[13] It pursued this through establishing several cultural institutions[14] and launching international inventories and regulations of heritage, though these were later abandoned due to lack of funding.

Nonetheless, the momentum they established in the heritage sphere was maintained. Later, in 1931, the Athens Conference explored various theories of heritage conservation. All 118 participants in the conference came from Europe, except for one American archaeologist who lived in Athens. The numerous Italian and French participants re-orientated the outcomes of the conference, shaping an international agenda based on theories and practices specific to their countries of origin. Being the first event at which professionals in heritage conservation shared their experiences – establishing a common, internationally shared, base for heritage recognition – European heritage theories, practices, and frameworks became international standards. One of the main innovations of the Athens Conference was the idea that there existed masterpieces produced by human civilizations that were of the utmost interest to the global community. The conference participants defined the value of these masterpieces as being of 'outstanding heritage meaning', and pledged to establish procedures that would enable institutions and organizations to submit requests for their preservation (Esposito and Gaulis, 2010).

The internationalization of heritage management began with this pledge and continued with the creation of UNESCO (1946). This international organization endorsed the idea of a 'universal heritage' composed of exceptional masterpieces, which was expressed in a speech by André Malraux[15] (8 March 1960) at the launch of the first UNESCO campaign in Egypt and the Sudan for the preservation of Abu Simbel:

13 The International Museum Office published 'The Draft Declaration concerning the protection of historical buildings and works of art in time of war' (1938) as well as a booklet setting out measures for reducing the negative impacts of warfare involving monuments (1939).

14 These included the International Committee for Intellectual Cooperation (ICIC); the International Institute of Intellectual Cooperation (IIIC), under which was placed the International Museum Office (IMO); and the International Commission of Historic Monuments.

15 André Malraux was a French intellectual, writer, and politician. He was arrested for smuggling Cambodian antiquities in the 1920s and wrote a novel about Angkor called *La Voie royale*. Later, he was Deputy Minister at the Presidency of the Council in 1958, and became the Minister for Cultural Affairs in 1959. In 1962, he sponsored the law for the protection of the 'safeguarded sectors' (*secteurs sauvegardés*) and, in 1964, he created the General Inventory for French Cultural Heritage.

> For the first time, human beings have discovered a universal language of art. We experience its strength clearly, even if we are not familiar with its nature. Without a doubt, this force is strengthened by the fact that human beings acknowledge for the first time that this treasure trove of art brings us the victory of human works over death. UNESCO is attempting to save Nubia's monuments because they are in immediate danger. It goes without saying that UNESCO would try to save other remarkable remains if they were threatened as well.[16]

The idea of the heritage of humanity would later be formally accepted worldwide, through UNESCO's Convention Concerning the Protection of the World Cultural and Natural Heritage (1972).[17] Through the establishment of cultural institutions[18] and the production of normative texts (such as recommendations, expert reports, and conventions), UNESCO founded a technocratic heritage system in which it became the main authority. Since then, it has initiated 26 international campaigns with an overall budget of nearly one billion US dollars (UNESCO, 1992-2013).

The cult of heritage, and its contemporary institutionalization and commercialization worldwide, largely drew on the global dissemination of the shared responsibility to preserve valuable works of art. Ambitious preservation projects led by the international community contributed to consolidating the idea of a responsible international community and the consensus around the conservation projects that it would undertake (Lowenthal, 1998). Conservation campaigns for remarkable sites were all centred on the equation of heritage with monuments and/or groups of buildings. UNESCO's publications confirmed the fundamental role of the heritage triad, as stated in the very first edition of the *Operational Guidelines for the Implementation of the World Heritage Convention* (1977), which immediately followed the World Heritage Convention, and by further

16 Cited in the speech by Anne Lesmaistre, 'Le CIC et Angkor', in UNESCO (2013), p. 15 (translation from the French by the author).

17 In what follows, I will refer to this document as the 1972 Convention.

18 ICOMOS (the International Council of Monuments and Sites), created by UNESCO resolution in 1964; ICOM (the International Council of Museums), created in 1946 as a non-governmental organization with a consultative status with UNESCO; ICCROM (the International Centre for Study of Preservation and Restoration of Cultural Property), founded in 1956 at the ninth UNESCO General Conference in New Delhi; and IUCN (the International Union for the Conservation of Nature and Natural Resources), established in 1948 on the initiative of the first Director-General, Julian Huxley.

documents, which sought to argue for the universal validity of boundaries as protective measures (UNESCO, 2008).

In the context of these discussions within the international community, Angkor was considered to be one of the highest expressions of the 'universal language of art'. Its extraordinary value pushed UNESCO to exert a long-term and powerful influence on the management of this 'symbolic site'.[19]

1.3 Shaping the legal and institutional heritage system for Angkor

UNESCO believed that international assistance for the conservation of Angkor was especially needed, as Cambodian institutions were unstable and under-equipped, having just been re-established with the support of the United Nations Transitional Authority in Cambodia (UNTAC). Moreover, Cambodia lacked a series of technical prerequisites that constitute the heritage system and are required by UNESCO for listing as a World Heritage Site: heritage legislation, human resources, infrastructure, a competent authority in the heritage field, and a management plan. For these reasons, UNESCO suggested that Angkor be added to the 'List of World Heritage in Danger', created especially for those sites considered to be under threat and therefore in need of urgent and extraordinary conservation measures. This 'prudent status' (Ryan and Silvanto, 2009) allows UNESCO to promote and disseminate the World Heritage label, while making its commitment conditional on a series of requirements to be satisfied by the nation states, which have not fully incorporated the principles and standards of the international heritage system. This was the case of Cambodia.

The special status of World Heritage in Danger established Cambodia's dependence vis-à-vis the international community represented by UNESCO. Because Cambodia had just gone through political turmoil, the international community exerted authority over its heritage affairs, an authority it considered to be legitimate for the sake of the conservation of the 'heritage of mankind'. The listing of Angkor as a World Heritage Site was of paramount importance for post-conflict Cambodia. National institutions pinned their hopes on the development of heritage-related tourism and on the recovery of funds and regional and international cooperation networks related to the UNESCO label. As Turtinen (2000) has argued, World Heritage sites are 'status symbols' with 'highly desired symbolic capital locally, nationally and

19 http://whc.unesco.org/fr/list/668 (accessed 6 November 2015).

internationally'. If cultural processes in the global community are based on centre-periphery relationships (Hannerz, 1992), Cambodia sought to achieve a central position by having Angkor listed as a UNESCO World Heritage Site. For this reason, its institutions showed a remarkable docility with respect to the notions, models, and personal advice of foreign consultants. They were fully committed to meeting the UNESCO requirements and hence to internalizing its theoretical and practical system of heritage conservation.

A protocol signed by King Norodom Sihanouk and the former UNESCO Director-General, Federico Mayor, made the advisory role of the international organization an official participant in Cambodian heritage affairs. French scholars and archaeologists from the EFEO, the École Pratique des Hautes Etudes, and the Association des Amis d'Angkor prepared the nomination file for Angkor on the behalf of their Cambodian counterparts, who were said to be 'less familiar' with this technocratic procedure. Two round-table discussions on the preservation of the Angkor monuments were also organized in Cambodia in 1989 and 1990, with representatives from UNESCO, the World Monuments Fund (New York), and Sophia University (Tokyo) (Chapman, 2013). The foreign influence on Cambodian heritage affairs was so extensive that the representatives of a former French colonial institution were allowed to define, on behalf of the national authorities, the outstanding value of their cultural properties.

The nomination file was positively received, and Angkor was simultaneously listed on the World Heritage List and as a site of World Heritage in Danger during the UNESCO World Heritage Committee's sixteenth session, in December 1992. Subsequently, UNESCO required heritage legislation as one of the conditions for definitively listing Angkor as a World Heritage Site.[20] The first Cambodian legal text (the Draft Resolution on the Protection of Cultural Property, 1993), prepared by the international lawyer Ridha Fraoua, substantially drew on the 1972 Convention to define heritage and proposed a system for its classification and inventory. In 1996, the law on the protection of cultural heritage (NS/RKM/0196/26) largely used the definition of cultural property in the 1972 Convention: a cultural property is 'any work produced by human agency and any natural phenomenon of a scientific, historic, artistic or religious nature which bears witness to a certain stage in the development of a civilization or of the natural world and

20 Regulations adopted before the establishment of the new government had an uncertain status in the new political context. The majority of the lawmakers considered that they were no longer valid (Fontaine, 2008) and for this reason the Cambodian legal system started to be completely redeveloped in 1991.

whose protection is in the public interest' (art. 4). The law also enumerates a set of values (scientific, artistic, historical, and religious), which are the same values recognized by the criteria for the designation of properties as World Heritage sites.

UNESCO also requested that the government create an institutional body in charge of the management of the archaeological site: this would form a 'national ally' for UNESCO, and would deal directly with an international body which UNESCO would preside over. Twenty-nine countries and eight organizations took part in the Inter-governmental Conference on the Safeguarding and Development of the Historical Area of Angkor, held in Tokyo in 1993, which launched the international campaign for the safeguarding of Angkor and created an International Coordinating Committee for the Safeguarding and Development of the Historic Site of Angkor (ICC-Angkor). Since then, this committee, a 'giant machine' of international cooperation, has brought together representatives of sixteen countries from four continents for a threefold purpose: ensuring the consistency of all the projects implemented in Angkor and its environs; defining the financial and technical standards for these projects; and consulting the parties involved in the various aspects of heritage management.

The ICC-Angkor model was based on previous experiences of UNESCO-directed international cooperation for endangered heritage sites. An executive committee for the conservation of the Egyptian and Sudanese monuments had been established in 1959, in which UNESCO played the role of coordinator between donors and the two national governments. The ICC-Angkor aimed to create a successful example of that model to export to further heritage sites.[21] Held in one of the most luxurious hotels in Siem Reap, admittance to the ICC meetings is by invitation only. The invited guests are experts in the fields of conservation and development.[22] They are called upon to give supremely qualified advice on the projects for Angkor and, by so doing, to construct what Smith has called an 'authorized

21 'We [the international community] are happy to observe that the international mechanism for cooperation which was shown to work for the knowledge, the conservation, and the development of Angkor [...] is used as reference for similar actions engaged throughout the World' (UNESCO, 2003, art. 16).

22 An ad hoc expert group on conservation has been active since the early years of the ICC's activity. It has advised on the philosophy and methods of conservation. An ad hoc group on sustainable development was created in 2006 within the ICC in order to 'make available their expertise in a large field of development, from tourism management, urban planning, to agriculture'. http://www.unesco.org/new/en/phnompenh/culture/tangible-heritage/ICC-angkor/ (accessed 6 November 2015).

heritage discourse' (2006), meaning one that defines dominant ideas about heritage and its management. However, rather than being a platform for genuine discussion and decision-making, this committee has become mere window-dressing: time for presenting and debating the projects is short, and some of the most controversial projects are not discussed at all.

The ICC's national counterpart was established in 1995 as the Authority for the Protection and Management of Angkor and the Region of Siem Reap (APSARA).[23] Jean-Yves Rossi, Chief Counsel at the *Cour des Comptes* ('Court of Auditors') in France, designed its administrative structure, using the model of the French state system. The idea was to create a centralized agency capable of combining a wide range of socio-economic expertise, which was traditionally split up among various ministries and provincial governments. After twenty years of turmoil, from 1993, all these institutions were being re-established in Cambodia, following the enactment of the new constitution. APSARA was established as a special national authority, supposed to exclude the ministries and provincial governments from operating in the area in question (hence 'Angkor and the Region of Siem Reap' in the APSARA title). It was formally in charge of all aspects of heritage conservation, tourism management, and the development of the broader territory of Siem Reap province. It was also made responsible for the urban development of the town of Siem Reap. Its competencies and tasks overlapped with those normally assigned to national authorities; it was to implement special administrative and institutional measures to strengthen the unique status of the archaeological park.

This 'institutional heritage system enshrined the dual ownership' of Angkor's heritage, which was endorsed by King Norodom Sihanouk. During the UNESCO Executive Board meeting of 1993, he stated:

> It is essential that technical and financial assistance to Cambodia should not only continue but also be expanded. In this way our country can overcome the difficulties it faces, in particular in the area of the conservation of its cultural heritage. Certainly this assistance cannot be directed only to historical monuments and their surroundings, but must also enable the Cambodian people to strengthen its capacity to manage and preserve its heritage, through the work of its own public officials.[24]

23 APSARA was established by Decree NS/RKT/0295/12 (15 February 1995). Its present structure was set up by Sub-decree No. 50 ANK/BK, August 2008.

24 Message by His Majesty Norodom Sihanouk during the 167th session of the Executive Board of UNESCO, No. 1389, 21 May 1993. Source: UNESCO (1993), p. 48.

Figure 1.2 The archaeological parks of Angkor, as defined by the World Heritage listing

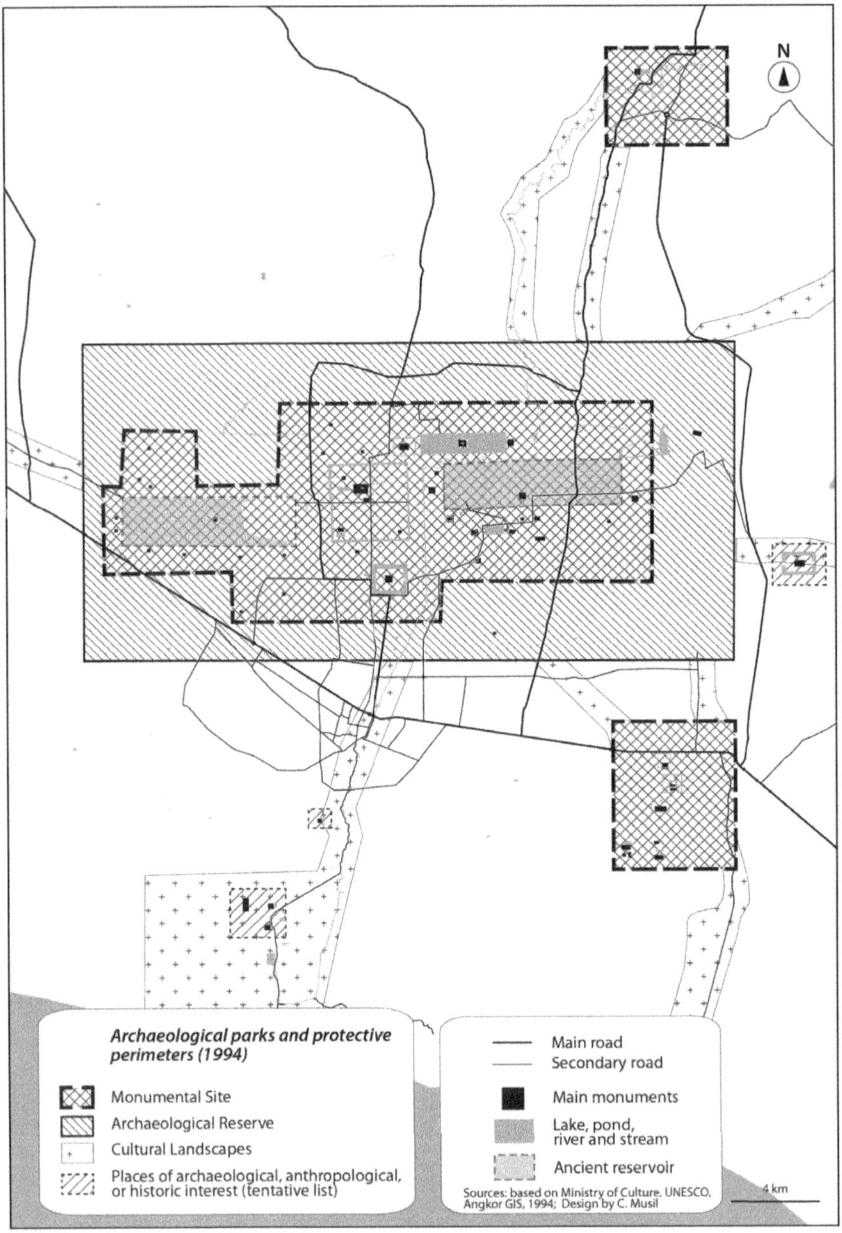

© Esposito 2016

In this speech, the king stated that the national management of heritage is of paramount importance. He identified two levels of authority over the heritage site (national and international), which have been the cause of tension between overlapping authorities and competing claims at other World Heritage sites (see inter alia Rakic and Chambers, 2008). In Cambodia, due also to its situation as a post-conflict country under reconstruction, the interference of foreign assistance in the heritage sphere was so strong that it resulted, according to Jean-Yves Rossi, in a 'new form of oversight' in line with old colonial models, which seemed to go counter to the process of political normalization taking place in the country.

1.4 Zoning a region shaped by Angkor's legacy

The World Heritage listing established three archaeological parks (Figure 1.2). Along with the park created during the colonial era, the new ones include additional archaeological sites and have broader boundaries. The first and biggest incorporated the major monuments of Angkor Wat and Angkor Thom, as well as the Western and Eastern *baray* (artificial lakes). Two smaller parks were defined around the archaeological site of Rolûos and the temple of Banteay Srei.[25] Ridha Fraoua envisaged that these areas would be surrounded by buffer zones, the size of which would depend on the importance of the monuments and the archaeological interest of the areas that still had to be excavated.

The World Heritage listing included additional monuments, while maintaining the conservation triad that delimits a heritage space. Like the archaeologists who, since the beginning of the twentieth century, had gone in search of Khmer monuments to be inventoried, Ridha Fraoua designated Cambodian heritage as 'a group of cultural properties which form a homogeneous complex and which as such possesses historical, architectural, and scientific value' (Fraoua, 1992, p. 11). In line with this statement, the World Heritage Committee defined Angkor as 'remains from the seventh century and, especially, numerous traces of the various Khmer Empire capitals built between the ninth and fifteenth centuries'. 'In Angkor', the Committee added, 'one can follow the history of the Khmer religious architecture, which has considerably influenced Thai art' (UNESCO, 1991, p. 52). Homogeneity, historical representativeness, and high artistic value

25 Banteay Srei, located to the northeast of Siem Reap, is a temple for the worship of the God Shiva. It was built in 968 by King Jayavarman V.

1969; Tambiah, 1976). The geographical distribution of buildings, urban areas, and the site as a whole was based on systems of concentric moats and geometrically aligned infrastructure (roads and canals), which marked the separation between sacred and profane spaces. For instance, the royal city of Angkor Thom, built by Jayavarman VII (1181-1220), was an area three kilometres square surrounded by moats and centred on the Bayon temple. Avenues orientated north-south and east-west cut the city into four sections. Infrastructure built facing the four points of the compass, moats surrounding minor temples, and aligned plots of land marked the boundaries between sacred and profane space.

> The establishment of a capital as an imitation of a celestial archetype in the way that has been described also required its delimitation and orientation as a sacred territory within the continuum of profane space. This was customarily effected in relation to that point, the holy of holies, whence the sacred *habitabilis* had taken its birth, and whence it had spread out in all directions. This central point, the focus of creative force, was the place where communication was achieved most easily between cosmic planes, between earth and heaven on the one hand, and between earth and the underworld on the other. It was through this point of ontological transition that there passed the axis of the world, represented in most instances by the capital city. (Wheatley, 1969, p. 7)

Referring more generally to the 'traditional cities' built by ancient civilizations such as the Maya, Miles (1957) described this type of settlement as the 'extended boundary city', where a 'focally situated ceremonial complex served a population scattered through the surrounding countryside'. This type of settlement and the successive urban foundations left remarkable remains in the Angkor area: a large number of monuments, but also hydraulic and urban infrastructures, the surviving boundaries delineating the plots of land, and minor temples that still preserve the outlines of these sacred organizations of space. The ZEMP study aimed to take this multi-layered and extended legacy into consideration, as well as its interactions with an inhabited and evolving region, which would soon experience intense tourism development. It sought to protect 'traditional patterns of natural resource use', to 'maintain landscape values', and to recreate 'Khmer archaeological features, such as canals and *barays*' (Wager, 1995, p. 520). Its ambition was to expand the heritage system to the periphery of the World Heritage site initially defined by UNESCO, in order to encompass a broad inhabited area with a rich legacy from Angkorian times.

Figure 1.3 Archaeological map of the Angkor region

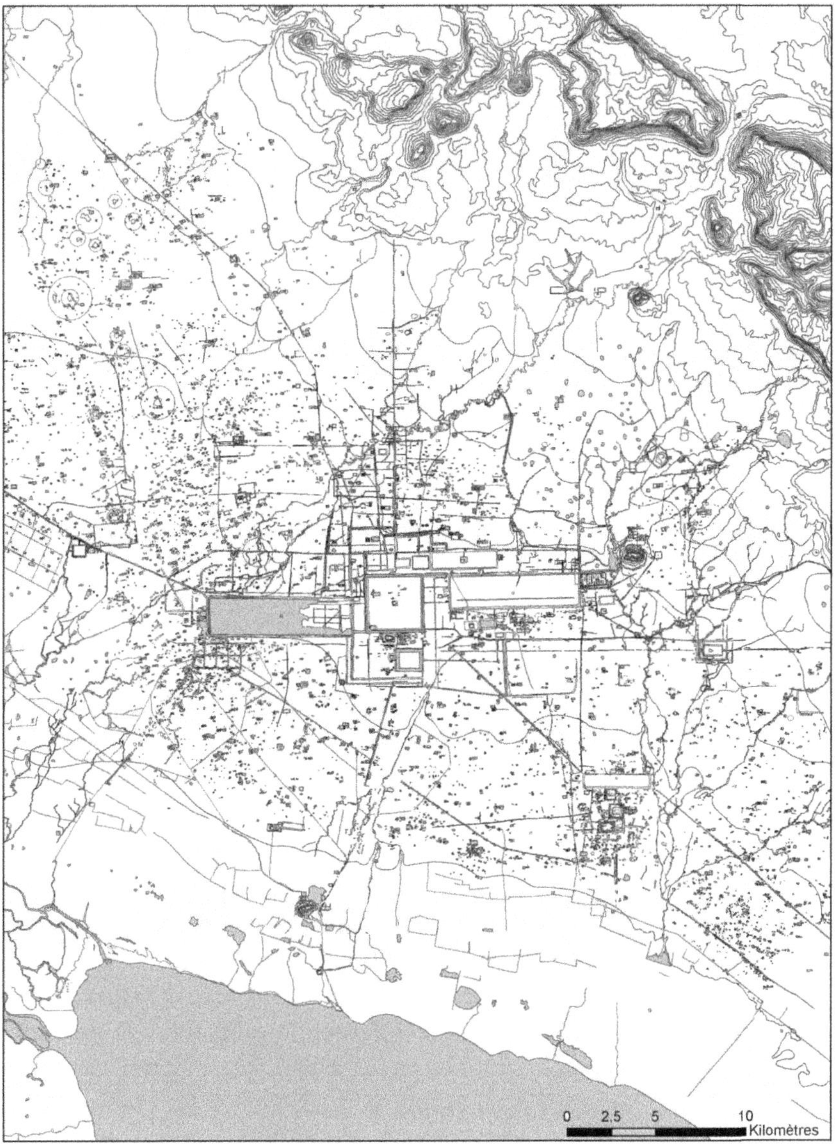

Evans et al., 2007

1.5 Expanding the heritage system: From the monument to the landscape

This strategy met the objectives of a heritage system based on the notion of cultural landscape, which was gaining momentum internationally as a new framework for understanding heritage. Originally coming from the Dutch word *landschap*, meaning a region or piece of land, the notion came to be associated with paintings of outdoor scenes and described picturesque English gardens between the mid-eighteenth and the beginning of the nineteenth centuries. Cultural geography has employed the term since the beginning of the twentieth century, when Carl Sauer (1925) wrote that 'a cultural landscape is fashioned from a natural landscape by a cultural group. Culture is the agent, the natural area is the medium, the cultural landscape is the result' (pp. 309-310).

In the 1960s, the International Union for the Conservation of Nature (IUCN)[27] began a debate on the preservation of nature, protected areas, and landscapes. In 1962, the UNESCO General Conference adopted the 'Recommendations Concerning the Safeguarding of the Beauty and Character of Landscapes and Sites' (Rössler, 2015), the first global instrument for the protection of landscapes. Rowntree (1996) notes that in the 1970s 'a humanistic geography arose that resurrected the cultural landscape concept as a major vehicle for analysing the ties between culture and environment' (pp. 133-134). In 1970, ICOMOS established the International Scientific Committee for Cultural Landscapes, together with the International Federation of Landscape Architects (IFLA). In 1982, ICOMOS adopted the Florence Charter of Historic Gardens. This process culminated at the 1992 Rio Earth Summit (United Nations Conference on Environment and Development), which stressed the interaction between human actions and the environment. This led to the incorporation of the notion of cultural landscape as a criterion for World Heritage listing into the UNESCO Operational Guidelines. Although the 1972 UNESCO Convention aimed to conserve both natural and cultural properties, it had not led 'to substantial considerations of landscape protection' (Rössler, 2015, p. 61). UNESCO officially defined cultural landscapes as 'the combined works of man and nature' and the outcomes of their interactions. The notion was incorporated into UNESCO's Operational Guidelines at the same session of the World Heritage Committee which agreed to list Angkor as a World Heritage Site in Danger (Santa Fe, sixteenth session, 1992). Two years later, UNESCO also adopted an Action

27 The IUCN had been established by UNESCO in 1949.

Plan to encourage state parties to revise their tentative lists[28] for the purpose of nominating or re-nominating properties as cultural landscapes (Akagawa and Sirisrisak, 2008).

Cultural landscapes usually encompass broader geographical regions than traditional conservation zones; however, some authors (Jones, 2003; Rowntree, 1996) argue that the definition of the term has been problematic. Hartshorne (1939) argued that it is useless to refer to landscape as 'cultural': with the exception of those landscapes that are untouched by humans, every landscape is made up of cultural and natural components. In opposition to Sauer, others have added that it is impossible to know fully what the 'original' natural landscape was like, as nature is continually changing, and humans were present in the landscape for so long in prehistory that it is impossible to know all the ways in which they have physically affected the landscape (Jones, 2003). The term's ambiguity allows a diversity of uses that research on cultural landscapes has only intensified. The concept is intended to get beyond the 'monument paradigm' and widen the scope of conservation to the relationship between the human population and the built and natural environment. It seeks a more inclusive idea of heritage, which would include the legacies of ordinary people and their interactions with daily life environments. Such a broad definition potentially embraces the diversity of cultural expression throughout the world. UNESCO has promoted this notion through conferences, workshops, and expert meetings worldwide in order to right the imbalance of the World Heritage List, which included a great majority of Western properties (Akagawa and Sirisrisak, 2008).

Although the concept of cultural landscape contained the seeds for reform of the heritage system, the ZEMP study still considered zoning as a crucial tool for achieving resource compatibility in the Angkor region. The word 'zoning' was used to mean something broader than the act of defining geographical areas and subjecting them to specific regulations. The ZEMP extended zoning to areas not subject to strict measures of heritage conservation (see Chapter 2). It divided the Siem Reap/Angkor region into five zones corresponding to specific levels of protection (Lesmaistre and Cavalier, 2002, p. 120) (Figure 1.3). The World Heritage Site was to correspond to the first four zones listed by the ZEMP, but the management plan for the site was to cover the whole of Siem Reap province. The major archaeological buildings were included in the 'monumental site' (zone 1), which included

28 Tentative lists contain the properties that nation-states would like to nominate to the UNESCO World Heritage List.

the three archaeological parks. The 'archaeological reserve' (zone 2) was a buffer zone in UNESCO terminology: a rectangular area surrounding the main archaeological park, whose purpose was to protect the environs of the monuments and the visual and aesthetic integrity of the archaeological remains through strict regulation of new building and the transformation of the landscape. The 'protected cultural landscapes' (zone 3) covered the ancient water and transport infrastructure; they also included all of Siem Reap town at the beginning of the 1990s, when it was spread out along both banks of the river. The 'points of archaeological, anthropological, or historic interest' (zone 4) were to be identified through further research at the time of the ZEMP. Finally, the perimeter of the 'social, economic, and cultural development of the Siem Reap-Angkor region' (zone 5) covered the rest of Siem Reap province, which was mainly used as rural and agricultural land (Figure 1.3). General guidelines were given for this region concerning agriculture, new buildings, and economic functions. UNESCO was to re-list Angkor in order to take into account this expansion of the heritage site and to acknowledge that Siem Reap province was involved in the social, spatial, and economic dynamics related to the World Heritage listing.

The notion of sustainable development, as shaped by the United Nations through various organizations, events, and documents,[29] infused the planning philosophy. The ZEMP reports said that this region should be managed 'with a focus on social and economic development through the sustainable exploitation of natural resources and the development of cultural tourism. The aim is not only to make development, but also to ensure that development is located in an appropriate way and that heritage conservation is taken into account' (UNESCO, 1993, p. 24). Conservation and development were intertwined in each of the five zones. For instance, in zone 5, intended for socio-economic development, some specific areas were to be preserved for agriculture and urban heritage conservation, while others were to be developed as new parts of the tourist city.

This approach to area management was inspired by the regional master plan sponsored in the 1970s by the Japanese International Cooperation Agency (JICA) for the Buddhist sanctuary of Borobudur in Central Java

29 Wager (1995) explicitly refers to the following organizations, events, and documents as inspiring the notion of sustainable development which underlies the ZEMP planning philosophy: World Conservation Union (IUCN), United Nations Environment Program (UNEP), World Wide Fund for Nature (WWF), the UNDP Handbook and Guidelines for Environment and Sustainable Development (1992), the Earth Summit (1992), and, lastly, the IIED/IUCN National Sustainable Development Strategies and Other Comprehensive Environmental and Development Strategies – A Guide to Implementing Agenda 21.

(Gaulis, 2007), which became a UNESCO World Heritage Site in 1991.[30] Borobudur, built between the eighth and ninth centuries, is located at the centre of a sacred landscape delimited by volcanoes (Merapi, Merbabu, Sumbing, and Sundoro) encircling the temples at the four points of the compass. While previous research and conservation programmes had focused on the temple itself, the JICA master plan encompassed 'a broad scenery zoning diagram that covered "mountainous skylines" forming "the visual edges from the Borobudur Park"' (Nagaoka, 2014, p. 238). Like the ZEMP, which covered the whole provincial area of Siem Reap where the ancient Khmer kings built cities as imitations of the 'celestial archetype', the layout of Borobudur drew on Buddhist philosophy, according to which the temple and the surrounding mountains formed a sacred mandala, a holy representation of cosmic order on earth. This 'cosmographic arrangement' allowed the preservation of local cultural values including architectural monuments and broader sacred landscapes (Nagaoka, 2014). The JICA plan for Borobudur also comprised five zones in concentric circles around the main shrine with decreasing levels of protection. The extension of the mandala centred around Borobudur corresponded to the surface of the protected area. Nagaoka (2014) explained that the notion of cultural landscape was central to this plan, although UNESCO had not yet introduced this notion into its theoretical framework. For him, the benchmark was Japanese heritage legislation, which had 'acknowledged the link between cultural monuments and landscapes' (p. 236) since the beginning of the twentieth century.

The notion of cultural landscape, as used to interpret the heritage of Angkor, has been formed at the intersection of various current concepts and experiences. Wager (1995) noted that the discussions conducted by the organizations associated with the UN were of paramount importance for linking cultural landscapes and sustainable development. Concomitantly, the Japanese experience at Borobudur laid the foundations of an approach to heritage that would connect spirituality and spatial planning. From Japan through Java to Cambodia, the notion of cultural landscape worked its way in as a new tool for reintegrating the local sense of sacredness into heritage, a dimension marginalized in the Eurocentric systems that claimed the superiority of scientific knowledge and technical rationality (Harrison, 2013).

Moreover, a heritage system based on the notion of cultural landscape would have incorporated important physical survivals such as agricultural

30 The plan was established in collaboration with the Indonesian Directorate-General of Culture and authored by two Japanese consulting firms, Pacific Consultants International and Japan City Planning.

practices, villages, and ancient infrastructures . However, the expansion of the area concerned by heritage recognition did not lead to developing new protective mechanisms. The Japanese model for Borobudur continued to use protective boundaries and the delimitation of heritage parks. According to JICA's plan, the conservation zones spread out like an oil spill to include a surface of 26 square kilometres surrounding the Borobudur temple. At Angkor, the boundaries of the monumental site and archaeological reserve were drawn arbitrarily: they did not correspond to any physical or locally relevant administrative limits and did not include the totality of the archaeological remains, which are actually scattered across the whole province. The only criterion for defining the limits was the spatial concentration of the major archaeological monuments; their perimeters were therefore drawn along latitude and longitude lines. In doing this, the ZEMP confirmed what the document nominating Angkor itself stated, that the perimeter of the three archaeological parks is 'represented in the field by a series of signposts' (UNESCO, 1991, p. 2), while some stones laid along the boundaries of the park indicate whether one is inside or outside the heritage space.

1.6 Contracting the heritage system: From the landscape to the archaeological park

Neither Angkor, nor Borobudur have ever been re-listed by UNESCO as cultural landscapes. In both cases, the World Heritage listing only retained those zones that contain the monuments and the buffer areas immediately adjacent to them, while neglecting those areas that include 'ordinary' historical remains, such as villages, waterways, and ancient infrastructures. By 'ordinary', here I mean the heritage that is shaped and given meaning by inhabitants and city dwellers who constantly contribute through micro-actions to building and transforming human settlements. They are distinct from the monumental heritage, which is the expression of the culture of the elites and given extraordinary value and status nationally and internationally.

Borobudur was listed as a World Heritage Site in 1991, before the introduction of the notion of cultural landscape into the UNESCO Operational Guidelines, and was never re-listed as such despite JICA's claims. In practice, only zone 1, 'for protection and prevention of destruction of the physical environment', and zone 2, 'for provision of park facilities', have been treated as central to institutional policies of heritage conservation, while the surrounding villages and natural environments have been socially, culturally, and economically marginalized (Kanki, Adishakti, and Fatimah, 2015).

At Angkor, the ZEMP zoning system has never obtained international recognition, even though the World Heritage Committee has congratulated the government for fulfilling UNESCO's requirements in the field of planning (Decision 19COM VII.C.126). Indeed, although the zoning system was given legal status at the national level (Royal Decree NS/001/1994) and the first four zones established by the ZEMP received the status of National Protected Cultural Sites (Wager, 1995), the zoning system as such was never implemented. The perimeter of the protected site did not encompass the whole area protected as either Archaeological Reserve or Cultural Landscape (Wager, 1995), but included the three archaeological parks and, in particular, the collection of 65 monuments inventoried in the nomination file (UNESCO, 1991). Thus, the site perimeter reinstated 'the previous Parc d'Angkor of the EFEO, in terms both of its boundaries and the attitudes and approaches towards Angkor's spiritual heritage that it enshrined' (Baille, 2007, p. 126).

The listing of Angkor as a cultural landscape was not further considered, although the site's nomination underwent a new phase of evaluation by UNESCO (2004), which removed it from the 'endangered heritage' list. Consequently, it came to be implicitly identified with zones 1 and 2 of the ZEMP, and, more specifically, with the three archaeological parks, which actually cover a surface of 401 square kilometres. By 'implicitly', I mean that the crystallization of this partial and selective concept of Angkor as a collection of ruins and an archaeological park resulted from a collective endorsement of the contemporary notion of a historic monument and a concomitant rejection of the notion of cultural landscape as a new framework for understanding heritage. Evidence of this crystallization process is provided by the Order of the Royal Government of Cambodia (No. 02/BB, 23 June 2004), which immediately followed the movement of Angkor 'from a world heritage in danger into a world heritage in sustainable development'.[31] The Order states that 'about conservation, the priority shall be given to the maintenance and the protection of the site of zone one, which is the "monument site", and zone two which is the "archaeological park to be protected". The size is 401 square kilometres located in the Siem Reap region and could be spread into five zones determined by the conditions for using land and various constructions'.

The rootedness of the idea of Angkor as an archaeological park underlies the social construction of a partial and selective heritage that finds

31 Angkor was removed from the list of 'World Heritage in Danger' during the thirteenth technical meeting of the International Co-ordination Committee for the Safeguarding and the Development of the historical site of Angkor, on February 2004.

expression in multiple ways; these range from defining a strict regulatory system specifically for the archaeological site, to producing a tourist map that emphasizes the visual evidence of the archaeological parks while showing the areas outside them in lighter colours. Representatives of the international community have focused their attention on the projects being implemented in this core space. International consultants have only reinforced this, designating the heritage space as 'the archaeological zone of Angkor' and 'the historical area of Angkor' (UNESCO, 1993). This process was marked by official documents, regulations, and distribution of tasks among Cambodian institutions and international stakeholders. It has also been supported by the tour operators who publicize the image of the archaeological parks as the main tourist destination, and by tourists who want to visit the top ten attractions of Cambodia. The repetition of this social construct of Angkor has, in fact, made it even stronger, not only in the minds of active supporters of this concept of heritage, but also among those, including tourists, who could be defined as recipients of the 'authorized heritage discourse', and who actually contribute to the reification of the image of the archaeological parks (Figure 1.4).

In the case of Angkor, in other words, the notion of cultural landscape has not yet influenced heritage theory sufficiently to be used as a management tool. The weakness of this notion is visible in other more recent cases,[32] as protective boundaries are still used to define heritage sites, creating the conditions for a permanent centre-periphery relationship. Boundaries, however, are inconsistent with the notion of cultural landscape, which evokes in both historical and scholarly terms the open-ended idea of a terrain and the ever-changing relations of inhabitants to their environment.

Why is the heritage triad (monument, boundary, and park) so strong that it resists recent attempts to move forward? The notion of human territoriality, as it was shaped by scholars in the field of human and political geography (inter alia Paasi, 2003; Storey, 2001),[33] offers some insights into

32 Such as the listing of the cultural landscapes of Bali (2012, Indonesia), which has recognized the value of the *subak* system for the cultivation of rice, as an expression of the sacred philosophy of Tri Hita Karana. These rice fields are visible in many parts of Bali; however, only five delimited areas are subject to safeguarding under the World Heritage system.

33 Two main schools of thoughts developed different understandings of the notion of territoriality. On the one hand, biologists, anthropologists, and psychologists support the idea that territoriality is a 'natural' behaviour that humans share with animals. It pushes them to secure the acquisition of a territory and impulsively defend it if necessary. On the other hand, the social sciences, and in particular human and political geography, conceive of territoriality as the product of social conditioning and power relations (Storey, 2001). I draw on the second school of thought in order to develop my argument.

the strategic underpinnings, which can explain the triad's persistence over time and across political regimes. The term 'territory' is generally defined as an area enclosed by a boundary line, whilst territoriality refers to those behaviours and practices that are related 'to the establishment and defense of territories' (Delaney, 2009, p. 196). Territoriality implies the existence of an institutionalized power, usually embodied by the state. It includes various ranges of activities that make state power visible, including regulations, spatial demarcation, classification, and communication about territorial boundaries, as well as sanctions applied when these regulations are infringed. According to Gottmann (1973), territoriality reflects the relationship between people and place and 'signifies [...] a distinction, indeed a separation, from adjacent territories that are under different jurisdictions' (p. 5). Sack (1983, 1986) defined it as 'the attempt by an individual or a group (x) to influence, affect, or control objects, people, and relationships (y) by delimiting and asserting control over a geographical area. This area is the territory' (1983, p. 56). Territoriality not only circumscribes a given territory, but also establishes 'differential access to things and people' (Sack, 1983, p. 55). It does this by transmitting information about the regulation of behaviour and by monitoring that behaviour. Human territoriality can occur on all levels (from a room to an international space) and can embody various degrees of control (1986). It is 'the attempt by any individual or group to influence or establish control over a clearly demarcated territory which is made distinctive and considered at least partially exclusive by its inhabitants or those who define its bounds' (Smith, 1986, quoted by Johnston, 1995, p. 482). It is the result of a human strategy that enables the state to exert surveillance through the establishment of a hierarchy of areas in which various degrees of control are exercised. It is also a symbol of group membership, and a means for regulating social relations. Thongchai Winichakul (1994) analysed the relation between the act of delimiting the national territory of Siam, its representation through maps, and the exercise of the political and military power within this territory: nationhood is grounded in the creation of a 'geo-body', a physical territory delimited by national frontiers which is the prime manifestation of national identity. The 'geo-body' serves as a basis for projecting a wide range of values, feelings, and social aspirations. Territoriality is also said to be a meaningful structure existing throughout history which reveals 'the resistance of the sacred cows of society' (Grosby, 1995). However, it can also generate violence and exclusion (Delaney, 2005): performed by controllers, it is experienced – and sometimes endured – by those who are controlled, and who can react with compliance and conformity, but also with resistance and transgression.

The establishment of boundaries may hide ambiguities, uncertainties, and irrational wills, which lead to the defence of territorial integrity.

Recent developments in the concept of territoriality focus on the discursive nature of territories, which can be conveyed by physical structures, linguistic markers, and rules establishing dominant interpretations at particular historical moments (Delaney, 2009). Communities define their heritage and identity with reference to the physical remains present in the territory where they live. In this context, the interrelation of heritage and territoriality emerges as a still under-explored but promising field of investigation. The state plays a leading role in defining heritage sites in which regulations based on territorial hierarchies are in force, and authorized heritage discourses (Smith, 2006) are projected onto physical space. These sites, especially if they enjoy national and international celebrity, contribute to the establishment of 'heritage territorialities'. Heritage sites are bounded spaces established in close connection with their cartographic representations in the management plans, which determine the areas in which the special powers of international and national institutions (the ICC and APSARA in the case of Angkor) are in force. Maps and plans contribute to making the power of the state visible through the identification of extraordinary heritage spaces, which catalyse national pride, cultural meanings, and sense of identity. Heritage territorialities thus consolidate the power of the state through a twofold strategy that projects a set of 'geographical imaginations' (Delaney, 2009) onto the heritage site, while applying specific levels and types of regulation to it. The establishment of heritage territorialities can also generate non-heritage spaces that are marginal in the production of discourse about the cultural roots of the nation and are subject to lower levels of control by the state. At the same time, these spaces are granted more freedom within the framework of a territorial strategy, which makes them more malleable by processes of spatial transformation carried out by different categories of agent.

Angkor is a major heritage territoriality for Cambodia and a globally iconic site. It embodies strong cultural values, which serve as a foundation for national pride, identity, and international endeavours in heritage conservation. The regulations of the World Heritage property of Angkor are not applied specifically to a group of cultural properties (i.e. to each monument), but are in force throughout the bounded area in which these objects are located. As Sack argues, 'territoriality classifies at least in part by area, rather than by type' (Sack, 1983, p. 58). Territoriality thus imposes different regimes of ownership and competency. Land, for instance, belongs to the public domain within the protected site and special regulations constrain its use.

Significantly, the villagers have been banned from rice cultivation within Angkor Thom. Collecting resin and forest products is also forbidden within the grounds of the ancient royal capital, although these activities were formerly fundamental to the villagers' livelihood. Other prohibitions concern cattle, which cannot be brought into the monuments, the use of water from ponds and *baray*, and the performance of plays at Angkor Wat for Khmer New Year (Tunprawat, 2009). Not only has the daily life of people living within the heritage territory been deeply changed, but the religious and spiritual values that lie at the basis of the relationship between the people and the site have been neglected. At the core of heritage management and conservation, 'Western ideologies rooted in objectification and rationalism' give little importance to religious values (Baille, 2007, p. 124). This process of desacralization began in colonial times with the establishment of the EFEO's dominating role in the management of Angkor and the creation of the first archaeological park. It was confirmed by the World Heritage listing, which failed to consider the role of the *sangha* in the maintenance and daily life of the temple (Baille, 2007), leaving the actual management of the site in the hands of the APSARA authority and the ICC committee.

Moving on from these connections between human territoriality and heritage spaces, one has to ask why, to whom, and for what purposes heritage territoriality would be so useful that it is maintained, despite attempts to introduce a new heritage paradigm. The argument that I shall develop throughout this book is that heritage territoriality supports and provides certain forms of political and economic power and allows the legitimation of that power both nationally and internationally.

Let me provide some preliminary evidence for this from the discourse of the international coordination committee (ICC-Angkor), which, together with the APSARA authority, is empowered to examine every project to be implemented in the area of the archaeological parks. Between 1993 and 2003, the ICC-Angkor focused its efforts on the conservation of archaeological heritage in zones 1 and 2. This allowed UNESCO to give a positive evaluation of its achievements when the results of a study of the Angkor landscapes were presented in 2005: 'the report stated that the situation is satisfactory in zones 1 and 2. Despite constant and growing pressures, [...] the landscapes and the Angkor heritage values have not been irreversibly altered. [...] Angkor is considered as a remarkable example, a success story in the field of heritage conservation' (ICC, 2005, p. 17). In another example, in 2003, Ambassador André Libourel delivered a positive assessment of the first ten years of international cooperation at Angkor: 'Between 1993 and today, this committee has followed the development and management of the site. [...] So, let us celebrate a resounding success and pay no attention to those who say that it could have gone better' (ICC, 2003, p. 8). This positive evaluation applies strictly to the two zones that are officially part of the World Heritage Site. It was possible for the ICC to exert a reasonable level of control on spatial transformations in this limited space and thus to protect the archaeological heritage. The restriction of World Heritage recognition to the archaeological park, and the focus on ancient remains, strategically allows a positive self-evaluation of the international campaigns for Angkor, legitimizing the involvement of international players in Cambodian heritage affairs. Consequently, the physical space omitted from international authority and monitoring sees a concentration of the negative consequences of development; one of these is urban development, which appears to be a difficult process to control in a country opening up to a market economy and seeking to attract as many investors as possible.

The management plan for Angkor is both the primary visual representation of the heritage site and environs and the most important means for the enforcement of the heritage conservation system based on zoning. Reproduced in a simplified way on numerous tourist maps, the limited protected zones are immediately associated with Angkor by the general public. Heritage is thus given explicit graphic visibility. This makes it easily recognizable for visitors looking for a significant tourist experience that is generally compressed in time. Also, the graphic visibility of the archaeological park facilitates the identification of Cambodian heritage with a bounded geographical area – a 'territoriality' – that is entitled to enshrine the essence of national cultural values and identity. The simplification of the complex archaeological reality of Angkor (which is actually made up of scattered ruins and territorial survivals over a wide region) is strategically orientated towards the enforcement of a system of control and its continuing positive assessment. It establishes a socially constructed meaning for Angkor over the long term. The cartographic representation of Angkor, through which institutional control is successfully enforced, celebrates national organizations who construct a visible image of the national heritage, consolidated through the various media that disseminate it. The proper management of the parks exemplifies the authorities' ability to impose their power in the most symbolic sector of the nation. Such a major heritage site concentrates, in a bounded and thus recognizable space, the essence of the geo-body, and for this reason becomes an important cultural reference for the Cambodian people.

Sack argues that territoriality 'provides a means of *reifying* power. Power and influence are not always tangible as are streams and mountains, roads, and houses. Moreover, power and the like are often potentialities.

Territoriality makes potential explicit and real by making them "visible"' (1983, p. 59). In this situation, power never comes to be associated with those people who have and perform it, but rather takes the form of a set of impersonal rules applied to a territory itself. In the case of Angkor, these rules take the form of a complex set of heritage management regulations for zones 1 and 2, concerning, for instance, land use and construction activity. Although these regulations have been socially constructed by generations of institutional actors, they appear to have their origins in a universal shared ethics of conservation which aims to protect the authenticity and integrity of monuments from disrespectful development. Heritage conservation, understood as a 'good practice' (Smith and Waterson, 2009), represents an ethical system that, like a religious belief system, consists of positive or negative judgements. This is why the 'authorized heritage discourse' (Smith, 2006), sustained by the standard-setting proclamations of UNESCO, seems to be above criticism: its deepest foundations, the value and representativeness of certain forms of heritage such as the monuments of Angkor, are perceived as intrinsically good. This discourse cannot easily be overturned because, shaped as it is by political and cultural elites, it cannot be reformed without calling into question the very idea of World Heritage. In the name of this ethics-based system, Angkor as a bounded entity comes to be accepted as the accurate representation of a real thing, not as a social construct, and even functions to reinforce the legitimation of power by national and international bodies.

The outcome of this process is the construction of two distinct categories of space. The first is the heritage space, which corresponds to the archaeological parks and is subject to an international regime of protection; the second, the rest of the Angkor region, is a non-heritage space (identified by the ZEMP with zones 3-5), which is subject to 'ordinary' Cambodian law, institutional control, and administration. A non-heritage space is one whose qualities and traditions are not valued. As defined here, it differs from spaces that are simply not concerned by heritage recognition in that it suffers the consequences of the proximity of a celebrated heritage site. Within this space, heritage as an institutional practice is negated, in order to allow developments that will support tourism and economic growth, but will destroy cultural inheritance. Other forms of inheritance located within the non-heritage space, including temples, hydraulic and transport infrastructures, local systems of land use, human settlements both urban and rural, and also people's attachments and associations, will therefore be marginalized. In the case of Angkor, this marginalization is particularly visible, as the institutions in charge of heritage management tend to overlook the numerous projects implemented outside the archaeological parks since these fall under different categories of ownership and management responsibility. In this way, the non-heritage space comes to be viewed both as an unregulated area (where territoriality is not enforced) and as an insignificant space that exists in the shadow of the heritage site. This dualism, shaped at the institutional level, frames the perception of Siem Reap-Angkor shared by a wide range of actors in architectural and urban design.

The non-heritage space is the other side of the coin in the process of heritage-making, and nowhere is this clearer, perhaps, than in the urban development of Siem Reap, the small town on the doorstep of the archaeological site, where increasing tourism-related investment began to transform the urban landscape without the framework of any planning mechanism.

1.7 Fragile and malleable Siem Reap

At the beginning of the 1990s, Siem Reap, six kilometres from the main temples of Angkor, was a small town of approximately 30,000 people. Its population had almost tripled after the Khmer Rouge period. In the late 1970s, the population had been forced to move and work in the countryside, but after the fall of the Khmer Rouge regime in 1979 a number of refugees from the rural areas decided to settle in the town. At that time, its small urban core, composed of a collection of villages and two districts created during the colonial period, was all included in the area that the ZEMP later defined as a 'cultural landscape' (zone 3) (Figure 1.4).

Siem Reap existed before the twentieth century, located at the intersection between the river, which was used as a canal in the Angkor period (Pottier, 1998), and another canal entering from west of Angkor. It was then nothing more than a conglomeration of villages scattered over roughly ten kilometres along the watercourse. It was situated on a plain with a wealth of survivals from the Angkor period, such as canals, roads, villages, ponds, and religious sites. The symbolic centre of the town was the Neak Ta Ya Tep, the home of the spirit-protector, located in the northern part of the conglomeration (Figure 1.5). The villages that composed Siem Reap were built of wooden houses on stilts, surrounded by luxuriant vegetation, vegetable gardens, and a capillary network of canals and retaining ponds. Historical sources do not record when they were founded, but the first European travellers to Angkor described the idyllic landscape of villages already buried in vegetation during the second half of the nineteenth century (see Chapter 4). However, human settlement in the area was much older: the majority of the pagodas to be found in the villages had been established on ancient Angkor religious sites. Archaeological maps show an ancient economic centre on the east side of the river, close to the Wat Bo pagoda (Hetreau-Pottier, 2008).

The two colonial districts were planned between the 1920s and 1930s along the Siem Reap river, and were almost completely developed under the French Protectorate. Compared with other colonial districts in Southeast Asia, they were rather small, because Siem Reap was nothing more than a provincial capital. On the maps, these two districts look like exogenous additions with brick and concrete buildings, the first signs of the modern town in a rural environment (Rabinow, 1995). Though small, they presented some of the typical features of European urban planning in the colonies: functional specialization (commercial and administrative neighbourhoods were separated), a well-ordered street grid system, and buildings designed with neoclassical stylistic features. They contained the facilities that a provincial centre must have, including a prison, a hospital, and a post office. At the end of the 1920s, a grand hotel and park were also built to welcome the first tourists to Angkor. The hotel was situated on National Highway No. 6, an east-west road built by the French Protectorate to link Siem Reap with the Thai border and Phnom Penh.

The administrative district was composed of large plots of land with plantations, on which villas were erected. Some of these housed the offices of the colonial administration. The dense commercial district was centred on the market hall, and composed of blocks of two-storey shophouses. This type of housing is ubiquitous in Southeast Asia. It probably originated from southern China and was developed by the colonial powers in the region (Viaro, 1992). Generally, the ground floor of the shophouse is used for commercial functions, while the second floor is the residence of the trader's family. Shophouses are built on adjacent oblong parcels of land, with a narrow façade on the street where traders display their wares or extend a restaurant into the public space with tables and stools. This was true of the shophouses of Siem Reap's commercial district. They had different architectural styles, as some of them were built even after Cambodian independence, and were all abandoned during the Khmer Rouge period. They then officially fell into the public domain, and were subsequently offered to the military officers who had contributed to the re-establishment of the national administrations.[34]

After Cambodia became independent in 1953, buildings such as the prince's villas, the stadium, the courthouse, and schools were constructed in

34 Personal communication with owners of shophouses, summer 2008.

Figure 1.4 IGN map 1962 reworked by ARTE (1995)

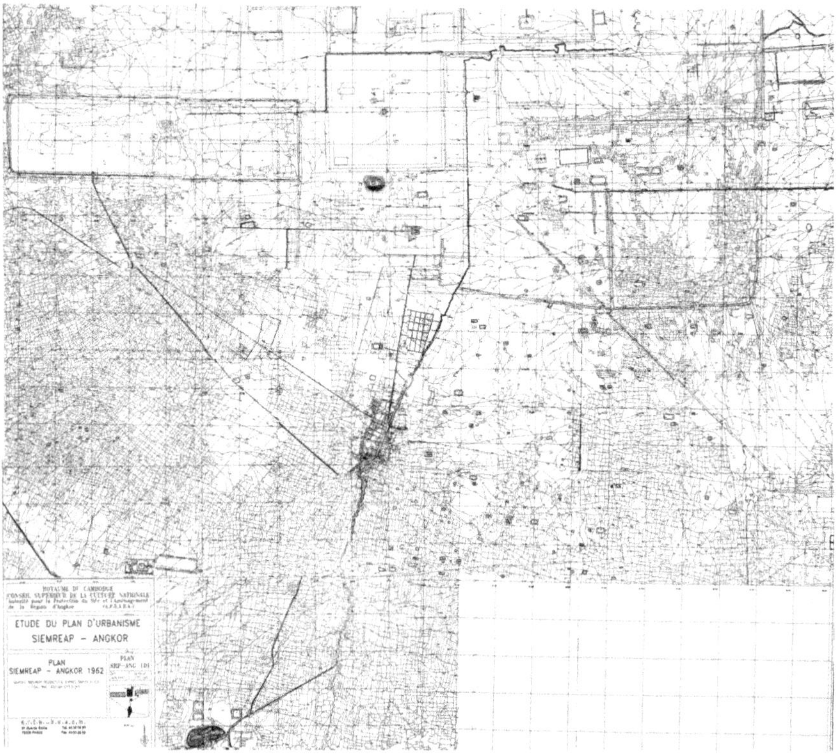

Plan de la région de Siem Reap' (map of Siem Reap region). Scale of the original document: 1:10.000

Siem Reap. Despite the faltering development of tourism (with an average of 50,000 visitors per year in the 1960s), the first hotels were established, such as the Hotel de la Paix and the Air France Hotel, whose construction close to Angkor Wat was interrupted by the advance of the Khmer Rouge. Public works expanded agricultural infrastructures such as irrigation networks. Projects initiated under the Sangkum Reastr Niyum[35] were all stopped after the military coup of the 1970s; some buildings were constructed but later destroyed by the Khmer Rouge. The Khmer Rouge were active in Siem Reap well before occupying Phnom Penh and emptying it of its inhabitants. Siem Reap lay between two combat zones until it fell in 1975.

35 Sangkum Reastr Niyum is generally translated into English as 'the community of the common people' or 'the people's socialist community'. It is a political movement founded by Norodom Sihanouk in 1955 which succeeded in holding power under his administration until 1970.

Figure 1.5 The Neak Ta Ya Tep, the spirit protector

Photo by the author, 2015

The population started to return to the town only at the beginning of the 1980s, soon after the 'liberation' by the Vietnamese. Although Siem Reap was a defensive zone until 1992, several important developments date from this period, 'including a defensive dike built around the city as well as the present "south circular road" which, for the first time, delimited the town to an area of approximately 25 km^2' (Hetreau-Pottier, 2008, p. 7). The old colonial market remained closed, but two new markets were created: the Phsar Leu (upper market) in the northeast of the town (which became the largest market in the province), and the Phsar Kraom (lower market) in the south. Both were located within the defensive line but far away from the town centre, for security reasons. Phum Thmey, the new village, was founded in 1990, on an area of 900 hectares, to house refugees seeking shelter. The Khmer Rouge period had completely overturned the urban structure and organization, and the slow return of the people to the town had compelled them to occupy new urban spaces and reorganize urban life.

The pace of urban development was slow until the beginning of the 1990s. Villages had been gradually absorbed as the town expanded, but were still recognizable in the urban landscape. Public facilities had been built without altering the provincial status of Siem Reap. The town had maintained its hybrid urban-rural character, with large rice fields served by a network of canals and retaining ponds. At the beginning of the 1990s, Siem Reap was a malleable environment. The colonial districts had lost their raison d'être. Commercial functions had moved to the periphery of the town, while the administration, closed down during the Khmer Rouge period, had to be entirely re-established. Hotels were in a bad state of repair. The first foreign consultants stayed in an empty grand hotel, enjoying its decadent luxury at low prices. Commercial and tourist facilities were empty shells hoping for new uses.

Siem Reap was also a fragile environment. Its wooden architecture, dense vegetation, and open-air urban infrastructures formed a thinly populated living landscape. Praised by foreign visitors during colonial and postcolonial times, the villages were looked upon as peaceful, beautiful environments where tourists could relax and get in touch with a spiritual dimension often forgotten in the Western world. However, these landscapes required constant care by the resident population; for instance, the perishable materials of wooden houses have to be regularly replaced. The charm of such a landscape relies on the luxuriant vegetation and the omnipresence of water, features owing their existence to the predominance of agriculture in the region, the slow pace of development, and the primary role played by the population in giving form to the urban environment. All these factors were to be eliminated by the development of Siem Reap as an international tourism hub. The town fell out of the hands of the inhabitants into those of the developers, with the connivance of the authorities, and under the eyes of the powerless foreign consultants who were requested to design the best of all possible towns in Siem Reap.

2 The arena of urban planning and the idea of the city

Siem Reap has been the backdrop of urban imaginings since the early 1990s. Various teams of foreign-sponsored planners have designed what they considered to be the most desirable development path and pattern for a small town that was going to become an international tourism hub. In this chapter, I analyse the politics of urban planning on the doorstep of the archaeological site of Angkor, with a twofold objective: firstly, to examine the ideas, models, and patterns of the tourist centre shaped by planners from different cultural and professional backgrounds; secondly, to explore the social, political, and economic struggles, which eventually led to the abandonment of all the urban plans designed for Siem Reap.

Planners who engage in designing the development of a tourist city face a serious dilemma. As Judd and Fainstein argue, 'a city that tries to build an economy based on tourism must project itself as a "dreamscape of visual consumption"' (1999, p. 7). Such a city needs facilities and infrastructures; it needs to modernize and equip its urban environment in order to facilitate consumption, but it also has to maintain a local flavour in order to satisfy the tourists' quest for the dream of authenticity (MacCannell, 1973; 1976). This twofold programme can be a source of contradiction. Infrastructure projects may endanger the integrity of inherited landscapes; conversely, the maintenance of landscapes may put a brake on the development of the hotel industry and thus limit the influx of tourists. The conservation versus development dilemma is particularly acute in Siem Reap because of its location within a non-heritage space that is largely ignored by the management system for the World Heritage Site of Angkor. Siem Reap is a vulnerable urban environment, as it was built on a rural substrate that is now coveted by the developers who seek to build and speculate. How can this fragile environment be modernized while maintaining an idyllic atmosphere that will attract tourists? Is Siem Reap's urban fabric, with its large cultivated plots and open-air canals, adapted to hosting massive influxes of tourists? What would be the best pattern for the urban development of a provincial town that is supposed to become an international tourism hub?

These are the pressing questions asked by several generations of planners. I use the word 'generations' because, over a period of only twenty years, different ideas of the city emerged, supported by successive teams of planners. Bilateral and multilateral development assistance programmes sponsored nine urban plans for Siem Reap between 1992 and 2009,[1] in addition to the numerous projects for the management of tourism and sector-specific projects for urban infrastructure, which were also funded by international aid. The government officially commissioned these nine plans, but implemented none of them. Consequently, twenty years after UNESCO had listed Angkor as a World Heritage Site, Siem Reap still lacked a legally approved master plan. Nevertheless, the town has expanded quickly; multiple disconnected projects by small and large developers have thoroughly transformed its urban fabric. Donors have continued to provide money and technical assistance for updating the urban plans, which were unable to keep up with the rapid pace of development, as well as for designing new planning instruments.

The contrast between the continuing commitment of international assistance and the lack of implementation gives some insight into the conflicting interactions between donors, consultants, and Cambodian institutions. Research on international assistance in Cambodia has mainly focused on governance, rural society, and the infrastructure sector. Few studies have been concerned with the relationship between international assistance and the politics of urban development (Huybrecht and Mauret, 2011; Fauveaud, 2015a). In this chapter, I illustrate the social and political complexity of the politics of urban planning through the metaphor of the arena, as developed in the field of political anthropology (Dartigues, 2001). This metaphor has been interpreted in different ways. Kasfir (1976) has broadly and neutrally defined the arena simply as the place where political activity takes place; Geertz (1983) sees it as the structural centre of social order, Long (1989) as a critical point of intersection between social systems; Olivier de Sardan and Bierschenk (1993) describe it as 'the place where heterogeneous and strategic groups face each other, driven by material and symbolic interests that are

1 The Zoning and Environmental Management Plan (1993-94); the Urban Reference Plan, by the consulting firms ARTE and BCEOM, sponsored by the French Development Agency (1995); the Land Use Plan and Urban Regulations (*Documents d'urbanisme réglementaire*), by the consulting firm Groupe 8, sponsored by the French Development Agency (1999); the Master Plan for Urban Transportation, by Tractabel, sponsored by the European Union (1999); the Plan for the Management of Siem Reap-Angkor 'Conservation and Development', by UNESCO, APSARA, and Groupe 8, sponsored by UNESCO and the French Development Agency (2003); the Study on Integrated Master Plan for Sustainable Development, by the consulting firm Nippon Koei Co. Ltd. and Kokusai Kogyo Co. Ltd., sponsored by the Japanese International Cooperation Agency (2006); the Land Use Plan, by the German Service of Cooperation DED, sponsored by the Adenauer Foundation and the European Union's Asia Urbs Program (2007); the Draft Statutory Zoning Plan, by Siem Reap's provincial department of the Ministry of Land Management, Urban Planning, and Construction, and the APSARA authority (2010); the 'Adressage patrimonial de la ville de Siem Reap' designed by Groupe 8 and sponsored by the French Development Agency (2012).

more or less compatible'; Darré (1996) puts the accent on the encounters of allies, which occasion the exchange of material resources and ideas and the unintentional convergence of interests.

Planning in Siem Reap occurs at the intersection of three social spheres: international donors, with their programmes and priorities; consulting firms and teams of consultants; and Cambodian institutions, which were completely re-established between 1993 and 1994, after the pro-Vietnamese government left the country. The metaphor of the arena is intended to illustrate the alliances and conflicts between members of these three spheres with respect to supporting or rejecting urban plans for Siem Reap, as well as the nature of the social and political relations between them and their specific objectives and intentions.

My analysis will be framed within the discipline of the anthropology of development, which examines the ideas governing international assistance in emerging countries and the social and political reality of aid programmes. More particularly, I draw upon the approach initiated by Norman Long, which seeks to build 'an ethnographic understanding of the "social life" of development projects – from conception to realisation – as well as the responses and lived experiences of the variously located and affected social actors' (Long, 2001, pp. 14-15), and to analyse the interactions between 'actors who have various statuses, heterogeneous resources, and dissimilar goals' (Olivier de Sardan, 2005, p. 12).[2] My research draws on this avenue of investigation, examining the various plans in close conjunction with the planning communities, that is, the foreign-sponsored teams of consultants who visited Siem Reap for shorter or longer periods in order to envisage its future development. In the process, I address Mosse's critique of development policy analysis, which he argues has often been disconnected from the communities of experts who generate and organize (or are organized by) policy, and which has privileged documents 'over the process that generated them' (Mosse, 2011, p. 2). To do this, I analyse urban plans as texts that happen 'in time and place and as integral to organized sequences of action'. A text is 'an occurrence embedded in what is going on and going forward' (Smith, 2006, p. 67). Similarly, plans can be seen as coordinated sequences of actions along a timeline going from a first draft up to (attempted) implementation, in close conjunction with the cultural backgrounds and behaviour of the teams of consultants and donors who author them.

2 According to Olivier de Sardan (1993), two other approaches may be distinguished. The first has unpacked the ideological constructions underpinning development programmes, pointing the finger at colonial cultural inheritances that are renewed in development programmes (inter alia Escobar, 1995). The second approach defends indigenous knowledge and encourages its close study.

2.1 Everyone wants a slice of the pie

'There are so many people who would like to help Cambodia!' an urban planner exclaimed when I interviewed him in his office.[3] 'Donors, consultants, and experts, they all want their slice of the pie. There is too much money and too many projects in Cambodia', another planner told me.[4] Cambodia is indeed 'among the most aid-dependent countries in Asia' (Sato et al., 2011, p. 2093), and the reconstruction of the national economy was highly dependent on international sources. Between 1993 and 2003, these flows of money contributed an average of thirteen per cent of national GDP annually (Ear, 2006). Between 2001 and 2011, international donors provided more than 50 per cent of the government's annual budget (Springer, 2011). The country received US$38 per capita in 2005 and US$43.5 in 2015, more than double the average of low-income countries, which was US$17 and US$20.7 respectively. In 2008, 35 official donors were established in the country. Between 1998 and 2006, 100 project implementation units operated in Cambodia every year, as well as '400 donor missions, reviews, and studies, duplicated technical cooperation and funding' (Chanboreth and Hach, 2008). Cambodia received a total of almost 13 billion US dollars in official development assistance (ODA) between 1991 and 2015, with an average of 518 million US dollars per year and a maximum of 808 million in 2013 (Table 2.1).

In spite of the large amount of aid, evaluations of its impact are often negative. Ear (2006) argues that international assistance has low economic efficiency, when it does not actually worsen governance. Olivieri, Jourde, and Sudrie (2009) present a negative assessment of French technical cooperation in Cambodia. As the country dramatically lacks capacity, consultants cannot transfer their knowledge to their local counterparts. Cambodian institutions bear a share of the responsibility for this. According to Bayart (2004), donors are not in a position to inculcate their philosophies, models, and best practices, because they have to follow the route established by their Cambodian counterparts. Drawing on an interview with Steve Heder, Bayart argues that donors are no more than the travelling companions of the Cambodian institutions. This means that they have little power: even if their economic assistance sustains the country's collapsing economy, they still have to endorse their counterparts' programmes and priorities.

Ear (2006) offers some insights into the reasons why the government welcomes foreign assistance even if it is not receptive to its programmes. He

3 Personal communication, 2008.

4 Personal communication, 2010.

Table 2.1 Net official development assistance and official aid received by Cambodia between 1991 and 2015

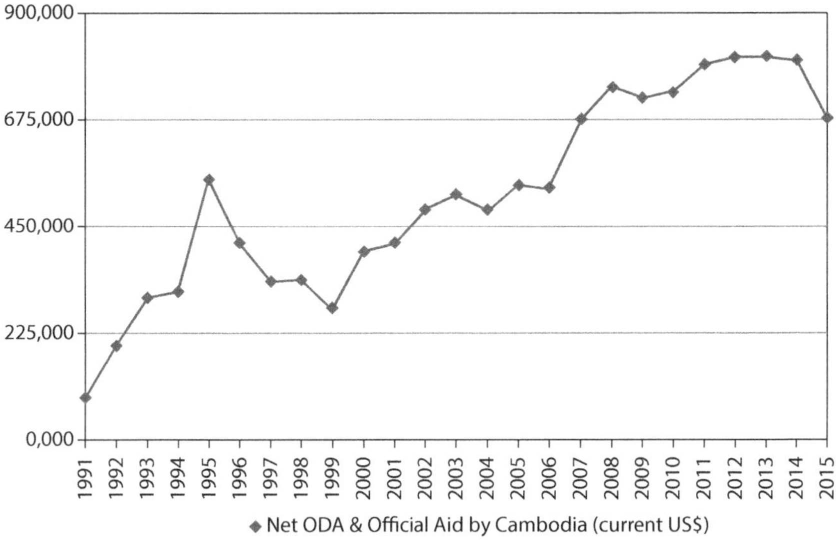

Table and graph by the author; data from the World Bank online database: http://data.worldbank.org/indicator/DT.ODA.ALLD.CD?end=2015&locations=KH&start=1991&view=chart, retrieved 11 May 2017

argues that this assistance is seen as proof that foreign donors trust the royal government and hence as a form of legitimation of the regime. In an official speech, Prime Minister Hun Sen announced that Cambodia had received US$600 million in official development assistance, along with US$50 million from NGOs, whereas it had only requested US$430 million. This generosity, he said, 'is a vote of confidence in Cambodia. It is an important encouragement for the government efforts in bringing peace and political stability, strengthening the foundations of democracy and human right respect in the society [sic], and especially in promoting sustained economic growth and substantially reducing poverty'.[5] This speech shows that the politics of financial and technical assistance form part of the kingdom's international diplomacy. For this reason, project implementation is not the only relevant criterion for evaluating the usefulness of international aid. This criterion has to be considered and evaluated within a broader strategy which helps the kingdom to build political support and credibility. For example, in late

5 Hun Sen, 'Address at the Launching of the Cambodia Socio-Economic Development Plan. 2001-2005. SEDP-II', 29 July 2002. Quoted by Ear (2006), p. 73.

2015, the alleged diversion by the Cambodian People's Party of Japanese aid initially intended to sponsor a drainage project in Phnom Penh, which was seemingly denounced by the opposition, was strongly denied. In order to maintain credibility, the prime minister went so far as to say that the donor was to blame for corruption and not the Cambodian government, which was not responsible for budget management.[6]

In the field of planning, donors provide money to design plans that they do not 'officially' implement: that is to say, they do not follow the procedure established by law to turn these plans into legal instruments.[7] However, the government continues to request new plans, and local authorities willingly accept the permanent presence of foreign consultants in their headquarters. Land and Morgan (2008) state that 'officials in the Royal Government of Cambodia almost invariably did not refuse external offers of technical assistance (TA) personnel including those that they suspected might be unnecessary or dysfunctional' (p. 43). Through the passive acceptance of foreign assistance, good diplomatic relations are maintained with the donor countries who offer a free workforce to local institutions.

Donors in Cambodia have to face criticism. Bayart (2004) notes that they are disconnected from the social and economic realities of Cambodia. Hugues (2009) observes that donors tend to project failings onto 'internal actors'. This allows them to exculpate 'external actors' in order to retain the moral upper hand. Looking at the master plan and the 30 sector projects designed by the French cooperation agency since 2007, Fauveaud (2015a) points out that owners, powerful individuals, and clans can make a plan fail if its measures run counter to their interests. Also, it is not uncommon that internationally sponsored programmes are abandoned by the Cambodian counterpart as soon as foreign support wanes (Paling, 2012) or the foreign experts providing assistance leave the country.[8] In this situation, international experts distance themselves from local politics and focus on the objectives that they were hired and paid to accomplish, even if this

6 Pech Sotheary, 2015, 'Use of Foreign Aid Free of Corruption: Premier', *Phnom Penh Post,* 6 November 2015: http://www.phnompenhpost.com/national/use-foreign-aid-free-corruption-premier?utm_content=buffer93970&utm_medium=social&utm_source=facebook.com&utm_campaign=buffer (accessed 7 November 2015).

7 Land use plans for Cambodian cities have to be approved by the National Committee for Land Management, Urban Planning and Construction in order to be legal: Law on Land Management, Urban Planning and Constructions (Kram/04NS94/10Aug94), art. 9. However, this committee has never delivered official approval for plans designed for Siem Reap. In this case, local authorities' hands are tied.

8 Personal communication, 2008.

attitude detaches them from the social challenges faced by contemporary Cambodians.

The French experts' desire to design a global planning strategy for Phnom Penh thus appears to Fauveaud (2015a) as an 'urban utopia'. In contrast, Olivieri, Jourde, and Sudrie (2009) claim that consultants ought to be forces of cultural influence in the host country, and that only the local appropriation of their knowledge and capacity guarantees the efficiency of technical assistance. Cambodia is unique in that the culture of urban planning, developed at the time of the Sangkum Reastr Niyum, was lost during the Khmer Rouge regime, when the majority of the educated class was killed. The director of the APSARA's department of the development of urban heritage told me that 'Vann Molyvann was the one who first used the word "urbanism" in Cambodia at the beginning of the 1990s after the approval of the Zoning and Environmental Management Plan'.[9] The director stressed that the education of Cambodian civil servants in the field of planning was virtually non-existent at the beginning of the 1990s. Faced with a drastic lack of education and capacity, international donors invested funds in urban planning. However, the firm commitment of donors and consultants to planning the development of modern Cambodian cities allowed for only limited collaboration with undertrained public officials and uneducated local populations, and resulted in a top-down approach to urbanism which left little space for local initiatives.

The unsuitability of the ideas and models of development that Western assistance has tried to disseminate (Sato et al., 2011) is revealed by the failure of 'rationalist planning' (Fauveaud, 2015a) in Phnom Penh. The authorities seem to be deaf to cultural influences from the West which might leach into overall models of urban development. In line with the national socioeconomic planning implemented in Cambodia since the second half of the 1990s, the development of infrastructure, the involvement of private parties, and a focus on 'results' rather than on 'processes' were given priority (Fauveaud, 2015a). Accordingly, Cambodian institutions are more open to funding and expertise for the construction of technical infrastructure, mainly sponsored by China, India, South Korea, and Thailand (Sato et al., 2011). These countries provide assistance in this area, which responds to the pragmatic needs of an emerging country, without interfering with Cambodia's development philosophy. Because private parties and special interests have such a strong influence in Cambodian urban politics, only consensual projects have a chance of being implemented. This is true of projects for the development

9 Ibid.

of hydraulic and transport infrastructure: in Phnom Penh and Siem Reap, these are implemented more easily because they actually increase the value of land and thus indirectly benefit urban speculators. These trends have re-orientated international aid towards sector projects and 'strategic planning', while the hard questions surrounding land management and speculation have been deliberately ignored (Fauveaud, 2015a).

The major argument of this chapter is that urban planning shaped by international assistance is a process of negotiation and combination of three competing elements: planning tools, which owe their global dissemination to historical trajectories of transnational and international circulation and transfer of experience; local architectural and urban forms, which inspire and fascinate foreign planners; and the philosophies, strategies, and regional programmes of international donors, which are adapted (to a certain extent and depending on the donor) to the specific locality where the donors invest and operate. The nine plans for the city of Siem Reap offer an intriguing object of analysis, helping us to understand the crucial importance of these negotiations at a time when urban planning is trying to catch up with a fast-moving urban reality and cities are becoming the prime movers of the national economy.

2.2 Planners as cultural brokers

Vann Molyvann is one of the most renowned modern architects from Cambodia. Previously, the de facto state architect under the Sihanouk regime, he was in exile in Switzerland during the Khmer Rouge period. During that period, he served as a public official for the UNDP programme and only returned to his country in 1989. Thanks to his close relationship with the political powers, his authority, and his energetic engagement, he was elected to the Council of Ministers in 1991, tasked with land management and urban planning across the country, with responsibilities equivalent to the mayor of Phnom Penh. Molyvann had founded the Royal University of Fine Arts (RUFA) in the 1960s. He became a close acquaintance of Jean-Marie Charpentier, then a 30-year-old French architect who got his first position as an assistant professor at RUFA. In 1969, Charpentier founded the architectural firm ARTE,[10] based in Paris, where he employed five Cambodian architects. These architects were unable to go back to their own country when the Khmer Rouge took over, and continued working

10 ARTE stands for Architecture, Research, Technique, and Respect for the Environment.

at ARTE. Among them was Ros Borath, at that time a student at the École de Chaillot,[11] who was later nominated as the director of the APSARA's department of Monuments and Archaeology. Pierre Clément, who had a doctorate in ethnology and was fascinated by the architecture and cities of Southeast Asia, was also a key member of the architectural firm.

At the beginning of the 1990s, Molyvann believed that planning the urban development of Siem Reap was of paramount importance for the reconstruction of his country. He was involved in the development of a strategy for the management of the Angkor region within the ICC-Angkor and had a say in the design of the ZEMP.[12] He asked Charpentier to work with him for the preservation and development of the Angkor region, and Charpentier appointed Clément to analyse the urban fabric of Siem Reap and design a plan for it.

Clément had started his career in Laos. He had received degrees from the Institut des Langues Orientales (INALCO) and the École des Hautes Etudes en Sciences Sociales (EHESS). His PhD dissertation in ethnology, written together with his wife Sophie Clément-Charpentier, studied the construction and spatial organization of Laotian wooden houses (Clément-Charpentier, 1990). With this background, he approached Southeast Asian cities with an interdisciplinary approach at the crossroads of architecture and anthropology. At the beginning of the 1990s, he was teaching at the École d'Architecture de Paris-Belleville (ENSAPB). Together with two other professors, Charles Goldblum and Yong-Hak Shin, he formed the core of a research team devoted to the study of Southeast Asian cities, based at the Institut Parisien de Recherche: Architecture, Urbanistique, Sociétés (IPRAUS) of the Architecture School. Clément organized a series of workshops on architecture and urban design in Phnom Penh and Siem Reap, which were addressed to MA students and early-career architects. Hundreds of first-year students from the recently re-established RUFA were also involved in these workshops under the more experienced guidance of

11 The École de Chaillot is a postgraduate institute founded in 1887, which delivers professional training for state architects and architects specializing in the conservation of monuments, historical sites, and 'ordinary heritage'.

12 However, Molyvann was said to oppose this plan. According to journalist Sarah Horner, Molyvann 'was known not to favor the ZEMP scheme and it appears his opinion has prevailed'. She explained that during the first meeting of the ICC-Angkor (21-22 December 1993), the ZEMP was dismissed in favour of a 'plan of action of the Royal Government of Cambodia', made up of a collection of projects to be sponsored by international assistance. Horner, Sarah, 1993, 'ZEMP Downplayed at Angkor Meeting', *Phnom Penh Post*, 31 December 1993: http://www.phnompenhpost.com/national/zemp-downplayed-angkor-meeting (accessed 24 August 2015).

the ENSAPB students. The first ideas for the future development of Siem Reap emerged in these occasions, under the watchful eye of Molyvann and the two French architects.

Molyvann arranged for King Norodom Sihanouk to make an official statement requesting the commitment of French technical cooperation for Siem Reap's urban planning. This request was timely, as France and Cambodia had favourable diplomatic relations at that time. In 1979, President Chirac had founded the International Association of Francophone Mayors (AIMF). As the only francophone city in Asia, Phnom Penh enjoyed a privileged status, and, by extension, Cambodia was viewed as a primary beneficiary of French international cooperation. Although a cooperation agreement between the two countries was only signed in 1994, France had already started to send technical assistants from the Atelier Parisien d'Urbanisme (APUR)[13] to design the urban development of Phnom Penh.

Molyvann received UNESCO's support and secured funding from the French Development Agency (AFD), the financial institution that is 'the main implementing agency for France's official development assistance'.[14] The agency opened a bidding process and selected ARTE, together with the engineering firm BCEOM,[15] to design Siem Reap's urban plan.[16] In Molyvann's view, this needed to be implemented quickly: Siem Reap urgently needed a master plan in order to counter the potentially disruptive effects of tourism development. He collaborated closely with Clément, who headed the design team for the Urban Reference Plan at ARTE. However, one urban planner told me that Molyvann 'considered this plan as his own'. This is confirmed by his writings, which claimed that the plan fully reflected his ideas for the development of the city (Molyvann, 2003).[17] He strongly encouraged ARTE and the AFD to sign a contract on 14 July 1994, a national holiday in France, in order to be able to start the process of urban design as

13 The Council of Paris created the APUR in 1967 with the twofold objective of analysing how urban and social evolutions interact with urban policies and becoming involved in urban design for Paris' metropolitan region.

14 Source: http://www.afd.fr/lang/en/home (accessed 24 August 2015).

15 BCEOM is a French engineering firm which was merged into the holding company EGIS in 2007.

16 Previous plans had included a report by Molyvann on the overall development of the Siem Reap-Angkor region with some broad indications on how to shape Siem Reap, and an urban report, signed by Ros Borath and Aline Hétreau-Pottier (1993), which was integrated into the ZEMP plan.

17 In his book, Molyvann's constant use of passive verbal forms to describe the design process for Siem Reap and failure to acknowledge the sources of images tends to mask the names of the authors of the guidelines contained in the Urban Reference Plan.

soon as possible. He played a role of paramount importance as a mediator between the consulting firm and the donor, and together with Charpentier and Clément he obtained funding and support.

The profile and role of these three men correspond to the figure of the cultural broker. Clifford Geertz (1960) defined cultural brokers as people who achieve leadership thanks to personal and social skills and who, caught between two worlds, master different cultural systems. Molyvann, for instance, is Cambodian, trained as an architect in France, and worked for several years for the United Nations. They know how power relations work in different political and social situations and are acquainted with several different communication codes and reference systems. Geertz's research in Indonesia showed that the *kijaji* (the Muslim teachers) are powerful individuals who play the role of 'translators' and cultural mediators between the peasantry and the political and cultural elites, two groups who grew further and further apart after Indonesian independence in 1945.

At the beginning of the 1990s, Charpentier, Clément, and Molyvann enjoyed this role thanks to their personal commitment, their passion and fascination for Southeast Asia, and their personal and professional acquaintance based on mutual respect and trust. The two Frenchmen combined sound knowledge about Cambodia and about urban planning, which reinforced their position as skilful mediators. Molyvann benefited from high standing in interpersonal relations, which enabled him to become powerful among the Cambodian political elite and to express a paternalistic and visionary perspective on the development of Cambodian cities.

Thompson (2003) writes that Molyvann's guiding principle was 'love for Cambodia', which 'takes the form of a double exigency: at once infinitely respectful of the past, and moved by an indefatigable hope for – and investment in – the future; an unusually deep knowledge of the cultural heritage and an extraordinarily modern creative force; a pride in and concern for things uniquely Cambodian and yet a deep commitment to a certain internationalist, and I would even say universalist perspective' (p. iv). Molyvann believed in the power of international organizations and supported the transnational transfer of models for urban and regional management: for example, his rehabilitation project for Phnom Penh's Beng Trabek neighbourhood drew on his experience as a UNDP official in Vientiane.

These human encounters are fundamental for understanding how the first spatial layout for the development of Siem Reap emerged and gained momentum in the local professional milieu. However, cumbersome political rivalries undermined the authority of the cultural brokers. Though officially a member of the Cambodian People's Party (CPP), Molyvann owed allegiance to King Norodom Sihanouk, for whom he had worked for decades, as well as to the international community of donors headed by UNESCO. When the bipartite government was dismissed and the CPP became the sole ruling party in Cambodia, Molyvann's authority declined. In 2002, a decree from the Prime Minister's office (Kimsong and Reed, 2001) obliged him to leave the APSARA authority, which he had headed between 1995 and 2001. He was later appointed as 'senior advisor of the Cambodian King', but this honorary office concealed a lack of effective power. Molyvann's decline entailed the failure of his ambition (shared by the planners who worked with him) to control, order, and develop a large urban and rural area. This was one of the factors that eventually led to the failure of the urban plan designed by the three-man consulting team.

2.3 Spatial layouts and ideas of the city

Since the early 1990s, planners have striven to create an all-encompassing spatial layout for the development of Siem Reap. Two schools of thought, represented by French cooperation (through the French Development Agency, AFD) and Japanese cooperation (through the Japanese International Cooperation Agency, JICA), have emphasized the advantages of two different patterns of urban development: the 'vegetal' city[18] and the compact city. My analysis mainly focuses on the plans produced by these two donors, as they were fundamental in defining the guidelines for urban development, which were then followed in the plans.

In addressing the factors that contributed to the emergence of two ideas of the city and their development into spatial layouts, I show that the vegetal city and compact city appear to be two diametrically opposed approaches to the development of Siem Reap: the first draws from the past (inherited local construction techniques, spatial layouts, and localization strategies) and adapts tradition to present needs; the second looks at the future and plans to lead Siem Reap towards modernization through spatial innovation. Far from considering it as a small town at the periphery of the world economy, ideas for its development reflect global questions about the future of cities in the twenty-first century. Issues of sustainability, balanced exploitation

18 Although the term 'vegetal' is rarely used in English, I use 'vegetal city' here as the most direct translation of the French expression *la ville végétale* that designates specific built forms, spatial organization, and relation to the environment and landscape defined by the ARTE urban planners.

of natural resources, and responsible energy consumption are central to the work of the two foreign cooperation agencies, which deal with these pressing questions in completely different ways. The analysis of urban planning uncovers the process through which Siem Reap has moved out of its marginal position, as a small town and a peripheral space in the shadow of Angkor, to become the object of successive flights of imagination inspired by global debates about the future of cities.

2.3.1 The vegetal city

The Urban Reference Plan,[19] co-authored by ARTE and BCEOM, viewed water and vegetation as the two main ingredients of urban planning for Siem Reap, to be maintained and adapted to modern requirements. At the beginning of the 1990s, plantations and open-air water infrastructures structured the urban fabric of the town. This system had its origins in the Angkor period. Bernard-Philippe Groslier (1979) speculated that the Angkor capitals were 'hydraulic cities' with intensive agriculture enabled by these networks. More recent discoveries have called the validity of this sweeping theory into question, but without dismissing the strong link between ancient urbanism and water networks. The latter suffered from silting up, which would have made such rich harvests impossible. Recent archaeological discoveries have demonstrated how urban elements were connected to a capillary system of canals and artificial reservoirs. In particular, the seminal contribution of Gaucher (2004) on the capital of Angkor Thom has retraced the network of canals and ponds and the placement of the houses built along them on embanked plots protected from periodic flooding. The architects sought to give new life to this inherited system and to use it as a major resource for contemporary planning.

The architects saw two other characteristics as fundamental to the future development of Siem Reap, namely, the hybrid of rural and urban elements and the presence of agriculture inside the town. Since these qualities already existed in the urban fabric, as shown by the planners' descriptions of Siem Reap's villages, they only needed to be preserved and expanded: 'these neighbourhoods, which are urbanized only on the façades visible along the river and the main roads, extend through a zone planted with fruit trees

19 In French urban planning, a 'reference plan' (*plan de référence*) is an instrument which underlies the planning of a municipality or group of municipalities over a five-year period of development. It generally draws on a preliminary analysis and recognition of the challenges faced by the municipality.

towards land still used for agriculture deep within these large plots of land' (ARTE-BCEOM, 1995, vol. 1, p. 1).

The idea was to preserve these qualities and use them to plan the urbanization of Siem Reap: future urbanization, it was argued, needs to maintain the rare environmental balance of the vegetal city over the long term. With this purpose in mind, land was reserved for agriculture in the southwest part of the city, where previous geological investigations had shown the soil to be the most fertile. New housing, to be developed in the southeast, was to be built on large plots that included vegetation, with canals structuring the new neighbourhoods. A 'green belt' marked the boundary between the town and the archaeological park. It restricted the extension of the town northwards and, at the same time, increased the size of the area allocated to vegetation (Figure 2.1).

Briefly, the four characteristics of the vegetal city are dense vegetation, open-air water infrastructures, hybrid urban elements at the intersection of the village and the city, and the presence of agricultural land within the city's boundaries. These characteristics were not unique to Siem Reap, but were central to urbanism in many Southeast Asian cities.[20] Ancient Southeast Asian agrarian cities, as defined by Lombard (1970), were established in the hinterland and commanded vast areas. They owed their survival to surrounding agricultural land served by a capillary system of water infrastructures. Cities such as Pagan, Sukhothai, Modjopahit, Mandalay, and Amarapura developed this model until the end of the fifteenth century. More particularly, in his research on Hanoi, Clément praised the 'fragile and unstable balance between earth and water', which 'illustrates a foundation myth, many times renewed, about the productive struggle between these two elements which ensures the survival of humankind' (2001, p. 9). Dense vegetation was common to many cities of the region, which enjoyed a tropical climate. In Chiang Mai and Luang Prabang, for instance, orchards and plantations were interspersed with the urban features, which were developed on rural substrates: the town has emerged from the village but has not erased its legacy.

The Urban Reference Plan for Siem Reap updated these principles into guidelines for modern urban design, proposing that the contemporary urban development of the town re-model the legacy of the past to accommodate present and future demands. Large-scale tourism facilities would

20 Pédélahore (2014). Communication at the round-table discussions 'Vietnam: continuités/discontinuités' (30 September 2014), organized in connection with the exhibition 'Réemergences vietnamiennes. L'invention spatiale au quotidien'.

be concentrated in an enclave called the Hotel City, located in the northeast on the town's driest land (Figure 2.2). In this way, the city could be built according to inherited construction techniques and patterns, which were adapted for a small, slow-growing, and mainly agrarian urban population. Obviously, the maintenance of these principles – low density, open-air water networks, thick vegetation, and rural features – presupposed the development of a well-regulated tourism system, which would accept only the number of visitors that existing infrastructure and facilities could efficiently sustain. In line with a report on tourism written in synergy with the Urban Reference Plan (Détente, Score, GIE-Villes Nouvelles, 1994), Siem Reap-Angkor would not be a site of mass tourism. At least in the first instance, high-end and luxury tourism would be encouraged in order to maximize revenues without compromising the fragile environmental and urban balance of Siem Reap (Gaulis, 2007).

The planners reversed a widespread approach that tries to impose international models and standards, unsuitable to local situations, on recipient countries. This approach has been widely criticized by anthropologists of development who have addressed the shortcomings of aid and the gaps between discourse and implementation, when planning tools and ideas draw on exogenous models and not on the careful consideration of local specificities. In contrast, respect for local heritage led to the harmonious integration of the priorities of the French Development Agency (AFD),[21] which operated in Cambodia under the terms of an agreement on 'cultural, scientific, and technical cooperation' signed by the French and Cambodian governments in 1994 (decree No. 95-816, June 1995). This agreement put the emphasis on the 'historical bonds of friendship' developed since colonial times. A substantial ingredient of these bonds was the research carried out by the École Française d'Extrême Orient (EFEO) on Angkor since the beginning of the twentieth century (see Chapter 1). The EFEO amassed an impressive amount of knowledge, not only on the Angkor monuments, but also on the patterns of water management and urban development in the region. The AFD funding programme, organized around the two key concepts of heritage and development, renewed ties with this scholarly tradition, as it concomitantly sponsored the restoration of monuments, the management of the archaeological park, urban and hydraulic infrastructure, and planning for urban and regional development.

21 At the time of the Urban Reference Plan, the AFD was called the Caisse française de développement. In the interests of clarity, I use the agency's current name.

Figure 2.2 Urban zoning as proposed by the Urban Reference Plan

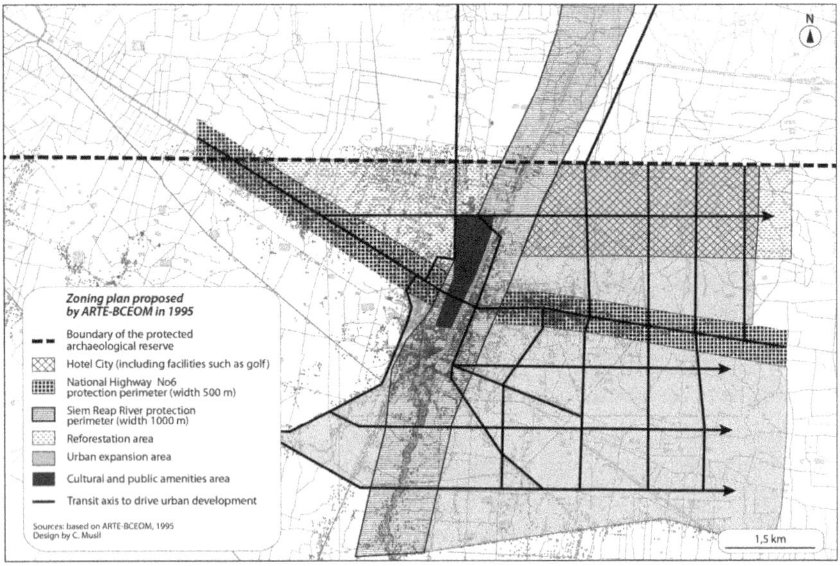

ARTE-BCEOM, 1995; © Esposito 2016

Clément and later Gaulis, one of his affiliated researchers at IPRAUS, noted that Angkor 'had lessons to teach' to contemporary urbanism (Clément, 2001; Gaulis, 2007). By designating Siem Reap as a vegetal city and invoking the more general principles of urbanism in Southeast Asia, the Urban Reference Plan potentially raised the future plan for Siem Reap town to the level of 'good practice' that ought to be followed by other cities in the region. Moreover, in developing the vegetal city as a pattern for contemporary urban development in general, the planners laid the basis for this concept, which did not take on material form but survived throughout the following two decades in the minds of the international planning community and of successive generations of Cambodian and foreign planners.

As one example of this, the report of the Second Intergovernmental Conference on the Safeguarding and Development of Angkor (2003) included the following description: 'as the starting point for tours of the Angkor temples, Siem Reap is a garden town with two main structuring features: the *stung* (Siem Reap river) and National Highway No. 6, crisscrossed in the downtown area by a grid pattern of right-angled streets. Richly endowed with trees, the town has a number of reservoirs or *trapeang* which serve to regulate variations in the water level throughout the year while lending a distinctive touch to its landscape' (UNESCO, 2003, p. 3). Although Siem

Figure 2.3 Replica of a noria and wooden bridge in the Old Market area

Photo by the author, 2015

Reap's urban configurations had started to change in those years under the effects of the first urban developments, the idea and image of the vegetal city still permeated the discourse of the international community. In 2010, when Groupe 8[22] was requested to develop a set of urban heritage regulations for Siem Reap, the consultants quoted the same description in their report (p. 53), in order to describe the town's valuable legacy. In the same way, Cambodian planners working for the APSARA authority still designate Siem Reap as a vegetal city in personal communications (2007-2009).

In a time of intense urban transformation, this image is especially necessary as a reminder of the urban features that need to be enhanced, both as an issue of identity and as the tangible expression of the local flavour that Siem Reap needs to maintain in order to satisfy tourists' desire to make a real connection with the locality. With tourists especially in mind, the APSARA authority suggested that the qualities of the vegetal city should be revealed and recovered through various means, including reproduction and re-creation. The authority presented the ICC-Angkor committee (2006) with a project for the re-establishment of canals (*preak*) and small artificial

22 Groupe 8 is a Paris-based consulting firm that mainly provides expertise in the field of urban development in emerging countries.

lakes (*trapeang*) along a two-kilometre-long section of National Highway No. 6; this was implemented in subsequent years. In order to increase the surface area available for building, hotel developers had cut down trees and filled up open-air watercourses which originally ensured the rice fields' water supply. However, the great majority of tourists access Siem Reap from this highway, and the series of giant hotels they immediately encounter compromises the image of the vegetal city they have learned to expect from travel narratives and guides. In order to reinstate the lost qualities of the vegetal city, and hence increase its attractiveness in the eyes of tourists, the APSARA has planted new rows of trees and dug canals to separate several traffic lanes. In this project, the modernization of traffic management goes hand in hand with the re-creation of a lost image for the sake of foreign visitors. The APSARA has indeed limited the extension of the plantations and canals to the section of the National Highway commonly used by tourists. In a similar vein, the APSARA has built a wooden footbridge and a noria, a type of water wheel that traditionally supplied water to the canals connecting the river with the rice fields (Figure 2.3). Over time, these wheels have been destroyed, and only a few are still to be found in the southern villages. However, this noria is not operational. Standing in the centre of Siem Reap, it is positioned in the opposite direction to that which would allow it to pump water, disavowing its real function and imposing a purely decorative one. The bridge and the new noria recreate a commodified reproduction of the heritage of Siem Reap for the use of tourists. They are a reminder of a disappearing vegetal city, reconstructed in a new physical form. The echoes of the vegetal city in discourse and projects show that this idea does have reverberations within planning circles. It persists as an image of a city increasingly disconnected from the reality of the urban fabric.

2.3.2 The compact city

The conditions for the emergence of the idea of the compact city lay in the rapidity and intensity of urban transformation starting at the beginning of the new millennium, when the improved political stability of Cambodia increased developers' expectation of high returns on investment (see Chapter 3). Urban planners lost faith in the idea of controlling the dynamics of urban development. The Urban Reference Plan was dismissed at the end of the 1990s, when the political climate turned against its implementation. Molyvann had been the only Cambodian representative during the planning process, even though the plan had been officially submitted to the

Cambodian Supreme National Council[23] and to the recently established planning authority, APSARA. Molyvann had persuaded Prince Norodom Ranariddh[24] to sign the plan. After the first general elections of 1993, the royalist party FUNCIPEC and Hun Sen's Cambodian People's Party (CPP) had allied to reach the 60 per cent majority required by the Cambodian constitution. The two leaders became joint prime ministers in the new government. However, political conflicts undermined the stability of this government, and it was overthrown by the military coup of 1997. Since the subsequent general elections (1998), the CPP has governed Cambodia alone. Prince Norodom Ranariddh was exiled, and without him the Urban Reference Plan lost the political support needed for its implementation. Moreover, only the highest political authorities had approved the plan, with no collaboration from the local authorities[25] who had been re-established in the provinces in 1994. This meant that the success of the plan strongly relied on the ascendancy of two individuals, Molyvann and Norodom Ranariddh, who had faded away by the turn of the century.

During the following years, Cambodian institutions showed no will to effectively implement the urban plans which succeeded the Urban Reference Plan and endorsed its provisions. Among these were the provisions crafted by Groupe 8 in 1999 with the aim of developing a land use plan, and the 1997 master plan for urban transport sponsored by the European Union. The latter argued that the Cambodian authorities should choose development routes to be carefully followed in order to find a way to sustainable development. One of these routes could be the maintenance of the vegetal city, which required strict control over tourist volume. However, other directions would have to be taken if the government wanted to develop mass tourism (Tractabel, 1997). In an impartial manner, which did not recommend any one development route as the best, this sector plan laid the foundations for the emergence of another idea of the city, which appeared full-blown in the JICA Master Plan designed between 2004 and 2006.

23 The Paris Peace Accords established the Supreme National Council (1991). This was the sole legitimate body and source of authority in which the sovereignty, independence, and unity of Cambodia were enshrined during the transitional period. The SNC was placed under the leadership of Prince Norodom Sihanouk. It represented Cambodia at the United Nations and delegated power to the United Nations Transitional Authority in Cambodia (UNTAC) until the establishment of the new government.

24 Prince Norodom Ranariddh is King Norodom Sihanouk's son, and leader of FUNCIPEC.

25 Namely, the provincial delegation of the Ministry of Land Management, Urban Planning, and Construction. The Law on Land Management, Urban Planning, and Constructions (Kram/04NS94/10Aug94) established that a committee within the provincial delegation of the Ministry should design land use plans that would then be approved at the national level.

Japanese planners working at the beginning of the twenty-first century found more similarities between Siem Reap and the crowded conurbations of developing countries, with their problems of urban infrastructure and services, than between it and the villages surrounded by vegetation that inspired the idea of the vegetal city. In their minds, Siem Reap reflected a broader problem encountered in the different Asian situations where JICA operates: on the one hand, cities are 'the cause of environmental degradation and resource depletion'; on the other hand, they 'drive economies' and 'it is within them that innovation occurs and an increasing part of global output is produced' (Jenks and Burgess, 2000, p. 17). From this dilemma emerges the challenge of sustainable development.

Siem Reap is increasingly expanding on land originally devoted to agriculture. However, land is not an unlimited resource: in the north, the archaeological park put a brake on urban development, since no new construction is officially allowed in the protected areas; in the south, land is subject to periodic flooding during the rainy season. The city is thus expanding mainly towards the east and west, with disconnected architectural and urban projects forming miscellaneous urban elements. The planners from the German Development Service (DED), who designed a land use plan in 2007 in collaboration with the JICA master plan,[26] drew a parallel between this recent expansion trend and the traditional pattern of human settlement in the region, both being characterized by low density. Their report stated, however, that 'further development in the traditional settlement pattern is ineffective as it creates problems in terms of infrastructure (road, supply system, etc.)' This pattern is likely to lead to high and unsustainable demand for land, especially in the suburban and rural areas (DED, 2007, p. 41).

The idea of the compact city has emerged as a reaction against the over-exploitation of land resources: 'the land use plan [...] devices the concept of a Compact City so that the city would not spread too much to outwards which would lower the efficiency of infrastructure development and the intra-urban transport more time and energy consuming' [sic] (JICA, 2006, vol. III, pp. 1-16). Planners chose the compact city for its efficiency in organizing movement and economizing land area. The idea that compact cities are efficient, more specifically in developing countries, is rooted in an entrenched belief that 'compaction will result in reductions in travel distances and thus vehicle emissions, and that high densities can create greater viability for

26 While JICA funded a master plan for Siem Reap province, the DED was asked to design a land use plan for Siem Reap district. The two agencies acknowledged that their tasks overlapped and collaborated to draw up two consistent land use plans.

service provision, public transport, waste disposal, healthcare and education' (Jenks, 2000, p. 18). In the same vein, Hofstad argued that the compact city 'secures socially beneficial, economically viable, and environmentally sound development through dense and mixed use patterns that rely on sustainable transportation' (2012, p. 3). The current interest in policies of compaction arose in the late 1980s, when the Brundtland Commission Report (1987) and the UNCED Agenda 21 (1993) stressed the importance of achieving sustainability through forms of urbanism. Their major concern was 'the environmental and socio-economic consequences of energy production and consumption for urban development' (Burgess, 2000) on a global scale.

Although recent research has criticized the 'compaction myth' (Neuman, 2015), Japanese researchers still offer a positive perception of the compact city. For instance, Kii and Doi assume that 'it is widely accepted that one of the most promising solutions for achieving sustainability in towns and cities is the implementation of the compact city, that is, a high-density mixed use, and intensified urban form' [sic] (2005, p. 485). This prolific literature shares a common perspective, according to which the development of a strategy for compact cities based on a set of standardized indexes and spatial models can be applied in Japan and throughout the world. The trust in the compact city pattern is reflected in urban policies across Japan (see, for instance, Lee and Kurisu, 2015). Japanese cities have faced challenges to sustainability since the start of the twenty-first century, as a result of depopulation, urban sprawl, and municipal financial crises. In reaction, local authorities have adopted counter-measures in the form of the development of compact cities.

The Japanese International Cooperation Agency consequently developed a cooperation strategy for urban development in emerging countries. Drawing on 'Japanese experience that overcame rapid urbanization and disasters' and on 'Japan's development know-how', this strategy was said to channel 'the energy of urbanization into the right direction'. It aimed to transform urban structures by applying the 'compact city model', which prevented 'chaotic urbanization (including expansion and dispersion)' while keeping 'the key urban activities within the appropriate size of the city' (JICA, 2013, p. 8). In Ulaanbaatar, Mongolia, for instance, the 2007 JICA Master Plan proposed that a compact city should be created in order to stop urban sprawl triggered by migration.[27] The development of such a strategy illustrates Mosse's and Mitchell's critique of international development assistance, in which as they see it, 'the work of professionals of all kinds is precisely to establish

27 Sanjo, Akihito, 'Towards the Low Carbon City in Developing Countries': siteresources.worldbank.org/.../Day1_P7_2_JICA.pdf (accessed 26 August 2015).

(against experience) the notion that social and technical change can be and is brought about by generalizable policy ideas, and that "global knowledge" produced by international organizations occupies a transcendent realm "standing above" particular contexts' (Mosse, 2011, p. 3, citing Mitchell, 2002).

Occupying this 'transcendent realm', the Japanese planners designed Siem Reap's urban plan, into which they introduced elements of a general discourse about developing cities that identified 'informality' and 'unplanned development' as two problems to be solved. JICA's planning narrative was constructed around dichotomies of order and disorder, sprawl and compactness, formality and informality. For instance, describing the residential and tourism neighbourhoods built by small property owners in the western section of Siem Reap, the planners commented that 'the road grid has not yet been completed because of the disordered expansion of the residential area' (JICA, 2006, vol. III, Chapter 1, p. 3). They identified 'unlawful human settlements [...] in some areas along the Siem Reap River' (Ibid., p. 7). Finally, they diagnosed 'the symptoms of urban sprawl with narrow, unpaved and winding, and often disconnected roads, and generally the lack of much infrastructure' (Ibid., p. 13). On this basis, JICA's master plan put the emphasis on regulation and reordering of the urban environment, achievable through the control of density, the building of infrastructure, and the commodification of the central districts for tourism. The implementation of the compact city was a way to order the urban fabric through the controlled densification of existing neighbourhoods and the rational urbanization of new urban sectors, adequately provided with urban infrastructure and basic services.

Furthermore, the Japanese planners viewed Siem Reap's urban fabric through the lens of analytical categories formed to describe metropolitan development, centred on the designations of 'urban area', 'urbanized area', 'peri-urban area', 'urbanizing area', and 'rural area'. These categories, however, failed to take into account the hybrid character of Siem Reap's urban features and their rural heritage. They also interpreted urban development as sprawling from a centre, identified as the colonial districts, towards a periphery, the urbanizing area, misunderstanding the historical evolution of the town, which actually originated from the conglomeration of villages along a belt of land approximately ten kilometres in length.

The analysis of Siem Reap's evolution according to the centre-periphery model is a preliminary step in the implementation of the compact city pattern. The commercial district, built during the French Protectorate, does indeed offer a local reference that, in the planners' minds, evokes the positive qualities associated with the compact city:

> With the population of 139,000 in 2004, the urbanized area of Siem Reap falls in a compact area within radius of about 2 km [...] The urbanized area extends between Sivatha Street and the Siem Reap River. The road grids were constructed during the French protectorate, and are well devised within this area today. This area accommodates a number of hotels, commercial facilities, and government buildings, and is relatively well planned. The area around the Old Market [...] is an active downtown area with a number of restaurants and pubs, retail shops including souvenir shops and service providers' offices. This area is becoming the core of the tourism activities after the visits to the ruins during the day [sic]. (JICA, 2006, vol. III, pp. 1-11)

This excerpt is representative of a planning narrative that celebrates the rationality of compact forms, seen as bringing order and efficiency to the daily functioning of the urban fabric.

The urban development strategy consisted of the expansion and adaptation of this pattern to the other areas of the city, with the goal of controlling urban sprawl through a land use plan, maximizing the efficiency of infrastructure, and minimizing energy consumption. Along with overall land use planning, numerous infrastructure projects were proposed, for transport, drainage, potable water, and pavements.

The focus on infrastructure is typical of JICA, as is reflected by other projects for Siem Reap[28] and by its general strategy for developing countries. European beliefs about development assistance had their roots in the ideology of the colonial 'civilizing mission' supposed to assist the cultural and material development of the colonized. The origins of this attitude, in turn, were to be found in the missionary goal of leading the natives along the path of moral progress and teaching them how they ought to live and improve their society (Blaise, 2006). However, as King and Grath (2004) have noted, Japan has never promoted Christianity; on the contrary, it was itself the object of missionary efforts. Additionally, when Japan occupied Korea the violence of its interventions in the social and educational spheres was condemned. This controversial past awakened sensitivities in Asia that 'seem to have confirmed a Japanese preference for their aid to support technical and infrastructural areas and not the so-called softer fields, such as human resources planning and governance' (King and Grath, p. 159). Moreover,

28 Already in 1992, JICA had produced an executive report for a master plan which carefully listed Siem Reap's technical malfunctions. JICA's funded projects in the region since then have mainly concerned potable water, wastewater treatment, and road improvement.

when Japan received international assistance after the Second World War, its official discourse about aid claimed that it was able to overcome this difficult period because the government defined its own development priorities, independent of the orientations of the donors and lenders (Nishigaki and Shimomura, 1996), and used aid to modernize its technical equipment. Drawing on these experiences, Japan has developed an aid philosophy that provides assistance in technical fields, such as industrial infrastructure, but does not interfere with the development directions chosen by the recipient countries (Soderberg, 1996). In this way, Japan leaves the recipient country with the responsibility of choosing the development model that fits best with its ideals and expectations; this is echoed by the Japanese Official Development Assistance Charters of 1992 and 2003, which stress the importance of the self-help efforts developing countries need to make (Watanabe, 2006).

The two Japanese companies working in Siem Reap shared a threefold focus on technology, innovation, and problem-solving. Founded in the aftermath of the Second World War, Nippon Koei Co. Ltd. and Kokusai Kogyo Co. Ltd. both operate in the engineering sector. The first has provided 'comprehensive services in the field of technical assistance to developing countries since its foundation in June, 1946' and aims to contribute to society 'through technology with sincerity'.[29] It stresses the importance of finding solutions that apply 'superior technology' and 'technical specialties' throughout the world. Established as a network of ten branches in the global 'South' (with the exception of an office in the United Kingdom and its headquarters in Japan), the company devotes almost all of its major projects to infrastructure building.[30] The second was founded in 1948 and specializes in geospatial information technology expertise, road and railway expansion planning, and disaster management. It focuses on developing cutting-edge technologies and innovation, applied both in Japan and in 'Asian markets'.[31]

The orientation of Japanese aid in Siem Reap, as reflected in the consulting firms' profiles and activities, illustrates the emphasis put on efficiency, technology, modernization, and economic development. The team appeared to be a coherent and cohesive group which drew both on the donor's philosophy and on a pragmatic (and disenchanted) awareness of the political reality of Cambodia. The implementation process in this case was dependent less on

29 Statement by the company's president, Noriake Hirose. Source: http://www.nipponkoei.com/ (accessed 16 June 2015).

30 Source: Japan's Infrastructure Development Institute website: http://www.idi.or.jp/english/idi_members/n_koei.htm (accessed 16 June 2015).

31 Source: http://www.kkc.co.jp/english/company/message.html (accessed 16 June 2015).

unpredictable political connections than on the daily work of persuasion, accomplished by several consultants who succeeded each other over time. Some were members of JICA's regular staff, others were senior volunteers; all were appointed for several years and based within a Cambodian authority. This organization reflected Japan's aid system, which gives weight to the 'person-to-person transfer of skills, technologies, and attitudes' (King and McGrath, 2004). However, according to Blaise (2006), Japan's claim that it does not impose a philosophy is fallacious: Japan does try to transfer its model to less developed neighbouring countries, as it requires them to imitate its own approach to defining development objectives. This is even more obvious with regard to the compact city model, which travelled from global ideas about the desirable pathways of urban development, through the experience of Japanese cities, to the developing world.

2.4 The buttresses of planning

Ideas and spatial layouts for Siem Reap have evolved over the last twenty years. However, planners have continued to use two instruments that appear to be fundamental elements of the grammar of urban planning, namely, functional zoning and heritage inventories. Both can be considered as 'travelling rationalities' according to the definition given by Craig and Porter (2006): that is, instruments that are the object of unanimous consensus by the class of international experts. Through them, 'the universal [is asserted] over the particular, the travelled over the placed, the technical over the political, and the formal over the substantive' (Craig and Porter, p. 120). Rationalities travel, circulating across time and space and asserting their technical efficiency over the uncertainties of local policies. They align aid instruments but tend to conceal 'the regional, institutional, agency or sector specificity of the development process' (Mosse, 2007, p. 1). I argue that the survival of zoning and inventory-making is due to global consensus about their validity as planning instruments. For this reason, I call them the 'buttresses' of planning: they are claimed by generations of planners to be relevant and efficient tools despite the failure of previous master plans, intense urban development, and the succession of consulting teams over time. Planners, caught between local concerns and global practices of urbanism, understand these instruments and their scope in different ways. Zoning and inventory-making are flexible instruments which can be adapted to the role that planners attribute to themselves and to the rules they choose or have to comply with.

2.4.1 Zoning

In *Modern Khmer Cities* (2003), Molyvann writes that 'in order to develop an efficient and practical policy for protecting and improving the environment of the Angkor/Siem Reap Region in general, as well as to institute the best possible land use, it is necessary to delimit zones and management areas which, while always responding to the needs of the monuments, also recognize existing forms of land use and land cover' (p. 74). Similarly, Jonathan Wager, the ZEMP team leader, argued that 'the whole Siem Reap Province is to be managed as a multiple-use zone in which guidelines, administered by the Angkor authorities, protect the archaeology and ecology, promote sustainable use of rural resources and concentrate development for tourism in selected areas' (1995, p. 520). Again, the urban plan for Siem Reap set out by Hetreau-Pottier and Ros (1994) and integrated into the ZEMP, bounded the area within which the urban extension of Siem Reap was permitted, and identified distinct zones for social and economic development, tourism infrastructure, and the conservation of cultural landscapes.

The use of zoning echoed the goal of combining the entire city into a 'larger conceptual unit' (Sundaram, 2010) formed of distinct but complementary areas. In the minds of the planners who approached Siem Reap at the beginning of the 1990s, zoning was a powerful tool that was thought to be capable of determining the overall development of the city. It was an instrument of authority which presupposed a perfect relationship between the planners' goals and a strong political will. In line with this idea, planners were seen as the deus ex machina of urban development. Molyvann's growing ascendancy in the Cambodian political sphere and his acquaintance with Prime Minister Prince Ranariddh added credibility to this idea.

Zoning was introduced in Cambodia during colonial times. The plans for Phnom Penh developed by Daniel Fabré in the 1890s and Ernest Hébrard in the 1920s legislated 'new patterns of space in response to what they perceived to be the disorder of the capital and its social structure [...] Ethnic districts, first created in the 1890s, were codified in the 1920s' (Nam, 2011, p. 57). Similarly, the colonial power separated commercial and administrative functions in Siem Reap. More broadly, the idea of separating urban functions emerged in the Western world in the nineteenth century, as an attempt to give some order to the new conurbations, which were undergoing vast changes at the time of the Industrial Revolution. Zoning introduced a 'scientific pattern of spatial organization' and an 'a-priori framework for urban behavior' (Choay, 1969, p. 98). Related to principles of order and discipline, zoning was soon associated with an ethic of progress and hygiene.

In his utopian plan for an industrial city, Tony Garnier (1917) classified space in terms of zoning and demonstrated the great utility of a tool 'that was soon to become one of the hallmarks of modern planning' (Rabinow, 1995, p. 226). For Ernest Hébrard and Hendrick Andersen, two associate winners of the prestigious Prix de Rome, 'zoning was the first principle', as 'the city of the future needed residential, business, and industrial quarters' (Rabinow, p. 246). Hébrard was later to introduce zoning as a general tool for urban planning in Indochina, especially in the plans for Hanoi, Phnom Penh, and Dalat, which he personally designed. Widely implemented in colonial territories in the wake of the Athens Charter, which recognized it as the main force in urban planning, zoning brought into play a set of 'objectivized norms' that contributed to the rise of a worldwide 'class of experts' (Sundaram, 2010, p. 47) and to the association of Western planning with ideas of urban modernity (Robinson, 2006). Zoning became a dominant form of urbanism, as it condensed 'urban policy into a single, easily interpreted document' (Soderstrom, 1996). Consensus on the validity of zoning was based on ethical and social concerns about the development of a 'good', 'liveable', and 'modern' city.

The team of planners headed by Charpentier, Clément, and Molyvann retrieved the results of the UNESCO-led Zoning and Environmental Management Plan (ZEMP) in order to design a comprehensive plan for Siem Reap. In this case, zoning was projected onto largely rural land areas: in other words, it was applied to a malleable territory open to the planners' imaginations and ambitions. The town was organized into four large zones whose boundaries were marked by the right-angled intersection of National Highway No. 6 and the Siem Reap river. The allocation of functions was based on geological surveys of land fertility, drainage systems, and vegetal cover. Specific areas were allocated to agriculture, housing, tourism, and a forest reserve separating the town from the archaeological park. In particular, the establishment of an agricultural land reserve depended on a project designed to increase the storage capacity of the Western *baray*, built by Suryavarman I in the eleventh century, in order to irrigate the rice fields located in the southwest sector of Siem Reap. Based on projections of demographic growth from 60,000 in 1995 to 140,000 in 2010, a large land reserve was established in the southeast sector for the development of new housing. Corridors (linear zones) were established in order to protect the cultural landscapes around ancient roads and watercourses, and surrounded the totality of Siem Reap's urban heritage. A tourist enclave was to be built in the northeast part of the city (Figure 2.2).

The vision developed for this zoning system was the latest addition to a long tradition of French research in the region, of which the ARTE planners were the heirs, and to the priorities of French development assistance in Cambodia. Clément, persuaded that Asian cities can teach lessons in contemporary urbanism, reused ancient construction techniques and spatial layouts in zoning. The specialization of function was based on a twofold rationale: firstly the protection of inherited architecture, urban elements, and landscapes for Angkor and its associated cultural landscapes, and secondly the relation between zoning and geological and hydrological surveys. In the ARTE, the application of functional zoning brought together multiple perspectives related to common values and understandings of the Angkor site, along with the impact of diplomatic ties and the inherited research tradition of the EFEO, which had addressed the infrastructure and management of the Angkor capitals. The rejection of this zoning plan went hand in hand with the planners' abandonment of their ambition to reproduce the vegetal city in new developments. This double failure demonstrates the limitations of the paradigm of postcolonial dependence, in a situation where powerful Cambodians – Molyvann and Prince Norodom Ranariddh – had taken over control of foreign-sponsored policy, as long as the alchemy of national politics enabled them to perform their personal and relational power.

The idea of the vegetal city survived in further planning, though without being implemented; this pattern of zoning was reintroduced in the regulations proposed by Groupe 8 for a land use plan in 1999 (Figure 2.4). This plan took the control of urban development to an extreme: the list of 27 zones and construction regulations was as detailed as possible, in order to forestall any attempt at interpreting them in a way that might be disrespectful of the existing urban landscapes. According to the Groupe 8 consultants, the obstacles to the implementation of zoning lay in the lack of explicit and detailed guidelines. In other words, public officials needed extensive urban regulation in order to restrain the developers' freedom to operate. Zoning and associated urban regulation were viewed as the weapons for fighting the developers' thirst for unrestrained profit. The bureaucratization and technocratization of urban planning was aimed at resisting the unbridled pressure on urban space exerted by developers and the connivance of the national authorities. The proof of this is that legal approval of Groupe 8's regulations (sub-decree No. 35, 2000) was indeed followed by severe tensions with the developers. The sub-decree was repealed, revised several times with gradual loosening of the regulations, and never implemented (JICA, 2006). The domain of urban planning experienced waves of (failed) negotiations, showing that law is a volatile instrument in the hands of a political class when it is too closely associated with the interests of the business elite.

Figure 2.4 Functional zoning as proposed by Groupe 8 in 1999

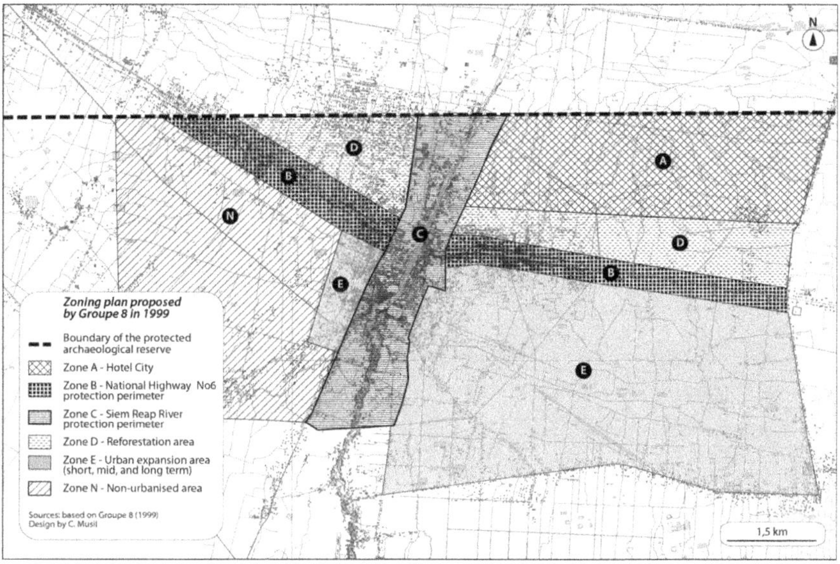

© Esposito 2016

In a situation shaped by multiple private-sector projects, planners who became aware of this institutional context still used zoning, but with different aims in mind. This trend began in 2002-2003, when the intensity of urban development and the controversial political environment opened the planners' eyes to the need to negotiate with the major players in the urban 'game' and to scale down their ambitions to control urban development.

This philosophy of Japanese development assistance informed the way the two Japanese consulting firms conceived of the guiding principles of their functional zoning plan for 2020. They tried to limit urban sprawl by defining the maximum outer perimeter that the city could reach by 2020 (Figure 2.5). However, they did not formulate an idea of the 'good city' to be developed. Instead, they acknowledged that urban development was being defined by multiple disjointed private projects, and encouraged these to expand further. This meant that the perimeter now surrounded already developed zones. Their aim was to identify existing urban functions and to encourage the specialization of function of urban areas, thus creating order out of what might look like anarchic development. By doing this, the planners acknowledged that Cambodian institutions had not defined any guidelines for urban development. They tried instead to negotiate land use with the strong private sector, through non-constraining zoning accompanied by

Figure 2.5 Functional zoning as proposed by JICA in 2006

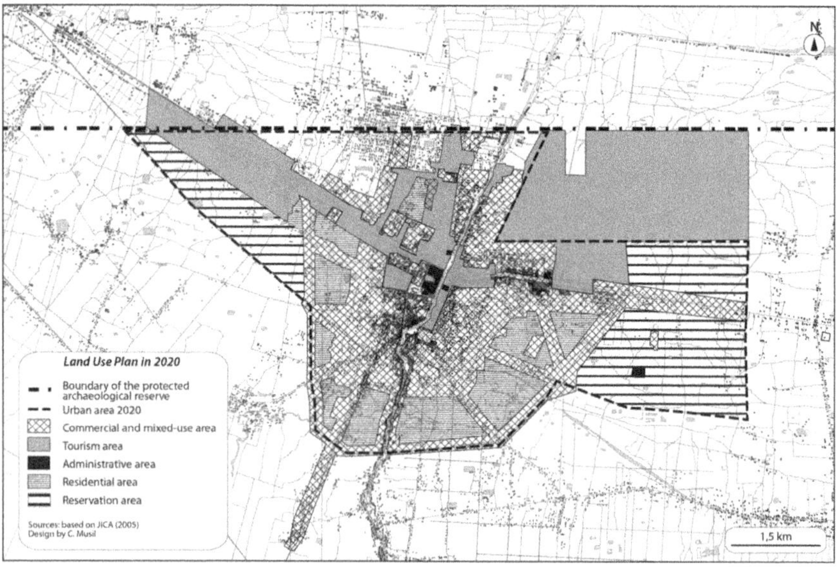

© Esposito 2016

a number of sector-specific projects. Most of these projects concerned infrastructure building designed to allow the efficient management of various types of flow within the city (including of people, vehicles, water, and waste) and hence to make development environmentally sustainable. The technical approach of the Japanese consultants positioned them as the ancillaries of the Cambodian authorities, since they were trying to facilitate a development process whose direction and guidelines they themselves had not originally established.[32]

2.4.2 Inventories

In the shadow of the World Heritage recognition of Angkor, planners recognized that Siem Reap town also had a heritage worth protecting. The ZEMP defined it as a 'cultural landscape' and, more specifically, as an

32 Similar approaches were followed by the German Development Service (DED), funded by the Adenauer Foundation and the European Union to design a land use plan for Siem Reap in 2007. The expert team discussed with JICA in order to achieve similar zoning, although they worked with different authorities: JICA collaborated with Siem Reap province, DED with Siem Reap district, and tried to incorporate participation by the local population.

'environment marked by human intervention across time' (1994, p. 2). The royal decree, which followed the ZEMP, established two conservation zones that protected a linear zone, 500 metres wide on both sides of the river, and a zone of 250 metres on both sides of National Highway No. 6 (sub-decree 79/ANKR/PK, 13 October 1995). Clément and his team of planners requested an inventory of buildings worth protecting (Mauret, 1996). Due to lack of funding, however, this inventory, ideally to be extended to several types of architecture, was restricted to wooden houses and colonial buildings to be listed as part of the national heritage of Cambodia.[33] The consultants identified inventorying and listing as the main tools for the conservation of the urban heritage, and the Cambodian state as the responsible agent of recognition and protection.

Inventories of cultural properties appeared at the beginning of the nineteenth century, and became popular in European countries (Chastel, 1990; Negri, 2014). Aimed at amassing knowledge and documentation of monuments, they also instilled a collective consciousness about the values of heritage, which could inaugurate a regime of legal protection. In Cambodia, the French Protectorate enacted a decree on 9 March 1900 on 'the conservation of monuments and objects of historic and artistic interest' which covered the same points as the French law on 'the conservation of historic monuments and works of art' of 1887. This text had regulated the first inventory of the Angkor remains, enabling the identification in 1887 alone of more than 300 objects from 32 regions of Cambodia (Mangin, 2006). Since the 1960s, inventories have become a global tool for heritage conservation. Other European countries started to develop heritage inventories based on the model of the French and Italian lists. The Council of Europe has supported a normalization process, which has improved the standards, methods, and criteria of inventory-making with the goal of encouraging countries to adopt policies for the protection of cultural heritage and, eventually, to create a common European heritage inventory (Negri, 2014). UNESCO has used the Council of Europe's guidelines in order to disseminate the 'good practice' of inventory worldwide, and international consultants widely refer to this in building inventories.

33 Cambodian law contains clauses about heritage listing. The Law on Land Management, Urban Planning and Constructions (Kram/04NS94/10Aug94) established that the royal government can draw up lists of 'immobile objects or resort places', which should be protected and promoted for their value. This list should be enacted through a sub-decree (art. 10). The Law on the Protection of Cultural Heritage (NS/RKM/0196/26) established that the boundaries of protected sites containing 'archaeological reserves or other sites of archaeological, anthropological or historic interest' are defined by sub-decrees of the royal government (art. 6).

Inventories have been used not only to protect monuments, but also to safeguard urban heritage within the perimeter of historic cities. The notion of urban heritage was first shaped by European architects and theorists around the turn of the twentieth century. In 1903, Alois Riegl wrote that 'age value' 'described a shift in the understanding of the monument [...]: the growing perception that not only individual monuments, but the everyday fabric of the city, was "historic" and worthy of conservation' (Lamprakos, 2014, p. 9). In *The Stones of Venice* (1851-1853), John Ruskin spoke out against the degradation of the urban landscape triggered by the Industrial Revolution: inherited cities had value since they rooted their inhabitants in time and space, and Ruskin criticized the transformations that undermined the awareness of collective identities. Camillo Sitte (1889) condemned the unaesthetic character of contemporary cities. He used urban morphology, a method of urban investigation that he had invented, to show that inherited urban forms had aesthetic value, and identified constant characteristics of urban spaces across time, which, he argued, should be reproduced in nineteenth-century additions in order to make them beautiful. All these authors expressed their fears for the loss of local, regional, and national identities and contributed to the idea that the 'historic city' was distinct and fundamentally different from the 'modern city' (Lamprakos, 2014), a distinction that the Italian architect Gustavo Giovannoni analysed in *Vecchie città ed edilizia nuova* ('Old Cities and New Building'), arguing that these two entities should be brought into harmonious relation through planning. Giovannoni coined the expression 'urban heritage' (1931), a notion that encompassed material legacies from the past as well as the social and cultural meanings attached to them. In his view, 'ancient' and 'modern' cities ought to coexist, spatially separate but governed by a common set of rules.

The first experiments in the conservation of historic districts date back to the colonial period, when European powers separated the districts inhabited by the natives from those of the colonizers. One of the purposes of this policy was to safeguard indigenous culture and attract tourists. Measures for urban heritage conservation were also introduced in the zoning plans of some American cities, such as Charleston, in the early twentieth century. However, international charters and national legislation started to incorporate the notion of urban heritage in the aftermath of the Second World War. The war had had disastrous effects on urban landscapes. In France, '460,000 buildings had been destroyed; out of 8000 listed buildings of national importance 1270 had been damaged' (Jokilehto, 1986, p. 409). Reconstruction work across Europe aimed to restore historical significance and national identity, but generated questions about how urban conservation and reconstruction should be carried out. As a result, historic towns and urban environments became the object of increasing attention, captured by the work of Italian theorists including Benedetto Croce, Giulio Carlo Argan, and Roberto Pane.

The Venice Charter (1964), written by the Second International Congress of Architects and Technicians of Historic Monuments, made a seminal contribution to the conservation of urban heritage thanks to its worldwide distribution. It stated that 'the concept of historic monument embraces not only the single architectural work, but also the urban and rural setting in which is found the evidence of a particular civilization, a significant development or a historic event. This applies not only to great works of art but also to more modest works of the past which have acquired cultural significance with the passing of time' (art. 1). European countries have gradually adopted measures for the protection of their historic centres. With the introduction of *secteurs sauvegardés* (conservation zones) in France (in the Loi Malraux of 4 August 1962), descriptive inventories for each building made it possible to extend protected status within historic centres. In Italy, in reaction to massive urban reconstruction and new housing developments, municipalities have started to sponsor programmes for the conservation of historic areas, even in minor urban centres, since the 1970s.

Large Asian cities have followed a similar path. Since the 1970s, they have undergone processes of intense urban development driven by economic growth. The conservation of urban heritage has not been a priority, and city dwellers are fascinated by the architectural innovations that express ideas of modernity. In Singapore, for instance, massive areas of dilapidated shophouses were destroyed during the 1970s, to be replaced by high-rise buildings. Here, consciousness of the value of urban heritage was already emerging at the end of that decade, but the Urban Redevelopment Authority implemented the first Conservation Master Plan only in 1986 (Loo Lee, 1996). In Kuala Lumpur, the preservation of areas designated as ethnic historic districts currently goes hand in hand with the destruction of large parts of the historical fabric to make room for condominiums and tower developments.

Medium-sized Southeast Asian cities began to join global economic networks in the 1980s and the 1990s, and also started to experience the destruction of the urban heritage under the impact of modernization. In Southeast Asia, the fear of losing cultural roots and local identities emerged, as in Europe, as a consequence of the rapid destruction of the urban legacy (Choay, 1992). This fear triggered the introduction of policies and laws on urban conservation, the listing of several historic areas and cities as UNESCO World Heritage sites, and the promotion of cultural tourism in the region.

Cambodia was not yet part of this trend. While other countries in the region were experiencing significant economic growth, Cambodia was a closed country under the Khmer Rouge. Between 1975 and 1979, the regime spread hatred of cities as hotbeds of moral corruption and emptied them of their inhabitants. After the 'liberation' by the Vietnamese army, refugees started to look for shelter in the cities. However, the vast majority of them were not the same people who had been evacuated in 1975, since many of those had died. The refugees from the countryside who settled in the cities had no memories of the built environment and felt no emotional attachment to it. On the contrary, historic buildings, which had been left to decay for decades and were now randomly and spontaneously occupied by new city dwellers in need, were closely associated with bad memories of poverty, obsolescence, and poor hygienic conditions (Clément-Charpentier, 2008).

In this impoverished community, there was no way for the notion of urban heritage to take root. Moreover, at the beginning of the 1990s, the country had no culture or knowledge of urbanism, and the University of Fine Arts had yet to be re-established. Cambodian national institutions focused on the idea of the historic monument to reconstruct national identity, and Angkor offered a grandiose legacy for this purpose, with immediate benefits from tourism. At the same time, they played the card of urban development and modernization through investment in the property sector. This thirst for development recalls a similar frenzy in the large Asian cities starting in the 1970s: urban heritage conservation was neglected until urban society realized that it risked losing essential identity values along with the erasure of the historic urban fabric.

Proposals for the establishment of an urban heritage policy based on inventory had no leverage in this context; this was especially true of those proposed for Siem Reap in the wake of the Urban Reference Plan (Mauret, 1996), which aimed to protect inherited buildings for their intrinsic architectural value and said nothing about occupation, use, and possible profitable conversion. In the heritage inventory of 1996, valuable buildings appeared as beautiful but empty shells (Figure 2.6). Echoing the depiction of landscapes since colonial times (see Chapter 4), human beings were absent from drawings and pictures, undermining the notion of cultural landscape as the interaction between human beings and their living environment. The inventory was another dehumanized instrument in the hands of planners who drew up lists of the buildings' history, physical characteristics, and state of conservation, with various degrees of value, which were to be associated with particular urban regulations in order to conserve their authenticity and integrity. Planners viewed inventory as a fundamental and generally valid instrument for heritage identification, and its utilization went without question. Derived as it ultimately was from positivism and essentialism, the concept of the inventory implied that historical and aesthetic significance is inherent in objects. Planners, the carriers of this heritage culture who function as cultural brokers, considered themselves to be the legitimate producers of heritage recognition in Siem Reap and the spokespersons for Cambodian institutions. By setting the boundaries of a conservation zone, their conservation philosophy echoed the principle of the preservation of native districts in colonial times and aimed both to protect the 'lifestyle of the people' (ARTE, 1995) and to attract tourists to the area; new developments were to take place outside the historic city. In other cases, this approach to heritage was met with criticism, as 'the standards designed for monuments cannot be applied to a living social-cultural fabric, which has to change and evolve' (Lamprakos, 2014, p. 10). The inventory of Siem Reap's urban heritage is thus representative of a broader tendency to treat historic districts as collections of monuments and impose the same kinds of regulation for their conservation.

However, urban development trends made it impossible to create an inventory that would conserve the historic city purely for the sake of cultural values. Other planners took a more realistic attitude and endorsed a strategy reflecting worldwide discussions of how conservation could be combined harmoniously with development goals. These discussions rejected the widespread idea that 'various aspects of development threaten to degrade and destroy heritage and its inherent values' (ICOMOS, 2011). Already in 1978, ICOMOS had sown the first seeds of this during the Moscow-Suzdal conference on the protection of historic cities and neighbourhoods within the framework of urban development. Historic monuments were seen as supports for economic and social development. Other events (e.g. the 1999 conference on the wise use of heritage in Mexico) and charters (e.g. the international cultural tourism charter of 1999) contributed to creating an 'authorized heritage discourse' (Smith, 2006), which sees development as an opportunity to enhance heritage resources and benefit from them. In 2002, the World Heritage Committee adopted the Budapest Declaration, which emphasized the need 'to ensure and appropriate an equitable balance between conservation, sustainability and development, so that World Heritage properties can be protected through appropriate activities contributing to the social and economic development and the quality of life of our communities'.[34] Of course, the idea of development had shifted from an economics-centred concept towards an inclusive understanding of human satisfaction: development was 'understood not only in terms

34 Source: http://whc.unesco.org/en/sustainabledevelopment/ (accessed 8 September 2015).

of economic growth, but also as a means to achieve a more satisfactory intellectual, emotional, moral and spiritual existence', in the words of the UNESCO Universal Declaration on Cultural Diversity (2001, art. 3). UNESCO's Operational Guidelines incorporated the notion of sustainable development in 2005, stating that, 'the protection and conservation of natural and cultural heritage are a significant contribution to sustainable development' (UNESCO, 2005, I-B, 6). The links between heritage and development have been strengthened in recent years through the ICOMOS Paris Declaration 'On Heritage as a Driver of Development' (2011), which viewed development 'as an asset to heritage conservation, to the dissemination of its inherent values, and to the cultural, social, and economic development of communities' (ICOMOS, 2011, p. 1).

JICA's plan for Siem Reap (2006) relied on this approach, treating heritage as a tourist resource. It suggested that downtown Siem Reap should be converted to tourism functions and that only a few buildings in the historic urban centre needed to be inventoried and strictly protected for historical reasons. Later, the urban plan by Groupe 8 (2011) followed the same trend, endorsing the modification of the historic core of Siem Reap for tourism and commercial activity. In spite of this change of perspective, these two plans still used the inventory as a tool for heritage recognition. The consultants inventoried approximately 50 buildings (*éléments isolés*), along with five zones of protected landscape, using the Council of Europe's inventory standards,[35] which had been specifically crafted for inventorying heritage not yet listed at the national level. Groupe 8's planners wrote that 'the inventory of the urban heritage of Siem Reap has not been made yet. The royal decree of 1994 has not yet been completed by a definition of "protected cultural landscape" which would justify listing part of the town as zone 3 [...] Therefore, the first step is to make an inventory of this urban heritage, or at least to outline it' (Groupe 8, 2011, p. 19).[36] Once the inventory was made, Cambodian institutions would impose regulations concerning different heritage categories such as 'Angkor heritage', 'Buddhist heritage', and 'colonial heritage'.

The consultants' discourse showed that the narrative concerning heritage inventories has changed, introducing a less rigorous, more development-orientated idea of the function and future of legacy buildings. The survival

35 The Committee for Cultural Heritage of the Council of Europe developed these standards in 1992, following the Granada Convention (1985) on the conservation of European urban heritage (Lavecchia, 2003; Groupe 8, 2011, p. 27).

36 Translation from French by the author.

Figure 2.6 Sample of inventoried building

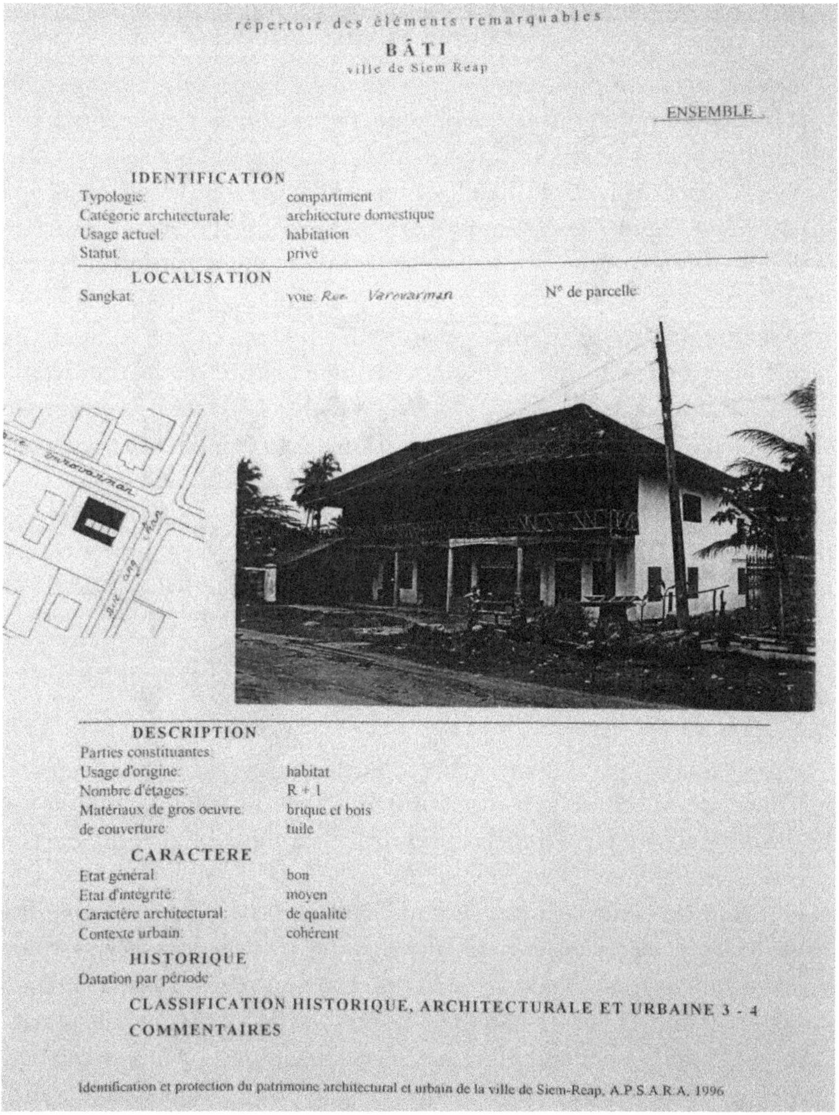

répertoir des éléments remarquables
BÂTI
ville de Siem Reap

ENSEMBLE

IDENTIFICATION

Typologie:	compartiment
Catégorie architecturale:	architecture domestique
Usage actuel:	habitation
Statut:	privé

LOCALISATION

Sangkat: voie: Rue Varovarman N° de parcelle:

DESCRIPTION

Parties constituantes:	
Usage d'origine:	habitat
Nombre d'étages:	R + 1
Matériaux de gros oeuvre	brique et bois
de couverture:	tuile

CARACTERE

Etat général:	bon
Etat d'intégrité:	moyen
Caractère architectural:	de qualité
Contexte urbain:	cohérent

HISTORIQUE

Datation par période:

CLASSIFICATION HISTORIQUE, ARCHITECTURALE ET URBAINE 3 - 4

COMMENTAIRES

Identification et protection du patrimoine architectural et urbain de la ville de Siem-Reap, A.P.S.A.R.A. 1996

Mauret, 1996

of this 'buttress of planning' relied on a centralized, top-down approach, which viewed the state as the primary force for heritage recognition and conservation, overlooking the global trends in conservation that promote participatory approaches and community involvement (Schofield, 2014). The evidence of Siem Reap's rapid urban development did not prompt questions about who has stakes in the urban heritage game: in the planners' minds, heritage recognition was still a procedural process entangled with categories, sets of criteria, and grids.

The fundamental shift, however, did not really concern the heritage tools themselves but rather the planners' hopes to have them implemented. The planners who worked in Siem Reap since the 2000s did not seek to move on from theory to practice. Their long-term acquaintance with Siem Reap's institutional framework[37] taught them that foreign-sponsored plans are systematically abandoned. However, money was still provided by the French Development Agency, and a new generation of planners from Groupe 8[38] was again requested to design a plan for Siem Reap. In this context, the recent plan tells more about the planners' own culture – what they would ideally do if they could – than about their ability to adapt this culture to the challenges and obstacles of the local situation. Planners do their work as if it is an exercise. They express the principles and guidelines that they perceive as good, and position themselves as the powerless bearers of a useful culture of planning, helpless in the face of the local power games and development processes that go beyond their (limited) agency.

2.5 Projects

The projects for the construction of a tourism enclave in Siem Reap and of a harbour on Tonlé Sap lake sponsored by international assistance are both ambitious undertakings that would substantially transform tourism practices in the Siem Reap-Angkor region. While the first project would concentrate the majority of tourists in a special district in close proximity to the Angkor park, provided with all necessary facilities, the second would create an alternative cluster of tourist attractions around the lake. In both cases, the planners terminated their work when they delivered the project report to their Cambodian colleagues. Subsequently, they could only follow the project from a distance, as outsiders to its implementation. Later events, however, perverted the projects' initial scope and compromised the donors' strategies. The projects were not abandoned, nor, as in the case of the vegetal

37 This began in 1994, with the involvement of some consultants from Groupe 8 in the Urban Reference Plan.

38 The previous generation of planners, who had been involved in the 1999 land use plan, had already retreated.

city, viewed as theoretical discourses disconnected from the reality of urban development. Instead, they were dismembered and reassembled into new programmes that exploited international assistance in various ways, to the advantage of other categories of participants. These two projects can be seen as representative case studies for analysing international aid as a process entangled in the controversial arena of tourism and urban development.

2.5.1 A tourist enclave

With the purpose of 'preserving the city and maintaining its atmosphere' (Molyvann, 2003, p. 94), the first generation of urban planners thought of building an enclave that would be the only place in the town where large hotels and tourism facilities could be built. This idea emerged with the first plans for Siem Reap (Hetreau-Pottier and Ros, 1993; Bouchaud, 1994) and culminated in the Urban Reference Plan. Molyvann (2003) explains that the enclave, called the Hotel City, had to be built in the northeast sector of Siem Reap, where the soil was too poor to support large forests. The Hotel City was designed on a 560-hectare rectangular plot of land, its boundaries marked by longitude and latitude coordinates (Figure 2.7). A royal sub-decree (No. 79/ANKR/PK, 13 October 1995) established a land reserve that could potentially be expanded to an area of 1000 hectares, should tourism demand increase in the following years.

Judd and Fainstein (1999) define 'tourist bubbles' as well-defined perimeters that separate tourism space from the rest of a city. In the United States, these enclaves were built starting in the 1980s in order to preserve the tourists from the sight of criminality, poverty, and decay. Tourists stay in this 'public parts of town' and are 'shielded from and unaware of the private space where people live and work'. The tourists are enveloped in these bubbles so that they only move 'inside secured, protected, and normalized environments' (p. 36). Tourism studies have widely used the 'tourism bubble' as a heuristic model to analyse the spatial layouts and social impacts of specialized districts and enclaves (inter alia Smith, 2007). The arguments developed using this framework draw on broader discussions of the relations between hosts and guests. MacCannell (1976) argues that tourists would like to have genuine contact with local people and places; however, they can only experience 'staged expressions of authenticity', while 'real life' takes place behind the scenes, away from the localities artificially created for them. Smith (1989) problematized the deep impact of tourism on the local populations: 'tourism is often a mixed blessing: the tourist industry creates jobs and increases cash flows but the tourists themselves can become a physical and a social burden, especially as the numbers increase' (p. 11). Smith identified various strategies that reduce the stress of the interaction between hosts and guests, including the limitation of the number of tourists admitted to a site or country, the careful selection of the aspects of culture that 'can be marketed as "local colour" without serious disruption' (pp. 15-16), and the staged reproduction of heritage and traditions. MacCannell and Smith's arguments concerning the problematic impacts of tourism and the unsatisfied quest for authenticity have been discussed and nuanced by further research. In particular, Winter, Teo, and Chang (2009) have called into question Asian tourists' desire to experience authenticity and argued that the reproduction of the typical characteristics of a locality sometimes responds to this demand. Also, the interaction between hosts and guests can be a source of mutual benefit, and especially of economic profit for the locals (Dahles, 2001).

Following these debates, the idea of establishing a tourism enclave relied on the evaluation of the negative impacts that the interaction between hosts and guests might generate. High-end tourism facilities were designed to attract 'tourist elites', who were supposed to be more respectful of the local context (Gaulis, 2007), while mass tourism and its disruptive effects were discouraged. Architectural design for tourist facilities drew on the typical features of Cambodian wooden architecture, which was particularly adapted to the tropical climate. Buildings were scattered among meadows and plantations of trees in order to benefit from a pleasant microclimate (Clément, 1996). The architecture was supposed to reproduce a staged environment for the tourists in which they would experience a mediated, easier, and more secure contact with the locals (Détente, GIE, Score and Villes Nouvelles, 1995).

The model for the Hotel City was found in Bali's Nusa Dua project. In 1971, the Indonesian government approved a French-designed regional tourism plan for the island which incorporated a 425-hectare tourism enclave. The project aimed to maintain a clear separation between natives and tourists (Picard, 1995). In line with the paradox described by MacCannell (1976) and Smith (1989), tourists in Bali expected to find unchanged cultural expressions, preserved from the attacks of modernity, while they themselves were partly responsible for spreading modernity across the planet. In other words, their presence compromised the object of their quest. In order to avoid this, the decision was taken to separate the residents from the tourists. Residents of Buala village, located on the area designated for the project, were compelled to sell their land (Shaw and Shaw, 1999). The newly established Bali Tourism Development Corporation (BTDC) coordinated several stakeholders, including the United Nations Development Program (UNDP), which sponsored the project, the World Bank, which was responsible for managing land transactions at market value, a Japanese firm, which provided assistance for the development of the programme and its implementation, and various governmental agencies, companies, and local Balinese organizations (Inskeep and Kallenberger, 1992). The tourism enclave was located in Nusa Dua in the southeast part of the island of Bali, and mainly targeted wealthy Westerners who wanted to spend a few days on the beach.

The development of the area was split into three phases. New roads linked the tourism enclave with the airport and the major tourist destinations in Bali. Infrastructures were provided by the BTDC, together with a Japanese firm, for a budget of US$36.1 million. The enclave included a convention centre, parking areas, a park, a golf course, several condominiums, and the National Tourism Education and Training Centre for Balinese staff. A set of construction regulations was established to fix maximum density, minimum distance from the shore, and height limitations[39] (Inskeep and Kallenberger, 1992).

Due to the Indonesian government's restrictive air travel policy and the reluctance of the first developers to be pioneers on undeveloped land, the project encountered some start-up difficulties. However, the first hotels opened in the mid-1980s. To help the development of the enclave, until 1985 the government limited the number of hotels built to international standards outside Nusa Dua to 1600. Ten five-star hotels eventually opened in the enclave. They were run by foreign hotel chains, Sino-Indonesian consortiums based in Jakarta, and members of President Suharto's family. The BTDC soon appeared to be a profitable venture. However, Nusa Dua discourages 'both economic and cultural interaction beyond the resort gate in order to maximize corporate profit margins', as the wide offer of services, events, and products aims at reducing the tourists' desire to get outside of the enclave and visit Bali (Shaw and Shaw, 1999, p. 75). Local people and companies thus do not benefit directly from tourism development in the area.

Siem Reap's Hotel City largely drew on this model in its form, management, and implementation process. Two roads at right angles to each other connected the enclave to the airport, the city, and the archaeological park of Angkor. A new entrance gate to Angkor was established at the intersection of the road with the archaeological park. The project for the Hotel City included

39 Height limitations were the same as in the rest of the island: buildings could not be higher than the trees (15 metres), so that hotels could blend into the natural environment.

hotels, a visitor centre, a shuttle bus station, and a botanic garden. Construction regulations specified that hotels could not be higher than coconut trees.

The APSARA authority was made responsible for regulating land occupation[40] and transactions in the area. However, a jurisdictional conflict soon emerged, when the Phnom Penh-based Ministry of Tourism signed a Memorandum of Understanding (MoU) with the Malaysian YTL Corporation establishing a private-public joint venture. YTL was responsible for building infrastructure, while developers were to lease and develop plots. Although this MoU disappeared from view a few years later, the conflict shows that land ownership and management was a delicate issue in Cambodia. Institutions competed for power and rights which afford economic benefits. Projects sponsored and designed by international organizations can be 'appropriated' by developers who sign separate agreements with Cambodian authorities.[41] In this particular case, the conflict between 'ordinary' national institutions and the APSARA (acting as the intermediary with the international organizations) was played out, showing how Cambodian institutions behave as developers want them to, and establish alliances with companies that give them land privileges in exchange for economic resources.

In later years, the APSARA again became the main executor of the Hotel City project. However, Cambodian institutions did not possess the will to overcome the obstacles that eventually impeded its implementation. The French Development Agency donated 25 million francs (approximately 3,85 million euros) and lent 35 million francs (5,38 million euros) to build infrastructure on a 50-hectare plot in order to implement the first phase of the project. Work had to be completed in 1999, when the APSARA and the Cambodian Superior Council of National Culture (CSCNC)[42] were to launch a call for tenders to select the company to carry out the infrastructure work. However, Cambodian budget legislation formally forbids public institutions and intergovernmental agencies to take out loans. Officially, the APSARA could not accept the donation portion. Moreover, the APSARA did not have an independent budget at that time, and received its funding from central government. Under these conditions, it could

40 Although it was undeveloped, some villagers had settled there and had to be compensated for relocation.

41 Rabé (2009) examined land sharing projects in Phnom Penh. He explains that advisors to the Phnom Penh Urban Poverty Reduction Project 'engaged in participatory planning of technical design and procedures of the land sharing projects, as part of a joint process with groups of community residents and leaders and representatives of commercial developers and local authorities', while 'a separate top-down process was underway between senior officials of the Municipality and developers that would ultimately determine the *real* project design' (p. 430).

42 The CSCNC was established by the Royal Decree n° NS/RKY/0295, 19 February 1995.

not legally guarantee that it would refund the loan portion. Lastly, no money was being offered to compensate the villagers who occupied land on the site of the Hotel City. The French Development Agency's general regulations stated that national governments had to absorb that expense. However, the government hesitated to allocate funds for this purpose, because financial calculations had shown that no short-term benefit would result from land expropriation and leasing at market value.[43]

These were the official reasons why the implementation of the project was postponed. They mask an implicit institutional resistance to the project, which the French planners were unable to locate at a specific governmental level.[44] The government was thinking like an investor, aiming to make a profit from the project. At the same time, it did not actively commit to its implementation, as it refused to engage financially on the side of the foreign donor. This resistance prevailed over the French planners' enthusiastic commitment to acting as the deus ex machina of urban development.

Measures were taken to overcome these institutional obstacles in the following years. To benefit from an independent budget, in 1999 the APSARA signed a contract with Sokha Hotels concerning the Angkor admission ticket system, which had been managed by the Ministry of Tourism. Sokha Hotels is a branch of the private company Sokimex, which has also invested in petrol, tourism, clothing, housing, and helicopters. The Vietnamese-Cambodian 'Okhna' Sok Kong owns the company.[45] The agreement established that the private company would manage the ticket system and pay an advance amount of one million US dollars to the Cambodian government, with a fifteeen per cent automatic increase per year for the next five years. Initially, the sum was shared between the APSARA (US$800,000), the Ministry of Tourism (US$150,000), and the Ministry of Culture (US$50,000) (Molyvann, 2003). In August 2000, the agreement was revised: as Miura (2005) notes, since 2001 the APSARA has received 70 per cent of the profit if the total revenue exceeds US$3 million, 50 per cent if less (p. 12). In official pronouncements

43 Information on the expropriation process is rare, but the average price was estimated to be US$3/m^2.

44 Personal communication, July 2010.

45 'Okhna' is an honorific title originally reserved to the nobility. A sub-decree resurrected it in 1994, establishing that the title would be given to individuals who make a US$100,000 donation to the Cambodian Government and show 'an ostensible commitment to direct some of their wealth towards the greater good'. In 2014, more than 400 citizens had been granted the title: Sek Odom and Henderson, Simon, 2014, 'As Okhna ranks grow, honorific loses meaning', *The Cambodia Daily,* 21 June: https://www.cambodiadaily.com/archives/as-oknha-ranks-grow-honorific-loses-meaning-62057/ (accessed 15 September 2015).

(e.g. the ICC-Angkor reports), this agreement was presented as a step forward in the empowerment of the APSARA and the construction of the Hotel City. In fact, the alliance between the government and Sokha largely favoured the latter, which enjoyed the direct exploitation of the national heritage of Angkor. However, this alliance came to an end in 2016, when the contract with Sokha ended; a ministerial body has replaced it, providing larger amounts of money to the state coffers (Channyda and Turton, 2015; Sor, 2016a).

The agreement between APSARA and Sokha arrived too late, as the Hotel City had already lost its attractiveness in the eyes of potential developers such as Novotel, YTL, and Beta Mekong, who had initially shown interest in building hotels there. In 1997, the Council of Ministers allocated a concession on a public plot of land directly on the route of the road intended to link the Hotel City with the airport, for the Swiss Agency for Development (SDC) to build the Kantha Bopha pediatric hospital. In front of the hospital, members of the Cambodian People's Party acquired land for a shopping mall, which was finally completed in 2007. These developments contributed to the failure of the Hotel City project, whose attractiveness largely depended on a fast and easy connection with the airport. The humanitarian purpose of the hospital forestalled criticism, but the purely commercial shopping mall project showed how little the members of the leading party really supported the construction of a tourism enclave.

Developers began requesting building permits from the Ministry of Land Management, Urban Planning, and Construction to build tourism facilities outside the Hotel City area. Seventeen hotels were built in Siem Reap during the 1990s. In spite of this, the French did not give up the idea of the tourism enclave. The French Cooperation Agency donated twenty million francs (approximately three million euros) to build the access avenues to the Hotel City, but the east-west road had to be interrupted at the intersection with the Siem Reap river because of the Kantha Bopha hospital. Straight, wide avenues bordered by tall lampposts and canals were traced on flat, empty land. They intersected at a roundabout where a celestial dancer faces those coming from the town towards the new entrance of the archaeological park. No developer responded to the invitation to build on this malleable but deserted site (Figure 2.8).

The APSARA renamed the project in order to give it new life. The Hotel City became the Angkor Gateway, as the former name was said to sound like a ghetto (APSARA-UNESCO, 2002).[46] Along with the name, the

46 This was especially true in French, where the word *cité* has come to mean the new developments built after the Second World War on the edges of cities, mainly housing low-income, working-class and migrant communities.

programme changed. The tourism district was subdivided into a grid of sixteen rectangular plots. Those located near the main road reproduced typical Cambodian landscapes, ranging from the rice paddy to the jungle, separated by portals. Tourists were given a glimpse of them as they were driven towards Angkor in order to get a synthetic and all-encompassing picture of Cambodia's cultural and natural heritage. The Angkor Gateway included culture and leisure facilities, condominiums, shops, and hotels of all categories, which, unlike those built in the town in the meantime, would comply with international standards. One of the objectives of the project was to induce the tourists to stay longer in Siem Reap-Angkor and to engage in other activities than the visit to the archaeological park. More broadly, such a district would bring in not only tourists, but also wealthy Cambodians and foreigners who would enjoy a new lifestyle in the condominiums and facilities of the new district.

The Angkor Gateway did not get built either, and the APSARA gave up the idea of establishing a land reserve. By 2002, it had only bought 140 hectares, while 60 more were 'under acquisition'. Incapable of going further, it suggested that it would lease the land that it officially owned to developers. The 60 additional hectares would be developed by the actual occupants. With the rental income from the land, the APSARA planned to develop the district further. Another idea was to delegate the development of the area to a single developer, for instance a joint venture between a Cambodian and a foreign firm. Cambodian institutions needed knowledge about the management of international-standard hotels and facilities. At the same time, the foreign partner would need know-how about the complex functioning of the Cambodian bureaucracy. In this new configuration, the APSARA would be simply the landowner. This idea too was later abandoned, but it indicates how uncertain the Cambodian authorities are about the strategies to be adopted. This was even more evident when the project was again renamed in 2004, as the Cultural and Tourist Angkor City.[47] The new name went along with an extreme simplification of the programme, aiming to attract developers who were reluctant to comply with any form of constraint. The programme consisted of an easily understandable set of urban regulations for the attention of developers, with no specific requests about the types and standards of the facilities. As a reminder of Khmer architecture, the buildings' roofs were to evoke the saw-toothed pagoda roofs: this was the only feature representing Cambodia's cultural heritage. The presence of

47 This new name appears on the APSARA's proposal for a decree on urban regulations, which was submitted to central government in 2004, but has never been officially adopted.

an architectural style with little connection to the locality, close to the symbolically significant archaeological site of Angkor, was thus legitimized.

The project for a tourist district failed as an enclave that would have reduced tourist pressure from the town; however, it is still included in the APSARA's strategic programme. In line with this, foreign planners continue to include the land reserve in the most recent land use plans.[48] The Cambodian authorities would obviously lose credibility and compromise relations with the French agency that donated money for the project if they were to admit that the tourist district will never exist. But like the vegetal city, the idea of establishing a tourist enclave today is an imaginary one, existing purely on paper.

In the meantime, the land has begun to be developed, but by different organizations with different intentions. The Angkor COEX of Royal Angkor World opened its doors in 2009 to host conventions and commercial exhibitions. Run by a Thai company, SMDC Co. Ltd., it also served as temporary headquarters for the APSARA in 2009-2010 and was then converted into a theatre for the show 'Smile of Angkor'.[49] Two other developments were under construction at the end of 2015, when I conducted my last fieldwork trip: Sokha Hotel was building a hotel complex of 600 rooms on 23 hectares of land, which will be able to accommodate 15,000 people at a time; Palais Angkor SA, a company based in Luxembourg, had only just fenced off a land plot. After several rounds of relocation, the APSARA and Siem Reap province headquarters eventually settled down in this area. All these new buildings echo APSARA's preferences for architectural design. The aim of mixing 'Khmer traditional style' with 'some modern style', expressed by Soka's spokesman (Thik Kaliyann, 2014), is reflected in a series of similar buildings, which imitate sculptures and moulding from Angkor and pagoda roofs covering low-rise buildings plastered in white (Figure 2.9). However, the area is always deserted. People who work in the offices do not stay out in the sun, and there is no street restaurant or shop in the area because only large-scale development can take place there, as a result of negotiations with the national authorities. In such a dehumanized environment, the buildings look like virtual, immaterial images floating over a desolate landscape.

Several museum facilities were also built in the area, all sponsored through Asian bilateral cooperation. The Preah Norodom Sihanouk-Angkor

48 Namely, JICA's 2006 and DED's 2007 land use plan, as well as the Draft Statutory Zoning Plan jointly designed by the APSARA and the provincial bureau in 2010.

49 'Smile of Angkor' features ancient Angkor history as a 'Grand Epic'. Tourists enjoy the performance while having a buffet dinner, according to a formula widespread in southeast Asia.

Museum was designed and built by Sophia University of Japan between 2006 and 2007. The museum houses a collection of 274 Buddhist statues, which had been buried in a pit at Banteai Kdei[50] temple and were excavated by the university.[51] However, tourists rarely visit it. The museum is isolated, badly advertised, and displays many fragments and broken statues that do not interest the average tourist. A journalist from the *Phnom Penh Post* wrote in 2010, 'The museum itself is in danger of becoming a museum piece. It has a sorry air, it's dusty and drab, the surrounding gardens are mostly untended, and the building itself is slowly declining into disrepair. It's rarely visited and little wonder because, apart from the overall air of neglect, its display is boring' (Olszewski, 2010).

The Asian Traditional Textile Museum opened in 2014. It was built by the Mekong Ganga Corporation (MGC), a cooperative network between India, Thailand, Myanmar, Cambodia, and Vietnam.[52] The overall cost of US$1.7 million was largely covered by the Indian government's one-million-dollar donation. An Indian ambassador explained that India has grown interested in the project since it has exerted a strong influence on the development of textiles across Southeast Asia. As textiles further connections between peoples through trade and cultural exchange, so the museum is a landmark of present-day intercultural cooperation among Asian countries (Wilkins, 2014).

Finally, the North Korean government provided US$15 million to build the third and most expensive museum (Figure 2.9). The Grand Panorama, which opened its doors at the end of 2015, houses a collection of 150 contemporary works of art by the Mansudae Studio, Pyongyang's production centre of official art. Mansudae was founded in 1959 and brings together approximately 1,000 artists and 4,000 staff in the North Korean capital. Art produced at Mansudae expresses North Korean ideology and the studio aims at disseminating it internationally. Art works are sold through an art centre established in Shanghai, an Italian company that represents the studio abroad, and the Mansudae Overseas Projects Group, which operates outside North Korea. The latter is responsible for the construction of many sculptures and edifices in African countries, including Namibia, Angola, and

50 The Banteai Kdei temple was built by King Jayavarman VII between the end of the twelfth and the beginning of the thirteenth century.

51 AEON Credit Services Co. Ltd., the 'philanthropic arm' of AEON 1 per cent Club funded the million-dollar museum, which is built on the APSARA land reserve and officially managed by the Cambodian authority.

52 The MGC develops regional projects in the fields of tourism, culture, education, and transport, and was established by an inter-ministerial meeting in 2000.

Figure 2.7 Project for the Hotel City

ARTE-BCEOM, 1995

Botswana. Working abroad is both a way to obtain foreign currency, which is highly needed by such an isolated country, and to foster cordial diplomatic relations with those countries who agree to cooperate with North Korea.

The museum is a highly politicized enterprise, renewing the traditional diplomatic links between Cambodia and North Korea. The friendship between King Norodom Sihanouk and the North Korean dictator Kim Il-Sung dated back to the 1960s, when the two leaders used to meet at non-aligned summits. Sihanouk was a close acquaintance of Kim Jong-Il and enjoyed several retreats in Pyongyang's luxurious palaces. Under the Khmer Rouge regime, the North Korean regime recognized a resistance coalition which included Sihanouk, and the exiled Cambodian king often resided in Changsuwon Palace. The relationship between the two countries faded after Kim Il-Sung's death and the king's abdication, but economic links are still active.

Figure 2.8 The main axis, which passes through the land reserve of the tourism district and gives access to the archaeological park

Photo by the author 2009

Two North Korean restaurants operate in Siem Reap, and a recent visit was paid by a North Korean delegation to its national embassy in Phnom Penh (Strangio, 2011).[53]

The Angkor Panorama Museum is a massive symbol of incipient diplomatic cooperation between the two countries. Sok An, the president of the APSARA, stated in his inaugural speech that the museum further strengthens 'the friendship and cooperation between the two nations'.[54] On the doorstep of a World Heritage Site, the museum also represents an open challenge to the widespread international hostility towards North Korea. The museum is a stain on the positive image of the site, and for this reason not much fanfare surrounded its construction.

53 Strangio, Sebastian. 2011. 'North Korea's New Friend?', *The Diplomat*, 14 August. http://thediplomat.com/2011/08/north-koreas-new-friend/ (accessed 10 March 2016).

54 http://www.japantimes.co.jp/news/2016/01/18/asia-pacific/mysterious-north-korean-museum-opens-cambodia/#.VuGVO8dFOV6 (accessed 10 March 2016); http://www.nytimes.com/2016/01/26/arts/design/cambodias-new-angkor-museum-created-by-a-north-korean-art-factory.html?_r=0 (accessed 11 March 2016).

Figure 2.9 The Grand Panorama Museum

Photo by the author 2015

The North Koreans will be in charge of management for approximately ten years, after which the museum will become Cambodian property under the authority of the APSARA. The question arises as to whether it will actually attract enough visitors to make a profitable return on the investment, as hoped by both governments, who have put their trust in the inevitable growth of tourism at Angkor. However, according to the press,[55] only twenty to 30 tourists a day cross the threshold of the museum and pay the fee of fifteen dollars for foreigners or eight for Khmer citizens. Why Mansudae invested so much money in the construction of a museum overseas remains unclear.

The tourist enclave has become the space where the geopolitical relations between Cambodia and other Asian countries are celebrated through cultural landmarks. The supposed tourism function of the three museum facilities is countered by the low number of visitors and masks their role as monuments in the original meaning of the word (Choay, 1992, see Chapter 1): material evidence of something to be remembered, in this case the transnational agreements and diplomatic alliances contracted by Cambodia. The three sponsors have little visibility on the international scene and are absent from the debates on the management of the Siem Reap-Angkor region. Worse still, the North Korean delegation is highly controversial and could compromise the important economic cooperation between Cambodia and South Korea. In the shadow of the elite circles of international organizations that manage restoration and tourism development in the Angkor park, the enclave houses the physical signs of these subaltern alliances.

55 Ibid.

2.5.2 A harbour on Tonlé Sap lake

The case of the Hotel City shows how a project initially designed with foreign technical assistance was abandoned. In contrast, the project for a new port on Tonlé Sap lake shows how foreign expertise was instrumentalized for the benefit of private developers.

During the nineteenth century, European travellers used to land at a rough harbour in Chong Kneas. At the beginning of the twenty-first century, the travel conditions had not changed much. The harbour was made of movable elements to accommodate flood levels and was used for the transport of both people and goods. Landing facilities relied on ancient earthen embankments and channels. At the start of the twenty-first century, Chong Kneas was a commune of seven villages, with approximately 5000 people in 700 families. Of these, 29 per cent came from Vietnam (Preuil, 2011). Families were poor: 60 per cent of the people lived on less than 50 US cents a day. They lacked basic sanitary and hygienic facilities, living on houseboats or wooden and bamboo houses on high stilts, whose location changed according to the lake flood levels (Figure 2.10). These types of housing, built with scarce resources, were adapted to the changing environmental conditions of the lake. In 2004, 56,500 long-distance travellers and 110,000 tourists used the harbour's facilities (Placenter Ltd., 2004). Many of them were backpackers who could not afford airfares. Cambodian companies managed long-distance ground transport and Chong Kneas villagers organized boat tours on the lake to the nearby floating village of Kompong Phluk or to a crocodile farm.

In 1997, UNESCO designated the Tonlé Sap as a biosphere reserve, which also includes Chong Kneas municipality. This designation was established in 1971 in the framework of the Man and Biosphere programme. It is not legally binding, but aims to build networks and share knowledge and experience on natural resource management. On 10 April 2001, the government enacted a national decree to protect the reserve. It established a zoning system, comprising three zones, to be managed as a natural park and with the threefold aim of sustainable development, the conservation of biological diversity, ecosystems, and landscapes, and the implementation of educational programmes. By law, Chong Kneas is located in the buffer zone, where human activities are required to be consistent with conservation aims. Within this framework, in 2002, the Asian Development Bank (ADB) offered technical assistance for a project on the environmental management of the UNESCO biosphere reserve. The government requested the bank's assistance again to plan the creation of a new harbour on the lake, designed by three consulting firms.[56]

The three firms' teams designed two separate harbours, one for tourist boats and one for the landing of goods, as well as two markets. The 1,150 villagers living on houseboats or in stilt houses were to be relocated to a 25-hectare solid platform, to be subdivided into 13m by 8m individual house plots. Villagers would be given prefabricated 'shell houses' to live in. Open space was left for gardens and communal areas. Educational and sanitary facilities would be built. The road grid followed a radial pattern, which converged in the direction of the Phnom Kraom hill, where a temple had been built during the reign of Yaçovarman I (889-912).

The objective of the plan, as laid out in the consultants' report, was to improve the population's living conditions. First, the facilities would offer basic social and health services. Second, tourism development and the markets would provide employment opportunities. Lastly, villagers would enjoy ownership rights to their plots. Living in houseboats or wooden stilt houses, they occupied public property. The consultants interviewed the villagers, asking whether they would like to own land. The answer was, of course, unanimously positive, especially considering that Cambodia is a country where the allocation of land often disadvantages the most needy (Blot, 2013). The consultants commented that 'resettlement, in the vast majority of the community living on the lake, offers an escape from insecurity, social isolation and poverty. The pressures caused by increased growth of population and the threat of diminishing lake resources heighten the need for this escape route' (Placenter et al., 2004, p. 19).

Poverty reduction is the mission of the Asian Development Bank and has three principles: 'pro-poor, sustainable economic growth; social development; and good governance' (ADB, 2004, p. iii). Drawing on the recent history of Asia, the ADB's strategy states that there is a 'complex relationship between economic growth and poverty reduction' (p. 6). Economic growth enabled East Asian 'miracle' economies to get rid of poverty between the 1960s and 1980s. Since labour is said to have a stronger impact on poverty reduction, the ADB favours growth that creates a positive environment

56 The consulting firms are Placenter Ltd., Pacific Consultants, and Sawac. The first is a Japanese engineering consultation firm. The second is a Japanese firm founded in the aftermath of the Second World War, working on transport infrastructure, disaster prevention, the development of new markets, and land issues. The third is a consulting firm originally based in the Netherlands, which has conducted many projects in the field of water management. In 1995, it collaborated with the ADB and PADCO (a company of the AECOM group) for the development of urban infrastructure in the Cambodian towns of Pursat and Battambang.

for the private sector and increases employment opportunities, especially for women and marginal social groups. The ADB also believes that the construction of infrastructure helps to reduce poverty, as it gives access to social facilities and creates new jobs.

The ADB's strategy and programme for Cambodia between 2005 and 2009 reflects its regional goals, as it aims to achieve 'sustainable poverty reduction through broad-based inclusive economic growth, social development, and good governance' (ADB, 2011, p. 2) in four main categories, namely governance, private sector development, gender, and environment. It is aligned with the government's Rectangular Strategy on Growth, Employment, Equity, and Efficiency (Royal Government of Cambodia, 2010), which has been implemented since 2006. The latter strategy is based on four 'strategic rectangles': 'the promotion of agriculture sector', 'the development of physical infrastructure', 'private sector development and employment', and 'capacity building and human resource development'.[57] Within this general framework, greater importance is given to the reform of fishing, the rehabilitation of the transport network, and the strengthening of the private sector.

These orientations reflect the global shift from the neoliberal structural adjustments of the 1990s to softer poverty reduction and good governance agendas based on the consensus formed around 'market-led growth and poor countries' integration into global capitalism' (Craig and Porter, 2006, p. 16). During the 1990s, development had been perceived as a counterproductive and Eurocentric concept. Only open markets would be able to integrate countries and regions into the global economy. However, the Asian economic crises of 1997-1998 showed the limits of this theory. Unregulated markets could damage societies and had to be re-embedded within a regulatory framework if more balanced development processes were to be pursued.

Poverty reduction as conceptualized by the United Nations Development Program's Poverty Reduction Millennium Development Goals (MDG) has sprung from this context; it promotes a 'three-legged agenda' based on 'economic opportunity through global market integration, and enhanced social and economic security and empowerment through innovative governance arrangements for local delivery of health, education and other poverty-reducing services' (Ibid., p. 4). The main idea of the MDG is that market integration have to be sustained by social services in order to achieve poverty reduction.

57 Source: http://www.cambodiainvestment.gov.kh/content/uploads/2013/11/2013-Rectangular-Strategy-III-En8.pdf (accessed 12 May 2017).

The project for a new harbour on the Tonlé Sap reflects this strategy, which has achieved an 'unprecedented expert consensus' (Mosse, 2011, p. 3) in that it has focused on the provision of basic social services and the incorporation of backward, rural regions into the mainstream of development through measures which improve the local economy. It also bears witness to the global concern for the growth of informal sector economies, caused by an under-resourced state, which generate economic opportunities and human settlement for the poor entirely outside government regulation, and therefore with uncertain ownership and social status. For these reasons, the harbour project's focus on land rights, social services, and the development of new, well-regulated economic opportunities for the villagers was meant to free them from their subaltern status.

However, the translation of this global discourse into measures for the villagers of Chong Kneas revealed shortcomings related to ignorance of the pitfalls of the Cambodian legal apparatus and the social inequalities that it can generate. While the Cambodian Government Rectangular Strategy aimed to offer guarantees of efficacy and stability, the political context in which urban planning and programmes for territorial development are supposed to be implemented is rather unreliable. Hesitation between control and laissez-faire undermines the consistency of Cambodian institutional behaviour. Project implementation depends on volatile institutional support and a complex, sometimes overlapping distribution of powers, making urban governance (Goldblum and Osmont, 2008; Goldblum, 2012) particularly unpredictable. The positive goal of providing security to the villagers through land rights contrasts significantly with the weak methods deployed to achieve it. According to the project, the resettlement platform will belong to the private domain of the state and villagers will be entitled to 99-year-lease agreements, to be renewed every ten years. However, recent governments have not hesitated to sell land from their private domain even if it was covered by a lease.[58]

Moreover, the harbour project did not explicitly specify the conditions under which the leases would be granted to the Vietnamese fishermen, who generally do not hold Cambodian citizenship and are deprived of basic social services and advantages in Cambodia. This grey zone functioned to endorse the anti-Vietnamese sentiment, which has historical roots and is still

58 The Renakse Hotel in Phnom Penh is a well-known example of this practice. This colonial building was first leased out to a Cambodian manager under a long-term contract and then sold to a private firm for redevelopment. However, the manager contested the dispossession so strongly that the demolition was indefinitely postponed; the building is at present unoccupied.

strong in contemporary Cambodia, where, for instance, ethnic Vietnamese are often prevented from voting.[59]

The consultants demonstrated their good intentions by including the villagers in the decision-making process (seeing them at least as relevant informants). However, they seemed to be unaware of the concealed threats to land security and social empowerment in the Cambodian political context. This shortcoming raises the question of how planners appropriate and adapt global discourses and strategies to specific local situations. Green (2011) argues that poverty has become a well-entrenched category of the 'development imaginary' and now encompasses 'understandings of the proper way to go about designing an approach, a perspective which is simultaneously moral and technical' (p. 37). However, the Tonlé Sap case showed that such moral and technical approaches to poverty have to cope with local complexities and the readiness of local authorities (in this case, the Ministry of Public Works) to acknowledge social, political, and economic conflicts that may endanger the effectiveness of the donors' strategies.

The very category of poverty is problematic in the Chong Kneas case. According to the consultants, the poor lack income, basic social services, and profitable employment opportunities. This way of understanding poverty reflects the ADB's focus on income, which is, in turn, based on the World Bank's estimation of global poverty (Guanghua and Iva, 2011). However, not only does this definition not take into account the cultural capital of the people of Chong Kneas, represented by their ability to build houses adapted to the climate and to interact with and benefit from the lake environment, but it views the material evidence of this know-how as a constraint on development: 'the range of employment opportunities available to the population of Chong Kneas is limited by their nomadic lifestyle, the lack of land and lack of infrastructure' (Placenter et al., 2004, p. 4). Although the consultants described the lake environment as 'unique in many respects', because most of its residents 'live in house boats which move their location throughout the course of the year in response to the rise and fall of water in the lake' (p. 6), this environment had to be destroyed to make way for a development that would enable poverty reduction. A new idea of place, centred on connectivity, efficiency, and labour, would erase those human landscapes that are the present tourist resource of Chong

59 Anti-Vietnamese feelings have been rooted in Cambodia since the seventeenth century, when Cambodia lost territories on the Mekong delta and in Phu Quoc to Vietnam. Racism against Vietnamese nationals reached its peak in the 1970s, when first the Lon Nol regime and then the Khmer Rouge militia killed more than 300,000 Vietnamese. (IRIN, 2013).

Kneas. This project raises questions about the problematic relation between poverty reduction and cultural heritage, which seem to be incompatible realms of strategizing within the ADB framework. Development is projected onto the Chong Kneas community as a completely new conception and form of organization, a new world that would replace the old one, symbolically shifting from water to dry land.

However, this project has never been implemented as such. The Cambodian company Heng Development, which mainly works in the fields of construction, property development, restoration, and cars, began to construct a new harbour without giving any notice. As the company had not provided any compensation or relocation opportunities, the villagers contested the project so strongly that construction was eventually interrupted. However, the Council for the Development of Cambodia (CDC) subsequently granted a land concession to Sou Ching,[60] a Cambodian company chaired by the tycoon Var Chhouda. On paper, the company is supposed to develop a two-million-dollar harbour on a 30-hectare land concession now consisting of rice fields and flooded forest, which originally belonged to the public domain of the Cambodian state. Negotiations between the CDC and Sou Ching were secret. Not only were these negotiations excluded from the ICC-Angkor international symposium, but the project was not included in the annual statistics of national and foreign projects annually compiled by the CDC.

As Craig and Porter (2006) argue, 'territorial patrimony, not market exchange, becomes the basis of wealth and poverty' in the under-resourced state: 'the rich typically are closely interwoven with patrimonial governance, and can leverage territorial and economic assets and opportunities: land, water, cheap labour, trading positions, and natural resources. Their connections secure government contracts at high prices, and the protection of the bendable rule of law' (p. 29). In the case of the harbour on the Tonlé Sap, the events controlled by the oppressive power of patrimonial governance undermined the strategy of poverty alleviation and showed how technical assistance can be instrumentalized and exploited for the sake of private interests and with the silent connivance of the state. Sou Ching did indeed exploit the technical results of the ADB's funded expertise in geological and hydrological exploration, which helped them to choose the best location for the harbour. The company paved a road, built a concrete ticket office, and dug a drainage canal, but did not make provision for the construction of a relocation platform

60 The company has repeatedly collaborated with South Korean consulting teams and investors. It has been involved in other tourism-related projects in the Angkor region, such as solar buses and lighting projects at the temples of Angkor.

for the villagers. Instead, the company director allegedly asked the governor of Siem Reap province to help them fight 'against the illegal occupation of the land involved' (Preuil, 2011, p. 184). Villagers could indeed be formally considered as squatters according to Cambodian law, as they occupied public property.

Despite these threatening initial statements, the treatment of villagers in subsequent years has been based less on the land status that they used to enjoy before the implementation of the project than on their origins. As Vietnamese fishermen cannot claim rights on land, they have continued to live on houseboats, which they are allowed to moor along the canal or on the lake, depending on the season. In contrast, Chong Kneas commune has given land titles to Cambodian citizens. Those who had already resided in the commune for several years have started to construct houses along the new road built by the company, before the gateway marking the edge of the piece of land covered by the economic land concession. Newcomers have started to urbanize the surroundings of Phnom Kraom hill[61] (Figure 2.11). Precarious straw huts and houses made of metal scraps and waste materials have gradually been replaced by wooden and concrete houses. Thus, the construction of the road has indirectly facilitated the stabilization of the population on firm land. However, it has also exacerbated social discrimination against the Vietnamese who, as illegal workers, have no means to improve their quality of life.

The idea of developing a 'tourist marina'[62] had not yet been implemented during my last fieldwork trip at the end of 2015. The company's owner initially wanted 'to build a Disneyland, with restaurants, hotels, shops, and a shopping mall'. However, 'he is rarely happy with what he has built and often destroys the constructions that have just been erected'.[63] Buildings going up and down give the appearance of an incoherent patchwork of projects. While some see this constant construction activity as a way to avoid paying taxes,[64] other informants believe that the volatile personality of the company's owner is the reason so many successive projects are implemented. Between 2009 and 2015, the small ticket office and straw huts where street vendors were obliged to stay have been replaced by a concrete building accommodating offices and souvenir shops. In front of this building, a vast car park is used by tourist buses. This infrastructure enables the company to function as mediators between the growing number of tour groups and the families that

61 Personal communication with representative of local NGO, 2015.

62 Posters attached to the construction site, 2008.

63 Personal communication with former employee of the Sou Ching Company, 2015.

64 Taxes are due only on finalized projects.

Figure 2.10 Movable houses on the Tonlé Sap

Photo by Dato Tarielashvili, 2007

previously organized tours on the lake. These families still carry tourists on their boats, but they have to deal with the centralized harbour management. They have established an association of boat owners, headed by a local leader, which manages a rotation system for the organization of tours.

The case of the harbour on the Tonlé Sap is a striking example of the permissive freedom that individuals in a position of ascendancy can enjoy in Cambodia. Expatriate informants involved in the project report that, in Cambodia, it is possible to reinvent one's profession, and to acquire new skills through unregulated experimentation. Such freedom, however, depends on the degree of power that an individual or community can secure through personal or mediated relations. Within this social and political system, hierarchical relations structure the distribution of benefits far more than concepts of social justice.

Figure 2.11 The changing Chong Kneas landscape

Photo by the author, 2015

2.6 The power of action and the power of ideas

The Japanese planner who worked at Siem Reap's provincial offices for two years after the finalization of the JICA report on the master plan in 2006 did not speak Khmer, but had a translator who was always at his side. He spoke English with a strong Japanese accent, and his translator was shy. However, both were absolutely devoted to the implementation of the master plan. Even though this plan had not been legally approved by the Cambodian Council of Ministries – and it probably never would be – they patiently toured all of Siem Reap's institutional headquarters in order to present it, to make it known to the local authorities, and to convince public officials of the importance of supporting at least one of the 70 smaller and more modest projects that it contained. The fundamental difference between the JICA's master plan and previous planning documents was that it not only provided an overall development strategy based on zoning, but also a series of sector projects that could be implemented separately and independently of each other. Almost half of these projects had begun to be implemented in 2010 (JICA, 2010); they included the construction of urban infrastructure, the renovation of markets, urban plantations, sewage and drainage, and urban signage. The commitment of the Japanese expert to the local authorities shows that the planning approach is evolving in Siem Reap, from an exclusive top-down perspective, which views the locals as the receivers of planning, to a growing concern for local involvement which has expanded in subsequent years.

The fragmentation of the master plan into a constellation of projects is a strategy used by the Japanese partners in order to enhance the possibility that they will see some of the plan's proposals implemented. Similarly, in Phnom Penh, the French-designed master plan has never become a legal instrument, although several guidelines have been implemented by local authorities (Fauveaud, 2015a). Their Cambodian counterparts are not deaf to this strategy, as they have given a positive reception to projects for infrastructure and urban services that create better conditions for economic growth (for instance, building a road increases land values) without restraining the developers' freedom to occupy, transform, and benefit from urban space. Tools such as zoning and inventory constrain this freedom and, for this reason, are systematically rejected, as is shown by the various unsuccessful attempts to mandate urban regulations for Siem Reap. Furthermore, through the implementation of sector projects some nuances can arise to modify the critical position widely shared by the expert community, who call into question Cambodian institutions' ability to act, disparaging their lack of capacity, training, resources, and power (*inter alia* ICEA, 2005).

The selection of successful projects confirms the argument presented by Sato et al. (2011) concerning South Korean and Chinese aid, according to which the 'Cambodian government accepts aid from emerging donors despite associated transaction costs not as a passive willingness to "accept whatever aid is offered", but rather as a part of a carefully considered strategy that views the new donors as providing alternatives important to the country's balanced development' (p. 2099). By contrast, the government seems to be inclined to refuse aid from traditional donors. Sato et al. interpret this refusal as a response to the inability of Western donors to acknowledge the importance of economic growth in the national strategy: Cambodian institutions are reluctant to impose a regulatory framework on urban development that would restrict opportunities for corporate profit. The selective attitude of Cambodian authorities towards international organizations is also shown by Rabé (2009), who has examined land sharing projects in Phnom Penh. Rabé argues that the Phnom Penh municipality listened only to some of the advice from UN experts with respect to land sharing schemes, readily accepting those which regulated the procedure of implementation while rejecting those which concerned contracts and design. From a critical standpoint, this situation confirms Bayart's argument (2004) that donors behave as Cambodian institutions' 'travelling companions'. In such a context, only those projects that accompany and galvanize the unrestrained market economy can be implemented in the international tourism hub of Siem Reap. Cambodian institutions and developers create alliances in order to use foreign assistance to achieve economic benefits.

Here, it remains to be asked whether foreign-sponsored urban planning is anything more than a large basket from which pieces of a puzzle are pulled out to be reconfigured outside their original context, in an uncontrolled, fast-developing city. This chapter has shown that various discourses, tools, and patterns of development converge in Siem Reap. In their attempt to harmonize discordant needs, the planners of the tourist city give form to urban design by drawing on three reference systems: a system of international planning tools circulating on a global scale, local architectural and urban traditions, and donors' philosophies, strategies, and ethics. The interplay between local specificities and global knowledge shows that planning is a field in which foreign professionals act both as mediators and interpreters. Mosse and Lewis (2006) argue that the role of aid is not limited to the power of action but also concerns the power of ideas, that is to say the power to inculcate and assert one's ideas and thus make them so popular that they become internationally shared and accepted. Looking at the case of Phnom Penh, Fauveaud (2015a) argues that planning documents, even if not implemented, have contributed to the dissemination of knowledge and know-how in the field of urban management. In Siem Reap, the ideas of the city expressed by the various urban plans have not been put into practice. Nevertheless, such plans act as pioneering disseminators of spatial cultures in a place where architectural and urban knowledge was destroyed with the killing of the great majority of the intellectuals and professionals. In that situation, the planners do seek to acquire power over actions and transformations of space, but only as a secondary, medium- to long-term goal.

3 The city as developers' playground

A young Khmer man opened the door of the concrete villa surrounded by lush vegetation. I entered the hall together with another doctoral student who was accompanying me. The interior was dark and smelled of old cigarettes. He indicated the office with polite gestures, and we walked in. The ceiling was low and the desks covered with messy paper folders, old computers, and empty beer cans. The South Korean developer was sitting in front of a computer screen, smoking. My objective for the interview was to get some insight into developers' tactics in Siem Reap, and in particular those of the South Koreans, who were one of the most powerful groups in the Cambodian property sector. My colleague and I took a seat in front of him. I began to ask the series of questions I had prepared about the projects that the construction team was developing in the town. We were shown a drawing representing five identical shophouses on a white page, surrounded by nothing more than a grey line indicating the level of the ground. However, this block of houses was not to be built on empty land, but would replace a series of one-storey wooden shop houses close to Wat Damnak, a pagoda in the southern area of Siem Reap. The shophouses were to be located at the roundabout between the north-south road along the river and the bridge, which leads to the old market area. Shophouses made with industrialized materials are cheap to build. In a climate of property speculation, they provide rapid returns on investment as they are easy to sell or rent out. Out of a sample of 349 requests for building permits in the period 2000-2009, 80 were for the construction of shophouses. Neither the urban environment, nor architectural design were important to the developers, as they had found a successful formula to make money.

Siem Reap's urban landscape has rapidly changed with the proliferation of these shophouse projects. Naturally, I disliked their uniformity and the fact that they erased many examples of vernacular architecture. However, during this interview, I tried not to overtly show my feelings, because informants are generally very sensitive to judgements. Developers in particular, who often negotiate the law in order to further their personal interests, are reluctant to provide information as soon as they grasp that the researcher has an accusatory attitude, even if indirectly or unconsciously expressed. My colleague, however, had a different understanding of the situation. She had worked as an architect and had also served as a consultant for one of the plans sponsored by an international development assistance project. She had been closely following recent urban dynamics and was deeply disappointed by the failure of any attempt to plan the overall development of the city. Consequently, she was fiercely critical of the projects that contributed to these dynamics.

Suddenly, she spoke up and asked: 'Why is the drawing of the shophouse so rough, and why does it lack so many construction details?' Without showing any sign that he was taken aback, the developer explained: 'Requesting a building permit is a pure formality in Cambodia. So it is not necessary for us to add more construction details, because we will be able to make additions and changes afterwards, during the construction stage, if we wish to.' My colleague replied: 'So why did you take the time to draw a glass roof over the courtyard? In such a tropical climate ventilation will be impossible!' The developer avoided answering the question directly, but said that the courtyard under the glass roof would be a commercial plaza, an extension of the shops on the ground floor of the shophouses. I understood that his concern was to convey an image of urban modernity through commercial facilities perceived as innovative in Cambodia. Shopping malls, covered markets, and galleries were mushrooming in the town to encourage consumption by tourists and help to construct narratives about social status targeting the rising Cambodian middle class. Concerns about energy consumption had no part to play in such a collective rush towards urban modernization in which air-conditioning is viewed as the new standard of comfort.

While feeling disturbed by my colleague's judgmental attitude, I realized that this meeting was even more informative than a regular interview, as it created the opportunity for an exchange between consultants like her and developers, two categories of people who seldom have the opportunity to engage in discussion in Siem Reap. The arena of urban development is silent but filled with conflict. Stories about failed projects and illegal developments are passed around by word of mouth. However, public consultation and dialogue about the development of Cambodian cities is almost entirely absent. The attitude of the two participants in this spontaneous debate gave me some insight into the significant power possessed by developers in the politics of urban formation. My colleague was extremely disappointed by the developer's unfair freedom to flout the regulations, while he was confidently serene in expressing his attitude towards Siem Reap's urban authorities.

This chapter enquires into the foundations of this confidence. My analysis of the developers' rationales is framed by De Certeau's (1984) analysis of tactical behaviour. De Certeau described a 'tactic' as

> a calculus which cannot count on a 'proper' (a spatial or institutional localization), nor thus on a borderline distinguishing the other as a visible totality. The place of a tactic belongs to the other. A tactic insinuates itself into the other's place, fragmentarily, without taking it over in its entirety, without being able to keep it at a distance. It has at its disposal no base where it can capitalize on its advantages, prepare its expansions, and secure independence with respect to circumstances. The 'proper' is a victory of space over time. On the contrary, because it does not have a place, a tactic depends on time – it is always on the watch for opportunities that must be seized 'on the wing.' Whatever it wins, it does not keep. It must constantly manipulate events in order to turn them into 'opportunities.' (De Certeau, 1984, p. xix)

Tacticians seize the opportunities offered by favourable situations in order to achieve individual profit, but cannot plan their actions in the long term. The intellectual synthesis of their practice is the decision itself and the specific way in which they use opportunities to their advantage. Tacticians do not construct discourses (that is, they do not convey their behaviour through structured verbal communications). Their rationale can be investigated chiefly through the analysis of their actions.

Implicitly adopting De Certeau's notion of the tactic, developers often obtain power over areas of land through underground negotiations that undermine the power of the state as the overarching regulator of urban terrain for the public good. On one plot of land after another, they fragmentarily acquire the power to act, which was denied to the planners. In a time of property speculation, developers do not keep what they gain, because they immediately reinvest their capital when they find opportunities to increase it. They ingeniously turn the unstable and confused political and legal environment into opportunities for deriving benefit, making the tide turn in their favour. Their collective behaviour can be investigated through the analysis of processes and procedures that explain their actions and the effects these actions have on the urban environment.

In contrast, for De Certeau, a strategy is 'the calculus of force-relationships which becomes possible when a subject of will and power [...] can be isolated from an "environment". A strategy assumes a place that can be circumscribed as *proper* (*propre*) and thus serve as the basis for generating relations with an exterior distinct from it [...]. Political, economic, and scientific rationality has been constructed on this strategic model' (p. xix). The analysis of projects (see Section 2.5) has shown that Cambodian institutions do not act in conformity with a strategy in the arena of urban development. Rather, they behave as the developers' allies and reason in terms of economic benefits that they can quickly obtain through and thanks to privately sponsored projects. They sometimes tacitly support projects that contravene the law, if this allows them to establish partnerships with donors and with national and foreign private sectors. Planners, in contrast, constantly try to secure the 'proper' from which to construct patterns of urban rationality. However, the very existence of this 'proper' is repeatedly compromised by multiple, covert tactical alliances. Lack of institutional support undermines the role of planners as strategists. Planners stubbornly go on playing the part of the strategists, but their calculus of force-relationships proves false, because they have no power in a situation where they are only discursively supported by the institutions, who would like to build political consensus without compromising the profit that they can derive from tourism-driven urban development in Siem Reap.

The analysis of the politics of urban development in this chapter shows that the Cambodian state has not been built on rational institutions (Weber, 1964). Cambodia is a neopatrimonial state, featuring a combination of modern bureaucracy and patrimonialized patron-client relationships within a traditional system of patrimonialism, with no clear differentiation between the public and the private (Kheang Un, 2011). The political elites who rule the country have incorporated part of the Khmer Rouge's revolutionary class and have concentrated both political power and economic accumulation in their hands. Despite UNTAC's attempts to create a new state of constitutional democracy in Cambodia, this elite has maintained a power system based on kinship. This type of organization has also been inherited from the Khmer Rouge authoritarian regime (Bayart, 2004) and has consolidated its patronal power since the 1980s. In this context, patrons and clients are organized into 'interlocking pyramids' (Heder and Ledgerwood, 1995, p. 5) and seek crucial means of gaining access to resources and increasing their status: 'patronage relationships are often characterized by suspicion and distrust, especially in the political realm, where the stakes for power, money, and prestige are high' (Hinton, 2005, p. 125). The rulers' power depends on their ability to attract and maintain the loyalty of the political elites. As patrimonial relations are based on reciprocity, rulers distribute fiefs and benefits in order to guarantee the stability of their power (King, 2000, p. 609). Corruption is institutionalized at the highest political levels and the weakness of the judicial system prevents it from punishing cases of corruption. Keang Un (2006) describes Cambodia as an 'unconsolidated democracy' that lacks both vertical and horizontal accountability.[1] In unconsolidated democracies,

1 'Horizontal accountability refers to the responsibility of one state institution to another, while vertical accountability refers to the responsibility of elected officials not only to voters but also to civil society organizations between election cycles' (Keang Un, 2006, p. 226).

elements identified with democratic governments, such as a liberal constitution and fair elections, can coexist with 'authoritarian and traditional practices, such as a lack of rule of law, rampant corruption, widespread patronage and executive usurpation of power' (Keang Un, 2006, p. 225). Little effort is made to undertake reforms, as the existing system benefits the elites in power. The development of civil society is not encouraged, since it forms a major threat to the stability of such a system.

The association of neopatrimonialism and liberalization has substantially influenced processes of urban development in contemporary Cambodia. New agents, markets, and inter-urban competition shape the evolution of cities, especially Phnom Penh (Fauveaud, 2011). Social fragmentation is increased because only a minority of the urban population can benefit from new residential and commercial developments produced by private capital. Since the early 1990s, a serious lack of institutional will for implementing urban planning explains developers' lack of concern for the integration of their projects into comprehensive planning. The tactical securing of institutional support through alliances with public officials and politicians has been given more importance as a guarantee of the success of development projects. In the neopatrimonial system, alliances proceed along family and clan lines (Springer, 2011; Fauveaud, 2015a). Because these alliances are frequently illicit, the origin and amounts of invested capital are often difficult to assess, as is the composition of the investment groups and joint ventures behind a number of urban projects. Neoliberalism in Cambodia is characterized by its 'secretive' nature (Springer, 2011), which obscures the connections between capital and patrons. However, it is possible to observe the impact of these connections on the urban space. Massive privatization has been achieved during the last decade. In central urban locations in Phnom Penh and Siem Reap, 'institutional facilities, such as ministries and police headquarters, are exchanged for cash and privately held lands on the periphery of these cities' (Springer, 2011, p. 2559). Urban land is often sold to local tycoons who offer it for lease or sale to private companies (Springer, 2011). Powerful groups revolving around major political and economic figures have control of land management. City centres have become coveted spaces for these elites for symbolic reasons. In Phnom Penh and in Siem Reap, central land plots on which public spaces, facilities, and administrations were once located have often been exchanged for peripheral, but larger land plots in order to facilitate privately led urban redevelopment. Under the pretext of 'cleansing' and 'beautifying the city', undesirable individuals and communities have been evicted in order to make land available for the production of commodified urban space, used to communicate ideas of social order, comfort, safety, and profit (Springer, 2010). Tools of negotiation, such as land sharing (Rabé, 2009), are only used in exceptional circumstances to solve conflicts and accommodate the informal population. Internationally sponsored programmes aimed at giving land titles to this population face a number of difficulties due to disputes and overlapping claims (Khemro and Payne, 2004). The neoliberal city, conceived as a showcase of images of urban modernity and internationalization (Fauveaud, 2014b), relies on the establishment of a new urban order that Fauveaud (2014b) calls the 'ordopolis'. This order is maintained through symbolic violence and coercion, which push the disadvantaged segments of the population towards the periphery of the city. Far from guaranteeing the establishment of the rule of law, the reconstruction and strengthening of the legal system has legitimized various forms of institutionalized violence (Springer, 2011). While high-ranking officials, patrons, and clans control the reins of the land system, low-income people do not master the procedures of land registration, nor do they have the power and tools to resist eviction and privatization. Paling (2012) observes that while, in other countries, 'popular opposition to state-sanctioned developments may be strengthened by the reality of the threat of being punished at the ballot box [...] this threat is much weaker in the Cambodian context, where the urban poor are greatly outnumbered by the rural population, who have consistently returned the ruling party to office with increased majorities' (p. 2905). In contrast, the powerful and wealthy succeed in accumulating land and securing their rights in accordance with the law. In this sense, the law favours them: it allows the establishment of an 'organized impunity' (Springer, 2013) instead of protecting the population as a whole. Social disparities contrast with the widespread 'language of empowerment that accompanies the neoliberal doctrine' and the political discourse of Cambodian institutions (Springer, 2010, p. 4). They hinder processes of democratization, which are suffocated by authoritarianism. Largely deprived of legal protection, the population cannot abandon the 'survival mentality' generated by war and genocide, and submits to the patronage system as the only 'security blanket' (Springer, 2013) able to provide some tactical advantage. They thus contribute to the persistence and reproduction of a system that harms them.

In this chapter, I examine how tourism has triggered the development of a property market in Siem Reap that has flourished at the intersection between the patrimonial system and the liberalization of the Cambodian economy. I argue that the participants in Cambodia's urban development have collectively shaped a series of tactics that successfully help them to negotiate with the legal establishment for their personal benefit. Understanding these tactics is reframed within a comprehensive overview of the politics of tourism development in contemporary Cambodia, which explains how and why tourism has become a primary field of investment, with Siem Reap-Angkor as the main tourism hub in the country. Taking a closer look at the rationale and dynamics of property speculation, I examine how foreign investors negotiate land rights in a country where land ownership is officially restricted to Cambodian citizens. From these analyses emerges a web of alliances and collusion between the political and economic elites, often established at the expense of low-income urban residents, who not only are excluded from benefiting from tourism revenue, but are also evicted from their dwellings in the urban centre. Little space is left for local associations to contest the developers' power grabs. Moving from social behaviour to spatial transformation, I address the processes of urban development and the impact of construction projects on the urban space in those areas that have been most coveted by developers and have consequently experienced the most intense tourism-driven urban transformation. In contrast, urban development managed by Cambodian families and foreign individuals who have converted residential areas into tourism and commercial neighbourhoods maintains the hybrid mix of rural and urban features which characterized the vegetal city. Political or forced relationships and the phenomena of urban development are two entangled threads, which are together responsible for the transition of Siem Reap from a group of villages to an international tourist city.

3.1 Our potential field is tourism

Tourism is now the second largest source of revenue for the Cambodian economy, after the garment industry. In 2014, it generated total revenues of US$2.2 billion and contributed 23.5 per cent of GDP (World Travel & Tourism Council, 2014). Visits by tourists have climbed from 50,000 in 1992 (Cheeang, 2008) to 2.1 million in 2008 and 3.6 million in 2012 (OECD, 2014). There are 1,690,000 jobs directly or indirectly related to the tourist industry, accounting for 20 per cent of total employment (World Travel & Tourism Council, 2014). These figures confirm the strategic importance of tourism to the national economy. In order to understand why and how it has become a primary economic sector for contemporary Cambodia, we need to look at the development of tourism within the framework of the transition from a planned economy to a free market, which took place by degrees after the fall of the totalitarian Khmer Rouge regime (Hugues, 2003).

In earlier times the contribution of tourism to the national economy was marginal. The French Protectorate had tried to establish a tourism industry in the colonies through the construction of roads and tourism facilities (Demay, 2011). In the 1910s, a newspaper article imagined that one day major crossroads, commercial and agricultural centres, and tourist centres would coincide in Indochina. A few years later, another article compared tourism to a network of channels of economic wealth that ought to be spread widely in the colonies.[2] This capillary dissemination, it was said, would be symbolically highly significant in evaluating the success of the colonial administration in Asia.[3]

By the end of the 1930s, road construction had made Angkor accessible from Bangkok and Saigon throughout the year. The colonial authorities also built the commercial and administrative facilities needed to make Siem Reap into a provincial capital. Between the 1920s and the 1930s, the Grand Hotel replaced the bungalow situated close to Angkor Wat where the occasional tourists had been lodged. The EFEO called for the construction of a hotel in order to protect the archaeological monuments from the pressure of tourism, which was expected to increase in the years to come. Through this project, the colonial authorities started to establish tourism facilities in nearby Siem Reap, as a first step in the development of a tourist hub on the doorstep of the archaeological site.

However, the reality did not match up to the expectations. Although 25,000 kilometres of roads were built in Indochina by 1931, 9,000 of them in Cambodia, only 952 tourists visited Angkor between January and June 1931, of whom 423 were French people who had previously lived in Indochina. A few years later, in 1935, a total of 1613 foreigners visited Angkor, of whom 736 resided in the region.[4] The main reason was that transport and tourism infrastructures were still underdeveloped in Indochina compared to other Asian countries (Zytnichi and Kazdaghli, 2009), so the region was unable to capture the tourists who went to the Far East.[5]

2 'Le tourisme en Indochine', *Le courrier de Haiphong*, 23 July 1924.

3 ANC No. 4992, 'Les transports au Cambodge. Notes sur le tourisme au Cambodge. Articles de presse', *Le courrier de Haiphong. Le tourisme*, by Gaston Valran, 1924, 'Notes sur le tourisme en Indochine'.

4 ANC No. 11838, 'Tourisme indochinois. Mouvements touristiques des premiers semestres 1931-1935 sur Angkor', 1935, by the Angkor Tourist Office.

5 Only 20,000 people visited the French colonies in 1936. ANC No. 7812, 'Lettre du Gouverneur de l'Indochine à Messieurs les Chefs des Administrations locales', 22 February 1936, by René Robin, in *Dossiers relatifs au tourism au Cambodge* (*Angkor et autres*).

Immediately after independence in 1953, tourism development was not a national priority. Public investment was largely directed towards building infrastructure for other sectors of the economy, such as manufacture and trade (Hall and Page, 2000). Limited funds were nevertheless provided for the development of the hotel industry, which contributed to building a modern image of the country. In spite of low investment, tourism propaganda formed part of the government's foreign policy, which promoted the country as an 'oasis of peace' in a troubled region affected by political tensions. At the 1955 Bandung Conference, Cambodia had espoused a policy of international neutrality and refused to join the Southeast Asia Treaty Organization (SEATO), which had been established with the purpose of protecting member states from the advance of communism.[6] In Norodom Sihanouk's view, Cambodia's position between countries aligned with the Western bloc (Thailand and South Vietnam) and the Eastern bloc (China and North Vietnam) would contribute to international balance (Dauphin-Meunier, 1965). These arguments contributed to enhancing Cambodia's attractiveness to tourists vis-à-vis other Southeast Asian countries, which were experiencing political turmoil and regional conflicts.

Tourism did not reach significant figures during the years of the Sangkum Reastr Niyum. Only 18,650 foreigners visited Cambodia in 1960; the number slowly grew to 22,284 in 1964 (Krippendorf and Perrin, 1969).[7] Tourism started to gain prominence in the government's strategies only at the end of the 1960s, when a national sector plan for the development of this industry was introduced for the years 1968-1974. This policy was in line with similar initiatives taken in other countries in the region, such as Indonesia (Dahles, 2001), where the development of international air traffic opened up ambitious prospects of international tourism development. However, the rise of the Khmer Rouge compromised the implementation of this programme. The regime closed the country to foreign visitors and many projects, such as the Angkor Hotel, which was to be built in close proximity to the temples, were abandoned (Collins and Grant Ross, 2006).

During the 1980s, an economic transition took place in the context of the civil war between the pro-Vietnamese regime established in Phnom Penh and the Khmer Rouge resistance, which was present in force at the Thai border.

6 The Bandung Conference took place on 18-24 April 1955. It brought together the delegates of 29 decolonized countries of Asia and Africa who had chosen a policy of non-alignment with respect to the two blocs defined at the end of the Second World War.

7 By comparison, Thailand received 211,924 visitors and Singapore 90,871 during the same year (Riman, 1968).

Early in the decade, the restoration of privately farmed plots of land preceded the re-establishment of 'market relations in all economic spheres in the late 1980s' (Collins and Grant Ross, p. 1). Hun Sen became prime minister in 1984 and triggered the economic opening up of the country; when the Vietnamese troops started to pull out of Cambodia and Thailand, Thai Prime Minister Chatichai Choonhavan expressed the desire to 'turn battlefields into market-places'. Subsequently, head of state Heng Samrin signed a contract with the Vietnamese state company Saigon Tourism, which allowed international tourists to visit Cambodia in combination with Vietnam, starting in 1986. Several Cambodian tourism companies opened in Siem Reap and Phnom Penh. In 1989, the new land law allowed private land ownership and a series of legal reforms promoted a market economy and foreign investment. Cambodia abandoned socialism and was defined as a neutral and non-aligned country. All these initiatives prepared for its return to independence and the establishment of a neoliberal economic system, which was confirmed by the Paris Accords of 1991.

The state administration and constitutional monarchy were re-established after twenty years of turmoil. The United Nations Transitional Authority in Cambodia (UNTAC) imported cutting-edge technology and encouraged the opening up of Cambodia to foreign aid, which had started to arrive in the late 1980s. Cambodia experienced sudden international dynamism, triggered by the 22,000 members of the UN delegation and numerous NGOs, donors, consultants, and investors who had started to take an interest in the country.

At a time when capitalism was triumphing over communist regimes, the transition of Cambodia from a planned to a market economy followed the ten economic policy prescriptions known as the Washington Consensus, crafted by the International Monetary Fund, the World Bank, and the US Treasury Department to develop crisis-torn emerging countries. These measures, designed in accordance with John Williamson's principles (Williamson, 1990), included prescriptions on macroeconomic liberalization, economic opening up to trade and investment, and the expansion of market forces within domestic economies. Hugues (2003) argues that Cambodia's transition from a planned economy to a free market 'has significantly influenced the possibilities for, and limits to' (p. 1) the transition from war to peace and from authoritarian rule to democracy. Taking this argument further, Bayart (2004) argues that there are few countries where the combination of the neoliberal paradigm and the global reshuffle of the international system has been as 'clear and dramatic' (p. 7) as in Cambodia, where economic liberalization coincided with the end of an international crisis and helped overcome the antagonisms between the United States, China, the Soviet Union, and Vietnam which had converged in Cambodia in the 1960s.

In this special framework of political and economic renaissance, tourism became the largest economic sector after the garment industry. However, compared to other countries in Southeast Asia it had to make up for lost time. The OECD noted that, even though Cambodia 'recorded the highest international tourism receipts of any ASEAN country as a share of GDP (15%)' in 2011, 'its regional ranking is low when it comes to travel facilitation and competitiveness' (OECD, 2014, p. 9). Progress had yet to be made in the development of infrastructures and facilities and, more broadly, in the improvement of the tourism management system, compared to other countries of the region such as Thailand and Indonesia, where tourism had become an industry and one of the sectors of national strategic planning (Hitchcock, King, and Parnwell, 2010).

However, tourism was not yet a high priority for Cambodian policy at the beginning of the 1990s. The 1994 National Program for the Rehabilitation and the Development of Cambodia did not explicitly mention this sector, while education, health, and the development of basic infrastructure, services, and agriculture, as well as the integration of Cambodia into regional and international economic dynamics, were seen as fundamental to reconstruction.[8] The assumption was that tourism could not be developed in a country that drastically lacked security and services for international travellers. At the same time, Cambodia needed capital to restart the national economy, which largely depended on international development assistance. Tourism, as a light industry, could provide this capital faster than manufacturing, which required larger and longer-term investment. Proof of this hypothesis was provided by the significant contribution of the UNTAC delegation to boosting the economy. When UNTAC left Cambodia, foreign exchange and private companies did not develop substantially, while foreign investment dramatically increased: the Cambodian authorities approved foreign-sponsored projects with a capital value of US$2 million in 1992, increasing to US$900 million the year after (De Vienne, 2008). In an unstable country like Cambodia, only one third of approved investment is generally implemented. However, such a significant increase indicated that foreign investment was to become fundamental to reconstructing the economy.

The designation of Angkor as a UNESCO World Heritage Site in 1992 sowed the seeds of a tourism revival that would enable Cambodia to follow a similar path to other Southeast Asian countries and give tourism a primary role in the national economic strategy. Between 1992 and 1993, Cambodian

8 This Program was established by the International Committee for the Reconstruction of Cambodia, which had been created after UNTAC's departure.

families opened the first guesthouses in Siem Reap to host the negligible numbers of audacious tourists, UNTAC delegates, and émigré Cambodian citizens who were coming back to visit their own country (Leiper, 1998). The first developers built some twelve hotels along National Highway No. 6. They were nothing more than concrete boxes with square holes for windows and saw-toothed roofs. When the volume of tourism facilities increased and tourism standards became higher, some of these were converted into sleazy karaoke bars. Others still look like dilapidated ghosts of bygone years. Some of the owners have increased the hotels' attractiveness through renovation work to appeal to an upgraded tourism market.

The sudden opening up of the economy and the subsequent privatization of most services and all industrial production (the only exception being the energy sector) encouraged the further development of the tourism industry. The dollarization of the economy amplified the economic boom and the presence of the UN delegation triggered real-estate transactions and development. The law on investment (03/NS94, 4 August 1994) constituted a clear invitation for national and foreign investors to implement projects in Cambodia. The law established the Council for the Development of Cambodia, which is responsible for evaluating investment proposals. It also established that all investors are equal before the law, that prices are not controlled, and that the use of foreign currency is allowed. A related sub-decree granted incentives to large and high-quality tourism projects. Small and medium companies were not even mentioned in the list of eligible entities included in the sub-decree's annexes. In the same way, labour and investment legislation has failed to mention small traders, thus shaping the contours of a legal establishment mainly concerned with protecting the interests of the financial elites.[9] Commenting on the investment laws, Thoraxy (2006) observes that unbridled open markets attract investors who do not appreciate having their activities limited by constraining regulations. While these neoliberal provisions have proved successful in fostering foreign and national investment, they have obscured the role of low-income households and small-scale, family-based, tourism workers, who were the first promoters of tourism facilities in Siem Reap, but who have not benefited from any incentive to go on playing a major role in the development of tourism infrastructure.

9 More precisely, 'complex tourism centers with hotel containing less than 100 rooms or tourist inns of less than 30 housing and resort of multiple services with size less than 10 (ten) hectares' [sic] are not eligible for tax exemptions. Annex 1 to the Sub-decree No. 111, ANK/BK, 27 September 2005, 'on the implementation of the Law on the Amendment to the Law on Investment', section 2 (DFDL, 2007, p. 129).

International donors encouraged the development of the tourism industry. In 1996, the World Bank sponsored a programme for tourism development in Cambodia. The expert report stated that tourism had a key role to play in the economy's transitional phase. As a light industry, tourism could provide a number of jobs and benefit countries with rich cultural and natural resources, whose poor infrastructure and technical facilities impeded, at least initially, the development of agriculture and manufacturing. The World Bank then forecast that Cambodia would reach one million visitors in 2000. Even if this estimate proved false because the international economic crisis and national political imbalances slowed the growth of this sector (only 466,365 foreigners arrived in 2000), Cambodia did finally reach the predicted figure in 2004, a few years after political stabilization encouraged both investors and visitors to flock to the country.

Tourism kept on increasing in the next few years. The First Socioeconomic Plan for the Development of Cambodia (1996-2000) considered tourism to be one of the key sectors for economic growth (JICA, 2002). This plan allocated 65 per cent of the national budget to urban centres, a percentage that reflects the government's desire to develop urban economies, even though agriculture was still the main economic sector and only fifteen per cent of the population lived in urban environments at that time. The official discourse accompanying the plan noted that the development of agriculture would directly benefit the population, but that tourism would also do so, as it was meant to provide capital which would be reinvested in the modernization of agriculture and thus would help reduce poverty. Tourism was seen 'not only as a catalyst of development, but also of political and economic change' (Sharpley, 2002, p. 13).

Speeches given by high-level political figures confirmed this strategy. Lay Prahas, Minister of Tourism between 2003 and 2007, stated that 'tourism is the only sector of the economy which can have a positive, almost immediate impact on poverty reduction through growth, unlike agriculture which needs a longer timeframe', adding, 'our biggest potential field in Cambodia is tourism', as 'tourism creates jobs and brings steady income for the nation and leads to development' (Chheang, 2008a, p. 292). Furthermore, Hun Sen constantly emphasized the positive role of tourism in the national economy: he argued that this industry was 'one of the most effective tools in poverty reduction in Cambodia through employment, tax revenues, and other spillover effects in other sectors, particularly agriculture, handicrafts and souvenir production, and construction'. For these reasons, he considered that 'tourism is one of the top five development priorities of Cambodia' (Chheang, 2008b, p. 91) and ought to be pursued to achieve long-term social benefits.

Until the end of the 1990s, the absence of political stability undermined the development of tourism. Investors did not fully trust Cambodia, despite the government's early efforts to regulate the national economy.[10] With the 1997 coup, which overthrew the government headed jointly by Norodom Ranariddh and Hun Sen, the process of political and economic integration of Cambodia into the international community was abruptly interrupted. ASEAN adjourned its meeting in Cambodia (which had received observer status in 1995); the UN seat reserved to Cambodia remained unfilled; the International Monetary Fund and the World Bank suspended their economic assistance. Combined with the international economic crisis, these events caused a sharp drop in investment and in tourist numbers, which had started to increase slowly throughout the 1990s: 118,183 foreigners had visited Cambodia in 1993, 260,489 in 1996, but only 218,843 in 1997, that is to say a fifteen per cent decrease (Chheang, 2008a). Several construction projects were suspended, leaving the skeletons of numerous unfinished hotels scattered across the Siem Reap landscape.

The fact that Siem Reap airport was not open to international flights was another factor limiting tourism development. Tourists had to land in Phnom Penh and reach Siem Reap through internal flights operated by Royal Air Cambodge (the national company, sold to Malaysian interests in 1994), or by other transport means such as buses or boats (Hall and Page, 2003, p. 3). In order to trigger tourism development in spite of the national and international crises at the end of the century, the government implemented an 'open sky' policy, which suddenly authorized international flights to land at the Siem Reap airport. This decision was obviously intended to counter the climate of political instability and boost tourism in Siem Reap. However, the government took this decision hastily and without a responsible evaluation of existing infrastructures, which were insufficient to sustain tourist arrivals on a large scale in Siem Reap. The government also counteracted projects then being implemented, such as the construction of a new domestic airport by the Asian Development Bank (ADB), which was intended to gradually increase the number of travellers, thus contravening the agreements made between the ADB and Cambodian Civil Aviation. In

10 These efforts included the establishment of reserve requirements, the liberalization of interest rates, and the creation of the International Committee on the Reconstruction of Cambodia. Starting in 1994, this committee produced annual plans for the reconstruction of the country. The Council for the Development of Cambodia was established as the authority responsible for the evaluation of the investment projects. The first five-year plan for the socio-economic development of Cambodia was approved in 1996, and since then a plan has been approved every five years.

2004, the French company Vinci was granted a concession to develop an international airport in Siem Reap and bought the ADB terminal, which became the domestic terminal.[11] Vinci developed a strategy designed to guarantee a positive return on its investment through a gradual, but sustained increase of tourist numbers. According to its estimate, 2.5 million tourists were expected in 2013. With this in mind, Vinci encouraged the Cambodians to develop adequate infrastructure and commercial activity in the Siem Reap-Angkor region, both being essential components of a successful tourist destination. In their view, Siem Reap-Angkor was a precious, fragile, but promising tourism product, which had to be carefully developed in order to keep attracting foreign clients.

The government did not listen to foreign planners' advice when it took the decision to remove the restrictions on air traffic. A diagnosis of the tourism sector, authored by the French consulting firms Détente, GIE, and Villes Nouvelles, had accompanied the Urban Reference Plan for Siem Reap in 1995. Among its main objectives, the report, *Mission Tourisme*, proposed that tourism-related earnings should be equally distributed between the province, the state, and the programme for the conservation of Angkor. Cambodian institutions would be responsible for using this money to improve social welfare and increase economic opportunities for the population. In order to avoid social disruption, high-spending tourists from Japan and the West should be given priority, because they would maximize benefits while minimizing tourism loads. This type of client would stay in the Hotel City and would choose tourism packages offering higher levels of psychological security to foreigners visiting a country recently at war. Complementary attractions, such as museums, sports, and shows, would induce tourists to stay longer. The plan deliberately neglected the emerging market in tourists from Asian countries, because Asian tourists, who generally travel in large groups and do not stay long, would substantially increase the tourism load without producing significant benefits. They would therefore only be welcome in a second phase of development, when they would use the same infrastructures and facilities created for wealthy Japanese and Western tourists.

In 1997, the European Union funded a transport master plan, which proposed that the government should choose a strategy of some kind to

11 The Vinci company established a branch in Cambodia, called SCA, which has operated Phnom Penh airport since 2001. Vinci signed a BOT contract (Build, Operate, and Transfer) for Siem Reap airport valid until 2040, after which it is supposed to deliver the airport infrastructure to its Cambodian counterparts.

enable consultants to design adequate plans. According to the consulting firm that drew up the plan, a 'good tourism product' was a destination where the infrastructure was appropriate to the number of tourists. Even mass tourism, if well planned, could be sustainable, because properly calibrated infrastructure would help to reduce the negative impact of the tourists on the environment, city, and cultural resources. If this was the government's objective, then a strategy of mass tourism ought to be rapidly implemented through a series of intelligent development projects. However, the government's sudden implementation of the open-sky policy did not form part of such a long-term strategy. Rather, it corresponded to a tactical decision to take the most effective steps with regard to the present situation in order to achieve rapid profits despite the national political crisis. Tourism development was vital for the future of the country and had to be pursued independently of any political turmoil. In 2002, Hun Sen confidently affirmed that the reduction of air restrictions 'is the key policy innovation that has enabled the rapid growth of our tourism industry'.[12]

This reckless appetite for tourism development revealed that the priority in Cambodia was economic growth with no concern for the consequences of massive tourist numbers in the archaeological park and the Angkor region. In this respect, tourism development and heritage conservation appeared to be two disconnected areas of political discourse and two parallel strategic sectors for the government. On the one hand, representatives of the government and the APSARA authority developed discourses, policies, and measures for the conservation of Angkor in line with the recommendations of the international ICC committee; on the other hand, a parallel discourse favoured the establishment of a neoliberal economy, a rapid increase in tourist numbers, and the thoughtless implementation of development projects in close proximity to the archaeological site. This disconnect generated a dualistic perception of these heritage resources: Angkor was seen as a bottomless honey pot and source of endless growth, but also as a milestone on the road to the construction of Cambodian national identity. This contradictory perception affected the way the government approached different and often conflicting groups of actors: it allied itself with national and foreign investors in order to get as much profit as possible from the exploitation of the Angkor site, while also endorsing the international community's efforts to establish a strong institutional system of heritage conservation. Consequently, the meaning

12 Speech by Hun Sen, 6 December 2002, quoted by Chheang (2008b), p. 94.

of 'quality' tourism changed over time, even in the minds of planners and donors who, as travelling companions of their Cambodian counterparts (Bayart, 2004), had to adapt to decisions taken on the spur of the moment. In recent years, quality tourism has come to be associated with the provision of suitable facilities and appropriate infrastructure, able to cope with an influx of tourists without drastically compromising the environmental balance.

When the political and economic environment became more stable after 1998 and Cambodia joined ASEAN in 1999, investors and tourists started to flock to the country. The development of Angkor became urgent, because Cambodia wanted to lose no time in benefiting fully from such a positive asset. The reins of tourism development were handed over to wealthy investors and developers who were able to develop large-scale infrastructures, in order to attract the highest possible number of tourists. Chea Sophorn, the head of the Cambodian delegation at the ICC-Angkor, asked the international community to understand the importance of investment that would transform Siem Reap-Angkor into a tourism hub complying with international standards:

> Angkor is sleeping! We will wake it up! Sites elsewhere in the world that have much less to offer are receiving millions of visitors a year, while we are getting only a few hundred thousand. Note the following figures: Château de Versailles, 6 million visitors a year; Borobudur temple, 2 million; the Eiffel Tower, 12 million. The Royal Government would like this to be looked into and that concrete proposals be arrived at quickly [...]. Without being untrue to its [the ICC's] mission to protect the Angkor sites, it must be flexible with regard to the needs of private enterprise, to the wishes and needs of the people, including those of young Cambodians now flocking into the labor market. (UNESCO-ICC, 2001, p. 8)

The exclamatory tone of the speech conveyed the government's determination to use Angkor as a powerful magnet for tourism-related investment.

Donors adapted to the will of the Cambodian government. In 2002, the ADB resigned itself to the sudden change in the air traffic strategy and sponsored a national tourism plan that focused on how to concentrate increasing numbers in the tourism hub in a sustainable way. In 2000, the government signed up to the UN's Millennium Development Goals and, in particular, committed itself to poverty reduction. In response, the ADB submitted a 'pro-poor' tourism management plan for its consideration. The plan proposed the creation of employment opportunities through small- and medium-sized companies and public-private partnerships. Micro-credits and small-scale consultancies would favour the people's active involvement in the tourism economy and the decision-making process (Goodwin and Roe, 2001). The main idea was that the dispersing of tourism would spread its benefits across a large proportion of the population. For this reason, tourists should be encouraged to visit not only Siem Reap-Angkor, but also Phnom Penh, Sihanoukville, and, later, the remote northeast provinces of Rattanakiri and Mondulkiri. Villages should be open to tourism and their inhabitants would manage guesthouses to host those visitors who do not require high-grade facilities but enjoy simpler accommodations.

In collaboration with the Ministry of Tourism and the Ministry of Culture and Fine Arts, the ADB created a database covering the whole country, identifying places with cultural and natural assets to be developed for tourism. This project could have been crucial in a country where heritage recognition had almost exclusively focused on archaeological remains. Under the pretext of developing tourism, the authorities agreed to compile an inventory of Cambodia's other heritage, including a range of valuable sites and cultural expressions around the country, such as villages, rituals, festivals, and handicrafts. However, this inventory grouped sanctuaries, casinos, and theme parks together. Heritage elements were not distinguished from other tourism resources, and their presence in the inventory depended purely on economic concerns, that is, on the possibility of developing them as tourist attractions. Moreover, the plan did not include measures for heritage conservation: the exploitation of cultural and natural resources for tourism was the sole concern, with the objective of achieving poverty reduction. This plan shows that heritage recognition in contemporary Cambodia has been mainly perceived through the lens of economic gain. Although the economic aspect of a country's heritage has proved to be ever more important in the global situation of greater circulation of investments and tourists, in other emerging countries in the region it is generally fused with competing concerns for the construction of national identity and political consensus, and communities' claims to social, cultural, and political recognition (Daly and Winter, 2012). In Cambodia, these concerns are very fragile compared to the dominating economic rationale of heritage development for tourism. Moreover, heritage-driven economic development drastically simplifies the interpretation of these heritage resources in order to conform to the interests of national and international tourists and, by exploiting heritage resources for economic purposes, deprives Cambodian citizens of the possibility of using their heritage to reconnect with their own history and identities.

3.2 Reconnecting the disenfranchised links of the economic chain

However, Siem Reap was still the second poorest province in Cambodia in 2007, and exhibited various standard poverty indicators such as high child malnutrition rates (Gebert, Samrach, et al., 2007).[13] Tourism development has been inequitable, failing to benefit the local population, and Siem Reap is the hub of this asymmetrical growth. This negative assessment is the starting point of the plan designed by the German Technical Cooperation Agency (GTZ), which has focused on improving the living conditions of villagers who live around the urban centre.[14] The GTZ observed that Siem Reap's hyper-specialization in tourism had disadvantaged agriculture. Agricultural means of production had been only marginally modernized since the early 1990s. Moreover, the tourism industry was not intelligently managed, since the majority of the handicrafts sold in Siem Reap markets were not produced locally but came from other Asian countries. The majority of the households in Siem Reap province depended either on a faltering agricultural system or on subaltern employment in the tourism industry.[15] In the funding request that the Cambodian government addressed to the donor, the project was called 'Green Belt'. This title evoked the image of an aesthetically appealing constellation of rural villages around the city; the aim was to encourage the sale of agricultural produce and handicrafts in Siem Reap's tourism economy.

However, the implementation of the green belt project faced a number of obstacles which eventually compromised its initial objectives. Firstly, many plots of land in Siem Reap province, which the plan had designated for agriculture, had become private property and were affected by regular cycles of land speculation. Secondly, the water and land quality was insufficient to produce fruit and vegetables suited to the sophisticated tourist demands. Finally, the German donor asked the Cambodian government to contribute ten per cent of the total project budget, the money to come from

13 Poverty rates throughout Cambodia were still high though improving in the decade 1993-2004; 56 per cent of the population remained below UN poverty standards in 1993. In 2004, 18.4 per cent of the population lived on less than one dollar per day and 34.7 per cent still remained below poverty standards. ADB, 2008, Fact Sheet: http://www.ADB.org/countries/cambodia/main (accessed 19 September 2008).

14 This shift coincided with an approach to urban planning which mainly dealt with the technical aspects of urban management such as infrastructure building (see Chapter 2).

15 In line with the 'one village-one product' strategy, promoted by the National Socioeconomic Development Plan (2006-2010), each village was to specialize in the production of a single type of handicraft or agricultural product.

Angkor entrance fees. However, the government delayed the payment for several years,[16] exposing its inadequate involvement in development and its position as a mere receiver of aid.

Between 2014 and 2017, the GTZ consultants launched a second phase of the project, the Regional Economic Development Program (RED), and benefited from additional funding from the Swiss Agency for Development and Cooperation (SDC). Because of land speculation and property development, they abandoned the idea of creating a green belt around Siem Reap. They started by concentrating their efforts on a few villages in Siem Reap province.[17] The project was eventually able to target all the twelve districts that compose the province, and a total of 100 communes, 936 villages, and 30,000 households. This has become a pervasive strategy for reintegrating the villagers into the agricultural value chain. It has striven to remedy the exclusive reliance on tourism of Siem Reap's economy, which so far has favoured investors and developers, as well as long-distance relationships with agricultural and handicrafts producers elsewhere in Southeast Asia. At the end of 2015, 30 per cent of the fruit and vegetables available in the Siem Reap markets was produced by villagers involved in the project. It would be difficult for this percentage to increase. Firstly, vegetables such as tomatoes and potatoes cannot be grown in Cambodia. Secondly, some sellers prefer to source their produce from Thai growers, who can easily deliver large quantities of food in a short time. Thirdly, the irrigation system is not fully developed in Cambodia.

Speculation no longer seems to be a problem for the implementation of the project. In 2007 and 2008, land prices continuously increased because speculation was seen as an effortless way of making money. Inexperienced investors bought large plots of land, which were sometimes unbuildable because of periodic flooding. The pressure on land was eliminated once investors realized the shortcomings of this investment tactic. The price of agricultural land consequently dropped around 2010. In addition, the villagers have become more aware of the value of their land, and are less eager to sell it to the first buyer in order to buy consumables such as motorbikes and cars.

Although the project mainly focuses on agriculture, it also includes measures for the development of tourism and handicrafts in rural and urban environments. For instance, the village of Banteay Srei is developing a tourism development plan that encourages tourists to visit the surroundings

16 At the end of 2015, the government had provided funding equivalent to 5-6 per cent of the total cost of the project.

17 Personal communication with project coordinator, September 2008.

of the famous temple. The Angkor Handicraft Association (AHA)[18] gathers together about 40 local producers in its centre in Siem Reap and has created a 'seal of authenticity', which can also be used to guarantee the local origin of handicrafts not directly produced by AHA members.[19] Implementation is facilitated by the emergence of an association of shared economic interests. The AHA is seen as a way to fight back against the domination of the foreign market in crafts and souvenirs that had disadvantaged the local producers. The seal is both a strategic tool for local empowerment and a symbolic way of affirming that the local association has the authority to evaluate the authenticity of the craft products.

The GTZ project is said to have substantially contributed to poverty reduction in Siem Reap province. It is estimated that the monetary advantage for the villagers will be equivalent to twice the money invested (nine million euros from the German donor alone) and that rural households have increased their average annual income of US$199 per year (GIZ, 2013). For this reason, the programme will be extended to two additional provinces, Banteay Meanchey and Oddar Meanchey, in the years to come (GIZ, 2015). The politics of this project reveal how fast social and economic conditions are evolving in Cambodia along with rural societies' perceptions of value. Projects change their name, as in the case of the Hotel City. GIZ consultants needed flexibility and resilience to make the best of this volatile but dynamic situation. Project implementation becomes possible as soon as it does not require the capacity to impose power from outside on the land itself. Rather than pursuing the unrealistic objective of creating a green belt, GIZ has adopted a capillary strategy of penetration of the rural economy of Siem Reap province, aiming to reconnect the weak and disenfranchised links of the socioeconomic chain.

In this instance consultants have respected the boundaries of acceptable behaviour in the socio-political context of Cambodia, where foreign entities are discouraged from disrupting existing structures of neopatrimonial power. Significantly, another project for Siem Reap province with similar objectives, sponsored by the World Bank, was delayed when the donor attempted to bring up major issues of land-grabbing in Phnom Penh.[20] This project, 'Livelihood Enhancement and Association of the Poor' (LEAP), aims at 'poverty alleviation through rural livelihood interventions' and

18 http://www.aha-kh.com/en/.

19 Personal communication with project coordinator, 2015.

20 New diplomatic agreements between Cambodia and the United States reached at the end of 2015 may reactivate the project in the new future.

working 'towards social and economic empowerment' in nine districts and 50 rural communes of Siem Reap province (World Bank, 2010, p. 2). Like the GTZ project, this plan shifted the focus of attention from the town, as shown by the map of the project location which represented the areas with high levels of poverty, those to be addressed, in shades of red, but left Siem Reap town white because the urban area was simply not included in the project. Its overall objective was to build 'a participatory process in order to create voice, space and power' for the poor (World Bank, p. 3). It aimed to assist households through micro-credits to be spent on animal farming and agriculture. Local products would then be sold in local markets. NGOs and community leaders would have led the plan's implementation and would have reported to provincial authorities.

The emergence of participatory approaches in planning laid the foundation for a shift of focus, from space to human beings. The first seeds of this approach can be found in a report written by JICA in 2002, which had recognized the fundamental role of the population in the Angkor region. The report noted that the people help to define the values of the archaeological site, with their beliefs, ceremonies, and prayers, in a unique landscape of rice fields, villages, and forests. This report encouraged the government to implement measures for increasing the villagers' involvement in the tourism economy. As a consequence, in 2004, a governmental decision forbade the eviction of villagers living in the Angkor park, although their activities were still restricted by a number of regulations (Miura, 2010). A few years later, the Siem Reap district land use plan, designed by the German Development Service (DED), involved the inhabitants in the identification of the major urban problems to be addressed in the district's 2007 master plan. This gradual shift of focus broke with the top-down approach to planning and to change. It echoed global enthusiasm for participatory planning, the safeguarding of intangible heritage, and the enhancement of cultural diversity, which UNESCO had expressed in its more recent conventions and which also marked the transition in the focus of international heritage discourse from material artefacts to the producers of cultural expressions.[21] Strategies for Siem Reap province reflected the heated debates that engage the international community, while the priority of planning for the poor became disconnected from the tourism industry, constructing a two-tier economy at the intersection of foreign investment and local concerns.

21 Namely, the Convention for the Safeguarding of the Intangible Cultural Heritage (2003) and the Convention on the Protection and Promotion of the Diversity of Cultural Expressions (2005).

3.3 An irrational property market

At the beginning of the 1990s, the families of small landowners carried out most of the construction in Siem Reap town. They built individual houses and shophouses in single or multiple units, and converted existing buildings into guesthouses to host the first tourists. Hotels were few in number and responded to the emerging demand for tourist accommodation.[22] This situation changed around 2002-2003, when the political situation stabilized and tourist numbers increased. Construction sites proliferated and property values went up dramatically. The proliferation of property developments, especially complexes of several hundred shophouses, extended the urbanized area. Each of these projects covered several square kilometres, more than the whole of Siem Reap's historic core (which was less than three square kilometres). Hotel construction began to intensify in 2000 and boomed between 2003 and 2004. Density became ever greater; the old market district was converted to tourism and business functions; areas that were still undeveloped started to be urbanized, with hotels, villas, and shophouses standing on empty land surrounded by dirt roads, bush vegetation, and rice fields. Siem Reap's landscapes were transformed as available plots were occupied by property developers. While the demand for tourist accommodation had been fully met by the end of 2004, hotel construction continued (EIC, 2008). There were 74 hotels in Siem Reap in 2005, growing to 130 by 2008. Consequently, occupancy rates decreased so far that the profitability of such construction projects became questionable: in 2005, only 46.8 per cent of the hotel rooms were occupied during the high season (between November and March) and 17.3 per cent during the rest of the year. Guesthouse occupancy rates were also very low,[23] at 43.4 per cent during the high season and 15.5 per cent during the low season (JICA, 2005). These data reveal that profitability could not have been the primary objective of these numerous construction projects. Some other rationale motivated the developers who built hotels in a town that needed no more of them.

Since the 1990s, investment in the Cambodian property sector has been perceived as a way to make money fast. In major cities such as Phnom Penh and Siem Reap, the growth of the urban population has meant increased demand for rental accommodation. Without having a sound knowledge of the market and the nature of this demand, many developers believed that they could rent out villas and shophouses to be used for offices, tourism activities,

22 Between 1994 and 1997 fewer than 200,000 tourists visited Cambodia (JICA 2010).

23 Author's inventory of tourist infrastructures and facilities (1992-2008), 2008.

and family groups. This trend started at the beginning of the 2000s, when greater political and economic stability enabled the steady development of tourism and the property market. The trend had still not reversed in 2015: developers continued to engage in projects costing several hundred thousand dollars without knowing exactly what kind of activity – a restaurant, a guesthouse, a travel agency, or something else – might be accommodated there.[24] However, the majority of the people who have migrated to Siem Reap have low incomes and generally cannot access the kinds of property that developers frantically built. The average annual earnings of a Cambodian citizen was approximately US$500 before 2011, according to UN statistics reported by JICA (2005), while a concrete shophouse in one of the newly built urban areas cost US$20,000-50,000 in 2007. The dynamism of the urban economy has led to a general improvement in household economic conditions in recent years, mirrored by the gradual occupation of the newly built shophouses.[25]

Many buildings stayed empty for several years, during which they were bought and sold several times. Sale regulations in Cambodia encouraged this kind of speculation, as a transaction can take place in several steps. Buyers initially need only five to ten per cent of the total cost of a property to secure the transaction. After a few months, they have to make a second payment. In the meantime, they can look for another buyer to whom they sell the property at a higher price, before actually becoming its legal owner. This practice has become very common, as it does not require particular financial expertise and gives a fast return on investment without a large initial outlay of capital. Due to the repeated application of this procedure, land prices constantly increased in Siem Reap during the first decade of the millennium.

The National Bank of Cambodia tried to put a brake on speculation in 2008, when land prices reached a peak, by establishing a control measure on bank loans. Since 2008, commercial banks have not been allowed to lend more than fifteen per cent of the total cost of an investment. This

24 Data on households' and developers' practices and money-lending provided in this section have been collected through semi-directive interviews with real estate agents, developers, and lawyers; statistics, real estate evaluations, and online promotional materials produced by real estate agents based in Phnom Penh and Siem Reap; and the author's survey of the transfer of hotel ownership, based on the lists periodically compiled by the Siem Reap headquarters of the Tourism Office, combined with the author's inventory of hotel facilities built in Siem Reap between 1993 and 2008.

25 The average price of a shophouse in Siem Reap was between US$135,000 and US$200,000 at the end of 2015 (personal communication with estate agent, 2015).

measure proved ineffective for several reasons. Firstly, the developers of large-scale construction projects generally have enough resources and do not request bank loans. Buyers, in contrast, often do need loans. This measure targeted them, as it was intended to prevent buyers from engaging in property transactions if they could not come up with 85 per cent of the total price at the start. However, not many people in Cambodia used banks at the beginning of 2000, as the banking system was still underdeveloped.[26] People were more accustomed to keeping their money hidden in cash, or investing in the property sector. In this particular situation, the measures against speculation had the opposite effect from that intended. They harmed the emerging Cambodian middle class with limited capital and regular income, who needed loans to buy a house, while investors were able to continue to buy and sell repeatedly with no interruption.

This measure did not succeed in stopping construction, which still relied on blind trust in a limitless expanding market. Developers believed in miraculous, never-ending growth ensured by the magnificent site of Angkor. This excerpt from the promotional material of an estate agency is a telling example of this widespread belief, disseminated by estate agents, in the value of properties in the neighbourhood of Angkor: 'Siem Reap's close proximity to the archaeological park of Angkor virtually guarantees that real estate properties in town will attract investors in the short and the long term. There is a public of visitors overseas, all demanding a place to sleep and eat. The number of visitors keeps growing and the perception of Cambodia as a tourist destination offering sufficient security for international tourism becomes more and more popular'.[27] The benefits of tourism would go beyond the profits directly derived from the exploitation of tourism infrastructures and facilities, since the popularity of Angkor would be unaffected by periods of crisis. These benefits supposedly extend to the whole property market and contribute to its indefinite growth. Estate agents believed that the market would continue growing in 2008, although the first symptoms of the international economic crisis were being experienced in Siem Reap: 'Considering the growth of all sectors of the real estate and property market during the last 2-3 years, the conclusion cannot but forecast that the perspective of growth for the next one or two years will be excellent'.[28] The

26 The Khmer Rouge abolished the banking system. In 1979, the Popular Bank of Kampuchea was the only bank to be reinstated. With economic liberalization, branches of foreign banks and private commercial banks have been authorized again.

27 Promotional materials produced by the estate agency CARE Angkor Real Estate, Siem Reap branch.

28 Ibid.

paradox of this projection is that it relied on very recent data. The economic evaluation of the property market lost its initial purpose, which is supposedly to anticipate trends in order to reassure investors about the health of the market. In fact, projections are used to push investors to act quickly, in other words to use tactics which will enable them to ride the wave of the present, perhaps volatile, situation. The idealistic trust in indefinite growth and the idea that one should act quickly in order to benefit fully from growth coexist, despite their apparent contradiction, and contribute to influencing developers' behaviour. Uncertainty undermines their confidence and drives them to implement hasty construction projects in which little time is spent on design and there is no overall vision for the city.

In this climate of blind trust in the market and land speculation, building hotels was viewed as a prestigious kind of business. Hotels introduce new international standards and models and thus showcase the wealth of the developer. Hotels were not directly involved in the speculation dynamics, which significantly concerned other market sectors: the capital needed to build or purchase a hotel is too substantial to be supplied by small investors. Speculative cycles have only marginally affected hotels. In 2008, only eleven hotels out of a total of 130 had changed ownership since they were built. However, a single change of ownership cannot be assumed to result from speculation, and multiple transactions are observable in only four of these eleven hotels. Owners generally do not advertise the sale of a hotel, because this would be perceived as a failure by the hotel manager and compromise his social image. Contacts and negotiations for the sale of a hotel take place via the owners' personal networks, and only rarely involve property agents. This social perception of hotels contrasts with the exploitation of other types of property for purely speculative purposes, and shows how competing rationales coexist to determine the programme of tourism-related projects.

Hotels play an important role in the growth of the property market. Building a hotel is a way to substantially increase the value of a plot of land. Developers have chosen central locations as far as these were available, in order to maximize the added value. By doing so, they collectively contributed to increasing the land values around the main transport hubs and in Siem Reap's historic centre. However, in 2008, empty plots and plots with hotels built on them were sold for the same price (approximately US$1250 per square metre) along National Highway No. 6 in the direction of the airport. Added value was not generated from the presence of a hotel but from the opportunity to develop city-centre properties intended for tourists' use, and the economic potential of these plots was confirmed by the large number of similar prestigious businesses.

Because added value is forward-looking (value is estimated depending on the development potential rather than the present state of a property), inherited buildings were widely perceived as burdens for the developer, who has to pay the demolition costs or adapt a construction programme to existing buildings. This perception at least partly changed between 2010 and 2015. In recent years, it was not uncommon for a developer to build on a plot just to increase the property value. Also, estate agents tended to assign surplus economic value to buildings they saw as having positive architectural qualities.

Even though the tourism market is saturated, developers have continued to invest in land and tourism because they believe that land values will continue to rise as they have done in the past. This rationale has become more important than the functioning of the tourism facility post-construction. Also, some developers certainly had to evacuate the uncomfortable traces of illegal transactions through hotel investment. A profitable hotel, even if the profits are small, generates clean money. Siem Reap has become the playground for these financial tactics, which have disconnected construction from the real economy.

The Cambodia National Bank regulations and then the international economic crisis of 2009 showed that unconditional confidence in the market was not well founded, as tourist numbers are extremely sensitive to national politics and the international economy. However, developers continued to build tourism facilities in Siem Reap. This excess capacity resulted in an increasing number of hotels and guest houses available for sale. At the end of 2015, a considerable number of hotels were owned or managed by tourism industry professionals. Many others, owned and managed by inexperienced individuals and families who sought to take up this new occupation, have become unattractive in this increasingly competitive market. Moreover, the success of a tourist facility depends substantially on volatile trends in taste disseminated by word of mouth. A guesthouse popular a few years ago can become completely outdated if a new one offers more comfort or more entertainment. As the property sector has become increasingly professionalized between 2008 and 2015, with several agencies opening licensed businesses, tourism facilities for sale have become more visible. A decreasing share of the market depends on networks of acquaintances and personal contacts. This professionalization undermines inherited perceptions of properties associated with the personal reputation of their owner.

Despite the hasty construction of an excessive number of buildings, Siem Reap's property market has not lost value. After a period of general stagnation in 2009, the only decrease was in speculation on agricultural land and open fields far from the city centre, while prices in the city centre continued to rise. Centrality and proximity to paved roads are the main factors influencing prices. Transportation master plans are seen as goldmines and potential investors treat all information about future road development as valuable. Significantly, the construction of a ring road around Siem Reap has led to increased prices in the area inside this road: by the end of 2015 no plots within this area cost less than US$80.

Discussions between the Cambodian government and the Korea International Cooperation Agency (KOICA) about the construction of the ring road started in 2003, but in this first phase they only concerned the upper part of the road, which bypassed the Angkor temples. The JICA Master Plan of 2006 then suggested that a southern ring road could join together fragments of existing unpaved paths and mark the limit of Siem Reap's urbanized area. KOICA and the Cambodian government followed this suggestion, and agreed on a southern extension of the ring road 20.5 kilometres in length, which was built between 2010 and 2012.[29] This example illustrates the reception of JICA's master plan. In the plan, the idea of the ring road was intended to prevent urban sprawl, and help implement the compact city model. For urban politics, however, the construction of this road has become both a discursive tool to celebrate the 'friendly spirit of Korea' and 'the symbol of growing partnership between the two countries' and also a powerful tool for property market profitability. At the end of 2015, rumours about the construction of a second ring road, which would further expand the area of profitable land, had already started to agitate the market. The urban area was being extended gradually, in a ripple effect.

Within the urban area, prices are determined by sales opportunities and negotiations between sellers and buyers, rather than reasonable assessments based on data and measurable parameters. A shared belief that property values will continue to increase produces a continuous general increase in asking prices[30] which can reach unexpected levels for a developing town. In December 2015, a block of shophouses in the Old Market area (2000m^2) was offered for sale for US$1,300,000 on the website of a local estate agent. However, as an estate agent sarcastically commented, 'If a grandmother has been asleep for two years, she will be willing to sell her shophouse for the

29 http://www.koica.go.kr/WEBZINE/2012-e_october/sub3.php. KOICA's total investment in the construction of the ring road was US$17.4 million.

30 The asking price is the price suggested by the owner, before negotiation with potential buyers. In Siem Reap, it can be much higher than the price at which the property will be actually sold. Communication with estate agent, 2015.

asking price of two years ago'.[31] The irrationality of the market is interpreted by foreign estate agents as the residue of traditional practices based on interpersonal negotiation and on naive and inexperienced assessments of the value of properties. Siem Reap's property market is still governed by fluctuating and volatile trends, megalomaniac expectations, and emulation.

3.4 Negotiating the land laws

The fact that the contemporary Cambodian economy is characterized by unbridled liberal openness does not mean that developers never have to comply with rules. In fact, developers know the formal constraints of the law and negotiate them in order to achieve their objectives and maximize the benefits of their investment.

The Khmer Rouge destroyed both Cambodian customary law, based on dispute resolution through conciliation, and the French law superimposed on traditional law in the colonial period (Donovan, 1993). After the Paris Accords of 1991, the majority of national and foreign lawyers agreed that previous laws had de facto been repealed. This meant that the Cambodian legal system had to be rebuilt from scratch (Fontaine, 2008). Due to the massive scale of the killings, however, Cambodia had only five fully trained legal professionals at the beginning of the 1990s. Foreign technical cooperation programmes provided substantial aid for creating a new legal framework. UNTAC presided over the promulgation of the new constitution of the Kingdom of Cambodia in 1993, along with 'the formation of a Constitutional Monarchy through elections, in which the concepts of political pluralism, human rights and the rule of law were introduced in Cambodia' (Peng, Phallack, and Menzel, 2012, p. 1). A number of laws were implemented under UNTAC direction in the areas of criminal law, judicial law, and press law. Between 1993 and 2002, the Cambodian government established the Council for State Reform, composed of a Council for Legal Reform and a Council for Judicial Reform, through which the royal government undertook legal and judicial reforms with the aid of various development partners.

The international consultants who directed the law-making process came from different professional and cultural backgrounds and different legal traditions. They generally spent short periods of time in Cambodia, and their Cambodian counterparts tended to blindly rely on those they believed to be experts (Fontaine, 2008). As a result, the current legal system

31 Personal communication with estate agent, 2015.

is a hybrid that draws on several traditions. It combines a civil code and civil procedure shaped by Japan, criminal law and criminal procedure shaped by France, and commercial law established under the influence of the World Bank (Fontaine, 2008). Donors compete to present their sometimes conflicting legal systems. Their fight to get their slice of the pie in the politics of law-making is reminiscent of similar conflicts in the field of urban planning, with different schools of thought trying to impose their ideas (see Chapter 2). The importation of legal systems inappropriate to Cambodia, together with a lack of coordination among different institutional bodies, made room for 'shadow zones' within and between legal norms and also in their implementation. Investors and developers ingeniously exploit these zones using tactics through which they negotiate regulations for their personal gain.

Private ownership of land was established in Cambodia at the time of the French Protectorate. The colonial power enacted a series of decisions based on the Roman legal tradition, which overlapped customary law in the same area and were subject to royal arbitration. According to customary law, all land belonged to the king, but could be spontaneously occupied by his subjects. Drawing on the 1808 French Civil Code, the 1884 Convention attempted to regulate customary possession rights claimed on the basis of appropriation. By the Royal Ordinance of 1897, the colonial government acquired the right to lease Cambodian land. The Crown Estate, over which the king had exclusive power, was henceforth distinguished from the colonial domain (*domaine privé de l'Indochine*), directly managed by French rulers. The land register, formally established in 1908, recognized the possibility of permanent land ownership rights. Consequently, customary possession came to be seen as a temporary and precarious right that needed to be secured. Communes (*khum*) were established in 1908 as subdivisions of larger indigenous territorial units (*srok*) to facilitate processes of land registration which transformed possession into ownership rights. However, Cambodians largely resisted the new bureaucratic system. While the French authorities took over the right to manage the national land register in 1925, many contracts were still concluded verbally. Temporary land occupation was still practised on the Crown Estate's vacant land plots, which could be farmed for several years before being abandoned.

Colonial regulations thus led to the formation of a dual land system; the gap between the two became ever wider as the French-inspired legal framework developed. After Cambodian independence, the 1956 Constitution recognized property rights. Colonial law was not substantially modified. However, lease agreements, temporary land occupation permits, and irregular or even illegal appropriation were still rooted in social practices. International observers believed that the existing legal system did not sufficiently address these practices, which nevertheless played a significant role in shaping territorial and urban development. In the 1950s and 1960s, the dual land system was confirmed: while wealthy Cambodians were able to secure large tracts of land, low-income people continued to appropriate land in temporary ways.

The shortcomings of land management helped the Khmer Rouge ideology to take root among the most disadvantaged.[32] When they came to power, the Khmer Rouge abolished this legal system. In Democratic Kampuchea all land became collective property owned by the *angka* (the 'organization') and urban residents were forced to abandon their property in the cities to work in the countryside. Under the Vietnamese administration, the 1981 constitution of the People's Republic of Kampuchea established that the state was the only landlord. But although land transactions and loans were forbidden, the socialist state allowed citizens to make use of land and transmit land rights to their children. People tried to return to their original places of residence. When this was impossible, they occupied vacant plots or empty houses without any immediate expectation that they would be able to own them (Springer, 2009).

Private ownership of land was reinstated in Cambodia through several steps over more than a decade. In 1989, a sub-decree (25 ANKR, 22 April) gave Cambodian citizens the right to own buildings. In 1992, the first land law established the right to own land individually and privately and the right to assert pre-emptive ownership rights over plots that households had occupied and used for more than five years. The process of land regularization culminated in the 2001 Land Law. This law abolished the provision concerning property rights established on the base of possession,[33] and

32 This account of the history of the establishment of the private property system in Cambodia draws on Carrier (2007; 2009).

33 In the time of Angkor, the right of possession of agricultural land was sustained if land was cultivated, cleared out, and fenced. Land could be used and transmitted to heirs without any additional formal requirements. In colonial times, the Civil Code of Cambodia (1920) regulated the right to possession, which remained similar to former Cambodian law. These regulations were still applicable at the time of the Sangkum Reastr Niyum but were abolished by the Khmer Rouge, who collectivized the land. In 1989, the 'Instruction on the Implementation of Land Use' prescribed that citizens should submit applications to register the land they possessed. This procedure was maintained by the 1992 Land Law which recognized possession rights over non-residential land and ordered villagers to regularize their situation and pay taxes. However, many people physically occupied land without fulfilling these legal requirements, especially in towns and cities. Also, communes followed different and sometimes conflicting principles

legislated that only the clauses relating to private property could regulate land tenure. The establishment of the land title registry (still under construction in Cambodia) helps to regularize land rights, since it improves the transparency and visibility of property transactions.

Three different categories of legitimation of land rights coexist in contemporary Cambodia: customary rules that still regulate life in the villages, the legacies of the socialist regime, and the recently established legal system. This coexistence results in a precarious social balance that generates violent confrontations, disputes between owners or competent jurisdictions, and evictions; in such a precarious and uncertain situation, law can be used as a guarantee that transactions are valid or, conversely, it can lose its initial function of regulating social life and be relegated to a marginal role as a 'false front' (*devanture formelle*), which legitimizes certain actions (Carrier, 2008). Carrier explains that the real mode of land occupation deviates from the official rules, because the vast majority of the rights exerted on land and other real property are not based on legal documentation. Tacit conventions rule possession of these rights, and the notion of ownership is fundamental to them. Taking possession is the first act that legitimizes property ownership and is initially established through the spontaneous occupation of land, marked by physical and visual signs such as fences, buildings, and milestones. The recognition of possession is only subsequently followed by legal regularization.

The uncertain status of much land requires estate agents, owners, and sellers to develop tools to give each of the parties a sufficient level of security and legality to engage in property transactions. Significantly, the still provisional character of Siem Reap's land title registry has led to the invention of three different types of land ownership, all in common use at the end of 2015. The first is the 'hard title', which includes a map of the sector where the property is located, showing the property boundary. This title is recognized by the Ministry of Land Management, Urban Planning, and Construction and is used for almost all large projects. Since the property boundaries have been approved, this type of land title can be a powerful legal tool to evict people who have not regularized their land rights. The second is the 'soft title': it is validated only by the local authorities and does not include a map. It is mainly used when the urban authorities have not

for the recognition of rights, some accepting claims of possession before 1979 and others only validating requests which followed the fall of the Khmer Rouge. These factors led to intense land conflicts which the 2001 Land Law has tried to solve by putting an end to the recognition of the rights of possession (Hap, 2010).

yet completed the land registry map. The third type of title is commonly described as 'intermediate' and contains a tentative sketch map of property boundaries that still have to be validated by the registry office. Validation requires that the office be able to establish rights of way on all land plots, which in some cases have been annulled by the redistribution of property boundaries. This means that the validity of an 'intermediate' land title can be called into question once the registry office establishes new boundaries.

In this uncertain yet flexible situation, Siem Reap's property market is open to tactics by the developers, who preserve a façade of legality while they get round the law. Tactics conceal the pursuit of particular interests that subvert laws under the mask of formal compliance. Drawing on peer experience, legal advice, and developers' knowledge of the national legal framework (and its gaps) and personal acquaintance with members of local and national administrations, these approaches become widespread because they have proved effective through collective experimentation and reiteration.

Land ownership is one of the areas where tactics are skilfully designed in order to generate substantial benefits from property development and speculation. Through analysing these tactics, we can gain an understanding of power sharing in urban spaces. We can also identify the fine line between acceptable and unacceptable behaviour in the politics of land and urban development. Regulations do indeed contain clauses and ambiguities that leave room for opportunistic manipulation. The existence and application of regulations sustains the credibility of the Cambodian state. However, these tactics function to make subversive, profit-orientated interpretations legal, and therefore applicable, even though these interpretations undermine the regulations' initial raison d'être.

The first shadow zone of Cambodian legislation with respect to the politics of urban development is created by the division of labour between various administrative levels. The national authorities play a dominating role in giving out construction permits, as they are entitled to evaluate large-scale investments without consulting the local authorities. According to the sub-decree on construction permits (No. 86/ANK/BK, 19 December 1997), the district, provincial, and national authorities share the responsibility for evaluating these requests, depending on the size of the buildings: the district evaluates requests for buildings under 500 square metres, the provincial authority those for buildings under 3000 square metres, and the Ministry of Land Management, Urban Planning and Construction (MLMUPC) those for buildings over 3000 square metres. In Siem Reap-Angkor, the APSARA authority also advises on large-scale projects; however, its opinion is not binding. The consequence of this administrative organization is that locally established authorities (both local authorities and special national authorities such as the APSARA) have no role in making decisions about projects whose large scale would lead to a major transformation of an urban landscape: these include golf courses, museums, tourist resorts, shophouse developments, and theme parks. The case of the Angkor National Museum (see Chapter 4) is significant in this respect. Built on state land along Avenue Charles de Gaulle, the road leading to the Angkor temples, the Thai-sponsored project has been only occasionally mentioned, but never actually discussed at the ICC-Angkor meetings, and has not been included in the national investment statistics annually produced by the CDC. The project was implemented through direct negotiations between the investors and the national Cambodian institutions. However, these negotiations are kept secret by the official sources.

The second shadow zone concerns construction regulations. As the South Korean developer whom I interviewed openly admitted, applying for a building permit is an optional formality in Siem Reap. The relevant sub-decree mentioned above indicates that developers have to comply with only a few generic construction rules in order to get permission to build.[34] All requests are accepted if they comply with these basic regulations; if they do not, public officials suggest modifications and the developers can carry out their project if they take these suggestions into account in the revised version of the building plan.[35] Despite the procedure's permissiveness, the building permits of a substantial percentage of Siem Reap's tourism facilities (28 per cent of the hotels and 71 per cent of the guesthouses operating there in 2008) were unavailable at either the provincial registry office, or the central MLMUPC headquarters. It is true that these offices have inefficient storage systems. However, the guesthouse percentage shows that a substantial number of the tourism facilities built in Siem Reap are informal; that is to say, they have not gone through the administrative procedure set up by Cambodian law. Moreover, although the sub-decree established that a permit has to be requested if the owner wants to demolish a building (art. 22, No. 86, 1997), such permits have never been requested in Siem Reap province. Landowners can destroy buildings with complete impunity, as no building in Siem Reap has been listed as a national heritage property. The sub-decree on building

34 These construction rules concern safety, public health, minimum distances, and maximum heights.

35 Personal communications with public officials working at Siem Reap's provincial bureau, 2009.

permits is a good example of the 'false front' (Carrier, 2008), purporting to show that the rule of law has been established in Cambodia but lacking normative force because it weakly regulates the field it applies to.

The third shadow zone concerns the land rights of foreigners. By law only Cambodian citizens are entitled to own land.[36] However, several tactics have been developed in order to give foreigners access to land rights that allow them to invest in the emerging property sector. One of these tactics is the 'nominee': a third party (a Cambodian citizen or company) buys a property in the name of a foreign developer. This procedure is generally legal in the Anglo-Saxon world but is forbidden in the Cambodian system. In spite of this, Cambodian authorities have widely tolerated it since the 1990s. Village chiefs, lawyers, estate agents, and sometimes even the provincial delegations of the MLMUPC serve as guarantors for this kind of procedure. In order to secure their rights, foreign developers keep the land title in their possession (or the document which recognizes property rights, if the land registry has not yet been established in the area where the property is located). Without this document, it is impossible for the official owner to sell the land. This procedure, however, is not considered completely safe, especially if disputes arise between the foreign developer and the Cambodian citizen.[37]

Another procedure is 'antichresis', which is viewed as a legal way to ensure debt reimbursement under the Cambodian Land Law (Chapter 13): a debtor gives a piece of land as collateral to the creditor until the debt is repaid. Antichresis was widely used to guarantee 70- to 90-year leases; the length of these leases has been recently limited to 50 years. The debt is equivalent to the price of the land, thus giving the foreigner long-term rights over it. Contracts can be automatically renewed in exchange for a symbolic sum of money (often one dollar). Joint ventures formed by Cambodian and foreign investors also use antichresis. In these companies, Cambodian citizens own at least 51 per cent of the share capital, in order to be entitled to own the land. However, the foreigners are often the real investors and use antichresis to secure their decision-making role in the joint venture. When the company is established, the Cambodian partners take out a loan from the foreign partners, the amount of which corresponds to the price of the land. The Cambodians share the amount of the debt among themselves and actually work as employees for the foreign partners. If their contract is terminated, they are obliged to give back a sum of money equivalent to the debt they contracted. Further contractual guarantees can be added in order to secure the power of the

36 Land Law, 1992, art. 2; Land Law, 2001, art 8.

37 Personal communication with lawyers based in Phnom Penh, March 2008.

foreign partners in the company; for instance, the Cambodian partners can be excluded from the right to vote on the joint venture's executive council, or they can be prevented from benefiting from or selling the land.[38]

Also, short- and long-term leases legally allow foreigners to access land rights. However, Cambodian law does not clearly specify foreigners' rights to buildings they erect on leased plots. It seems to tolerate foreign ownership of these buildings at the end of the lease, but also states that the owners must return the land along with the buildings when the lease ends.[39]

Lastly, economic land concessions can give foreign developers land rights. The law states that 'a land concession is a legal right established by a document issued under the discretion of the competent authority, given to any natural person or legal entity or group of persons to occupy a land and to exercise thereon the rights set forth by this law' (art. 48). More specifically, economic land concessions 'allow the beneficiaries to clear the land for industrial agricultural exploitation of land in the territory of the Kingdom of Cambodia'.[40] In order for the concession to be legal, the land must belong to the 'private domain of the State', which can be subject to such transactions.[41] 'Public state land', by contrast, is supposed to be used for public and collective facilities and cannot be alienated. However, Cambodian law also authorizes the modification of state land status from public to private, if the public properties lose their public-interest use. Only when public institutions such as hospitals, schools, and the like have been moved to another site altogether is the 'transferring of State public property to State private property' permitted. In cities such as Siem Reap and Phnom Penh, public state land is often located on prime urban sites. Developers often exchange large plots located on the periphery for smaller plots on these sites. In exchange for acquiring land rights, they often bear the costs of infrastructure. Public-interest facilities on these plots are then displaced towards the city's perimeter and necessarily go into decline (see section 3.4.2). The status of the land can then be changed in accordance with the law, in order to make it available to developers. In these cases, the regulations concerning the status of public state land are diverted from the initial raison d'être, the protection of plots for public and community facilities.

38 Land Law, 2001, art. 108. Personal communication with lawyers based in Phnom Penh, March 2008.

39 Ibid.

40 Land Law, 2001, art 49: economic land concessions are distinct from social land concessions, which 'respond to a social purpose' and 'allow beneficiaries to build residential constructions and/or cultivate lands belonging to the State for their subsistence'.

41 Land Law, 2001, art 14.

The Law on the Provision of Ownership Rights over Co-owned Buildings (NS/RMK/0510/066) aims to facilitate 'foreigners investing in the Kingdom of Cambodia' and 'investors' business in the field of construction', and to respond to 'the expansion of the property market in the Kingdom of Cambodia' (art. 2). This law allows foreigners to own a property as long as it is not located on the ground floor or basement of a building. It specifies that an owner can divide a building into multiple individual units and sell up to 70 per cent of the whole building in this way. According to the MLMUPC, the law supports economic, social, and legal interests, and helps integrate Cambodia into the global and regional economy.[42] Foreigners enjoy 'ownership rights over private parts' of the buildings, and 'rights to use and enjoy benefits in the common areas of a co-owned building' (art. 1). It was primarily conceived for residential buildings, especially newly built condominiums where many foreigners live. However, if the co-owned building were to be 'totally destroyed by a human act or by force majeure', and the Cambodian owner consequently decides to sell the land on which it is located, the building's co-owners cannot contest this decision, but will only receive 'sale proceeds based on their right to use and enjoy the common areas according to the proportion of the surface area of their private units or according to a previously made agreement or the internal rules' (art. 18). Phnom Penh's property market has immediately benefited from the implementation of this law, as the numerous apartments available in the recently built high-rises have also been targeted to foreign owners. In contrast, Siem Reap's market has not yet been affected by the possibility of acquiring so-called strata title to property. Potential owners prefer to buy houses rather than flats, given the considerable number of available individual houses, but selling flats is a profitable activity only in high-rise buildings, and developing these is still forbidden in the proximity of the Angkor temples.

3.5 Invisible investment

Foreign direct investment (FDI) is an economic source of paramount importance for the Cambodian economy. Only one year after the enactment of the law on investment, the Council for the Development of Cambodia (CDC) approved projects sponsored by FDI to the amount of US$2.3 billion. In 2008,

42 Meas Sokchea and Steve Finch, 2010, 'Law on Foreign Property Passed', *Phnom Penh Post*, 6 April: http://www.phnompenhpost.com/national/law-foreign-property-passed (accessed 24 September 2015).

this increased to US$10.89 billion, with US$8.7 billion invested in tourism. This is a remarkable sum considering that only US$106.73 million was spent on agriculture.[43] Between 1999 and 2005, approximately 25 per cent of FDI was invested in tourism, 40 per cent in industry, 30 per cent in other services, and only 4.6 per cent in agriculture. In comparison, tourism in Thailand received only 5 per cent of FDI during the same period. In absolute dollar amounts, that 5 per cent is almost double the amount of tourism investment in Cambodia over the ten-year period. However, tourism in Thailand has been actively developed and promoted for 30 years and destinations are spread across the country. Tourism development in Cambodia is recent and investment has been almost exclusively concentrated in the region of Angkor (De Vienne, 2008). Malaysia was the major investor during that period (48.1 per cent of FDI), followed by China (14.3 per cent), and Taiwan (11 per cent). Currently, major investors in the country are China (23.97 per cent) and South Korea (10.68 per cent), followed by Malaysia, Taiwan, Hong Kong, and Thailand.[44] Cambodia's neoliberal economy attracts floating capital from other Asian and especially ASEAN countries.[45] These investors accept the high risks of investing in an unstable country. In return, they ride the wave of speculation and obtain substantial benefits in short periods of time.

Despite the great importance of FDI in the national economy, the statistics annually produced by the CDC are structured in such a way that they give only a limited picture of its actual impact. This lack of transparency, partly related to the ambiguous status of foreign land ownership rights, forms another shadow zone for covert negotiations and secret alliances. Since 1991, national statistics have recorded FDI.[46] These statistics make it possible to estimate the participation of foreign and Cambodian investors in the field of tourism. Between 1995 and 1999, 39 per cent of the capital invested in tourism projects was Cambodian, compared to 61 per cent from foreign investors (Thoraxy, 1999). Between 2001 and 2009, only 19 per cent of the capital invested in tourism came from Cambodia.[47] During the first period the major investors were the United Kingdom (22 per cent), Thailand (21 per

43 CDC website: http://www.cambodiainvestment.gov.kh/investors-information/fdi-trend.html (accessed 21 October 2015).

44 Ibid.

45 In contrast, industrialized countries funded the majority of tourism projects in Thailand over the same period (1998-2005).

46 The National Committee on Investments produced these statistics for 1991-1993. They were published by Chap Sotharith, 1994, *An Assessment of Foreign Direct Investments in Cambodia*, MA thesis, Asian Institute of Technology, Bangkok.

47 Statistics compiled by the Council for the Development of Cambodia for 2000-2009.

cent), Malaysia (16 per cent), and France (16 per cent); in the second period, the major investors were Malaysia (16 per cent), Thailand (15 per cent), and Singapore (13 per cent), followed by Russia and South Korea (8 per cent each). The number of countries investing in Cambodia has gradually increased between 1992 and 2009, but Western countries are now in the minority while Asian countries have increased their total contribution.

However, these statistics do not fully describe the impact of FDI. First, some major investments are missing, such as the project for the construction of a new harbour on Tonlé Sap lake by the Cambodian company Sou Ching (see Section 2.5.2). Second, the statistics record the investment that the CDC has approved, not the projects effectively implemented.[48] Significantly, a peak of FDI is observable for the year 1995, due to the Malaysian company Ariston's US$1300 million investment for the construction of hotels, resorts, and golf courses in the south of Cambodia (Table 3.1). However, this development was never implemented.[49] Also in 1995, an investment of US$39 million by Singapore was supposed to underwrite a five-star hotel in the proximity of the Phnom Penh Olympic Stadium, but this was also abandoned.[50]

Because Cambodia is an unstable country where many projects are abandoned before being initiated or completed, statistics are not a reliable source of information on tourism-related construction activity. While the CDC provides inflated statistics (Table 3.2), it also fails to record a large amount of foreign investment, including that concealed behind Cambodian nominees. For instance, South Korean investment is said to be of paramount importance by Siem Reap's estate agents, but is almost invisible in the CDC statistics (at 8 per cent) and in the requests for building permits presented by the official Cambodian owners.

An additional source of uncertainty is the involvement of foreign capital, which depends on the application of Cambodian commercial law. As explained above, foreigners often obtain rights to land through partnerships with Cambodians and the establishment of joint ventures. When a new company is created, it declares the amount of its capital, which is supposed to be shared proportionately by all its partners, but this does not necessarily reflect the actual contributions of the partners to investment costs.

48 Sources are also fundamentally unreliable: for instance, the number of investment projects for 1995-2005 listed by the Economic Institute of Cambodia is higher than the figures provided by the CDC for the same years.

49 In general, Malaysian projects are a large contributor to FDI, but only a small percentage of these projects are successfully implemented. Of the US$1890 million in Malaysian investments proposed before 1999, only US$480 million was actually spent (Thoraxy 1999).

50 Cambodian partners held nine per cent of the shares for this project.

Moreover, official documents often nominally attribute 51 per cent of this capital to the Cambodian partners in order to allow the joint venture to buy land. The share of capital also generally reflects the share of benefits derived from the exploitation of the property. However, in the case of Cambodian joint ventures, contractual guarantees frequently prevent the Cambodian partners from directly benefiting from the investment. The capital is thus falsely attributed to Cambodian investors. Furthermore, the statistics compiled by the CDC do not record the proportion of fixed assets within the total investment. In many cases, foreign partners bear the totality of this cost while the Cambodian partners are only nominees.

Lastly, CDC statistics only record investment projects of more than US$2 million. A sub-decree of the investment law (No. 17, 9 February 2005) established investment committees in the Cambodian provinces and municipalities, to be responsible for the evaluation of projects below US$2 million. However, the local authorities seldom publish investment statistics, thus indirectly contributing to the invisibility of part of the national economy.

In this situation, only individual case analyses can show how foreign investment and Cambodian participation are negotiated. I would like to describe two examples that give some insight into the complex financial structure of investment projects for tourism facilities. The first is a hotel built by a French developer between 2005 and 2006.[51] The developer put the capital together with contributions from several foreign individual investors. The group formed a company registered in the United Kingdom, whose capital was secured in a bank in Hong Kong. Then the foreign company contacted a Cambodian nominee company,[52] in which only 51 per cent of the shares are held by Cambodian citizens. The nominee company bought a land parcel and signed a long lease (70-99 years) with the foreign company. Its request for the hotel's building permits and the investment's declared sources mask the presence of foreign participants, since only the nominee company appears as the legitimate owner.

The second example is a Singapore-based company registered in the Cayman Islands, whose shares are sold on the London stock exchange. This company created a branch with an initial capital of US$220 million, which was invested in Vietnam and Cambodia. In 2009, it submitted two

51 Personal communication with the French developer, March 2008.

52 Personal communication with the hotel owner. Nominee companies, like those named by the French developer, can be listed by the Ministry of Commerce as operating in the property field, and also in other sectors. Personal communication with Siem Reap's Chamber of Commerce, July 2008.

Table 3.1 Incoming FDI to Cambodia by country of origin and sector

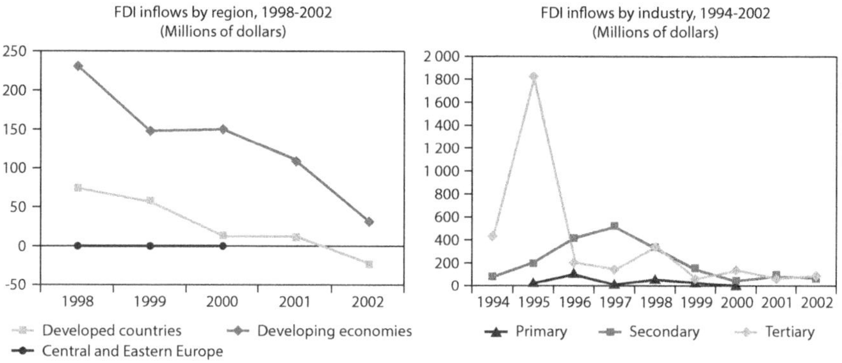

Data: UNDP, graphs by the author; © Esposito 2011

investment projects for Cambodia: a hotel in Phnom Penh and a commercial complex with a hotel and mall in Siem Reap. The MLMUPC and the Siem Reap provincial office received building permit requests for the projects, both of which were approved. However, the purposes of the two projects differed significantly. The hotel in Phnom Penh was a 'real economic activity', meaning that the company invested substantial resources to make it profitable. In contrast, the development in Siem Reap was purely a financial investment. No particular effort was expended to make it function well, because the only source of profits was expected to be the increase in the value of the company stock. In this case, Siem Reap's urban fabric was in effect treated as a façade for the investors' financial tactics.

The analysis of negotiations and shadow zones in the area of construction and land ownership shows that the seeds of unbridled liberalization are to be found in the technical intelligence, which makes the negotiation of law possible. Developers operate within a network of personal acquaintances, which they build on or consolidate in order to implement their projects. They act according to a set of rules established less by law and more by shared behaviours viewed as acceptable. Actions are accepted if they do not openly compromise the rule of law, since that would negate the credibility of the Cambodian state. Actions are rejected if they would undermine the fundamental principles of Cambodian law, such as the right to own land. By restricting land rights, Cambodians maintain their power over profitable land while negotiating the conditions under which both foreigners and Cambodian citizens take advantage of tourism and urban development. By only compiling investment statistics, the CDC presents a façade of

Table 3.2 Statistics of tourism investment compiled by the CDC, 1995-2009

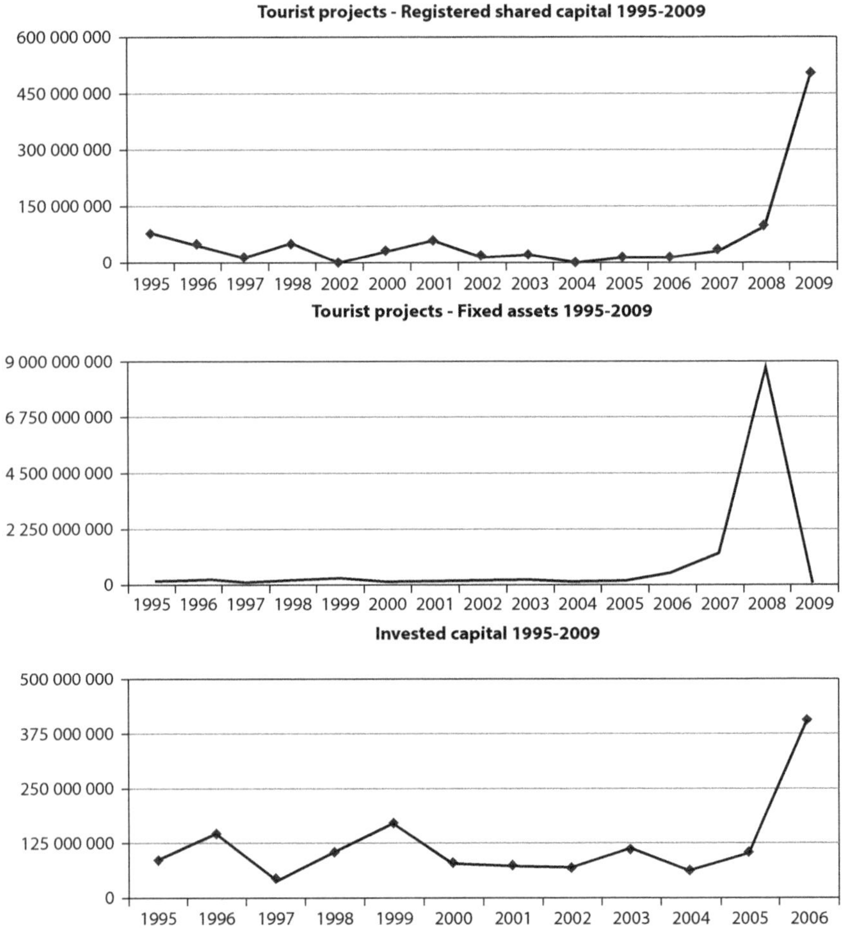

Top, registered shared capital of the projects approved by the CDC; middle, their fixed assets; bottom, invested capital (tables by the author). The term 'registered shared capital' designates the capital declared when the company was created. It assumes that the members of the company will distribute future profits proportionally but does not specify how the members will contribute to the investment costs. The term 'fixed asset' designates company assets that can be amortized. These are of three types: tangible (e.g. buildings and machines), intangible (e.g. licences), and financial (e.g. titles and deposits).
© Esposito 2011

transparency with respect to the projects it records, but this collapses as soon as an inventory of actually implemented projects reveals the discrepancy with the published statistics. From this perspective, the Cambodian state participates in the tactics adopted in the urban arena.

3.6 A dismal attempt at beautification

The international community made significant efforts to establish a liberal peace framework that combines democracy, free markets, and the rule of law (Richmond and Franks, 2007; Ojendal and Lilja, 2009). However, as in other developing countries where this framework was imported, the imposition of an external order served to create a weak state, which largely depends on foreign aid (Ear, 2006; 2009) and is subject to corruption (Richmond and Franks, 2007). Economic liberalization did not empower civil society as the international community had hoped. On the contrary, it reinforced the power of the elites (Hugues, 2003) and neopatrimonial social organizations. As in other Asian countries, economic growth through the influx of national and foreign capital was pursued as an end in itself and in spite of its social costs for the poor (Hugues and Un, 2011). In this framework, the capitalization of land has been a major source of profit. The reintroduction and consolidation of private property in Cambodia, especially following the enactment of the 2001 Land Law, has not made ordinary people's land tenure more secure, but instead has resulted in violent dispossession and property accumulation (Springer, 2009; Un and So, 2011). Speculation, dubious land title procurements, and forced evictions have marked the country's economic liberalization, with the massive sell-off of 45 per cent of the nation's land to private investors between 1993 and 2009. Since the new Land Law was enacted in 2001, land conflicts have gradually increased in number. Many concern rural land that has become the object of land grabs (Schneider, 2011) and economic land concessions to political elites and foreign investors (Neef, Touch and Chiengthong, 2013; Oldenburg and Neef, 2013). Even though Cambodian legislation includes 'communal land titles' that would allow villagers to collectively manage land, this possibility is limited to indigenous communities that have been legally recognized as such (Baird, 2013; Keating, 2013; Milne, 2013). In the years following the passage of the 2001 Land Law, ten thousand Cambodians were forced off state land that had been privatized or acquired by high-ranking officials. In 2009 alone, Cambodia experienced at least 27 forced evictions of entire neighbourhoods or villages, and the royal government gave 124,000 hectares of land in concessions to nineteen companies (Schneider, 2011). With the aim of widely improving security of tenure, the World Bank sponsored a project of systematic land titling (2002-2009). However, the project mainly targeted areas where people's tenure was already quite secure. It neglected areas where disputes were likely and areas that were covered by large economic land concessions (ELC) (Dwyer, 2015). The poorest and most socially disadvantaged households are the easiest victims of land grabs, forced eviction (Beng Hong and Payne, 2004), low financial compensation, and unattractive relocation in the cities' peripheries (Rabé, 2004; Blot, 2013, 2014; Fauveaud, 2015a).

In the course of my fieldwork between 2005 and 2015, I saw many houses disappear in Siem Reap: wooden houses, houses made of bamboo and scrap metal, houses perched on stilts, and houses of poor families built directly on the ground out of straw and waste materials. Some of them were destroyed overnight. It sometimes happened that no new building replaced them, and the land stayed vacant with only sticks to mark its boundaries. I was struck by the lack of information on these evictions, and contacted an NGO, based in Siem Reap, working on numerous cases of eviction across the country, hoping to get some understanding of this issue.

The NGO staff invited me to visit their headquarters. I reached the villa on the outskirts of town, where unpaved roads had been created to keep up with construction activity. When I came in, six or seven people were sitting around a big oval table, each with a notepad and glass of water. They invited me to sit and have some water, and calmly waited for my questions. Slightly intimidated by the number of people and their polite manners, I started to explain that I was conducting research on the urban development of Siem Reap and was surprised by the lack of information about the sudden disappearance of dozens of houses, especially in the town's periphery and main thoroughfares, where they were often replaced by hotels and other tourism facilities. I had observed that the press said nothing and the authorities were unavailable to speak to me. As soon as I asked this question, the atmosphere in the room became tense. My impression was that the NGO staff were offended. One of them acted as spokesman, while the others remained silent. He said that the NGO did not investigate any issues concerning the city of Siem Reap. I had the impression that this brief answer was meant to cut off further discussion or response on my part; however, I made bold to reply that the NGO was based in Siem Reap, and as they were all interested in helping the poor and the disadvantaged they could not be blind to the rapid changes of Siem Reap's social landscape. The same person replied, in a controlled, determined, but nervous tone of voice: he told me that no information was available on the displacement of these people, and that, in any case, it was not possible to talk about eviction in such cases, because the owners of the hotels and tourism facilities all possessed regular land titles. I was then asked to leave the room.

This was the shortest personal interaction I have ever had during my fieldwork, and the only one conducted without an exchange of smiles. For a long time I viewed this interview as the biggest mistake of my fieldwork:

Didn't I push hard enough? Didn't I ask the right questions? After I overcame my disappointment, however, I realized that such stiff resistance to communication was a source of information in itself, as it betrayed the tensions surrounding the taboo subject of eviction in Siem Reap.

Cases of eviction have become a matter of public knowledge in other parts of rural and urban Cambodia, whenever the resident community has been strong enough to put up resistance with the support of local activists (Hugues, 2008; Brickell, 2013; Sokphea, 2015). Researchers have given wide attention to these cases (inter alia Hugues, 2007; Springer, 2013a, 2013b; Kheang Un and Sokbunthoeun So, 2011, Formosa and Stock, 2016). In particular, Rabé (2009) has described how international organizations, coalitions, networks, and associations became involved in land management issues in Cambodia. He has traced the development of locally based legal rights groups such as LICADHO (Cambodian League for the Promotion and Defense of Human Rights) and ADHOC (Cambodian Human Rights and Development Association). Baird (2017) has recently shown how local forms of resistance to evictions resulting from extensive economic concessions on agricultural land may also not rely on organized activism or international NGOs. They can also be based on contingent reactions by local leaders or villages, grounded in narratives drawing on history, identity, and geography.

USAID estimated that 153,584 people were affected by land conflicts in 2005, whilst Amnesty International calculated that as many as 150,000 people were living under threat of eviction in 2008 (Un and So, 2011). However, these figures only tell part of the story. As Springer notes (2013), only a few of those forced to leave the land they occupy can be said to have been forcibly evicted by internationally accepted definitions. Significantly, Amnesty International does not view the displacement of people performed in accordance with the law, or in conformity with provisions of international human rights treaties, to be forced evictions. Since the vast majority of forced resettlements in Cambodia are performed through legal means, it can be said that national law authorizes 'institutionalized forms of violence' (Springer, 2013), which obscure a great many removals which are not acknowledged as evictions. In Siem Reap many people were simply swept away without a trace. This silence exposes their fundamental weakness in the face of the law of the market. Many of these vulnerable people used to occupy state land or had not carried out the legal procedures of land registration, and for this reason could not claim rights over it. The system of land transfer further disempowers them. Un and So (2011) describe it as 'quasi-formal' because it involves local authorities but is not recognized under the current Land Law. It is the product of the pre-war two-tier land management system, which reserved proper land ownership rights to a minority, while the majority of urban dwellers spontaneously occupied state land on which they could only acquire temporary possession status (Carrier, 2007, 2009). Under the 1992 Land Law, citizens were entitled to request the conversion of possession rights into ownership for residential purposes, based on durable and undisturbed occupancy of a land plot (Clerc, 2010). This measure was formally aimed at encouraging the stabilization of land occupation and protecting the population. However, 'because of bureaucratic red tape, corruption, fees and taxes [...] the legally required ownership transfer procedure' was not systematically followed. As in the past, a visit to the communal office was enough to confirm the transfer of rights from possession to ownership (Un and So, 2011, p. 305). However, this procedure does not ensure sufficient protection of the occupants: a developer can secure a regular land ownership title on a land plot where a 'quasi-formal' procedure has previously been carried out. Residents are sometimes uninformed about security of tenure: 'a majority of the people believe that if they are occupying land without conflict or controversy it is legally theirs, irrespective of whether they formally possess land papers' (Sophal, Saravy and Acharya, 2002, quoted by Rabé, 2009). However, Springer (2013) argues that, in these cases, 'evictees have virtually no recourse, as their "ownership" claims are not reflected in official documentation or legal entitlement but in traditional understandings relating to occupation, community consensus, and actual use' (p. 610). As local officials and village chiefs are often deeply enmeshed in the patronage system, which favours the ruling elites (Nissen, 2005; Roberts, 2009), these cases are not rare, especially in central urban environments where land has high market value. Inhabitants may easily be defined as 'squatters' by the authorities if they have not complied with the procedure (Rabé, 2009), or if they occupy public land that the government wishes to allocate to a new project (Roberts, 2008; Un and So, 2011). Moreover, urban dwellers have developed 'some sort of acceptance' of evictions (Blot and Spire, 2014, p. 14) because they are familiar with a history of forced displacement that started during the civil war and continued under the Khmer Rouge. When the population was finally allowed to come back to the cities during the Vietnamese occupation, it was often forced to relocate repeatedly because of housing opportunities or changes of status and use of the urban land (Fauveaud, 2015a).

In this situation, urban dwellers interiorized 'the absence of the right to hold a permanent place because of repeated coercive mobility' (Blot and Spire, 2014, p. 14).[53] In Phnom Penh, because of frequent and massive

53 Translation by the author.

evictions, urban dwellers have started to seek legal support and organize themselves as communities in order to better assert their rights (Rabé, 2009). The legal status of a community is recognized by local *sangkat* (neighbourhoods within a municipality). A community is represented by a leader who is in charge of negotiations with 'outsiders' (e.g. developers and public authorities).[54] When the community's land tenure status is uncertain its ability to resist evictions depends on various factors, including 'alliances with people's organizations, non-governmental organizations, human rights groups, political parties, and other types of organizations that may give the slum dwellers' cause more visibility' (Rabé, 2009, p. 127). Charismatic urban activists have emerged from collective fights against unfair relocations (Brickell, 2013; Formoso and Stock, 2016). In some cases, however, visibility and respect are not enough to protect them from eviction. The case of the Phnom Penh-based AB Preah Monivong Community, once established on the site of the hospital of the same name, is revealing (Rabé, 2009). Although it was awarded a Certificate of Appreciation by the municipality for being a 'model community', it faced eviction when the hospital's grounds were leased to a private company by the Ministry of the Interior in 2005 (Rabé, 2009).

In Siem Reap the situation is different, as urban dwellers have not taken part in any significant form of collective action and no neighbourhood had obtained the legal status of community by the end of 2015. Lawyers from a Cambodian NGO specializing in land rights recently reported (2015) that evictions in Siem Reap mainly affect a few households and not organized communities, which would probably be more able to fight back.[55] These lawyers justified the absence of engagement with evictions in Siem Reap by the fact that the donor sponsoring the NGO they work for gave priority to the protection of communities over individual households. This programmatic priority reveals the disconnection between the donor's philosophy and the social and political reality on the field. The NGO lawyers can consequently distance themselves from the limited outcomes of their own actions, which mainly consist of advising inhabitants about their legal rights. During both interviews, Cambodian law was used as a shield – another form of the use of legislation as a 'false front' – to protect the NGOs from attacks on their legitimacy. In this context, Siem Reap's irregular urban population appears to be at the earliest stage of collective organization

54 Rabé (2009) explains that 'the term "community" in Phnom Penh has a very specific official connotation: after an informal settlement is officially recognized and "organized" by non-governmental organizations and local authorities, the settlement is subdivided into a number of separate "communities", headed by a community leader. The size of a community depends on the settlement, and can vary from several dozen to several hundred families' (p. 304).

55 Personal communication with Cambodian lawyers, December 2015.

when compared to Phnom Penh, where NGOs and donors are more active, and is thus particularly vulnerable to relocation projects.

The eviction of a thousand families living along both banks of the Siem Reap River was the first in Siem Reap to obtain media coverage in the Anglophone press, as the inhabitants refused for many years to be relocated. The APSARA had sought to 'widen and embellish' the riverbanks ever since I first conducted fieldwork back in 2005.[56] Many of the families had originally moved to Siem Reap to find subaltern employment in the tourist industry or to open small shops. Some of them had been living along the river for 30 years. These families built their houses on very small plots with no direct access to hydraulic infrastructure. Officially, the land was the public property of the state. However, some of the residents claimed to have bought plots from individuals who purported to have rights to them. As the land title registry system was still under construction in Siem Reap, property rights were not always easy to determine. Astute individuals exploited this uncertain situation to take advantage of people of modest means with little understanding of the land management system. These people were given land titles by the false owners, which were obviously not recognized as valid by the provincial authorities. This is a current practice in Cambodia, especially in Phnom Penh, where individuals with good connections in the military, the police force, or the urban authorities squatted on public land, then subdivided it, sold it, or rented it out (Beng Hong, 2000, quoted by Rabé, 2009). Many informal residents believe that these kinds of title together with long-term and undisturbed land occupation are enough to guarantee security of tenure (Sophal, Saravy and Acharya, 2001, quoted by Rabé, 2009), until the land plot where they live is targeted for redevelopment.

The first time I went to Siem Reap as an MA student, my teachers and fellow students used to meet at an informal but popular terrace restaurant on the river, perched on tall stilts, and take pictures of these houses (Figure 3.3). Everybody in our group saw them as ingenious examples of vernacular architecture, showing how the production of space in 'informal neighborhoods' can express local know-how and innovations (Clerc, 2010). Some students drew them in order to understand how people could organize different functions within such a limited space. The inhabitants had adapted the construction patterns and spatial layout of wooden houses to the constraints of tiny dwellings. Internal spaces were arranged and rearranged for the different functions and activities taking place every day. Flexible, movable, lightweight bamboo

56 Personal communication with APSARA public officer, 2008. Similar vocabulary is used by officials interviewed by the *Phnom Penh Post* (Rann Reuy, 2009).

screens delimited the rooms. The inhabitants also occupied the tiny space between the houses and the road, using this as an extension of the house and furnishing it with hammocks and chairs. Some organized morning markets of second-hand clothes, fruit, and vegetables displayed on pieces of cloth on the ground. Others repaired bicycles and motorbikes, or opened restaurants where customers could choose a hot meal from five or six stews cooked in big pots.

Because they had no access to potable water, the residents used to take water from the river, which they boiled before drinking, and they poured waste water back into the watercourse. For this reason, the APSARA authority accused them of polluting the river. Civic officials designated this population as squatters,[57] as they had illegally settled down on public state land; the families were said to 'have lived illegally on government property, negatively affected the environment and polluted the river for many years' (Tik Kaliyann, 2013). The discursive construction of the informal population as 'squatters' echoes similar processes of social discrimination in Phnom Penh during the 1990s. In order to legitimize large-scale evictions, the municipality 'claimed that city squatters were "illegal" and labeled them as "anarchists" (*samnang Anna thibtai*) because they were allegedly occupying public and private land "to which other people already held the land titles"' (Rabé, 2009, pp. 93-94). In Siem Reap, as in Phnom Penh, informal settlements were seen as 'blots on the landscape' (Rabé, 2009, p. 108), which should be removed in order to beautify and sanitize the urban environment and make the city safer.

Rabé explains that this discourse began to change in Phnom Penh at the turn of the millennium. In 1998, the Chief of Cabinet of the municipality recognized disadvantaged groups as poor (*neak kray koh*). In 2000, Prime Minister Hun Sen replaced the term 'anarchist' by 'temporary resident' (*samnang bands asonn*) (Clerc and Rachmuhl, 2006). Even though this definition does not seem to recognize the urban poor as 'full citizens', it 'signaled progress' in public housing policy: 'the Municipality announced that it would henceforth resettle the urban poor in a more planned and orderly way, instead of by means of forced evictions' (Rabé, 2009, p. 99). Resettlements were presented as a means to reduce poverty by providing the poor with more secure land status and new houses (e.g. along river banks, railway tracks, pavements, and public parks). In some cases, the municipality committed to 'on-site slum upgrading as an alternative to resettlement of the urban poor, through its support for a multi-year United Nations technical assistance project based at the Municipality' (Rabé, 2009, p. 99). On-site

57 Civic officials used the term 'squatters' during personal communications with the author and in press interviews. See, for instance, Prak Chan Thul (2005).

pilot projects of slum upgrading were strategically used in the framework of the CPP's electoral campaign for the 2003 national elections. However, these did not provide an adequate response to the housing problems of the urban poor, due to abuses, speculation, lack of transparency, and the passivity of ordinary residents subdued by local community leaders (Rabé, 2009). Moreover, pilot projects undertaken in the course of the electoral campaign have not been followed by a consistent public housing policy.

In Siem Reap, the urban authorities continued to refer to informal urban populations as squatters during the 2000s. In an informal conversation, one public official told me that the settlements established along the Siem Reap riverbanks could not be thought of as vernacular architecture, because traditional Khmer houses were built on wide, open plots, whereas these houses were all jammed together on small pieces of land. Their residents had rural origins and were newcomers to the city, there to look for employment in the tourism sector.[58] They were not portrayed as 'poor', but as astute seekers of economic opportunity. This contradicted surveys that confirm the long-term occupation of the riverbank,[59] and aimed to discredit its occupants and justify their relocation. The official's vocabulary revolved around the oppositions of cleanliness and pollution, legality and squatting. The word 'cleaning' was associated both with the environmental purification of the river and the eviction of the people said to be responsible for the pollution, but who also tainted the positive image that the urban authorities wanted to convey to tourists. Similar campaigns of beautification had been undertaken by Governor Chea Sophara (1998-2003) in Phnom Penh, under the pretext that relocation upgraded public health and urban environmental conditions, while also improving the tourist image of the Cambodian capital (Hugues, 2003; Rabé, 2009; Fauveaud, 2015a). In contrast, low-income workers presented a tarnished image of a country with a severe absence of public housing programmes, and made social inequalities and the weakness of the Cambodian state strikingly visible. Poor urban residents, drug addicts, street children, people infected with HIV, ethnic Vietnamese houseboat communities, and sex workers have been perceived as social threats by representatives of Cambodian institutions and therefore 'removed' from the city centre. In some cases, they have been

58 Personal communication with APSARA's public spokesperson, 2008.

59 Surveys were conducted by the journalists who wrote articles concerning this case, published in *The Cambodia Daily* and *The Phnom Penh Post*. Surveys were also conducted by MA students from the Architecture School of Paris-Belleville (academic years 2004-2005 and 2005-2006), who chose these settlements as a case study and a site for designing a personal architectural and urban project. All these sources attested that some of these families had been living along the Siem Reap river for a long time.

provided with their own residential enclaves in the urban periphery, and kept out of the sight of tourists and foreign observers in order not to compromise the public and international image of Cambodia (Fauveaud, 2014b; Rabé, 2009).

The relocation of 500 families took place in 2012, funded by a US$40 million grant from the Korea International Cooperation Agency. The donor was also involved in the environmental improvement of the river. In 2013, the number of evicted families rose to 640, with 735 houses being destroyed. The displaced population received monetary compensation of 14 cents US per square metre, while the market price of land in that area was estimated at US$100-200 per square metre during the same years. They were also given US$200 per household 'as well as "unspecified assistance" in moving their belongings' (Tik Kaliyann, 2011). They were allocated land in the rural Sambour settlement, four kilometres from the city centre, where each family was given a plot on which to build a new house. The new settlement was equipped with a hospital, a school, a well, and electricity, but is not convenient for the families who used to sustain themselves by commercial and tourism activity. Relocation to remote urban peripheries is a common procedure in Cambodia. The resettlement policy for Phnom Penh launched at the beginning of the 2000s relocated informal dwellers to suburban areas intended for new developments. Evictions 'began to involve some form of compensation in the form of land, infrastructure and basic services' (Rabé, 2009, p. 102), and were presented as a way to secure the living conditions of the urban poor through complete ownership over a plot of land. In Phnom Penh as in Siem Reap, however, relocation sites remain isolated and disconnected from the city's urban dynamic.

Despite multiple inconveniences, the concession of a land plot to informal dwellers is seen as an amnesty and a gift in the eyes of Cambodian authorities, who portray these residents as immoral and inauthentic (Rabé, 2009). A local NGO tried to help the Sambour families after relocation in order to secure their land rights in the new village, but the inhabitants allegedly refused, since they believed their stability was no longer threatened in Sambour. However, the status of the allocated land plot, supposedly a governmental social concession, had not yet been authorized by law. The NGOs can only help to reduce the negative effects of relocation. The fact that the NGO could not intervene at a higher level to contest the relocation or negotiate its conditions reveals how powerless civil society organizations still are in Siem Reap, and the weakness of policies of social protection in Cambodia (Clerc, 2010).[60]

60 The action of this NGO in Siem Reap town and rural environs is limited to the analysis of land status and the assistance to peasants who would like to write letters to local authorities requesting, for instance, the improvement of the sewage and the road system.

Figure 3.3 Houses along the eastern bank of Siem Reap River

Photo by Marcel Morellec, 2005

The riverbank area that these people once occupied has been converted into a public park, funded by the French Development Agency via the APSARA authority and targeting 'road works for the development and beautification around the Siem Reap river banks' (AFD, 2009) close to three pagodas in the centre of Siem Reap. The park is actually a flat grassy space with benches, where the tourists can walk. The work consisted in the laying down of pavements and 1,100 metres of paved road, and the planting of 950 trees. Paradoxically, the tourists whom the urban authority sought to please used to take pictures of the lively, dense human settlement because they immediately connected it with images of tropical, exotic village environments (see Chapter 4), but now they rarely dare to take the walk that the APSARA has created for them. This walk is indeed far from pleasant, with motorbikes racing a few metres away and frequent interruptions at road intersections. Such a dismal attempt at beautification has served no purpose except to fulfil the APSARA authority's desire to convey an image of beauty and order and to exercise control over the urban space (Hugues, 2003; Rabé, 2009). However, in Siem Reap, where processes of urban development are largely driven by voracious market forces, APSARA

Figure 3.4 Maps of the applications for building permits for all types of project and for tourist accommodation and facilities issued between 2000 and 2009

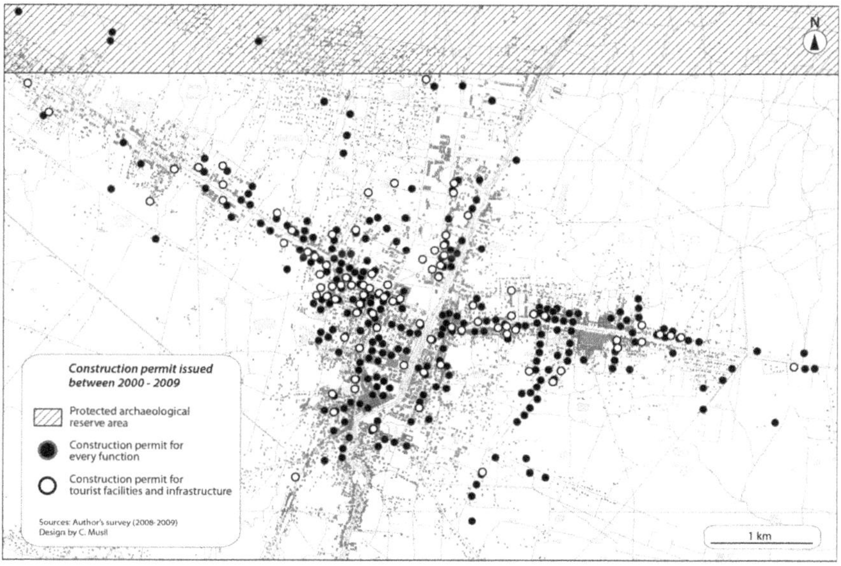

© Esposito 2016

is only able to play its part as an urban authority in the interstitial space of the Siem Reap riverbanks.

3.7 Material effects: Processes and impacts of urban development

Moving from tactics to the physical city, this section explores the way development has transformed Siem Reap's urban landscape. Tourism has played an important role in driving construction: 35 per cent of the building permits at the provincial level and 87 per cent at the national level have concerned tourist accommodation and facilities (Figures 3.4).[61] My analysis here focuses on major building and urban planning projects, sponsored by

61 As explained earlier, however, these building permits represent only part of the overall tourism-related construction in the town, as 28 per cent of the hotels and 71 per cent of the guesthouses operating in Siem Reap in 2008 were not included among the applications for building permits at either the provincial or national level.

Figure 3.5 10 January 1979 High School before transformation

Photo by the author, 2005

national or foreign capital, which have had the most drastic consequences, erasing large parts of the urban heritage.

3.7.1 The administrative district and Sivatha Road

The administrative district was the core of Siem Reap's local government. It was built between the 1920s and 1930s by the French Protectorate. It is bordered to the north by National Highway No. 6, to the west by Sivatha Road, to the east by the river, and to the south by the commercial district, also dating from the colonial period (see Chapter 1). In the 1990s, after fifteen years without regular maintenance, the district showed some physical deterioration. Vegetation had invaded the road, the road surface was damaged, and some buildings were decrepit. However, no urban rehabilitation was undertaken. The local government[62] gradually re-entered the abandoned buildings. The former post office was leased to a hotel company which

62 That is, the provincial offices and the great majority of the provincial branches of Cambodian ministries.

converted it into one of the first restaurants and high-grade hotels in the city, the Foreign Correspondent Club, headquarters of the expatriate community in Siem Reap. At the beginning of the twenty-first century, the land occupied by the administrative district was still publicly owned by the state. However, the entire area was then sold to one person,[63] who divided it into several plots which he sold to several developers. Dramatic spatial and functional transformation followed.

A first type of transformation concerned the reduction of the land area available for public facilities. The 10 January 1979 High School is a case in point. The first time I visited this school in 2005, it occupied a large plot in the administrative district. The main hall, built of concrete, was complemented by bamboo and wooden buildings surrounding a large, planted courtyard. A few years later, the section of the school's land that ran along Sivatha Road became private land and was used to build a complex of shophouses. The bamboo and wooden buildings (Figure 3.5) were demolished, new concrete classrooms were built in the remaining space, and the courtyard became narrower.

The second type concerned the replacement of public facilities and the eviction of informal markets in order to increase the commercial area available for sale or rent. The central market (Phsar Kandal) was completely rebuilt: rows of concrete shophouses border the roads and surround two market halls built of steel. Individual spaces inside the shaded halls were leased to merchants who try to attract tourists with extensive displays of similar souvenirs. The vegetable and fruit markets which used to occupy vacant plots and waste land under old parasols were evicted and replaced by blocks of shophouses organized around a new grid of right-angled roads. In the past, local families used to build their shophouses (or a small number of shophouse units) where they lived and engaged in commercial activity. In the new context of the market economy and increasing investment, developers built and rented out blocks of identical shophouses, as part of the process of commercial growth in the developing city. New shopkeepers opened travel agencies, souvenir shops, shoe shops, fast-food restaurants, and a number of commercial activities targeting tourists as well as the emerging Cambodian middle class. In the next few years, the tenants appropriated the built space of the shophouses, diversifying the decoration of the homogeneous urban façade and occupying adjacent public space. They extended their shops onto the pavements and put up large, brightly coloured roadside hoardings. At

63 Personal communication from a hotel developer established in the area of the administrative district, 2008.

Figure 3.6 Shophouses along Sivatha Road

Photo by the author, 2008

the same time, the APSARA authority disliked the concrete façade along the road, and planted a row of trees on the pavements, designed to hide it once they had grown enough (Figure 3.6).

During the 1990s, people had illegally built makeshift houses on available plots or on waste land on the edges of plots in the administrative district. They later left, leaving the space to several hotels that imitated the style, low height, and large gardens of colonial architecture. More recent hotels and condominiums, however, preferred more profitable compact five-storey buildings without interior courtyards. Between 2013 and 2015, the first hotel apartments began to offer short- or long-term rental opportunities to tourists and foreigners, and several art galleries and expensive craft shops were opened. Without following an overall planning strategy, the district has reproduced some of the characteristics that the French planners initially envisioned for the Hotel City, such as low-rise architecture, dense vegetation, and up-scale facilities. In this process of total reconfiguration, the road grid and the organization of plots of land were maintained; only a few plots were subdivided into smaller properties. The heritage of French urban planning is still visible in the organization of the road grid and the shapes of the plots, even though some administrative buildings were converted into hotels (Figure 3.7).

Figure 3.7 The evolution of land use in the administrative district, 2009 and 2015

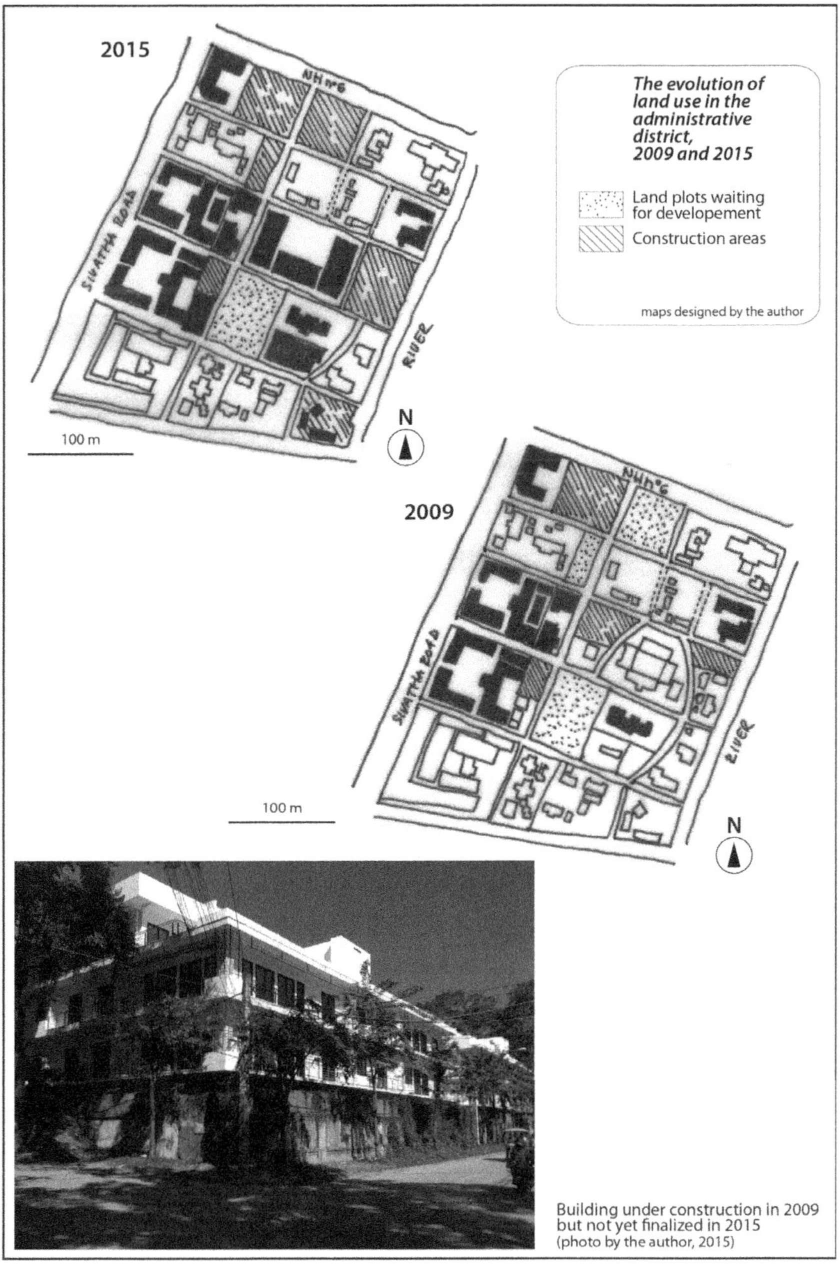

Building under construction in 2009 but not yet finalized in 2015
(photo by the author, 2015)

Map by the author; © Esposito 2016

Figure 3.8 Somadevi Hotel, Sivatha Road

Photo by the author, 2007

Along Sivatha Road, new hotels were built in the rear section of the plot. Two of them, the Somadevi Hotel and Prince d'Angkor Hotel, adopted the same construction model, which maximizes the benefits of the economic exploitation of the land. On the other side of a courtyard used as a parking area, an urban façade of concrete shophouses faces the commercial thoroughfare. These shophouses have been rented out to shopkeepers, providing regular, fast profits to the hotel developer. A large gate, with giant sculptures surrounding the name of the hotel on a huge sign, marks the entrance of each hotel. Each building is a massive five-storey block. Pillars, vaguely reminiscent of Greek architecture, subdivide them into identical units with balconies and French windows. Each hotel's lateral wings surround a second courtyard with a swimming pool and a bar, separated from the dilapidated urban environment of the administrative district by a tiny wall (Figure 3.8).[64]

64 Developers also found another way to maximize economic benefits through the coexistence of commercial and tourism functions on the same plot: they built shophouses on the ground floor of a hotel.

The construction of the first supermarkets and shopping malls of Siem Reap confirmed the commercial purpose of Sivatha Road. Angkor Market attracts the expatriate population looking for products from their home towns, while the upscale Lucky Market, with its boutiques selling expensive brands, arouses the curiosity of the town residents, who stroll along its alleyways without being able to buy anything. Along Sivatha Road the first imitation McDonald's was opened, where young people crowd in order to experience a taste of this symbol of modernity.

The removal of the local government offices followed in 2010. By order of the former Siem Reap governor, approximately one thousand civil servants were relocated to a new administrative centre in Ampil, some twenty kilometres from Siem Reap. The buildings they had occupied were allocated to a company which then constructed the 26 buildings of the new 42-hectare administrative headquarters. Land swapping is a current practice in Cambodia: 'through this mechanism private developers purchase or swap well-located public properties in the city centre in exchange for land and new construction for public authorities in the urban periphery, where these companies have large land banks. [...] Many of the swaps entail the sale and subsequent destruction of historic properties and the relocation of public institutions' (Rabé, 2009, pp. 133-134).

However, once Siem Reap province got a new governor, the decision was revoked. The civil servants had complained about the new location, which was too far away from their homes and obliged them to pay transport expenses that ate into their already low wages. Consequently, the provincial offices were allocated a new building in the Hotel City area, which had been meant to house the APSARA authority. The APSARA staff were, in turn, required to move to the isolated headquarters (Phorn Bopha, 2013), but were then once again relocated in the Hotel City area. Political change can lead to drastic reconfigurations because new alliances will be formed. The displacement of the local government offices from the centre of Siem Reap to its periphery is a clear symptom of the conversion and commodification of the city centre for tourism and commerce. Developers and civil servants do not perceive the centre as the hub of political life and social services for the local population.[65] They imagine it rather as a prime commercial location, the source of substantial economic benefit. The neoliberal frenzy has marginalized

65 This conception even led to threatening the removal of the provincial hospital, located on a plot separating the administrative from the commercial district, which provides basic health care to Siem Reap's population, in favour of another commercial complex.

the identity of Siem Reap as a city in the etymological sense of *civitas*, the political and civic association of the citizens, instead emphasizing its role as a place of consumption.

3.7.2 National Highway No. 6 (East)

The French Protectorate built National Highway No. 6 in order to connect Siem Reap with Thailand in the west and Phnom Penh in the east. During the twentieth century, urbanization took place along this road in both directions. Between the 1940s and 1970s, villages originally at a distance from the road started to expand to be closer to it. Wooden houses were linked to the road by dirt tracks near the Siem Reap River.[66]

When the Cambodian population was allowed to go back to the city at the beginning of the 1980s, the Old Market remained abandoned for security reasons, and new markets were established at the edge of the city (Hétreau-Pottier, 2008).[67] The Phsar Leu ('the upper market') emerged spontaneously on the merchants' initiative and gradually grew as new sellers arrived, until the provincial authorities built the first market hall in concrete and steel. This market attracts customers from all over Siem Reap province, from dawn to dusk. Even at night, street restaurants and vendors sell hot meals and fruit in front of the market hall.

The Phsar Leu triggered the urbanization of the surrounding areas. Inhabitants built their houses close to the market. Their wooden houses, wooden shophouses, and concrete villas formed a heterogeneous urban landscape that increased in density over time. One- and two-storey wooden shophouses surrounded the market hall (Figure 3.9). Behind them, dirt tracks connected two other rows of mixed buildings and led to the rice fields and open land. This neighbourhood has become the most dense centre of local life in Siem Reap, but few tourists set foot there. The market hall lacks basic safety and hygiene provision. The interior space is organized by types of product: gold and silver in the very centre, surrounded by tailors, household products, and hairdressers. Vegetable and fruit displays are located outside the market under canvas roofs and sunshades. Meat and fish are sold in the rear on big wooden tables, with no cooling system except for large blocks

66 As visible on the map designed by ARTE-BCEOM: Royaume du Cambodge, Conseil Supérieur de la Culture Nationale, Autorité APSARA. Etude du Plan d'Urbanisme de Siem Reap, ARTE-BCEOM. *Plan Siemreap-Angkor 1962-1994* (IPRAUS Archives, Paris).

67 During the same years, another market, the Phsar Kraom ('the low market') was established on the southern periphery of Siem Reap.

of ice chopped into small pieces on top of the coolers, often with the same knives used to cut up meat and fish. The narrow roads surrounding the market are often crowded, especially in the mornings and early afternoons, when people shop and load their bags onto the backs of motorbikes. Women selling their modest production of vegetables and fruit display their wares on pieces of cloth spread on the ground.

Some fifty metres away from the market hall, shophouses, and wooden houses on stilts made up a hybrid residential zone. Shared courtyards and water retention ponds were interspersed throughout the area. Not far away from these rows of houses built along winding dirt tracks, vegetation became denser and houses developed around low land that was periodically flooded during the wet season. This hybrid zone started to change between 2005 and 2009, when the neighbourhood began to display signs of improving economic conditions. As soon as families had enough money, concrete shophouses replaced the wooden ones. Empty plots were occupied by individual villas built of concrete, while several flooded areas were backfilled in order to be usable for construction.[68] The urban-rural frontier moved further and further away. New buildings were constructed along the roads that lead from the market to the southern axial road on the urban periphery.

The presence of the market has also triggered the urbanization of National Highway No. 6, from the city centre outwards in the direction of the Phsar Leu. A tightly packed row of concrete shophouses was built between the 1990s and 2000s, with a wide range of goods intended for Cambodian customers. Some hotels and guesthouses were built on this side of the road, mainly for Cambodian tourists and groups of visitors from other Asian countries. The space separating the buildings from the road (approximately seven metres wide[69]) is not used as a pedestrian pavement but for parking vehicles or as an extension of the commercial activity. These uses produce a gradual transition from the private interior spaces of the buildings to the public space of the road, which characterizes the urbanism of many Southeast Asian cities (Gibert, 2014; Kurfürst, 2011). The few tourists who dare to walk in the hot sun to explore the city have to zigzag uncomfortably among cars, motorbikes, tables, and merchandise displays, dangerously close to the urban traffic. Behind this compact urban façade, the forms of the buildings

68 This process of backfilling creates flooding problems in Siem Reap. As monsoon water cannot be collected in ponds and drained through connecting canals, which are also filled up, and no alternative system exists, Siem Reap is affected by frequent flooding in September and October.

69 Author's survey, 2008.

still recall those of the villages, and after two or three rows of houses the dirt tracks peter out in open spaces, waste land, flooded plots, orchards, and rice fields (Figure 3.10).

Beyond the Phsar Leu market, urbanization stretches towards the east. A huge hotel with the highest tower in Siem Reap imitates the towers of the Angkor temples. Standing at the intersection with the wide avenue that was supposed to lead to the never completed Hotel City, it seems to reflect the owners' desire to be as close as possible to the new tourism centre (Figure 3.11). Beyond this avenue, project implementation follows the rapid pace of land transactions.

New neighbourhoods have been built here from scratch in the course of a few years. Developers have bought and combined available plots, forming irregular areas where they build water and transport infrastructures. In some cases, they directly build hundreds of shophouses; in others, they sell prepared land plots where new owners can build their own individual shophouses in one of a series of allowed building types. Developers call these new neighbourhoods *borey*. The term derives from a Sanskrit toponymic affix designating cities or other urban spaces. It later became a separate word in Khmer, but there is no consensus about its origins and exact meaning. Fauveaud (2015b) notes that for many Cambodians the term designates the ancient Khmer capitals. For others, it is a bounded, rectangular inhabited space, sometimes surrounded by walls. A third definition associates the *borey* with ancient toponyms no longer used in Khmer.

After Cambodian independence the word was used for residential areas or groups of public facilities. Then, during the Vietnamese occupation of 1979-1980, it referred to public administrations and their residential estates where public officials lived. The contemporary meaning of the word as a housing complex probably stems from this period. Since the end of the 1990s, Cambodian developers have increasingly used the word and disseminated it across the whole country. The *borey* has come to designate residential developments composed of a dozen to several hundred shophouses. They are generally built by a single developer and are distinguished from the rest of the city by their spatial separation, independent services, and systems of management run by the developer himself. With the increase in the number and surface area of satellite cities in Phnom Penh in the decade of the 2000s, a sub-decree in 2011 regulated the duties and rights of *borey* developers. It also homogenized construction standards and encouraged cooperation between local authorities and developers.

Fauveaud (2015b) claims that *borey* have become a new urban model (*référence résidentielle*) in Cambodia, drawing on local urban knowledge

Figure 3.9 Shophouses surrounding the Phsar Leu Market

Photo by the author, 2008

Figure 3.10 Urban landscape along National Highway No. 6

Photo by the author, 2008

and practices. The main construction unit is indeed the shophouse, which developed in Cambodia at the beginning of the twentieth century. His claim calls into question the deeply rooted paradigm of dependence which assumes unidirectional transfer of urban models from Western countries to Southeast Asia. *Borey* negotiate international models via local urban practices, reflected in both the normalization of the construction activity and the diversification of the types of development across the country.

In Siem Reap groups of shophouses started to be built at the beginning of the decade of the 2000s and, as in Phnom Penh, real estate offerings gradually became diversified. Developers started to introduce educational, commercial, and leisure facilities in the complexes they called *borey*. The first one was Borey Seng Nam, whose construction started in 2004. It was developed by a Cambodian citizen along National Highway No. 6 (Figure 3.12). Shophouses were built along the main artery of the *borey* connected to National Highway No. 6. The other plots were sold to the new residents, who built their own houses, choosing among five possible pre-determined plot layouts. The developer also built urban infrastructure and installed basic services, including the market. In doing so, he replaced the local authorities, who, in spite of their supposed role as the regulator of urban development, failed to install infrastructure for future urbanization or to make social services available. He did not hesitate to take on this role, because the infrastructure increased the value of the plots and enabled him to profit from the sale of empty land to new residents in an area at the edge of the existing city. Similarly, in Phnom Penh, developers play an important part in the development of infrastructure and the daily management of the urban complexes. They often become 'sociopolitical referents' within the new urban spaces, dealing with a substantial amount of the administrative and management tasks normally carried out by public authorities (Fauveaud 2015b). The transfer of public powers to private parties who actually deliver better services than the local authorities contributes to the increased independence of the *borey* from the rest of the urban environment and to the perception that they are desirable places to live.

A French-Cambodian joint venture developed another urban satellite called Borey Sokleap (Figure 3.13). Construction started in 2008 on a 30-hectare plot. The whole project consisted of 600 shophouses, a cinema, a school, a market, guesthouses, condominiums, and public gardens. The developers designed a single model of shophouse which was reproduced in the entire development, the only variation being in the patterns available for the decoration of the façades. The joint venture's programme called for 300 shophouses to be built during the first phase of development, and the other 300 in the following five-month period. In July 2008, about six months after the start of construction, half of the shophouses had already been sold although construction was still incomplete. In the meantime, the value of the property had increased: when construction began, one shophouse cost approximately US$60,000, rising to US$80,000 for the same unit later in the same year. In 2015, however, only the western part of the plot had been developed with shophouses and no collective facilities had yet been constructed. The progression is similar to *borey* developments in Phnom Penh, where investors split up their development programme in successive phases, to be implemented only if the previous ones are successful. Collective facilities are usually left to last, even though they are invoked as major inducements from the beginning of the project. This tactic is used to reduce risk in the Cambodian situation, which is seen as volatile and unstable (Fauveaud, 2015b).

At Borey Sokleap, the residential estate lies along one main road with a gate at the entrance; however, a passageway for motorbikes (the most common mode of transportation for Siem Reap's residents) is always left open, and the guards passively look on as people pass through. The closing off of *borey* complexes also occurs in Phnom Penh (Fauveaud, 2015b). It is seen as a positive asset that attracts a relatively wealthy population looking for security and exclusivity. More broadly, the closing off of residential estates seems to be a general tendency in contemporary cities, inspired by the North American model of the gated community[70] now rapidly expanding in East and Southeast Asia (Leisch, 2002). Fauveaud (2015b), however, argues that *borey* are contextualized products that redefine local ways of living, the managing of residential spaces, and the relationship between inhabitants, developers, and local authorities.

As in Phnom Penh, Siem Reap's local authorities have been ready to define *borey* in legal terms. In a 2008 sub-decree, the APSARA authority called these developments 'satellites',[71] a word that suggests both their isolation in the midst of open fields and their connection to the city via the main roads. However, as the aforementioned cases reveal, *borey* built in Siem Reap sometimes include no public facilities, in spite of the objectives established in construction programmes. Also, the spatial and management mechanisms for ensuring security are only imperfectly implemented. I would argue that *borey*, as developed in Siem Reap, implement the urban model 'in a minor

70 A gated community generally designates a residential enclave with control systems at the entrance gates, in which public space is privatized.

71 Sub-decree No. 50/ANK/BK, art. 16, 'on the organization and functioning of the General Direction of the APSARA authority'.

Figure 3.11 The hotel with the highest pinnacle in town

Photo by the author, 2009

Figure 3.12 Road to nowhere: the main avenue of Borey Seang Nam

Photo by the author, 2015

Figure 3.13 Shophouses at Borey Sokleap

Photo by the author, 2015

mode'. Following Franck, Goldblum, and Taillard (2012), who argue that secondary cities display features of metropolization without becoming metropolises, I believe that local implementation of the new urban model leads to the imperfect adaptation of spatial forms and management practices, and pays more attention to formal resemblance than to effective function.

3.7.3 National Highway No. 6 (West)

Property price inflation played an important role in the urbanization of the section of National Highway No. 6 leading to the Siem Reap airport, where a number of hotels and tourism facilities were built to increase the value of the land. Before the advent of tourism, wooden and bamboo houses were built at some distance from the highway, with trees and ponds characterizing its landscape. New developments erased this landscape and backfilled the ponds in order to increase the surface of usable land.

Along this section of the highway, several 'urban sequences' with specific characteristics can be recognized. The first one was developed along the edge of the administrative district. The Grand Hotel and its gardens, built at the end of the 1920s, face the royal residence, followed by densely packed and formally heterogeneous shophouses housing small tourist restaurants and services. After the intersection with Sivatha Road, large-scale hotels are the most common architectural feature of the urban landscape. In the interstices of the hotel sites, some older buildings and shophouses survive, with their ponds and surrounding greenery (Figure 3.14).

When I saw these massive hotels on my first trip to Siem Reap, I instinctively compared them to a big, clumsy papier-mâché stage set. They all follow the same architectural model and spatial layout, with slight variations in the colours of the façades and the size and shape of the sites (see Chapter 4). They are huge compared to the average buildings of Siem Reap. For this reason, they look artificial, as if they came from another world and had been dumped onto this green, rural environment. At the same time, the cheap materials, shoddy construction techniques, and over-sized decoration call to mind a theatre set and convey a sense of fragility.

In front of each hotel building a lawn and an open space for cars to drop off clients marks the transition between the public space of the highway and the private space of the hotel. Each building is a massive block of four or five storeys. Due to height limitations,[72] the buildings extend horizontally in order to increase the number of rooms. Building a big hotel is proportionately less expensive in terms of construction costs per unit than building a smaller one. For this reason, the size of the hotel is not directly related to projections of average occupancy rates, but to the available capital to be invested in the construction. Like the hotels along Sivatha Road, all the buildings use the same basic construction module, formed by two pillars or columns on each side of a window or balcony. Differences among the hotels are confined to the façade decorations and shape of the entrance gates. The hotel roofs often imitate pagoda or temple roofs, but increase the dimensions of their traditional construction and decorative elements in order to fit the larger surface to be covered. These giant imitations are only a clumsy echo of their architectural origins. Behind each building, a garden with a swimming pool (and sometimes a bar) faces the open fields, separated from them by a fence or a green wall. A vacant landscape surrounds these gardens, which are meant to provide a comfortable, luxurious ambiance where tourists can relax. These developments are gradually urbanizing areas where only scattered houses used to stand at the beginning of the twenty-first century. Investors bought the most valuable plots along the highway and hotels mushroomed close together. The concentration of facilities in an area where they could benefit from shared infrastructure contributed to the overall increase in land values, making the development even more profitable. However, as prices became higher and higher and plots scarcer along the

72 Height limitations are imposed by the APSARA authority and are generally respected in Siem Reap.

Figure 3.14 Urban sequences along National Highway No. 6

Photo by the author, 2015

highway, developers started to build further back, transforming dirt tracks into paved roads. Privately constructed villas, guesthouses, condominiums, and hotels urbanized the land near the highway on both sides. Speculation stimulated the process: the majority of buildings were immediately available for sale or rent. The juxtaposition of these developments produced higgledy-piggledy settlements resulting from individual initiatives, which gradually consumed the most fertile land of Siem Reap.

The hotels established along National Highway No. 6 are mostly occupied by groups of tourists who purchase tour packages including several destinations in Southeast Asia, and who stay in Siem Reap-Angkor for only a few days.[73] As soon as these tourists land at the airport they go to their hotel, which is conveniently located along the highway. They generally have their meals in restaurants along the same road, and are driven down Avenue Charles de Gaulle to reach the temples. They rarely visit Siem Reap town, except perhaps for an evening stroll if that is a scheduled part of the package tour.[74]

73 The average stay was three days and two nights for hotels along National Highway No. 6. Author's survey, 2008.

74 Personal communications with travel agents based in Siem Reap, 2007-2008.

3.7.4 Avenue Charles de Gaulle

The French Protectorate built the Avenue Charles de Gaulle as the main access to the archaeological park of Angkor.[75] Because of the low-density urbanization of the area close to the avenue at the beginning of the 1990s, the Urban Reference Plan sought to re-afforest it in order to create a protective green belt at the interface of the town and the park. However, the land along the west side of the avenue was the public property of the state and had been the object of a number of transactions and concessions. International hotel chains opened along this avenue in the early 2000s. Sofitel and Méridien respected the principle of low-density land use and surrounded their hotels with dense vegetation in order to merge them into the urban landscape. On the other side of the road, the demarcation of plots is more irregular, because construction and usage have depended on the tactics of private and small-scale landowners. The luxuriant vegetation along the east bank of the river extends into these urban settlements.

Extremely dense complexes of shophouses have thoroughly transformed the avenue's landscape in recent years. Though these complexes are smaller, their rationales are similar to those of the urban satellites built along National Highway No. 6. The Charming Tourist City is one such complex, located on a six-hectare plot at the very edge of the archaeological reserve boundary.[76] Sponsored by Canadia Bank,[77] its construction was started in 2006. Like the Khmer equivalent *borey*, 'city' suggests the desire to create a new urban centre. The name is in English, as the developers want to promote the complex not only among new Cambodian residents, but also to international clients who would be attracted by its proximity to the archaeological monuments and would stay in local guesthouses. A grid of right-angle roads structures a series of compact blocks of shophouses with façade ornamentation supposedly reminiscent of European architecture, such as bow windows, wrought-iron balconies, and carved mouldings. The shophouses were designed to attract Cambodian clients: 60 per cent were

75 In 2000, a new entrance to the archaeological park on the east side of Siem Reap was opened on the north-south route to the Hotel City.

76 Promotional materials and project application for a building permit, Siem Reap land title registry office, 2005.

77 Canadia Bank is a commercial bank established in 1991 which connects the National Bank of Cambodia with Canadian investors in the Canadia Gold and Trust Corporation. In 1993, the company's name was changed to Canadia Bank Ltd., registered as a commercial bank at the Cambodian Ministry of Commerce. In 2003, its name changed again to Canadia Bank Public Limited Company.

Figure 3.15 The Charming Tourist City

Photo by the author, 2008

bought as primary residences, and 40 per cent as investments. At the centre of the area, the market has a circular layout and the covered central hall inside it is in the shape of a snail shell. The architect who coordinated the project's design team chose this unusual shape in order to 'introduce some innovations into local architectural forms'.[78] However, few tourists visit the Charming Tourist City and the market is mainly used by local merchants selling food and everyday products to the residents who settled in the shophouses (Figure 3.15).

3.8 Urban transformation by the local people

It would be inaccurate to say that Siem Reap is entirely in the hands of the developers. Families of local residents and small-scale promoters, both Khmer and foreign, contribute to reshape long-established neighbourhoods by introducing tourism-related and commercial facilities. Families seldom have recourse to an architect, but design the projects themselves with the help of a construction company. These projects do not break completely with the city's urban heritage, but have combined inherited forms with modern functions, new criteria of comfort and taste, and new construction.

78 Personal communication with the project's architect, 2008.

I conducted fieldwork in two urban areas where individual owners have undertaken projects for the conversion of residential neighbourhoods into tourist districts with small restaurants, businesses, and accommodation facilities. The first is Wat Bo neighbourhood, where families have been living since the 1980s.[79] They opened the first guesthouses at the beginning of the 1990s, taking advantage of the economic opportunity resulting from the presence of the UNTAC delegation. Wat Bo was originally a village area bordering the Siem Reap river on the east (Figure 3.16). It took its name from the Wat Bo pagoda, which was probably built before the nineteenth century. The French administration laid out a road parallel to the river and a grid of right-angle roads was orientated on an east-west axis. During the 1960s, the Cambodian government built various administrative facilities in the area. These low buildings were surrounded by luxuriant vegetation and wooden houses on stilts.

Khmer families opened guesthouses in the wooden houses where they used to live. At that time, they offered only basic services and comforts. As soon as the families accumulated enough capital, they built individual toilets, equipped the rooms with new furniture, and improved ventilation. They sometimes hired an architect or a construction company and replaced the wooden house with a concrete building copied from a construction catalogue.[80] In other cases, the Wat Bo families built concrete additions to existing houses, in order to increase the number of guest rooms.

In the block I focused on in my survey (Figure 3.16), the families initially all owned, managed, and lived in the guesthouses, with the exception of one family who had built a new house with the sole goal of renting it out. However, competition had become very fierce: there were 150 guesthouses in Siem Reap in 2008. Some Cambodian owners preferred to rent out their guesthouses for long periods, mainly to foreigners looking for opportunities to settle and work in the town. In this way, they secured regular income (the monthly rent) and avoided the risk represented by the average low

79 I conducted my surveys in Vat Bo between 2008 and 2009. I focused on one block of buildings in the north of the neighbourhood, which shares a border with National Highway No. 6, and contains eleven guesthouses. The survey consisted in the analysis of architectural projects (renovation, new construction), extensive interviews with owners and managers, and analysis of the transformation of the layout of the area through historical maps.

80 The majority of construction activity in Cambodia draws on construction catalogues, which propose various models of buildings to be adapted to specific sites. Construction companies and architects generally discuss the characteristics of projects with owners based on these catalogues. These standardized housing models have therefore rapidly expanded in Siem Reap. Architects and construction companies copied them on request of clients and introduced only slight changes in the decoration and colours of the façades.

Figure 3.16 Wat Bo: localization map, sketch and picture of the surveyed area

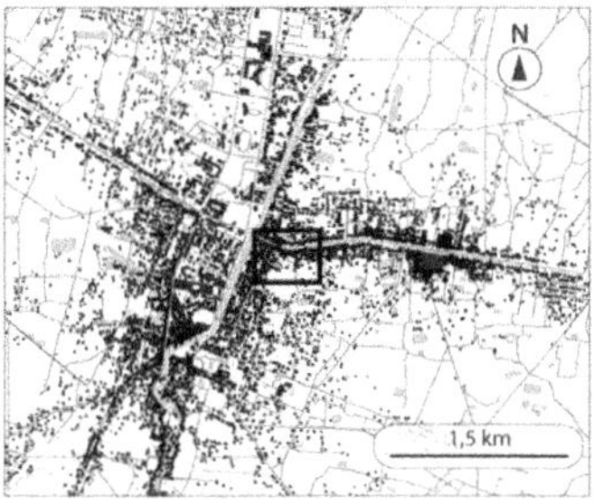

Vat Bo sector

Hybrid urban landscape at Vat Bo
A winding path passing through a block of guesthouses
(photo by the author, 2008)

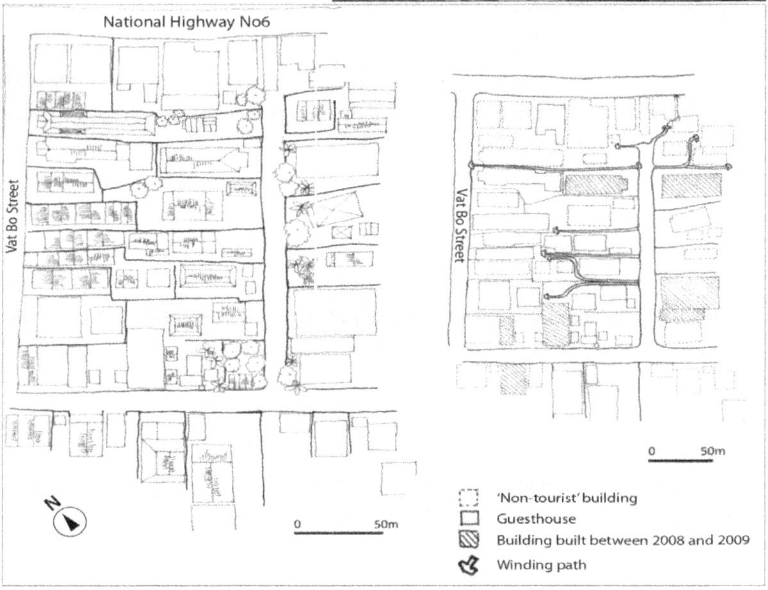

Sketch of the surveyed area in 2009 (on the left);
Functions of the buildings and winding path (on the right) (by the author, 2009)

© Esposito 2016

occupancy rates of the guesthouses.[81] Between 2004 and 2008, all but one family hired other individuals or families to manage the guesthouses in this block. Many European and Australian managers took over the guesthouses and employed young Khmer people to manage their day-to-day operations. Cambodian owners moved to the edge of the city where they could buy large plots and build big new houses. The only Cambodian family who still lived in the block built a separate house for family members. The social reshaping of the neighbourhood eliminated the defining characteristic of the typical guesthouse, the sharing of a residential space by hosts and guests.

The number of new concrete buildings and the destruction of many wooden houses transformed the neighbourhood. However, the replacement rate of the buildings was more rapid than the transformation of the urban layouts, which still maintain some of the features of a village. The vegetation was cleared from some of the plots in order to increase the buildable area. The density increased and owners built fences to mark the boundaries of their property. However, the flexible and blurred relationship between public and private spaces has been conserved, as have the system of winding dirt paths connecting with the orthogonal road grid, the dense vegetation, and the presence of farm animals. New buildings fronted on the road and blocked access to the back of some plots. Consequently, the rear rows of houses lost direct access to the main road network; only paths, sometimes too narrow for more than one person, meander among the houses and through courtyards where children play and chickens roam (Figure 3.16).

The second area where I conducted surveys is the Taphul neighbourhood, located at the intersection of National Highway No. 6 and a north-south orientated road called Taphul Road (Figure 3.17). The latter was no more than a dirt track during the 1990s. Responding to its intense use by local residents and increased commercial activity, the Ministry of Public Works widened and paved it. Along the side roads dense vegetation, scattered houses, and dirt paths still evoke a village. As in the Wat Bo area, some of the buildings have been gradually or rapidly replaced, but the landscape has maintained the hybrid mix of urban and rural features. Allison Hotel, a large-scale facility, was built on state land that was sold to a Cambodian developer. Its concrete lateral wings extend into the urban fabric and it sits close to the row of houses built along the north-south road (Figure 3.17).

I focused the surveys on a block located in the north of the Taphul neighbourhood because of the concentration of seventeen guesthouses over fewer than two hectares (Figure 3.17). At the beginning of the twenty-first century,

81 In 2010, there were 343 hotels and guesthouses in Siem Reap (Groupe 8, 2011).

owners built on plots that they had paid for in gold or purchased cheap land for US$20-30 per square metre. Subsequently, land prices substantially increased: around 2009, available plots were costing on average US$250 per square metre. Many guesthouse owners inherited land from their parents, opening the first guesthouses between 1998 and 1999. Following their encouragement, other family members acquired adjacent plots and opened new guesthouses in the 2000s. This collective strategy, based on the common perception of the tourism potential of the area, led to the concentration of a large number of guesthouses in a relatively small urban area.

Unlike Wat Bo, these owners generally reside in Taphul. In several cases, they have replaced inherited wooden houses with new buildings chosen from construction catalogues. In other cases, they have used the new buildings to house tourists, but have renovated the older houses for their own use. These families have built concrete houses only to suit what they perceived to be the tourists' desires and expectations of modern accommodation standards, but they prefer not to live in such buildings themselves, since they do not suit their lifestyle. Other families, especially those living along Taphul's main artery, have built concrete extensions to their main houses. Some owners have opened stalls built of concrete and metal sheeting, put up just in front of the family residence.

Two foreign managers (Swiss and Korean) rented houses from Khmer families, who moved to buildings on the rear sections of their plots. The foreign managers renovated the wooden houses for tourists, targeting a different market segment, namely those visitors wanting to experience local styles and living patterns. These projects inspired some other Khmer owners in the neighbourhood, who regretted having built concrete guesthouses. Innovations introduced by pioneer owners and managers have introduced models and investment strategies that other families would like to imitate. The collective practices of conversion for tourist industry purposes become established through imitation. For instance, some families opened guesthouses where relatives had already located theirs, and followed similar architectural models, which embodied ideas of innovation and modernity at a precise moment in Cambodian history. However, these ideas change quickly, and collective practices may change along with the evolution of taste and changing standards of comfort. These small-business owners are reconstructing a spatial culture in terms of architecture and urban reconfigurations in a number of ways: through hesitant experimentation, through projects that come to be seen as models to be reproduced, and through influences from abroad. This process goes through several phases of importation and appropriation. However, the availability of capital and the

Figure 3.17 Taphul: localization map, sketch and picture of the surveyed area

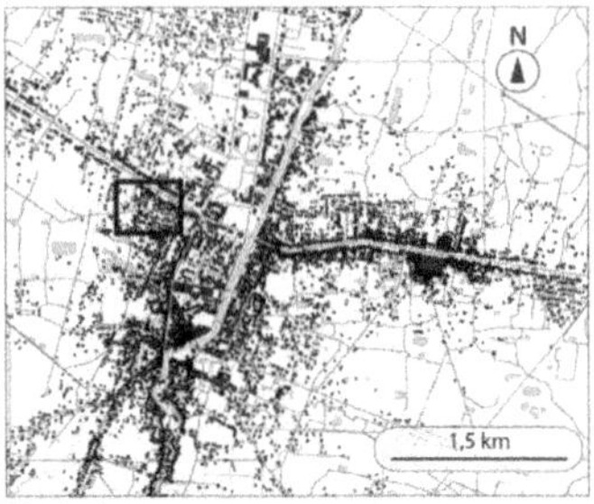

Taphul sector

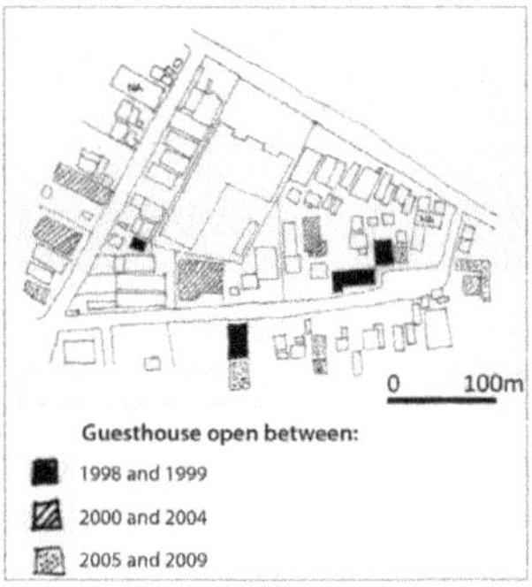

Guest-houses in the surveyed and years of construction (by the author, 2009)

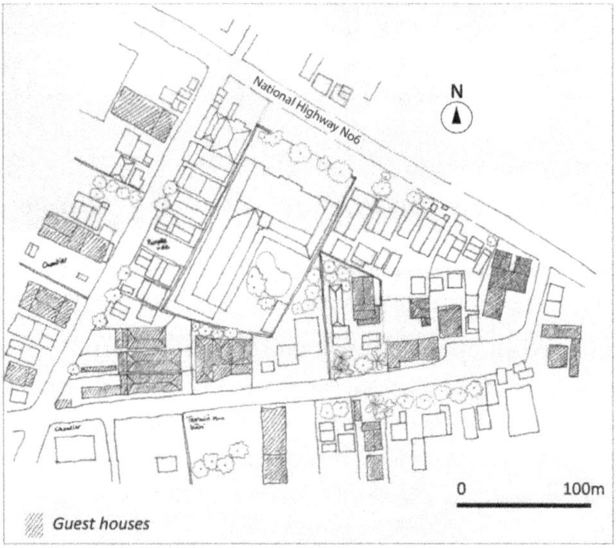

Sketch of the surveyed area in 2009 (by the author, 2009)

The Allison hotel and the other nearby features incluiding houses, guesthouses, and small shops in Taphul neighborhood (photo by the author, 2008)

© Esposito 2016

rapid growth of international tourism have produced a rush to reconstruction, which has deeply marked the urban landscape with a generation of look-alike buildings.

3.9 The trajectory of Siem Reap's urban transition

Siem Reap was a province (*kaet*) and a district (*sangkat*) before becoming a municipality in 2008. The municipality covers a surface of 47,273 hectares (including 12,287 hectares of agricultural land and 9,605 hectares of residential land) and includes thirteen communes and 108 villages with a total population of 230,000. Ten of the thirteen communes already formed part of the Siem Reap district, and the three others are former rural communes that have been added to the municipality (Figure 3.18). The recent designation of Siem Reap as a municipality is aimed at solving long-lasting problems related to overlapping jurisdictions in the field of urban development. It is acknowledged that it is experiencing rapid transition, which is transforming it into an international tourism hub.

In modern Khmer, the word for municipality is the same as that for city (*krong*). However, as shown by the figures above, Siem Reap encompasses some rural environments, that is, a number of villages and large agricultural areas. The hybrid coexistence of urban and rural configurations has characterized Southeast Asian urbanism for centuries. Nowadays, cities in the region are experiencing the growth of conurbations expanding into formerly rural areas. In 2008, the perimeter of the city of Hanoi had expanded to encompass a surface of 3344 square kilometres, two thirds of which is agricultural land; 3.7 million out of the 6.4 million inhabitants are peasants (Bui To Uyen, 2012). On a smaller scale, the recent designation of Siem Reap as a municipality illustrates a similar process. This poses questions about the idea of the city that the urban authorities aim to achieve through this administrative designation. In a decree of 2008, the APSARA authority stated that its task was to 'maintain the balance between the needs of the urban development concerning Siem Reap town and its satellites'.[82] This description conveys the idea of an urban core surrounded by an urbanized territory of scattered hubs undergoing development. The construction of three golf courses, several resorts, and a theme park on the outskirts of the city, as well as the displacement of the administrative headquarters to the

82 Sub-decree on the organization and functioning of the Directorate-General of the APSARA authority (French draft version, 8 May 2008).

Figure 3.18 Siem Reap province, district, and municipality

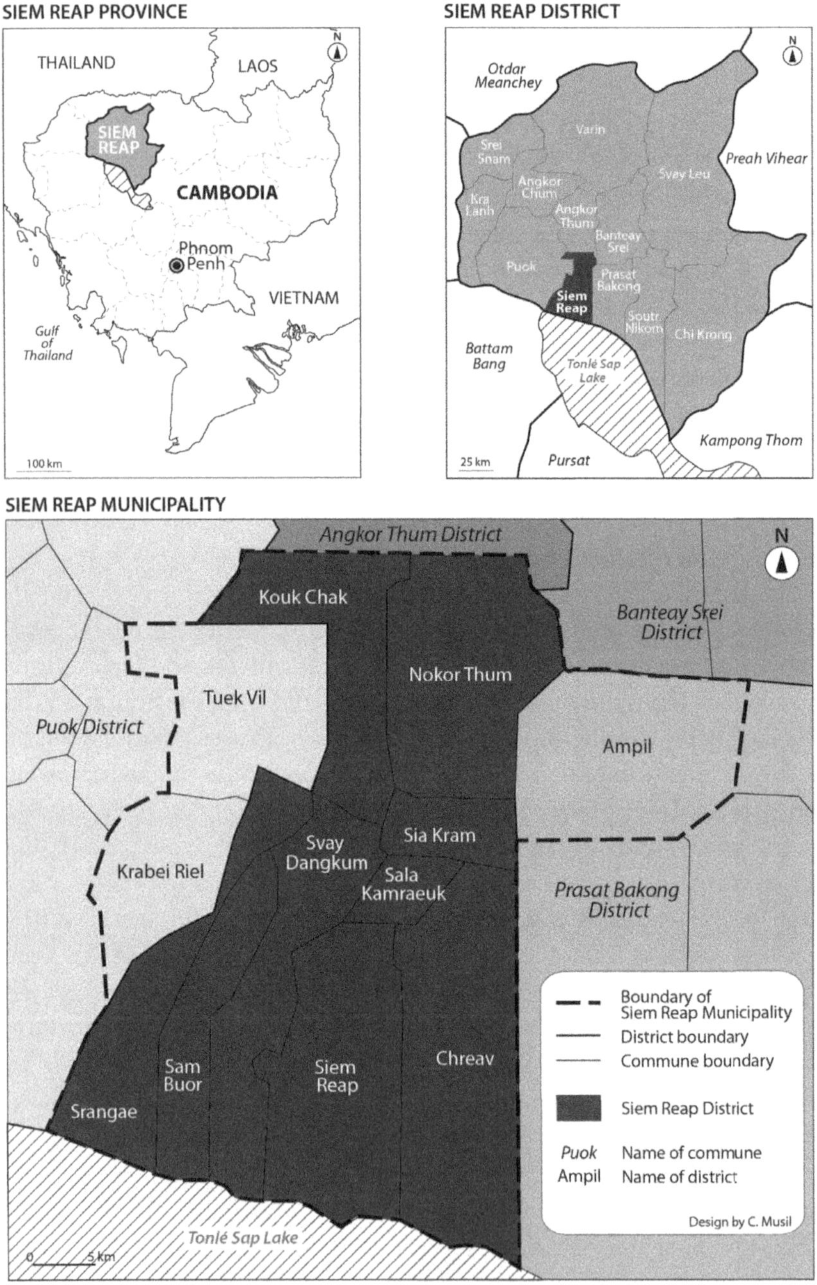

© Esposito 2016

periphery, confirms this idea. Architectural and urban projects collectively contribute to the explosion of the city into a constellation of hubs of activity, all centred on the tourist and commercial centre developed in the former colonial districts. The massive privatization of public land and market forces have been the two main drivers of these processes of urban change, and have overshadowed concern for urban identity, heritage, and the sense of belonging. Siem Reap will be what the sum total of privately managed developments will make it: this is the tacit position of the urban authorities who take the ideology of laissez-faire to extremes.

4 The architectural space

How contemporary design shapes urban identities and ideas of modernity

The previous chapter examined the conflicts between different parties that underpin the transition of Siem Reap from a village to an international tourism hub. I looked at the city as a battlefield where multiple parties strive to earn the right to implement their projects in close proximity to the archaeological site of Angkor. I analysed architectural and urban projects such as property investment, drawing attention to the economic, social, and political entanglements of urban transition. This chapter presents another perspective on the analysis of architectural and urban projects. It examines architectural design as a semiotic activity and explores the methods of production of architectural space from the point of view of the meanings and ideals that producers attribute to it (Reiner, 1982; Levy, 2008).

More particularly, I argue that contemporary architectural design in Siem Reap draws on images and narratives about Angkor and Cambodia that have been inherited from colonial times and deliver interpretations of national heritage, identity, and history.[1] Between the second half of the nineteenth century and the beginning of the twentieth, a first generation of European travellers initiated the production of images and narratives. They were naturalists, adventurers, artists, and naval officers who willingly undertook long trips for the sake of personal satisfaction or the progress of science, or were sponsored by national governments. They wrote travel narratives illustrated with photographs, maps, and engravings, which presented Angkor to the European public. Increasing European interest in Indochina was a way to build consensus about colonization; for this reason, the French colonial administration drew on these early narratives while also pursuing the production of images and narratives of its own. It organized colonial and universal exhibitions, which reproduced the monuments and typical built environments of the French colonies; it also sponsored or facilitated the production of promotional materials (tour

1 When I use the term 'image', I mean an iconographic representation of a place, object, or human landscape, such as paintings, engraving, maps, and photographs. By 'narrative', I mean a text which recounts past events or describes spatial or social realities. I use the term 'representation' to cover both images and narratives.

guides, press articles, book publications) aimed at attracting tourists to Cambodia and, more broadly, to Indochina. The various means deployed converged in the composition of a coherent narrative about the colonized territories and societies (Foley, 2006), which defined Indochina as a space of cultural production (Norindr, 1996). This chapter analyses the formation of images and narratives in colonial times through three major means – travel narratives, colonial exhibitions, and universal exhibitions – and the organization of the tourist experience through the planning of space and dissemination of tour guides. It also looks at how inherited representations were appropriated and reinterpreted at the time of the Sangkum Reastr Niyum (1955-1970), and how they influenced national programmes of tourism development.

These images and narratives played a fundamental role in forming the European idea of the region of Siem Reap-Angkor. They constructed the 'tourist gaze' (Urry, 1990), that is to say, tourists' expectations of places and societies which influence their practices, perceptions, and interpretations. Tourism promotion influences these expectations through the dissemination of images and representations that shape tourists' ideas of a place. It establishes tourism as a socially controlled practice occurring in a planned space. The construction of the tourist gaze is a collective enterprise, as parties playing different roles in tourism development (e.g. national governments, museum administrators, developers, tour operators) contribute to shaping representations and to reshaping those inherited from previous historical periods, through processes of selection, appropriation, and reinterpretation. Once on the site, the tourist's imagination looks for material evidence of the 'internal world of [...] ideas, images, myths, and fantasies' (Selwyn, 1996, p. 10), which has been constructed on the basis of images and narratives. The transformative power of representation lies in the space between it and reality: attempts are made to get tourism landscapes to conform in order to satisfy expectations.

The core of this chapter is an analysis of contemporary architectural design in Siem Reap. The power of images and narratives is particularly strong in reshaping the urban landscape of Siem Reap, for various reasons. First, Siem Reap is not the actual tourist destination, but a marginal space on the doorstep of a World Heritage Site. In order to increase its attractiveness, the tourism industry strives to recreate the environment of Angkor in Siem Reap. A stronger connection between the archaeological site and the town facilitates the expansion of tourism towards the margins of the heritage site and persuades tourists to spend more time and money in the town. Second, Siem Reap is a malleable space. At the beginning of the 1990s, wooden houses on stilts surrounded by dense vegetation and open-air infrastructure made up the urban landscape. These more natural built forms have been transformed, erased, and replaced without too much difficulty, due especially to the weak legal and administrative framework for construction and urban planning. Third, heritage recognition in Cambodia has been mainly driven by the intent to use heritage as an economic resource. In this context, developers and designers have largely drawn on inherited representations of Cambodian history, tradition, and heritage, drawn from the colonial period, which they supposed to be consistent with European tourists' perceptions of Angkor.

In the present-day creation of the tourist city, images and narratives encounter the global models and forms which underlie tourism architectural design. Originally, hotels, museums, bungalows, and theme parks were shaped by and for Westerners, but were later expanded to an international audience with the development of tourism and travel (inter alia Sanjuan et al., 2003; Giebelhausen, 2011; Kreps, 2003; Hollinshead, 2009; Clavé, 2007). They play a part in the cultural re-imagining and material shaping of Siem Reap: 150 hotels were built between 1992 and 2008 and their number never ceases to grow. Nevertheless, with a few remarkable exceptions (Sanjuan et al., 2003; Peleggi, 2005; Teo and Chang, 2009), tourism architecture has rarely been a subject of academic interest. This chapter aims to contribute to the analysis of tourism architecture as the object of convergence of various layers of meaning interconnected through local collections and combinations of architectural elements and spatial features.

4.1 Angkor: From discovery to commodity

Angkor was almost unknown to the West in the second half of the nineteenth century. Nevertheless, Portuguese and Spanish travel writers from the sixteenth century[2] had borne witness to the existence of the ancient Khmer kingdom. They had portrayed a mythical city hidden deep in the forest, which the Cambodian King Sâtha had rediscovered after the abandonment of the capital in the fifteenth century (Groslier, 1958; Chandler, 2008). In

2 During the second half of the sixteenth century, European missionaries, merchants, and adventurers were present at King Satha's court. The king surrounded himself with foreign intermediaries who helped him negotiate with the Portuguese colonizers in Malaysia and the Spanish colonizers in the Philippines. The number of Europeans at the royal court decreased in the eighteenth century in Cambodia as well as in nearby Laos and Siam (Chandler, 2000).

fact, Angkor had never been abandoned, as Khmer villagers living nearby had always taken care of the temples and viewed them as sacred places (Baille, 2007). Later, the French Sinologist Albert Rémusat translated and published the story of the visit that Tcheou Ta-Kouan, a Chinese ambassador, paid to Angkor in 1296-1297 (Fournereau and Porcher, 1890). This work, which included a vivid description of the daily life, beliefs, and political and economic life of the kingdom, went almost unnoticed except by scholars (Pelliot, 1951).

Henri Mouhot has long been seen as the discoverer of Angkor. Mouhot was a naturalist and explorer who travelled across Thailand, Laos, and Cambodia in 1858-1861 and visited Angkor in 1860. His travel narrative was published shortly after his death in the magazine *Le Tour du Monde* (Mouhot, 1863),[3] the same year that the French protectorate was established in Cambodia. Its publication coincided with the increasing interest of French naval forces in the coastal cities of Southeast Asia, where they sought to strengthen their presence in order to extend French control inland. The growing collective awareness of the existence of Angkor, given political significance by the French government's expansionist strategy, overlapped with Mouhot's individual experience of discovery. At a time when officials sought consensus on France's territorial expansion, Mouhot's narrative was strategically used to make Angkor more widely known and demonstrate that it would be in the interests of France to extend its authority over Cambodia (Dagens, 2008).

A few years later, in 1866-1868, an official French-sponsored expedition was sent to find the sources of the Mekong River in Tibet, in order to push China to open this route to foreign trade. The expedition was also supposed to gather knowledge about local political systems and to produce the first topographical maps of the region. Doudart de Lagrée, Louis Delaporte, and Francis Garnier, who were members of the expedition, published several articles and narratives describing in detail the first visit to Angkor. The photographer Emile Gsell illustrated these narratives with the first photographs of the temples. Louis Delaporte also published a book giving an account of this and later expeditions to Angkor, from which he brought back to France a substantial collection of Khmer art to be exhibited at the Musée Guimet.[4]

3 A few years later, his travel narrative was published in a book edited by T. Hodykin and Ferdinard de Lanoye (1866).

4 The collection of the Musée Guimet was begun by Emile Guimet, a manufacturer from Lyon who sought to open a museum of the religions of Egypt, classical antiquity, and Asia. He built up his collection through trips to countries of interest, and exhibited it in Lyon beginning in 1879. He built a museum in Paris, the Musée Guimet, which opened its doors in 1889.

Because only a minority of people knew about Angkor and only a few documents about the remains of the ancient Khmer kingdom were available in Europe, the first explorers who chanced to visit the temples wrote that these unexpected discoveries surpassed the bounds of the imagination. Their travel narratives described the depth of their aesthetic response.[5] After landing near the mouth of Siem Reap River, the travellers advanced through the jungle, without knowing when they would come across the temples they had heard of. Finally, standing in front of Angkor, they reacted with profoundly mixed emotions: fear, surprise, fascination, mistrust, and the impression of being crushed under the imposing weight of the temples. The grandeur of Angkor was more than they could grasp, and they felt overwhelmed by these remnants of an enigmatic history, both fascinating and intriguing.

Standing for the first time in front of Angkor Wat, Mouhot wrote, 'the mind feels crushed and the imagination overcome; I look, I admire, and filled with respect I fall silent' (1989, p. 192, author's translation). In a similar vein, Delaporte described the daunting path that brought the company towards the Angkor temples: 'A gigantic multi-headed monster, a fantastic dragon, rises half above the water at our side. It is a hundred times more terrible and more threatening than the crocodiles that inhabit this wilderness. We take the road, following a path worn by the wild beasts who are now the only dwellers in these ruins. My travel companions, for whom this spectacle is completely new, cannot restrain their cries of astonishment and admiration' (1880, p. 67, author's translation). Another of the travellers, De Carné, added:

> Pompous descriptions had been given to me; I had just re-read the pages of M. Mouhot on Angkor; but in spite of all, I felt overcome. I had, as it were, a shock of astonishment. I had hardly cleared the gate of the central pavilion when a second paved avenue, about 200 metres in length, opened before me to a huge building, the style of which is as different from any of our western forms of architecture as the Chinese fancies, of which I had already been able to study some examples. Wearied with the journey, and overcome by the heat, I thought I saw an incredible number of towers of strange outline dance before me, nothing supporting them in the air, and another higher tower rising above them. This kind of hallucination soon passed, and gave place to a just admiration. (1995, pp. 40-41)

5 Aesthetic emotions are said to be aroused by the beauty of a work of art or a spectacle of nature, and were conceptualized in the period of Romanticism.

The emotions the travellers experienced seem to have corresponded to the aesthetic concept of the sublime as put forward by Kant (1764) and later by Schiller (1801). For Kant, the sublime 'must be nature, or thought of as nature' (Ferguson, 1992, p. 4). He identifies two forms: the 'mathematical sublime', which occurs when imagination fails to represent the idea of wholeness, and the 'dynamic sublime', which arises in the face of savage, terrifying, and formless scenes. The first reveals the powerlessness of the human mind, the second its physical vulnerability. Kant argues that the sublime reveals our human condition, giving us a glimpse of what cannot be imagined. The sublime is transcendental, as the power of nature shows us that our ordinary concerns are insignificant. Drawing on Kant, Schiller argues that an object is sublime when the mental representation that we have of it enables us to experience the limits of our physical being, while our mind feels its superiority and fundamental freedom from limitation. The explorers could perceive the temples as 'natural', finding them deeply embedded in the jungle (Figure 4.1). Confronted with them, their minds were so overwhelmed by the astonishing sight that they fell silent. Their travel narratives expressed how threatened they felt by the savagery of the temples sunk in the jungle; they were afraid, trembling, and amazed. The sublime connects human beings with the fundamental quest for intensity and the absolute. This experience was possible for these travellers because of the particular conditions under which they visited the temples. The almost complete lack of previous knowledge about Angkor resulted in astonishment and surprise, the dangerous nature of the expedition aroused mistrust and fear, and the entangled ruins and vegetation increased the threatening aspect of the temples' and jungle's mysterious wholeness.

The production of knowledge and representations of Angkor along with the development of tourist facilities in the Siem Reap-Angkor region reduced the emotional charge that later visitors could be experience in front of the Angkor temples, because the strength of the original emotional experience depended precisely on the absence of expectations and previous frames of reference.

A few years later, Lunet Delajonquière wrote in an article published in *Le Tour du Monde* that Indochina was no longer 'the terra incognita which haunts explorers' (Delajonquière, 1910, p. 386, author's translation). In her description of her travels in Cambodia, Rose de Quaintenne, the wife of a colonial army officer in Cochin-China, wrote:

> Don't you think it a little ridiculous, dear readers, when tourists claim to inform their contemporaries about the character, the delights, the habits and customs of a country that they have only visited on a fifteen-day trip

> by steamer, hotel, sampan, ox cart [...] almost in a dream? What kind of new knowledge would the confidences of these chatty pilgrims produce? What original, personal observations could be made about the region between Saigon and Phnom Penh that have not been repeated a hundred times? I will thus attempt merely to provide a precise account of the impressions I have received during my trip to Angkor in 1907. (1909, p. 29, author's translation)

Rose de Quaintenne's dismissive portrait of the typical tourist shows how modest she was about her own experiences as visitor and narrator. However, her trip, like Delajonquière's article, dates back to the very beginning of the colonial enterprise at Angkor. It was only after 1907 that the École Française d'Extrême Orient was able to establish its headquarters in Siem Reap, following Siam's cession of Siem Reap province to Cambodia. Few travel narratives had been published at that time and no substantial development had yet taken place in the region. The radical change in the perception of the sites as expressed in the travel narratives – from amazing discovery to the limited experience of the already known – reveals the strength of the power of representations as constructed through narratives and images.

The tension between the original and its representation is a classic feature of the tourist experience. The sources describing Angkor show that two main forms of contradiction underpin this tension and keep it alive. First, tourists pursue the fundamental quest for intense experience. However, few of them are willing to face the fear of the unknown, along with the lack of familiar cues and comforts. For this reason, they content themselves with the commodified places and experiences that the tourism industry has developed for them. To respond to this ambivalent search for both intensity and security, the tourism industry produces representations which provide tourists with cultural anchors and prepare them to approach a new place. The industry also constructs 'tourism bubbles' (Judd, 1999) and secure environments, where the space is designed to manage tourists' contradictory desires, or where authentic expressions of local life are reproduced in order to arouse a surrogate experience of intense aesthetic feeling.

Second, representations are double-edged. While they offer substitutes for the original, they also shape observers' expectations, leading them to look for their concrete manifestation at the tourist site and to view any variation as an impurity and imperfection. In his travel writings, Pierre Loti described the frustration generated by the impossibility of recovering the intensity of the aesthetic feelings aroused at Angkor Wat. Loti was a writer and naval officer who travelled to Angkor at the beginning of the twentieth century, when the first publications about the ancient ruins and remote country had just been

Figure 4.1 Ancient road discovered in the midst of the ruins of Pontéay Preah Khan

Delaporte, 1880 © BnF

made available. He had learnt about the existence of the Khmer temples when he was only a child from a colonial magazine, which described the discovery of the ancient ruins by the first generation of European travellers. One image, he wrote, had made him shiver: 'There was one picture at which I stopped with a kind of thrill – showing great strange towers entwined with exotic branches, the temples of mysterious Angkor' (Loti, 1996, p. 6). He continued to be fascinated by this enigmatic image for many years.

When Loti eventually visited Angkor as an adult he recognized the towers that had fired his imagination as a child. However, he did not experience the emotion he had long expected. The feeling aroused by the image in the child's mind could not be aroused again in front of the original: 'Yet somehow I do not feel the emotion that I should have expected. It is probably too late in life, and I have seen too many of these remains of the great past, too many temples, too many palaces, too many ruins. Besides it is all so blurred, as it were, under the glare of the daylight; it is difficult to see because it is too bright. And, above all, midday is drawing near with its lassitude, its invincible somnolence' (1995, p. 29). Loti's frustration arose from the gap between the expectation built up on the basis of an image and the reality that failed to satisfy it. Implicitly claiming the superiority of the manufactured image over an imperfect reality, he illustrated the paradox at the core of the tourist experience.

4.2 Emotional authenticity

Colonial exhibitions were powerful engines for the production of representations of tourist sites in the colonized territories. Replicas of monuments, other buildings, and landscapes were constructed using techniques of reproduction that were to be fundamental for the later production of tourism architecture. Since 1866, European empires organized colonial exhibitions in order to show off the lands, products, and societies of the colonized countries in the 'mother country'. Universal exhibitions began to include a colonial section in 1867, when the Paris Universal Exhibition first included pavilions illustrating the architectural styles of the French colonies.

The Angkor temples as well as Cambodian villages and towns were first reproduced in colonial exhibitions in 1898, well before Siem Reap province fell under French control in 1907. Techniques of reproduction became more and more accurate over time, and found their most sophisticated expression at the Vincennes Colonial Exhibition of 1931, which attracted eight million visitors. Original pieces brought back by travellers, as well as heterogeneous compositions in which faithful reproductions of architectural and sculptural fragments were combined with fanciful reconstructions of the monuments' environment, represented the Angkor temples at several more such exhibitions.

In a similar vein, engravings by Delaporte portrayed sculptural and architectural fragments from Angkor found deep in the jungle (Figure 4.1). Following an artistic tradition established by Piranesi, who had engraved some of the first representations of Roman antiquities, Delaporte recreated a setting for the ruins. This setting was not realistic, but evoked a picturesque mix of nature and monuments: 'Only the artist's pencil could portray the picturesque effect of these beautiful fragments in the midst of the luxuriant vegetation which covers and envelops them. Wild vines with bright red leaves twist and turn everywhere on the piles of stone and the crumbling arches; countless creepers wrap around them in such a regular way that one might think a human hand had designed their embroidery' (Delaporte, 1880, p. 53, author's translation). Picturesque engravings and colonial exhibitions both presented credible reproductions of the Angkor ruins and their surroundings. In both cases, the replicas tamed the savagery of nature: the images, whether in two or three dimensions, reproduced reality but imposed a new order on it.

Two architects, Blanche father and son, reconstructed a full-scale model of the central tower of Angkor Wat at the colonial exhibition of 1931 (Figure 4.2). They also focused only on that section of the temple, admittedly a gigantic one: 'On the edge of the enormous road dotted with sacred "nagas", Angkor rose up fifty metres high, above its terraces and foundations, its central dome, an embossed tiara framed by four other domes flanked by two corner towers [...] At nightfall, the temple glowed with the splendour of a thousand flames and the bright halo of electric lights' (Deberny-Peignot, 1931, author's translation). On the outside, the architects attempted to create a faithful replica of the original. In contrast, the interior spaces of the replica were modern, to suit its function as an exhibition hall demonstrating the benefits of French colonization in Cambodia (Morton, 2003).

The narrative describing this pavilion called the reproduction 'Angkor' and 'the temple', although the copy was not perfectly accurate and had none of the functions of the original. Even for the less sophisticated reproductions in the exhibition of 1898, Edwards (2008) points out that in the eyes of the French government and the 26 million spectators, 'the pavilion *was* Cambodge. Its authenticity was bolstered by the deployment of Cambodians – possibly the artists that would have built it – in the villages, temples, and markets of the colonial section' (p. 33).

What made the close association between the copy and the temple possible was not its formal faithfulness, but rather the ability of the copy to evoke the original: 'Only one section of the incredible buildings which stand in the heart of the great Cambodian forest was reproduced, but this décor was effectively designed to have an emotional effect on the spectator' (Deberny-Peignot, 1931, author's translation). The copy was meant to arouse the emotions that an inexperienced spectator – the majority of the visitors knew little about Cambodia and the temples – would have felt in front of the temples. These emotions needed to be like those felt by the first generation of travellers: surprise, wonder, and admiration for the monumentality and beauty of the temples. Because they had to approach the intensity of these aesthetic feelings, they had to meet the criterion of emotional authenticity.

Authenticity is a recurrent theme in the history of European thinking about art and human creation. Walter Benjamin (2007) argued that three phases are recognizable in human history. During the 'traditional phase', artefacts are produced by hand.

> Authenticity was intrinsically linked to the original, created in the service of the magic or religious cult. The artefact was surrounded by an 'aura' which confirmed its uniqueness. This conception of authenticity was less linked to individual creation than to the traditional continuity in which each artefact was located. A second phase conceives art as a collectors' item. The unique and artistic value gained more importance than

Figure 4.2 Replica of Angkor Wat temple at the 1931 colonial exhibition

Studio Deberny-Peignot, 1931

> traditional continuity. Historically, rare examples of this approach could be found in ancient Egypt, where the statues of important monarchs were restored in order to keep their memory alive. However, art collection was accompanied by a new approach from the 18th century onwards, when art works began to be considered as historical documents to be conserved as sources of knowledge. Restoration had to respect the material signs, which made historical inquiry possible. Theories by Ruskin and William Morris stressed the importance of keeping the traces that each historical period left on the artefact. According to Benjamin, the advent of the instruments for mechanical reproduction such as photography and film blurred the concept of authenticity for the work of art: images can be manipulated, multiplied and disseminated. The link with the 'author', the original creator, is weakened. (Esposito and Gaulis, 2010, p. 51)

The relation between the original and the replica of Angkor reflected the blurring of the notion of authenticity at these colonial exhibitions. Accurate technical reproductions made it possible to remove the barrier separating the original from the copy. In this new context, the correspondence between the original and the replica was based on the shared ability of the original and the copy to arouse the emotions. In order to reach this objective, the copy had to reproduce the size, shapes, and materials of the original in a credible way. However, the details, which would not increase the emotional impact of the replica on the spectator, could be left out without difficulty. The replica produced a new order, assembling aspects and fragments of the original together with 'modern' interior architecture. The new architectural composition finds its coherence in the capacity of every shape and decorative detail to increase emotional authenticity, that is to say to immerse the observer-visitors in temporal and spatial otherness despite their physical distance from the original. Emotional authenticity, however, results from a triple form of commodification of places and objects: the combination of tradition and modernity; mediation through narrative; and domestication of the unpleasant aspects of the experience of foreign places. These three forms of commodification excise the 'fearful' component of aesthetic feeling for the benefit of visitors who are only seeking pleasure.

4.3 Taming exoticism

Other pavilions in these colonial exhibitions reproduced villages and local dwellings in the French colonies. The exhibition organizers had selected classes of similar buildings and human settlements whose common features, functions, and geographical origins made up a type.[6] Because they could represent the shared qualities of a class of objects while leaving out particular differences, types were seen as ideal models available for reproduction. Their ideal character was the result of generalization. A 'real' house was one which expressed the characteristics of the type, and only these characteristics, without individual variation. Thus, 'the' Annamite palace, 'the' fishing village of the Tonkin delta, 'the' ancient villa of Hue, 'the' palace of Cochin-China, and 'the' Cambodian pagoda were presented in an impossibly pure form.

Narratives were attached to these models. Types of dwelling and human settlement reproduced at the Marseille Colonial Exhibition of 1906 were described as picturesque (Malo, 1906). In the field of art, the term 'picturesque' refers to the harmonious coexistence of plants and small buildings

6 In a similar process, the 'science' of physiognomy superimposed images of human beings from the same ethnic group. The type was supposedly constructed from their common characteristics.

in English gardens as well as the representation of landscapes in painting. Historically, the term has also been given other meanings, including the representation of strange or unusual scenery (Pleșu, 2007) and of curious or burlesque human figures (Gilpin, 1794).

This representation of the colonized is consistent with the travellers' descriptions of Cambodian villages. Loti expressed his fascination with local houses on his trip from Siam to Cambodia:

> We are in front of a village, on a little river with flowery banks. Through the reeds the rising sun shoots its golden arrows everywhere. Little thatched houses built upon piles form a line along a pathway of fine sand. Men and women, half-naked, slender, with copper-colored bodies, move around amongst the verdure [...] The flowers perfume the air; an odour of jasmine, of gardenia, of tuberose. In the clear light of dawn this simple morning coming and going seems like a scene of the early ages, when man still had tranquillity [...] We pass through villages, peaceful and pleasing as in the golden age, where the inhabitants watch us go by with smiles of shy goodwill [...] After an hour we stop at Siem Reap, almost a town, but quite Siamese in character, with its little houses always perched on piles, and its temple bristling with golden finials. (Loti, 1996, pp. 27-28)

This description is characteristic of a broader tendency to depict Indochinese communities as mythical places, echoing the European notion of a Golden Age of humanity. The colonized lived in a desirable state of peace which, however, was also backward and isolated from the rest of the world. This characterization legitimized the presence of French colonizers, who would bring progress to the societies which also deeply attracted them. The narrative of the 1931 colonial exhibition presented this ambivalent position:

> Our arrival in the midst of backward populations, some still in a state of savagery or anarchy, others detached from general human evolution, is only justified if we bring them inner peace, moral and social progress, and economic advancement. Yet our actions will be considered effective only under the necessary condition that we do not believe too much in the infallibility and perfection of our own procedures and institutions, that we constantly keep our eyes open for what, among these different brothers of ours, might be better than at home, and that we remain permanently concerned to adapt to their status, traditions, customs, and beliefs: in one word, that we understand them. (Deberny-Peignot, 1931, p. 1)

Ambivalence was also at the heart of the sense of exoticism, which has been said to occur when the desire to get in touch with the otherness of colonized societies coexists with a feeling of repulsion for aspects of this otherness that the observers dislike (Segalen, 1986), for instance economic backwardness and poverty. Because of this partial repulsion, observers maintain an irreducible distance from the object of desire, which allows them to engage in distanced but fascinated contemplation of it while avoiding those aspects of diversity they may criticize. If they decide to merge with the other – to become insiders – the sense of exoticism will fade away. Observers then risk being lost in a dangerous otherness that they cannot survive, like Paul Bowles' protagonists in the novel *The Sheltering Sky*, who go crazy or die in the North African desert. Exoticism, and the detached and admiring observation that goes with it, thus preserves the identity as well as the mental and physical integrity of the observer.

The pavilions of the colonial exhibitions awakened the visitors' sense of exoticism. However, the process of typological reproduction also erased those aspects of the dwellings and settlements that might repel the foreign observer. For instance, the overcrowding and dirtiness that some travellers had criticized in Indochinese cities were eliminated from the replicas, producing an enjoyable and safe environment for the visitors. In this sense also, replicas were ideal models because they reproduced a purified environment, one which implicitly asserted the imperfection of the real world. For prospective tourists, the gap between the replicas and the real places grew even wider as the narratives assimilated the former to the latter, 'these busy natives who come and go, live there, dwell there, work there, as if they had been transplanted from their far-off village', as a commentator remarked after visiting the 1907 exhibition in Nogent-sur-Marne (Nozeroy, 1907).

'Natives' did indeed populate the microcosm of these exhibitions. Their staged dances, everyday practices, and traditions completed the transposition of the otherness accomplished by the architectural reproductions. Their activity was similar to photography, enabling visitors to transcend distance and travel by means of the imagination:

> Travelling is a luxury. Travelling requires effort. If luxury is not available to everyone and effort is not necessarily desirable, photography eliminates these obstacles in order to allow both the poor and the lazy [...] to see far-off countries. To access the 'elsewhere', certainly, but without being there; to benefit from the charms it offers the eye [...] without suffering the

> probable discomfort and weariness. In our age of 'universal locomotion' [...] photography inaugurates a new way to travel: this new image becomes a window permanently open on the world. (Gautier, 1856)

Both photography and colonial exhibitions were 'windows' opening on the colonies. The partial reality that the windows framed, and the cultural filters influencing perceptions of these tiny fragments, built up tourist expectations and, more broadly, affected how Europeans imagined Angkor and Cambodia. At colonial exhibitions, visitors moved rapidly and excitedly from one attraction to the other in the festive atmosphere of the show. They learned how to gaze at the reproduced monuments and landscapes in the curious but distracted way of those who have been taught what is interesting to look at but who have too little time to indulge in contemplation. Monuments and human settlements were made into a spectacular show, and the visitors complied with the trick. They were educated while being entertained, and would not criticize the artificial character of the reproduction when the experience was so enjoyable. Typological reproduction tamed the ambivalent exotic feeling. Travel by means of the imagination made representations and replicas into valid alternatives to the originals.

4.4 Representing and planning the tourist space

4.4.1 Spatial arrangements as manifestations of colonial power

At colonial exhibitions, visitors were viewed as recipients of images, narratives, and replicas prepared by the organizers. The tourist is given a similar status: unlike the traveller who explores an unknown country and produces knowledge about the places and societies encountered, the tourist is supposed to acquire knowledge in a form compiled and presented by communities of experts. The tourist moves within a space planned through the construction of infrastructures, facilities, tours, and attractions. The planning of the tourist space, like that of the replicas of original monuments and buildings at colonial exhibitions, uses assemblage, mediation, and domestication to produce a new spatial order. Through this process, the tourist space comes to reflect images and narratives, an equivalence reinforced by the production and dissemination of promotional materials such as tour guides. The planning of the space and the writing of tour guides also help to make tourism a socially constructed practice.

When Siem Reap province fell under French control in 1907, the French administration defined two specific areas of activity: monument conservation (see Chapter 1) and the planning of the tourist space (*l'aménagement de l'espace*). In colonial discourse, these two areas were brought together via the use of the expression *mise en valeur*, which applied to all activities that added or produced value for the archaeological and tourist sites. This expression is highly ambiguous, as Choay (2007) notes: it can refer to the value of a heritage that needs to be protected and disseminated, but also to the economic concept of added value. The planning of the tourist space and the related construction of the tourist gaze were intended to develop tourism as an industry which would benefit the owners and managers of tourism infrastructures and facilities.

With this in mind, the colonial administration first improved the accessibility of the archaeological park. Roads were particularly important because they made the archaeological site accessible all year around and were tourists' preferred means of transport. They connected Siem Reap with Tonlé Sap lake, where the boats from Vietnam and Thailand docked, and with Phnom Penh and Bangkok. A new canal made it easier for boats to dock on the lake shore. By the end of the 1930s tourists could get to Angkor from both Thailand and Vietnam. All-inclusive tours departing from Saigon were organized by the Compagnie des Messageries Maritimes.[7] Angkor was served by 2,800 km of gravel roads and 800 km of paved roads. Roads also linked the Angkor temples, making them easily reachable by car.[8] Tours were organized within the park: the *petit circuit* and *grand circuit*, connecting twenty of the main Angkor monuments, could be done by car. These were recommended by tour guides as the preferable routes to follow (Marchal, 1928). The French protectorate[9] also made provision for the construction of hotels. The Grand Hôtel was built in Siem Reap during the 1920s. During

7 The Compagnie des Messageries Maritimes was founded by Albert Rostand and Ernest Simons in 1851 and was initially called the Messageries Nationales. It took its new name in 1871. In colonial times, it managed intercontinental shipping lines for commercial communication and ensured the international mail service.

8 The construction of roads in the Siem Reap-Angkor region was planned within a broader programme for the improvement of transportation infrastructures in Indochina. In 1931, Indochina had 25,000 km of roads. In Cambodia, where there were only 300 km of roads in 1900, 9,000 km were built between 1900 and 1930 as a result of the establishment of a system of public forced labour to which the inhabitants were subjected.

9 In the first instance, because private initiative could not undertake major investments which would only be profitable after many years, the General Government of Indochina built hotel facilities run by managers. Then, in 1924, the colonial administration sponsored the creation of the Société des Grands Hôtels Indochinois, which was supposed to build and manage hotels.

the same period, the construction of the commercial and administrative districts gave Siem Reap the role of a provincial capital. These development programmes helped to determine its function as an international tourism hub and economic centre on the doorstep of the archaeological park.

Tourism-driven spatial arrangements can be understood as the manifestation of political and economic power. The tourism space is circumscribed and filled with functional and symbolic signs such as ease of transportation and accommodation, while it showcases the appropriation of the colonized country for economic exploitation. Spatial arrangements and urban development make it possible to manage movement, resources, and the occupation of space. They thus prove the colonizer's mastery of a geographical region and its economy (Zythnichi and Kazdaghili, 2009), the establishment of a human territoriality (see Chapter 1).

Control of space goes hand in hand with the control of perceptions, movements, and practices. Tourism takes place in an already delimited space. Significantly, Marchal's guide (1928) suggested that tourists should only visit a small number of the monuments on the *petit circuit* and *grand circuit* in one day, in order to have enough energy and concentration to view them unhurriedly, and that they should walk around in the park only during the coolest hours of the day. In contrast, savants, poets, and artists 'will be able to wander around the monuments at any time in order to study the varied and endlessly renewed impressions they provide' (Marchal, 1928, p. 4). These recommendations marked the difference between the travellers, who were also intellectuals and artists, and who were free to move around unguided, and the tourists, who had to keep to the beaten track.

Tourist guides written during the 1930s, when the development of infrastructure and facilities was smoothing the expansion of international tourism in Indochina, also prescribed which landscapes the tourists should look at and how they should perceive them. A promotional brochure about Indochina described Cholon, with 'its shops with their long hanging signage, its lively atmosphere all day and night, its Chinese restaurants where singing girls come to entertain the opium-smokers, the constant clicking of wooden sandals, typical of the whole Chinese city'.[10] This does not describe one street in particular but, like the colonial exhibitions, aims to encapsulate the very essence of the place as if seen through a window. In continuity

However, this company went bankrupt. The hotels went back to being the direct responsibility of the colonial government and were run by managers selected through a call for tenders.

10 'Le tourisme en Indochine 1. Son essor – son organisation, ses moyens d'action', in *L'information d'Indochine économique et financière* 1935, p. 3.

with the colonial exhibitions, tourists are invited to gaze at typical scenes as if they were looking at 'animated paintings', never dealing with the locals more directly. This fundamental distance is the sine qua non for keeping the sense of exoticism alive. Some tourists complained about the restrictions and constraints imposed on them. Geoffrey Gorer, who travelled to Bali and Angkor in the 1930s, described the advantages and disadvantages of travelling in a planned space:

> I travelled in considerable luxury; there were excellent hotels and (save in Indochina) very good cars and roads. Except for the fact that we travelled rather slowly, our journey differed little from that of other tourists; I saw little that other tourists couldn't see. [...] I naturally talked as much as I could with the chauffeurs and servants I had anything to do with, for they were the most interesting people in the neighbourhood; and whenever I had the opportunity I used to talk to strangers in the streets or the country; but after these encounters I always went back to the hotel or the car. Now one of the chief disadvantages of living in hotels and cars is that everything seen through their windows is likely to be couleur de rose; Europeans or Americans enjoying themselves present such a dismal and depressing spectacle that all people not connected with these rich pleasure-seekers appear by contrast to have all sort of desirable qualities. (Gorer, 1936, pp. 11-12)

The reasons why tourists agreed – sometimes with reluctance, as in Gorer's case – to have their experience controlled include the fear of the unknown, the difficulty of connecting with the 'locals' from their position as outsiders and their consequent need of cultural brokers to assist them, and, lastly, the influence of representations on their expectations, which the tourism industry attempted to satisfy through facilities which reproduced typical but staged environments.

4.4.2 Between reclamation and innovation of tourist spaces in postcolonial Cambodia

The colonial administration undertook a vigorous campaign to develop infrastructure and tourism facilities in Indochina. It promoted tourism in France, with Angkor as the main destination. The opening of the Suez Canal in 1869 and the subsequent improvements of intercontinental sea transport facilitated travel to the Far East. Nevertheless, Indochina received far fewer visitors than other Asian countries during the same period. In 1915, Japan had 20,000 tourists, Java 8,000, and the Philippines 4,000, whilst Indochina only attracted 150 (Rondet-Saint, 1916). Only 952 foreign tourists visited Angkor in 1931, 423 of whom were actually European colonists. Tourism growth at Angkor was slow, with only 1613 tourists in 1935, despite efforts to improve the accessibility of the archaeological park. Because the demands of tourism were low, planning for tourists in the urban space of Siem Reap did not substantially expand during the colonial years, apart from the opening of the Grand Hotel. However, the colonial regime created the foundations for a substantial reconfiguration of the town after Angkor was added to the UNESCO World Heritage List. It also began to construct the characteristics of the tourist gaze, which successive regimes and tourism organizations reinforced.

Norodom Sihanouk obtained the independence of Cambodia in 1953 and his political movement, the Sangkum Reastr Niyum, won the national elections in 1955. Tourism did not become an important sector in the national economy, although the government used the modernization of the country and the improvement of the road system and air traffic as its chief inducements for attracting tourists to Cambodia. The Société Khmère des Auberges Royales (SOKHAR),[11] established by government decree in 1959, organized tours, undertook construction, and managed up-market hotels in Siem Reap, Sihanoukville, and Kep. The private company Société Cambodgienne de l'Hôtellerie et du Tourisme (SOCHOT), created in 1952, also built and managed tourism infrastructure, including the main hotels in Phnom Penh. During those years, motels, chalets, and youth hostels were built in order to attract tourists on limited budgets. A few luxurious hotels opened their doors in Phnom Penh and Siem Reap, including the Monorom and Hotel de la Paix.

In spite of the small economic contribution of this sector,[12] tourism promotion flourished between the 1950s and the 1960s. Cambodian consular services in foreign countries along with tour operators were the main authors and disseminators of this promotion, directed at the primary countries of origin of international tourists (France, the United States, Hong Kong, Japan, and the Federal Republic of Germany). Tourism promotion also operated through Cambodian magazines written in French and English, such as

11 SOKHAR was a mixed company, the state and private investors sharing its capital. Later the company was completely taken over by the Cambodian state.

12 Only 12,195 tourists visited Cambodia in 1954 and 28,801 in 1967. In 1969, the number of tourist visits was close to 30,000, while Thailand reached 100,000 in the same year (De Vienne and Népote, 1993; Riman, 1968).

Kambuja, published during the 1960s. It clearly aimed to awaken a dormant industry for future development. It also served the political propaganda and foreign policy of the regime: by presenting a positive image of the national government, it fostered regional and international cooperation.

Promotional materials reclaimed images and narratives of tourist sites inherited from colonialism. Firstly, Angkor's history and legacy were viewed as the main sources of national pride. The cultural significance of secondary cities, such as Battambang, was related to their historical roots in the age of Angkor, which research at the time of Sihanouk aimed to recover. The theme of a forgotten history to be unveiled echoed the travel narratives' theme of discovery, and served to legitimize the political regime which made such a cultural enterprise possible. Secondly, the presentation of Cambodian villages and towns echoed the ambivalent colonial discourse, which contrasted the Orientalist representation of idyllic, secluded places with the rhetoric of economic development that colonization would bring to these backward countries. Following a similar narrative, tourism promotion described communities both as mythical, peaceful places in a timeless world and as economic nodes involved in ambitious programmes of economic development. However, according to postcolonial propaganda such a mythical state was not the result of backwardness and economic isolation; rather, it was a natural condition of the Cambodian people, who had preserved a state of inner peace which European societies had already lost.

Cambodian 'peace' can also be interpreted from a political perspective. At the Bandung Conference convened by Indonesia's President Sukarno in 1955, which brought together representatives from 29 decolonized countries in Africa and Asia who had joined the non-aligned movement, Sihanouk opted for international neutrality. Consequently, Cambodia became a buffer state between Thailand and South Vietnam, both allied with the Western bloc, and North Vietnam and China, allied with the Eastern bloc (Dauphin-Meunier, 1965). In this context, tourism promotion focused on the peaceful situation of Cambodia compared to the turmoil of neighbouring countries. Cambodia could be presented as an 'oasis of peace' and 'a land for work' (Ministère de l'Information, 1963) with a high level of social and economic development.

For the needs of tourism propaganda Siem Reap stood out among the towns of Cambodia. Hamel wrote in *Kambuja* magazine:

> Siem Reap in fact, is not a town that one visits like other towns in the world, large or small, and from which one takes away a few statistics, superficial impressions, or stereotyped ideas. It is rather a town in which atmosphere is all-important, and where the visitor must forget the preoccupations

> of everyday life [...] For Siem Reap is a town where everything conspires to enchant the visitor, and this enchantment cannot be easily conveyed by ordinary words [...]. The visual enchantment begins on the road at the edge of the town [...] the bridge which spans the Siem Reap river [...] well-planned and beautifully kept garden [...] quiet beauty on the banks of a picturesque river, which lends to it much of its charm [...] the dominant impression is of that utter peace and serenity which befit a site, where lie the glorious remains of an unrivalled civilization. Furthermore, this peace and serenity make Siem Reap an ideal place to rest, where everything invites the visitor to relax and meditate. (Hamel, 1965, p. 60)

The magazine goes on to describe the mysterious spell of the town, where foreign visitors can 'forget the vain preoccupations of our age' and develop a spiritually elevated state of mind through contact with its people. Hamel borrowed the image of the 'paradise lost' from colonial images and narratives. However, the colonial sense of superiority, which perceived the colonized as backward, gives way here to a positive perception of the local population. The dichotomy of archaeological park and tourist hub, established in colonial times, is rejected in favour of a representation of the town as an integral part of the spiritual landscape of Angkor:[13]

> It goes without saying that this serenity would be shattered were Siem Reap to try to provide the tourists with 'entertainment' in the proper sense of the world [...] Just imagine, for a moment, what Siem Reap would be if it offered what is needed for the 'night life' of the Occident. It would be difficult, moreover, to appreciate the atmosphere of 'night-clubs' after long hours of ecstatic contemplation in the forecourt of Angkor Wat. Siem Reap is a place where one comes to dream, to communicate with the past, to find aesthetic pleasure in the purest form, and also to re-discover oneself. It simply cannot be a place where one comes to be 'entertained'. (p. 60)

This shift shows how images and narratives could travel through time and space and be appropriated – and, at the same time, modified – to serve new causes and propaganda aims. By claiming that the Khmer people embody spiritual qualities that Westerners lack, the colonial representation of the idyllic village was used as a tool of empowerment for a postcolonial society

13 International tour guides and publications did not modify colonial representations in this way. Instead, they adopted the narrative of the mystery of Angkor yet to be unveiled (*inter alia* Fodor, 1964).

that sought to reverse the hierarchical relations established during the period of foreign control. The enduring presence of some of these representations leads us to ask how and to what extent they continued to shape the expectations of tourists from different parts of the world. I will try to answer this question through an analysis of contemporary tourism architecture.

4.5 All hotels want to be 'Grand'

4.5.1 The importation of a model

The Grand Hotel was the first tourist facility to be reopened in Siem Reap in the early 1990s. For the first consultants who arrived to plan the town's future, the hotel's poor state of preservation contrasted with memories of its past splendour. When it was built it could not compete with other grand hotels of Southeast Asia such as the Raffles Hotel in Singapore, being relatively small and decent, but not luxurious.[14] Nevertheless, this monumental concrete building must have astonished the urban population (Figure 4.3). The use of concrete was a clear mark of modernization: only a few years earlier, the bigger and magnificent Hotel Royal in Phnom Penh had been built of stucco-covered brick and thatch.

The hotel's design was inspired by the Lang Biang Palace, which the French colonial government had built in the Vietnamese tourist resort of Dalat in 1922. As in Siem Reap, the palace was located in a village and played a symbolic role in the foundation of a new urban entity, in a region that the French colonizers saw as almost untouched by civilization (Ascher, Cohen, and Hauvuy, 1987). The Palace in Dalat had drawn on the Hotel Negresco in Nice, designed by Edouard Niermans. The architecture of these two hotels, with their art deco motifs, represented luxury, and experimented with recent technical innovations in the construction industry (Jennings, 2003).

The trajectory of this architectural model, from France to Vietnam and then to Cambodia, illustrates the international migration of tourism architecture. The model of the grand hotel was created in the Western world in the nineteenth century, and imported into Asian countries under the influence of the colonial powers, where it was readapted to the programmes

14 According to the hotel manager, the Siem Reap Grand Hotel was a lodge, meaning a modern, comfortable residence built in a rural environment. Initially small, it could have been expanded to meet tourism growth. The garden was created between 1936 and 1937 (interview with Joseph Beghin, general manager, March 2008).

and objectives of local entrepreneurs and governments. The grand hotel can be distinguished from other types of tourist accommodation by its level of luxury, the high expectations of its customers, and the high quality and quantity of services (Sanjuan et al., 2003). Its invention was closely linked to the technological and economic transformations of the first Industrial Revolution. The development of travel, facilitated by the improvement of transportation systems, generated a demand for hotel accommodation which could no longer be satisfied by aristocratic mansions or cheap hostels.

This new type of accommodation was born in the United States in the 1820s. The Tremont House, built in Boston in 1829, was innovative in size, construction techniques, and high level of comfort and services. The St. Nicholas Hotel, built in New York in 1852, outshone it with its 800 rooms, a façade 92 metres long, and more modern technology. In Europe, the various universal exhibitions provided the opportunity to build the first grand hotels, such as the Great Western Hotel in London, opened in 1851, and the Grand Hotel du Louvre in Paris, opened in 1855.

Western societies developed three main types of grand hotel in the nineteenth century: the American hotel with its gigantic size, high standards of comfort and functionality, and central urban location; the tourist resort or spa hotel, which might be a long-term residence, in a magnificent natural setting; and the prestige hotel, generally smaller, modelled on the homes of the aristocracy, giving the impression of social elitism and intimacy (Ascher, 1987; Sanjuan et al., 2003). The grand hotel contributed to the processes of urban modernization and also to the construction of new urban spaces centred on monumental hotel buildings.

In Asia, colonial and national governments first imported these models around the turn of the century. In Japan, for instance, the importation reflected the ruling class's determination to reach a Western level of economic development. Architectural forms and social practices from the Western world were closely associated with positive evolution and modernization (Fiévé, 2003). Hotel design combined Western models with elements from Japanese architectural traditions. The British architect Josiah Conder, who designed the Rokumeikan hotel,[15] invented a neo-oriental style which made allusions to Japanese religious architecture. The Tsukiji hotel[16] took its inspiration from colonial architecture, with its U-shaped plan and covered galleries; but its wooden structure, mud walls decorated with white diamond

15 The Rokumeikan hotel was built in Tokyo in 1883 and was sponsored by the Japanese Minister of Foreign Affairs.

16 The Tsukiji hotel opened in 1886 in Tokyo's foreign district.

patterns, and tiled roofs, reproduced the typical elements and techniques of popular Japanese architecture.

The combination of elements from different cultural and functional universes allowed for the emergence of a hybrid architecture which integrated heterogeneous elements into a project at a high level of technical innovation. In particular, allusions to religious architecture were included in order to satisfy the foreign customers' desire to get in touch with the 'local culture'. In other cases, such as the Imperial hotel (Fiévé, 2003), allusions to local architecture were rejected, because the hotel was intended to reflect only an image of urban modernity.

These examples show how thoroughly hotel architecture has been charged with meaning and, in many cases, combines tradition and modernity. More especially in Asia, where the importation of the model showcased Asian countries' ability to reach Western standards, the hotel was imagined as the symbol and indication of modernization. However, it also had to meet foreigners' expectations of local traditions, and thus had to recreate them. As a result, the hotel was configured as a hybrid architectural object which amalgamated these ambivalent semiotic registers.

As in other Asian countries, the hotels of colonial and postcolonial Cambodia took up the challenge of reflecting the country's ambition to progress. However, unlike the rich countries of East Asia, these luxurious entities were out of phase with the general development level. Hotels appeared as 'plethoric objects' (Prud'homme, 1969), which contrasted with the wooden houses and straw huts of the towns and villages.

In Siem Reap, after the UNESCO World Heritage listing of Angkor, the construction of hotels drove urban development, and the majority of these hotels aspired to be 'grand'; that is, the model of the grand hotel was adopted when deciding on size, architectural shape, and services offered. However, the appropriation of the international model was in many cases over-hasty and only some of its distinguishing features were copied. Architects lacked experience, while developers very often considered themselves capable of designing their own hotels.

Many of the hotel buildings are monumental in appearance, with multiple storeys and a plan in an 'L' or 'U' shape. The lobby on the ground floor contains the main visitor services. A staircase leads to the restaurant on the next floor. The rooms are on the upper floors, along corridors. On the façade, a main portal generally features columns inspired by classical architecture, or decorations evoking Angkor temples. In front of the building, a transitional space with a garden or lawn separates the hotel from the road. Behind the building, the lateral wings enclose a garden with a swimming pool (Figure 4.4; Figure 4.5).

Construction materials are of poor quality, and the first signs of deterioration appear fewer than ten years after completion. Many of them offer views merely of open fields punctuated by mushrooming new real-estate developments.

The majority of Siem Reap's hotels thus imitated the grand hotel without giving new life to the international model. In a ripple effect, hotels aiming to be grand spread through the town, as developers sought to create buildings associated with progress and reflecting their own high social status. They copied each other's products more and more frequently, reproducing simplistic versions of the grand hotel with little variation in size and decoration. Another reason for the relatively careless way these architectural projects were pursued was the speculative nature of many of these investments. Developers wanted to spend money they had illicitly acquired in order to get clean money (see Chapter 3), and thus high-speed construction was a priority. It was of secondary concern that the hotel might not be attractive enough to bring in many customers.

4.5.2 Evocations of the past(s)

Given these considerations, one might suppose that no thought was put into any of this architectural production. However, the hotels of Siem Reap, like their Japanese predecessors, incorporate many elements evoking forms from the past. Combined with the model of the grand hotel, they generate a kind of hybrid style which connects several semiotic layers in the architectural fabric.

The most frequently recurring source of these allusions to the past is, obviously, Angkor. Since colonial times, Angkor has played a role of paramount importance in the construction of national history and identity. The extraordinary character of the archaeological remains has nurtured the imagination, evoking a glorious civilization in sharp contrast with later centuries of economic decline and foreign colonization. Travel narratives and colonial narratives described the astonishing glory of Angkor and the degenerate barbarism of contemporary Cambodian society in order to legitimize the foreign regime which would reinstate economic progress and better knowledge of ancient history (Edwards, 2008). Colonial exhibitions reproduced the temples, and tourism focused on visiting the archaeological monuments. In the postcolonial period, the excessive focus of national narratives on Angkor was continued, eclipsing other historical epochs (Winter, 2007). The UNESCO World Heritage listing in 1992 only confirmed the centrality of Angkor to Cambodian history and enshrined it as part of the heritage of humanity.

These are some of the reasons why Angkor has become a major source for hotel architecture. Moreover, because of its position on the doorstep of the archaeological site, developers see Siem Reap as the continuation of the tourists' experience at the temples. The city needs to recreate the temple environment in order to be perceived as such by the tourists.

Nevertheless, Angkor is not the only source of inspiration for hotel architecture. Though less often, hotel design alludes to colonial architecture and history as well as to the Khmer tradition of building in wood. Through the filter of inherited representations, these three sources are given new life in contemporary architecture. They are sometimes superimposed on or entwined with the model of the grand hotel in order to create buildings which look back to the past while concomitantly expressing the desire for modernization and innovation that the international model embodies in the eyes of developers.

There are three recurrent processes through which 'the past' becomes a source for contemporary architecture: the reproduction of spatial forms and objects, the production of narratives, and the re-creation of ambiance. By 'spatial form' I mean the typical built forms and also the organization of space – mainly copied from Angkor – reproduced in hotel layouts. These include the orientation of the temples on a north-south or east-west axis, the use of canals and moats, and the presence of symbolic elements with spiritual or religious meanings.

The plan of the hotel previously called the Hotel de la Paix, now the Park Hyatt, was designed by the international architect Bill Bensley. It has two square inner courtyards with walkways and shallow ponds, imitating the alternation of water and built forms in temple architecture. A sequence of portals along the walkways evokes the temple corridors. Internal moats suggest the canal system built by the Khmer rulers in the Angkor empire (see Chapter 1). In temple architecture, orthogonal axes lead to a central tower that represents the most sacred area of the sanctuary. In the hotel, the orthogonal walkways meet at a central point, where a tree has been planted (Figure 4.6).

The 'reproduction of Angkor' goes through two phases reminiscent of the methods of typological reproduction at the colonial exhibitions: first, the recognition of typical spatial forms to be found in several temples, which can thus represent Angkor as a whole; then the reproduction of the elements to be found in all these temples, and the exclusion of elements specific to only one of them.

By 'object', I mean here specific fragments of Angkor, such as sculptures or construction features, reproduced in new contexts of hotel architecture, which an informed observer would be able to associate with the original. For instance, one of the towers of the Bayon temple is reproduced in the courtyard of the Angkor Howard Hotel (Figure 4.7). The tower depicts the four faces of the Buddha and also the Khmer King Jayavarman VII, who was believed to have godlike status. The tower is incorporated into a new spatial composition made up of heterogeneous elements reminiscent of the reconstructions of Angkor at the colonial exhibitions and of Delaporte's picturesque engravings of the Angkor ruins lost in the jungle.

When I talk about 'narrative', I am referring to promotional materials that describe the relation between hotel architecture and heritage through text and images, even when this relation has not been made evident through the architectural form. The website of the Grand Hotel, now the Raffles Grand Hotel since its renovation in the 1990s, claims that its swimming pool replicates the basins of the Khmer kings at the Phimeanakas temple.[17] However, today, this is a roughly dug basin contained by walls of different heights and infiltrated by vegetation. Only archaeologists can say whether there is a real formal correspondence between this piece of archaeological heritage and the hotel's swimming pool. In other cases, the relation between the hotel and the heritage is established not through formal resemblance, but simply through some common characteristic that the narrative emphasizes. For instance, the promotional materials for the Goldiana and Angkor Paradise hotels juxtapose an image of Angkor Wat to the image of the hotel, as if they shared the same magnificence and splendour: 'Find serenity next to the grandeur' say the brochures of the Angkor Paradise, constructing the idea of shared monumentality.

By 'ambiance', I mean a quality much more immaterial than the previous ones, the re-creation of an atmosphere related to a particular environment of historical significance. For example, promotional materials describe the rooms of the Grand Hotel as immersed in 'the ambiance of Angkor' because they are decorated with objects that evoke the golden age of travel. The promotional materials of the Apsara Angkor Hotel illustrate a similar strategy:

> Apsara Angkor Resort & Conference built in the styles of the Khmer & Colonial Architecture and decorated like the home of the Khmers, it offers a unique charm of bygone Angkorian era, and complemented with the conveniences of today's luxury that has all the comforts of a home away from home. The hotel blends a traditional ambiance of the old-world elegance and modern convenience. As guests enter the lobby, they are reminded of the charm of the Khmer arts & civilization. It features an unusual traditional-designed chandelier and marvelous artworks by original Khmer Masters to make any stay at the hotel truly memorable of the past romance [sic].[18]

17 The Phimeanakas is a small temple in the form of a terraced pyramid, built in the tenth century (Glaize, 1993).

18 http://www.apsaraangkor.com/home.html (accessed 24 March 2016).

Figure 4.3 Raffles Grand Hotel

Photo by the author, 2009

Figure 4.4 A hotel that wants to be 'grand': façade; bottom

Photo by the author, 2009

Figure 4.5 A hotel that wants to be 'grand': internal courtyard

Photo by the author, 2009

Figure 4.6 Internal courtyard of the Park Hyatt Hotel, ex-Hotel de la Paix

Photo by the author, 2009

Figure 4.7 Reproduction of Angkor sculpture at the Angkor Howard Hotel

Photo by the author, 2009

Figure 4.8 Reproduction of colonial architecture and atmosphere at the Victoria Hotel

Photo by the author, 2009

Recreating an ambiance means treating hotel architecture as a stage set, furnished with objects and complemented with elements that involve senses other than sight, such as perfume, music, and food. The aim is to make tourists feel immersed in an authentic environment, as the Apsara Angkor illustrates with its focus on 'the home of the Khmers' and 'the traditional ambiance'.

In a similar vein, other hotels evoke colonial times. The Victoria is a significant example of this trend. Designed by French designers and owned by the French Société Electricité et Eaux de Madagascar, it draws on architectural forms, materials, decorations, and furnishings from the colonial period. In the hotel lobby, an old map shows the location of all the hotels owned by the Victoria company in Vietnam and Cambodia. Next to it is a picture from the travel narrative of the Duc de Montpensier, who visited Angkor in 1907 in spite of the very poor condition of the road system. In front of the hotel, two vintage Citroëns also pay homage symbolically to the Duc de Montpensier,[19] who had used a similar car to drive to Angkor. Behind the hotel counter, a picture from Mouhot's travel narrative depicts the towers of Angkor Wat deep in the forest, as they looked when the European explorers discovered them (Figure 4.8). Along the walls of the hotel's veranda, a series of paintings represents Cambodian village life, evoking a peaceful world of straw huts surrounded by vegetation, inhabited by a population with modest means but a serene outlook on life.

The influence of the travel narratives depicting the Cambodian population as living in a golden age isolated from the passage of time surfaces in these paintings. All the elements contribute to manufacture a credible re-creation of a colonial atmosphere. Like the colonial exhibitions, the hotel architecture succeeds in producing a 'temporal elsewhere', restoring a bygone era through an artificial re-creation. As with the colonial exhibitions, tourists are expected to accept the assimilation of the original to its re-creation in order to enjoy the offered experience of contact with a spatial or temporal elsewhere. More specifically, the re-creation of a colonial atmosphere invites tourists to identify with the explorers who discovered the temples or with the first travellers to Angkor who once experienced this kind of environment. Through the architecture and interior decoration of the hotel, inherited representations are reactivated in order to give the tourists a taste of the intense feelings of the first generation of travellers. In a similar vein, the reproduction of Angkor's architecture aims to extend the experience of the temples and the qualities of the World Heritage Site to the marginal place

19 The Duc de Montpensier travelled from Saigon to Angkor by car in 1908. He aimed to show that the Angkor region could be made accessible by road (Duc de Montpensier, 1910).

that is Siem Reap. The reproduction of spatial forms and objects seeks to arouse surrogates for the sense of the sublime that tourists may experience in front of the original works of art.

4.5.3 The arbitrariness of architectural signs

A Khmer owner told me during an interview that her family had imagined her hotel 'as traditional architecture recalling the eighteenth and nineteenth centuries, and as local architecture looking Cambodian'. She explained:

> Our parents wanted to build a hotel that looked like a pagoda. We decided together to build three wings arranged in the shape of a U because one single wing would have been too huge considering how many rooms we wanted to have. We imagined these wings as three big houses. We also wanted to put in a lot of wood (which we have used for the decoration of interior spaces), vegetation, and water, as you can see in the garden. On the plot of land there were already some palm trees which we decided to keep. So we organized the garden around the palm trees and surrounded it with the three buildings.[20]

This follows a common practice in Siem Reap, where the developers design the hotels themselves and only sometimes hire an architect to draw up and sign the plans required to obtain a building permit (see Chapter 3).

During the interview, the owner was particularly proud of the fact that her hotel drew on various architectural traditions – Angkor, the pagodas, and Khmer wooden handicrafts. A close examination of the building showed that its portal had been decorated with mouldings depicting elephants, mythical creatures, and *nagas*.[21] A small garden with tropical vegetation tries for a picturesque effect, but the open space is very narrow and almost completely occupied by the tiny swimming pool. A small wooden house accommodates complementary services (Figure 4.5).

Another developer showed a similarly positive attitude towards architectural eclecticism in presenting his hotel: 'As our family travels a lot, we have developed a style that is inspired both by French and Cambodian architecture, but that is neither colonial nor Khmer. This is what, in Montreal, we call "the Italian house"'.[22]

20 Personal communication with hotel owner, April 2008.

21 Mythical creatures in Hindu and Buddhist philosophy that take the form of water snakes.

22 Personal communication with hotel developer, April 2008.

Financial and economic reasons alone are insufficient to explain why developers are so keen to establish links with architectural traditions, or, more specifically, why they choose to combine them in the same building. According to Cody (2003), the multiplying of architectural allusions blurs the meaning given to them in the new hotel. The Mandarin Oriental in Hong Kong, opened in 1963, was initially a modernist building. Modernism reflected socio-economic innovation and modernization. It also represented the novel and ephemeral, the loss of stability of individuals who leave their usual residence in order to experience a transitory 'in-between'. But, later renovations of this hotel incorporated British colonial allusions as well as decorations based on Chinese art. This hybrid architecture avoids awakening nostalgia either for 'Victorian Great Britain' or an 'imaginary China' (Cody, p. 163). The association of eclectic allusions with a modernist building, which became even more sophisticated after the renovations, reflects the rapid evolution of postcolonial society as well as the uncertainties about its political and cultural identity.

A similar interpretation of the hybrid architecture of Siem Reap's hotels helps us to understand the developers' thinking. In the two cases presented above, the hotels reflect a clumsy attempt to construct ideas of a Cambodian identity that encompass the diverse expressions this identity may take. For instance, the second developer had lived in Canada for a long time: his reference to the name given to this particular form of hybrid in Montreal suggests a desire to incorporate the cosmopolitan culture of the Cambodian diaspora into his hotel project.

However, unlike the Mandarin Oriental, where the allusions had been emptied of cultural meaning, in my two examples the architectural elements and spatial forms are overloaded with identity-related features which their unsophisticated design communicates less effectively than a narrative would. There is a huge gap between the ways allusions are imagined and described verbally and the ways in which architecture and spatial forms express them. For instance, in the case of the second hotel only the façade expresses the mixture of French and Khmer architecture, which the owner presents as the leitmotiv of the whole project. Some allusions are merely stylized, like the roof of the first hotel, which simplistically reproduces the form and decoration of pagoda roofs. Because so many reproductions take the most simplistic forms, allusions become mere conventions, which, despite their approximate similarity can immediately be associated with the architectural type or the original monument both by tourists and by the residents of Siem Reap.

In other cases, there may be no concern with national identity. This is especially true when developers do not make reference only to local heritage and traditions (Angkor, the colonial period, and modern wooden dwellings and villages) but combine them with other cultural forms from outside Cambodia. For example, the French developer of the luxurious Héritage Hotel (Figure 4.9) in Siem Reap told me:

> I was inspired by the headquarters of the Phnom Penh sailing house which dates back to the 1920s. Only the façade of this building was left when I visited Phnom Penh [...] I took a picture of it and I replicated it on the hotel's façade. However, I modified the columns that I drew in a 'more conical' shape in order to accentuate the visual perspective. I also modified the carpentry because I believed it was rather crude in the original. Then I reproduced the same structure of the façade along the sides of the hotel. The building followed the construction techniques of the period with the exception of the foundations, which are modern. I copied the curves of the arches from the Paris metro [...]. I have actually imagined my hotel as a sequence of scenes inspired by Art Deco. For the rear part of the building, I imagined a shopping street, like the ones that you can find in Europe and especially in Italy. For example, I have copied Prague's lampposts – they are real gas lamps! I wanted to recreate the ambiance of the shopping street, I wanted symmetry [...] For the swimming pool, I drew on Balinese hotels, in particular the Begawan Giri Estate.[23]

The developer claimed that he faithfully reproduced originals. At the same time, he said that he had brought together reproductions of several spatial realities with different origins. Logically, these two statements cannot both be true; however, the developer did not detect any inconsistency in his approach. What these replicas have in common is the power to transpose 'elsewheres' into the hotel compound. Walking through the covered gallery, I found myself thinking that it looked like an Italian street – but which one? I could not say. The customer-visitor immediately recognizes the atmosphere of the recreated place and can connect with the memories, emotions, and ideas associated with it. However, these memories are socially constructed. The authenticity of the allusions claimed by the developer is undermined by their multiple sources. However, their power to instantly evoke atmospheres, places, and objects – in other words, their emotional authenticity – remains intact. The observer's capacity to associate the copy with one or several

23 Personal communication with hotel developer, February 2008.

originals is based on the same process of typological abstraction which was formed at the colonial exhibitions. This process reduces a family of similar objects to a synthesis of the elements that characterizes that particular family. In the colonial exhibitions, this process had pedagogic purposes, as it aimed to present the colonies to a public that hardly knew them. In the hotel, visitors are expected to recognize the allusions. It is not very important that the visitors should connect with a specific object, especially in cases where this object is not very well known (e.g. Phnom Penh's sailing house). It is more important that the symbolic association between the original and the re-creation connects them with an entire universe of reference, including the historic centres of Italian cities, colonial buildings, and Balinese resorts. Re-creations stand for symbols of these universes of reference, and symbols make multiple objects present simultaneously in the confined environment of the hotel. The customer-visitor can thus be transported to multiple cultural and geographical 'elsewheres'.

The case of the Heritage Hotel is both particular and characteristic: it is particular in that the developer has undertaken a multidirectional process of typological reproduction, and characteristic in throwing more light on the rationale that underpins the reproduction of cultural traditions. The promotional discourse of the Raffles Grand Hotel can help us to take this analysis further. Its promotional materials describe the hotel's rooms as permeated by the 'ambiance of Angkor', with decorations reminiscent of 'memories and artifacts' from 'the Golden Age of traveling'. The hotel's website states that the rooms have wood floors and marble bathrooms, and are furnished with four-poster beds. The correspondence between Angkor and the hotel is established on the basis of non-architectural common denominators: furniture, decoration, and luxury. Representations of the past and representations of luxury participate jointly in the construction of a consistent promotional narrative. Such consistency is only possible if the narrative moves beyond the historical dimension, which connects architectural allusions to the specific socio-cultural contexts they come from. This inevitable disconnection, however, does not rule out the possibility that the allusion will recall the past. That past can be local or foreign, but its evocative power is fundamental, because it represents a form of authority. Associated with the appeal of luxury and comfort, the persuasiveness of the promotional narrative draws both on enchantment and legitimation. Hotels' narratives are generally extremely terse when it comes to the practical details of the accommodation: their raison d'être is in no way limited to their function. Baudrillard's notion of 'functional simulacrum' (1981, p. 32) is helpful here. He argues that from primitive societies onward, the consumption of goods does not only meet functional needs, but also expresses symbolic values. He draws here on Veblen's theory of the 'leisure class'. Veblen (1989) argued that the division of labour has enabled higher-status individuals to be emancipated from productive work and to engage in symbolic activities which make their position in the social hierarchy visible. Through these activities powerful and wealthy individuals demonstrate that they can afford to waste time and money in unproductive activities, and to let others (servants, women) to do so on their behalf; he calls these social practices respectively 'conspicuous waste' and 'ostentatious prodigality'. Baudrillard draws on this to argue that consumption is 'a restrictive social institution that determines behavior' (p. 31) and to extend consumption from the realm of practices to the world of objects. On this basis, he argues that in contemporary societies 'objects never exhaust themselves in the function they serve, and in this excess of presence they take on their signification of prestige' (p. 32). Functionality and non-functionality coexist in tension, since two contradictory objectives – use and prestige – are intrinsic to the production of entire categories of object.

Hotels are characteristic examples of this conflict. Of course, they satisfy tourists' basic need for accommodation, but their narrative reflects a production of signification that goes far beyond the practical function of providing people with somewhere to sleep. Moreover, tourism is, by definition, unproductive. Like Veblen's leisure class, tourists acquire prestige, expending time and money on activities that demonstrate the higher social status of those who can afford to stay in hotels calling themselves 'Grand'. Hotels are 'not the locus of the satisfaction of needs, but of a symbolic labor, of a "production" in both senses of the term: *pro-ducers* – they are fabricated, but they are also produced as a *proof.* They are the locus of consecration of an effort, of an uninterrupted performance, of a *stress for achievement,* aiming always at providing the continual and tangible proof of social value' (Baudrillard, 1981, p. 33). The rhetoric of social prestige makes use of a semantics that considers heritage as a marker of authority and social legitimation, on the same level as luxury and decoration. Hotels can be seen as 'fetishes', as 'artifacts' resulting from 'a labor of appearances and signs' (Baudrillard, 1981, p. 91). Signs 'do not have a distinct reference to any reality. There remains only simulacra, as signs [...] lose contact with the things signified. The world of the consumer is seen as composed of pure simulacra, or the hyperreal, where just the signs themselves constitute the realm of experience' (O'Shaughnessy and O'Shaughnessy, 2003, p. 80).

When adopted for hotel design, allusions to heritage and tradition are emptied of their cultural content, as in the case that Cody (2003) examined:

Figure 4.9 The Heritage Hotel

Photo by the author, 2009

they are not introduced because of their real cultural, historical, or political character, but as signs of prestige. These criteria structure a new form of narrative and formal consistency that allows the juxtaposition and combination of elements from very different backgrounds. This process re-contextualizes replicas (spatial forms, objects, or ambiance) in a new semantics, in which they all function as signs of prestige. Furthermore, hotels offer the tourist a mediated experience of the real. Replicas – of villages, colonial environments, and temples – trigger emotions and fantasies about the past, blurring the distinction between reality and image. Hotel architecture thus encapsulates both an individual quest for pleasure, intrinsic to the tourism experience, and a social quest for legitimation. This work of legitimation is not limited to tourists. The developers and owners who can spend money to build a Grand Hotel (or a hotel that aspires to that status) are also flaunting their prestige, especially in a town undergoing a transition from village to international tourism hub. Paradoxically, this reaches its extreme expression when the hotel turns out to be unprofitable and survives simply as a giant, unproductive monument.

4.6 The quest for the local

4.6.1 Living in a 'house'

The desire to get in touch with 'the local' is another quest at the foundations of the tourism experience. The anthropology of tourism has frequently examined the ways in which tourism promotion creates expectations about the encounter with the local, and the ways in which the tourism space is planned in order to manage contact between tourists and their hosts. MacCannell (1973; 1976) argues that tourists would like to access the interior of tourist destinations and societies in order to touch the essence of the local; however, since local hosts are not continuously available to be exposed to the tourists' gaze and show them aspects of their culture usually reserved for insiders, spaces of staged authenticity are created. In these spaces, 'the local' is displayed and performed through re-creations and manipulations of heritage, while 'real life' takes place behind the scenes. The tourists' quest for authentic contact with the local is left unsatisfied. Other authors (Nyìri, 2009) argue that not all tourists necessarily look for such contact, but are happy with the performances and manufactured environments organized for them. Drawing on the example of Bali, Picard and Wood (1997) argue that tourism gives local societies the opportunity to decide which aspects of their culture they want to make available to an audience of outsiders.

Tourism architecture in Siem Reap responds to the quest for contact with 'the local'. Hotels that draw on local forms of housing, and more particularly on the Cambodian tradition of wooden dwellings, shape spaces of staged authenticity.

Since time immemorial, wooden houses on stilts have marked the landscape of Cambodian villages. Apart from minor variations in this form of housing introduced in the nineteenth and twentieth centuries (Prak, 2006), construction techniques have changed little over the centuries (Tenturier, 2006). Ideas of the sacred are embedded in the construction of a wooden house and the planning of the village to which it belongs (Népote, 2006). These ideas draw on the animist substrate of Cambodian society. It is generally believed that the house is a living organism, whose parts have names associated with the human body. A house can only be established after the savage forces of nature have been domesticated and the favour of the tutelary spirits obtained. For this purpose, rituals codify the phases of construction while ensuring that harmony between the microcosm and the macrocosm is achieved: 'the Khmer house is a deeply symbolic whole. It thus appears as the expression of a complex system that impresses social and cultural meanings on the space, like a technical solution to the need to protect, structure, and identify the family. It is the minimal unit of production, the result of a collective family endeavour. Each person has to repeat the actions learned from predecessors and build their own shelter at least once in their life' (Phuoeng, 1997, p. 88, author's translation).

Népote (2006) argues that 'many traditions concur in suggesting that there once was a particular type of rural dwelling, the *pteah rong daol*' (p. 108) from which all typological variations derive; for instance, types of house have been identified based on the form of the roof (Pan, 2003). The main partition wall of the house was on a north-south axis. The structure was a system of wooden columns and beams with spans of regular dimensions. A staircase gave access to a covered veranda, and a wooden frame supported the roof. The column standing in the centre of the house and supporting the ridgepole represented the male ancestor of the family. The sectors of the house's single floor were organized around this column and designated for specific functions and levels of privacy. The house was divided into four quadrants, the two most important being the public and the private, subdivided into various parts distinguished by function, activity, and category of people (women, men, guests, monks) who can occupy them. The space beneath the dwelling is divided into two main sectors, namely the space for everyday family activities and the workspace in which animals, plants and plant products, and weavers can be located. Nowadays, construction materials may vary, especially because wood is becoming a scarce resource following the massive deforestation of Cambodia. A majority of contemporary houses have two connected main spaces on the house floor, that is to say an enclosed room where the parents sleep and a big multi-use space for the children. The height of the stilts reflects the wealth of the family. If they are tall enough, the space beneath them can be used both for work and family life. The kitchen is generally a platform, only sometimes covered, located partway between the ground and the house floor, to the side, or behind the main building. In rural environments, plots are quite large and may include lateral annexes such as a rice granary and animal cages. Plants, trees, and wooden fences mark the limit of the plot, which is also the limit of sacred space (Tenturier, 2006). In villages that have been absorbed by urban development, plots tend to be smaller, and, increasingly frequently, walls are built to delimit private ownership. Also, in urban environments bricks and concrete walls enclose the ground floor in order to increase the liveable space.

Apart from typological variations, the stilts and the column-and-beam construction persist. Cambodians believe that living on an elevated structure allows free air circulation between the columns and the between the floorboards, and ensures that the house will be healthy and comfortable (Phuoeng, 1997). Because of their sacred value and longstanding rootedness in the life of Cambodian society, the conventional wisdom holds that wooden houses on stilts are the typical form of Khmer dwelling. Other forms of housing, such as the shophouse, have become widely developed in Cambodian cities, but are still largely associated with the descendants of Chinese and Vietnamese immigrants.

Discussion of the main features of wooden architecture has been developing in Cambodia since the 1990s. It is based on several scholarly publications by both Khmer and foreign authors, mainly drawing on morphological and ethnographic analyses (inter alia Tenturier, 2006). This discussion has started to extend beyond academia and to interest the general public. For instance, in 2013, the National Museum of Phnom Penh put on an exhibition of models of typical wooden houses. In 2008, the first issues of the architecture magazine *Khmer Home and Decor* published drawings illustrating the construction process of the wooden house. However, this discussion has not been orientated towards the conservation of existing wooden houses; instead, it has advocated for the construction techniques, materials, typical spatial layouts, and social and religious values associated with the tradition of wooden architecture.

In other countries of Southeast Asia, such as Thailand and Malaysia, a similar discussion developed when industrialization increased the divide between modernized cities and rural villages. Wooden houses came to be imbued with the nostalgic memories of urban dwellers who aspired to regain a peaceful lifestyle. They encapsulated the ideal of an idyllic rural environment and functioned as anchors for social memories, which needed to be preserved in order to maintain a connection with the foundations of the national culture. In Cambodia, the recording of oral traditions of construction that had never previously been formalized in treatises on architecture (Tenturier, 2006) is the first sign of an emerging discussion of national traditions and identity, which may take a similar direction in future years.

However, thus far, the production of wooden houses for tourist accommodation has been the main form in which the value of architecture in wood has been recognized. Once again, the discussion of Cambodian identity, heritage, and traditions is, at least initially, driven primarily by tourism. It is, for the moment, a discussion disproportionately focused outwards, that is to say towards the satisfaction of tourists' expectations of contact with 'the local'. While wooden houses are highly appreciated by tourists,

Cambodians generally prefer villas and condominiums, associated with ideas of modernity and improved social status.

The adaptation of local housing for foreigners has its roots in the global architectural culture of the bungalow (King, 1995). Back in the eighteenth century, the British adapted the Bengalese house into a new residential form – the bungalow – to suit the demands of colonial settlers in India. The local workforce contributed to the development of this housing form, which was suitable for the tropical climate, but also met the criteria of comfort demanded by British architects and future residents. The form of the bungalow diversified during the nineteenth century and was disseminated across the colonial world, incorporating ever more elements of Western origin. The bungalow was viewed as a cultural anchor for Western residents in the colonies and helped spread Western tastes and criteria of comfort across Asia.

A bungalow was the first tourist lodging built by the French administration at Angkor. It was called the Bungalow des Ruines and was a single wing, with brick walls and wooden floor, built on short stilts and covered with a sloping roof.[24] It replaced the *sala*,[25] a semi-open building on stilts, which provided only the most basic comforts to travellers. In postcolonial times, the 'bungalow hotel' in Kep, a seaside resort in southern Cambodia, was composed of two wings, called chalets, each divided into three rooms. The two buildings were linked around a central pavilion that contained the hotel service areas. Archival sources say that this building belonged 'to the widespread type of the *sala* with outbuildings for the staff'.[26] These examples from the history of tourism in Cambodia show that the *sala* and the bungalow have both drawn on local wooden houses, adapting them for temporary occupancy by foreigners, while gradually improving the level of comfort.

24 ANC, No. 15917 'Lettre du gérant de la Maison de Passagers à Angkor Wat au Commissaire délégué à Battambang', in *Dossier général sur le parc d'Angkor, la gestion du tourisme, horaires, subventions, travaux relatifs aux ruines*, 1909-1913.

25 *Sala* is a generic term in Khmer meaning house, building, hall, or school. Compound terms with the word *sala* designate different types of building, e.g. *sala kdei* = tribunal, *sala kaet* = provincial headquarters. At Angkor, the *sala* was not furnished and early travellers had to sleep on mats. Viscount Miramon-Fargues described it as a building 'painted blue, built out of planks, with a platform' which 'looks like the stage of a café concert' (1905, p. 362, author's translation). Pierre Loti described it as a wooden semi-open building on stilts 'like their houses, it consists of lattice floor with a thatched roof upheld by pillars of reddish wood. It has no walls, and to screen us, night and day, we have only the transparent curtains of our mosquito nets' (1996, p. 31).

26 ANC, No. 1833, 'Création à Kèp d'une station de repos', Protectorat du Cambodge, Cabinet du Résident Supérieur, Phnom Penh, 15 Mars 1916, Dossier cartes 1916-1917.

Today, both Cambodian and foreign owners and designers use the concept of the bungalow to design hotels that take their inspiration from local building traditions. The Angkor Village resort, built in 1995 by a French-Cambodian architect couple, was one of the first in this genre to be opened in Siem Reap. It makes explicit reference to the Buddhist monks' little houses, built in the pagoda precincts (Figure 4.10). They are traditionally built on short stilts, making the space below the building inaccessible to someone standing upright. A ladder gives access to a small veranda where the monks dry their clothes. The interior space is one single room. Like the families' wooden houses, the monks' cells are built with a column-beam structure that supports a sloping roof. At Wat Bo, as in many other Cambodian pagodas, the monks' houses are grouped together side by side in the rear area of the precinct. In the interpretation of this model in the hotel, 28 small houses are positioned along a main axis, while bigger buildings allude to the *sala* and house the hotel's services and restaurant. Ponds and plants surround the small houses. There are bungalows with one floor (20 square metres) and two floors (40 square metres), each with a veranda located under the eaves of the tiled roof. Overhead walkways bordered by dense vegetation lead to the houses and give the impression of a labyrinth of narrow paths (Figure 4.11).

Other more modest hotels establish a direct link with Khmer families' wooden houses. The two French owners of the Mystères d'Angkor hotel, for instance, did their own analysis of local types of dwelling in order to build their hotel in the village of Wat Polinka. They also drew on *Charpentes et tuiles khmères* (Dumarçay, 1973) to design the details and decorations of the bungalows, which are situated in a garden and surrounded by a swimming pool. In particular, they wanted the materials used and the shape of the roofs to reflect Cambodian architecture: 'in our charming tropical garden, in the shade of the coconut trees, we will welcome you to an authentic Khmer house [...] where in little dwellings which respect the local architecture, comfortable rooms with exotic decor await you'.[27]

The authenticity of these adaptations of wooden buildings for tourists is restricted to their architectural character and spatial forms. For instance, tourists stay in houses that take their inspiration from monks' cells, but do not have to endure the basic daily living conditions of the monastery. Similarly, at Mystères d'Angkor, the guests live in a village environment, but benefit from a vastly improved level of comfort.

27 http://www.mysteres-angkor.com/fr/ (accessed 30 March 2016). Translation from French by the author (the English version of the promotional narrative on the website does not correspond to the content of the text in French).

This process of selection recalls the ambivalence of the sense of exoticism. A cultural expression or a typical scene fascinates the foreign observer. At the same time, the observer is repelled by some aspects of this object of fascination, and has no interest in closer contact with it. The colonial exhibitions offered entertainment for European visitors, eliminating the unpleasant aspects of the sense of exoticism. Similarly, the bungalows are fabricated versions of local dwellings through which customers can sense an echo of exoticism without really touching it. They cannot recapture the emotional intensity experienced by the first travellers, who encountered Southeast Asian countries unprotected. Yet, they still long for that intensity, and it is this longing that brings them to choose the hotel.

Representations of 'the local' are central to architectural design. The desire to gaze at exotic Cambodian architecture has its roots in the idea of an unchanging tradition, which the relative stability of the wooden house typology only confirms (Tenturier, 2006). It is reinforced by the inherited representations of a static population[28] disseminated by colonial discourse, which postcolonial narratives appropriated and converted into the positive portrait of a spiritually elevated people.

During their stay in the bungalows, tourists encounter the historically stratified representations with which the hotel's built landscape is permeated. A sense of nostalgia may be awakened: not the sentimentalist attraction for a bygone past (as in the case of reproductions of colonial architecture), but rather a fascination with the human condition as it supposedly still exists in the Cambodian pagodas and villages. The tourist connects to the notion of the idyll described by Loti. Such a sense of nostalgia is rooted deep in the human quest for the original; the primitive house supposedly reflects the immemorial, instinctual wisdom of its makers. This wisdom is seen as timeless, speaking to what is universal in the human being (Rykwert, 1976).

In this twofold process of adaptation and idealization of local architecture, however, the sense of sacredness is eliminated from the replica houses, whose construction does not have to respect the rituals and spatial layouts dictated by animist beliefs. Imitating a feature found in several of the Angkor temples, the yoni is represented by a stone sculpture that brings a constant flow of water to a basin. In the temples, the yoni has a sacred value, fertility, and when it is penetrated by a vertical stone called the lingam, representing the male sex, it symbolizes the fundamental unity at the core of the universe.

28 Morton (2000) observes that colonial narratives presented the Cambodian population as backward in order to legitimize the colonial enterprise which was supposed to bring them progress.

Figure 4.10 Monks' houses, Wat Bo

Photo by Aline Hétreau-Pottier, 2007

Figure 4.11 Angkor Village hotel

Photo by the author, 2009

In the hotel, the replica of this sculpture brings water to the swimming pool around which the bungalows are positioned. Replicas empty such typical objects of their original and sacred meaning. Only the outward forms are maintained as reminders of local tradition. In a similar way, wooden houses lose the sacred and cultural meanings of their original context. They are reduced to empty shells, objects onto which the tourists can project their expectations. They are merely the material residue of representations.

Far from the idealizations associated with architectural re-creations of wooden houses, low-budget tourists look for contact with 'the local' by staying at a guesthouse. The way these guesthouses have developed raises more questions about the notions of the local and the authentic with regard to the evolution of Siem Reap's urban society and housing forms.

As its name suggests, the guesthouse is considered to be a preferable way to escape from 'staged authenticity', as it allows the guests to share the daily life of the inhabitants. In Wat Bo and Taphul (see Chapter 3), the owners have created guesthouses in the houses where they have lived since the beginning of the 1990s. A Khmer family opened the Mahogany Guesthouse on the land it has owned since the 1980s, when the grandmother paid for it in gold. Like many wooden houses in an urban environment, the ground floor is enclosed by walls and the plot is rather small. The guesthouse is a line of buildings with sloping tiled roofs, interconnected along the long side of the oblong plot. The façade has a large veranda accessible by a staircase. To the rear, the kitchen is a semi-open, detached building bordering the outside wall. When the guesthouse opened in 1992 with fifteen rooms available for rent on the first floor, the guests used to share the family's living conditions. In 1995, the number of rooms was reduced to improve the comfort level, with the construction of private bathrooms and toilets. With the commercial development of Wat Bo Road, the family opened a travel agency on the ground floor. The family members continue to live on the ground floor (only the grandmother keeps a room on the first floor), but the front space of the house has been converted into an office, now with advertisements 'decorating' the façade and making the wooden architecture less and less visible (Figure 4.12).

Mom's Guesthouse, also located along Wat Bo Road, started on the same basis, but its evolution has been rather different. First, a new concrete building was built behind the wooden house. Then, as soon as the family accumulated enough capital, the wooden house was destroyed in order to 'improve the guesthouse as tourism was growing' and to provide 'clean rooms with bathrooms, more comfort, and air conditioning'.[29] A Khmer architect showed the family a catalogue with several models of buildings with a concrete bearing structure and brick walls, and they chose one of them for the new guesthouse. That particular model was selected because it had 'columns and wooden mouldings'. The decorations of the façade do indeed aim to evoke classical architecture, with pairs of pinkish columns supporting a pediment decorated with sculpted flowers (Figure 4.13). The older concrete building in the rear of the plot has been converted into a restaurant, while the guest rooms have been located in the new building. A tiny swimming pool was also built. These successive alterations reveal the owners' intention to transform their guesthouse gradually into a small hotel, and illustrates, on a miniature scale, the same eclectic borrowing of allusions found in Siem Reap's grand hotels.

The guesthouse's advertising confirms this intention: 'Mom's Guesthouse opened in 1992. It initially started with 15 Khmer traditional wooden rooms. Thanks to our hospitality and excellent service, Mom's Guest House has become very popular for both local and international tourists. Our business is progressively growing. By early 2004, we were able to replace our wooden guesthouse with a brick building of 30 luxury rooms and March 2010 we build swimming pool' [sic].[30]

This narrative does not view the destruction of the wooden house as a loss, but as one of the necessary steps towards an improvement of the guesthouse's standing, the gradual acquisition of signs of luxury. The tourist who wishes to get in touch with the spirit of the local milieu will now recognize the desire for economic progress and the changing tastes of Siem Reap's inhabitants. This does not mean that values associated with the authentic and local are eliminated from the discourse these inhabitants produce about themselves and their tourist accommodation. On the contrary, the guesthouse's website shows pictures of the family members performing daily activities such as cooking, sitting together in the living room, repairing plumbing, washing dishes, and playing with children. These images seem to invite the observer (and prospective customer) to experience the most ordinary but authentic expressions of daily life. This un-staged authenticity of the local people is in contradiction with enduring representations of a static Cambodian society, and illustrates how the guesthouse owners appropriate images of modernization and luxury while also constructing a discourse about their own identity.

29 Personal communication with the guesthouse owners, February 2008.
30 http://www.momguesthouse.com/ (accessed 26 March 2016).

Figure 4.12 Mahogany Guesthouse

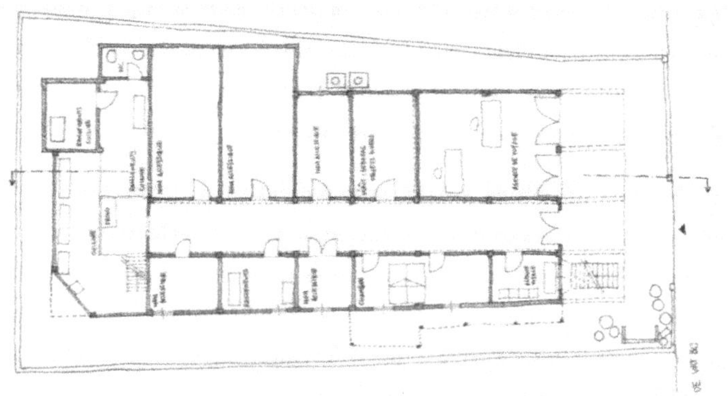

Map of the groundfloor

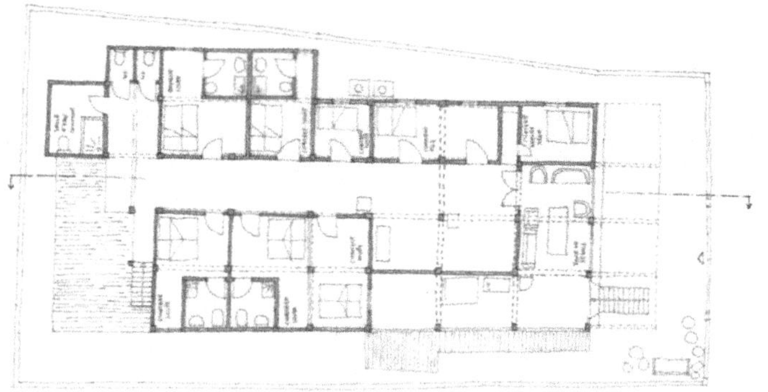

Map of the first floor

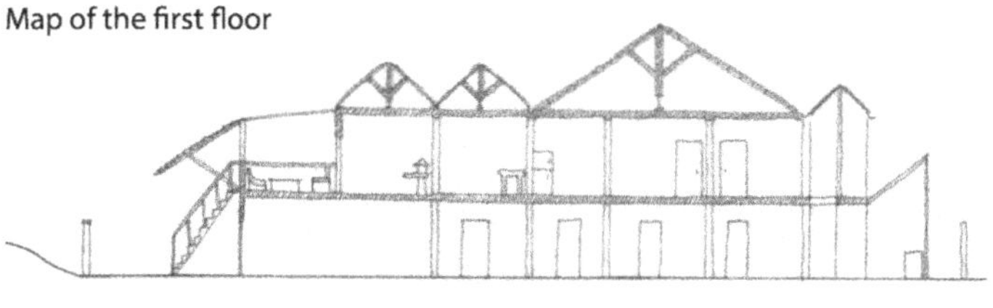

Longitudinal section

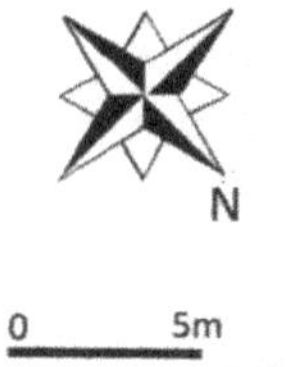

Drawings and picture by the author, 2008

Figure 4.13 Mom's Guesthouse façade

Photo by the author, 2008

4.6.2 Performing tradition in the Cambodian Cultural Village

The Cambodian Cultural Village is the first theme park to reproduce different types of Cambodian village and 'past lifestyles'. The park also features miniature reproductions of Cambodian monuments and a museum with wax models of historical figures, a collection of crafted items, and various models representing striking events from the Angkor period. Although this might look quite conventional from an international perspective, the opening of the theme park in 2003 represented a substantial broadening of heritage recognition in Cambodia, where the official recognition of national heritage had previously been almost exclusively focused on archaeology.

Three young Khmer architects were initially in charge of the project, though only one of them remained with it until the end, together with an archaeologist and an engineer. The team undertook one month of fieldwork across Cambodia, with a particular focus on Rattanakiri, Mondulkiri, and Siem Reap provinces. They made drawings of the different types of house they could identify. The archaeologist classified them by type, representing the different peoples and cultures of Cambodia. Finally, the architect designed the plan and elevation views of the buildings to be built in the park. The eleven reconstructed villages bring the largest Cambodian group – the Khmer – together with minority groups, diaspora, and descendants of foreigners (Figure 4.14). Descriptions of the types of dwelling, geographical situation, inhabitants' economic activities, daily practices, and religious beliefs accompany the reproduced villages and provide background information about these human settlements.

The selection processes are much like those that governed the reproduction of villages and towns in colonial exhibitions. Performances are staged in the reproductions in order to simulate daily life. Young Khmer dancers, unsure of their role and poorly trained, wearily perform the dances and rituals of ethnic minorities. Sometimes they cannot help laughing at the audiences of amused but unenthusiastic or somewhat distracted foreigners and Cambodians.

Despite this striking similarity with the colonial exhibitions, the Khmer architects did not use those as models. To get ideas on how to design a theme park, they travelled to Shenzhen, where the Splendid China Folk Cultural Village, opened in 1991, houses reproductions of 24 villages representing the 21 nationalities of China, with the main objective of promoting Chinese national culture. Close to this park, the older Splendid China, opened in 1989, showcases miniature replicas of major Chinese monuments.[31]

In China, the theme park industry first emerged in the 1980s. It developed rapidly, and there were already between 2,000 and 2,500 theme parks in the country by 1998 (Ap, 2008). With Japan and South Korea, China is among the first Asian countries where the Western model[32] of the theme park was imported (Clavé, 2007; Brannen, 1992), followed, in Southeast Asia, by Singapore. The global model of the theme park entered Asia through its most dynamic economies, at a time when domestic tourism was also developing. The Khmer architects followed the milestones in the dissemination of the theme park in Asia in order to imitate the forms and meanings associated with this global model.

The Khmer team adopted the building materials of original houses, but adapted the built forms to the context and constraints of the theme park. For instance, in one of the villages used as a model the houses were originally

31 A third theme park has been built in the Shenzhen special economic zone, but was not used as a source by the Khmer design team. It is the World's Window, which displays miniature replicas of famous monuments from everywhere in the world.

32 Its ancient origins lie in the fairs of medieval Europe and in the European and American amusement parks of the nineteenth century; it was developed as a recreational model by Disney in the theme park which opened in California in 1955, and was then emulated by various agents and corporations across the world (Clavé, 2007).

built in a row along a path. However, the plan for the tourist facility required the houses to be arranged around a square where daily dance and theatre performances would take place. Also, while there were discursive references to the lifestyles and house types from the past, architectural allusions made no attempt at historical accuracy: ancient and modern elements were combined in the same sample house. This atemporal reconstruction of Cambodian culture flattens history into a microcosm of heritage in which the present coalesces with the ancient and recent past.

One particular point is especially telling. The roof decorations of some of the houses imitate the dragons from the Angkor temples. Reacting to criticism by some of the visitors who thought they recognized Thai decorations on the roofs, the Khmer architects proved that every element of the houses' design came from Cambodia. The criterion used to support the legitimacy of the architectural allusions is neither the accurate reproduction of the originals, nor emotional authenticity, but simply the fact of Cambodian origin. Unlike the colonial exhibitions, which were only addressed to European audiences, the Chinese and Cambodian theme parks seek to build ideas and images of national identity that address both local and international audiences (Hitchcock, Stanley, and Chung Siu, 2005).

However, using Cambodian origin as a criterion poses problems of representativeness. A group of wooden pavilions around a Christian church represents the Khmer people living in the United States. This is the only Khmer diaspora community to be represented in the park. This special status is due to the fact that the developer of the Cambodian Cultural Village is a Khmer citizen living in the USA. The Chinese minority also benefits from a favourable position: the narrative which presents their village celebrates this community for the 'perseverance and good management' of descendants of Chinese immigrants, who have been successful in business and developed both agriculture and trade. In contrast, the Vietnamese ethnic minority, which makes up approximately five per cent of the Cambodian population, is not represented at all in the Cambodian Cultural Village. The reasons are left unspoken, but may relate to historically rooted racism and prejudice against the Vietnamese minority, still very present in Cambodian society. Lastly, the 'millionaire house' does not represent an ethnic group, but is rather the typical house of the wealthy families who used to live 'in Oudong in the past'.[33] It is an open invitation to the visitors to indulge in imagining the ideal wooden house, echoing similar approaches to the

33 Oudong was the former capital of Cambodia in the seventeenth century, and again between 1740 and 1746.

reproduction of such houses in hotel architecture. The selective nature of the park features undermines claims that it was designed objectively, and reveals the political character of the project, which uses the park as an opportunity to give voice to enmities and alliances as well as judgements based on personal preferences.

The microcosm of the Cambodian Cultural Village also includes reproductions of Cambodian monuments including the Royal Palace, the religious buildings of the ancient capital of Oudong, the Phnom Penh National Museum, and the Wat Phnom. With the exception of the reclining Buddha of the Baphuon temple (which was not yet open to visitors when the theme park was opened), none of the monuments are from Angkor. Through miniature replicas, the park extends heritage recognition to a collection of ancient and modern monuments, while at the same time reinforcing the role of Siem Reap-Angkor as a microcosm which can contain the totality of Cambodian heritage, even monuments located in other provinces.

This microcosmic representation of heritage blurs the conventional distinction between high and popular culture, confirming the park's dual purpose as an educational and leisure destination. Not only disparate monuments and dwellings are juxtaposed; the wax museum brings together kings, queens, generals, monks, and political figures with movie stars and singers from the 1960s. A controversial representation of an American soldier with a young Khmer girl was used to evoke increasing prostitution and the spread of the HIV virus at the time of the UNTAC, but had been taken out of the wax museum one year after my first visit in 2008.

The importation of the theme park model into Cambodia readily shows how international capital and tourists circulate in what was once a peripheral country. Through this flagship project, Siem Reap appears to be an emerging node of the global economy, thanks to the close proximity of a World Heritage Site, which helps the town to overcome its previous marginality on the international stage. The profiles of the people actually involved with the project, however, reveal the subordinate position of Siem Reap and Cambodia on this stage. A single individual initiated the project with funding from a Canadian and Cambodian joint venture (Canadian Gold & Trust Corporation), which founded the Canadia Bank, one of the first commercial banks to be opened in the country. Only three young Khmer professionals – the chief architect had only just graduated from the Royal University of Fine Arts when he was hired for this project – were in charge of the park's design. The Cambodian Cultural Village exemplifies the subaltern role of the state in producing a heritage discourse. Almost exclusively focused on Angkor, the state is not involved in the recognition

Figure 4.14 Reproduction of a village of the Kola, an ethnic minority originally from Burma, in the Cambodian Cultural Village

Photo by the author, 2009

of ordinary customs and traditions as constitutive of national identity. That task, which is particularly important for a nation only just emerging from war and foreign occupation, has been left in the hands of a group of developers and young architects.

4.7 Spectacular heritage: The museums of Siem Reap

The Angkor National Museum's façades echo temple architecture, with their towers, sculptures, and surfaces loosely imitating the pink stone of Angkor. However, when I touched the imposing pillars of the museum entrance gate, I realized they were hollow. The Angkor National Museum reminded me of a giant stage set. The sensory contrast between an image of solidity and a reality of structural weakness illustrates, in my view, the entire project for the museum of Angkor in Siem Reap (Figure 4.15).

Siem Reap had no museum. The École Française d'Extrême Orient established the Angkor Conservation at the beginning of the twentieth century as a permanent institution for the protection and restoration of items from Angkor. The Angkor Conservation was attached to the Cambodian Ministry of Culture after the country won independence, but remained under the EFEO's direction until the Khmer Rouge took over. In Phnom Penh, a national museum had been established in colonial times. It was first established in one of the buildings of the Royal Palace, made available by King Sisowath in 1905; a new museum building was constructed by Georges Groslier between 1917 and 1924, and part of its collection was opened to the public in 1920. Nationalized, like the Angkor Conservation, after Cambodian independence, it was opened again in 1994 in conjunction with the French-Cambodian Cooperation Convention.

Tourism development at Siem Reap-Angkor opened up the possibility of significant revenue from a more ambitious museum established close to the archaeological site. A Thai-based international company, Vilailuck International Holdings,[34] seized this opportunity. It established a Cambodian branch (the Museum Company Limited) and secured a Build Cooperate and Transfer (BCT) contract with the APSARA and the Cambodian Ministry of Culture and Fine Arts, which allowed the company to build a fifteen-million-dollar museum and manage it for 30 years, after which the museum is supposed to become Cambodian state property.

The company's objective was to establish a 'world-class museum', 'a cultural learning institute that would enhance artifact preservation, collection and restoration', 'a notable site of arts bringing community collaboration and commitment'.[35] A permanent Conservation and Restoration Workshop consolidated the image of the museum's scientific commitment, which is also promoted on its website, where several examples of restored pieces are published, together with information on their origin and characteristics as well as technical details of the conservation process. This narrative was a response to the harsh criticism that immediately followed the museum's opening. International experts, architects, and archaeologists complained about the exhibition choices and lack of compliance with international standards.[36] In response to these criticisms, the museum claims scientific

34 The company is chaired by Charoenrath Vilailuck, an Australia-educated Thai citizen. Its parent company is Samart Corporation, which has invested heavily in the Cambodian telecommunications sector in the last twenty years.

35 Source: website of the Angkor National Museum, www.angkornationalmuseum.com (accessed 4 February 2015).

36 Turnbull 2008; personal communication with archaeologists and architects based in Siem Reap, summer 2008.

credibility in order to legitimize its existence close to the UNESCO World Heritage Site.

When I first visited the museum a few days after its opening, the archaeological items were mounted on rough blocks of cement. Subdued light prevented the visitor from appreciating the details of the sculptures. Information about their history was skimpy and slightly inaccurate. In contrast, a great deal of effort had been made to create displays idealizing Angkor as a magical creation.

Before entering the exhibition area the visitor passes through a small theatre, called the Briefing Hall. The silhouette of Angkor Wat suddenly emerges out of darkness, illuminated by fluorescent lighting and accompanied by music reminiscent of American blockbuster films. The visitor is invited to sit back and relax, and watch a fifteen-minute film that briefly presents the history of Angkor Wat and the overall layout of the museum. The language of the video is similar in tone and vocabulary to those advertisements for spas that invite the tourist to indulge in a pleasant, effortless experience. Its spectacular special effects are supposed to amaze the visitor. When compared to the travel narratives of the second half of the nineteenth century, this seems like an artificial attempt to reanimate emotional intensity in surrogate form.

Next comes the Exclusive Gallery – a name suggesting a luxury hotel rather than a cultural institution – where a thousand Buddha images are exhibited to invite the visitor to 'reflect on Buddhism'. The museum recreates the Buddhist temple environment, where it is typical to exhibit a series of images of the Lord Buddha as objects to be venerated. This is followed by the Khmer Civilization Gallery where it is asserted that 'one of the mysteries is how the Khmer empire was established'. This claim marks the reappearance of the discovery myth in this contemporary project. Since colonial times, historians and archaeologists have gradually solved the enigmas of the Khmer temples; but the theme of mystery is reintroduced as a seductive argument to help the visitor to identify with the nineteenth-century adventurer. Discovery can then be experienced at the individual level, as the visitor moves through the galleries to learn 'what drove the ancient Khmer civilization to create the world's most colossal structure ever', to 'explore the Khmer people's faith in the great kings', and to 'delve into the stories of ancient wars that once ravaged these tranquil lands'.

After viewing some basic information about the chronology of the Khmer kings and the beliefs of the Khmer people in the past, the visitor enters the hall, which presents Angkor Wat as the 'most significant example of an earthly paradise' and Angkor Thom as 'the Pantheon of Spirits', the 'great capital', and an 'architectural masterpiece'. The museum narrative promotes Angkor as a great civilization. Stone inscriptions are exhibited as 'proofs that such a grand world once existed'. Historians and archaeologists have removed any doubt about the existence of the Khmer kingdom. Nonetheless, this narrative draws not on those scientific sources, but rather on the colonial images of wonder that constructed Angkor as a marvel.

The generation of aesthetic feeling and the inherited representations of Angkor – even though the re-creation is artificial – are supposed to satisfy tourists' expectations of finding a reality matching the images and narratives that have influenced them. However, a great many of the museum's visitors are Khmer families and groups of Asian tourists,[37] who we can assume, have not been influenced by the history of Western knowledge about Indochina. The use of these images and narratives shows that they are circulating among the international companies who today produce Siem Reap, and that they are also acquired by Asian tourists. In this recycling of inherited images, audio-visual technology lets tourists indulge in an entertaining and 'soft' cultural experience, which sacrifices the accuracy of historical information to the fascinating charm of a narrative.

The marketing of Angkor as a cultural commodity finds its place within the broader commercial context of the museum. On the street-level floor of the building, commercial space in a large shopping mall, evocatively called the Cultural Mall, was supposed to be rented out to shops and restaurants. However, due to the relatively low number of visitors and the peripheral location of the museum along Avenue Charles de Gaulle, the shops were permanently empty and all commercial activity soon closed down. During my second visit to the museum in 2013, I walked along the deserted, dusty alley, populated only by already tattered posters of smiling blond tourists eating pastries. The yet to be opened, but already obsolete building seemed like a striking illustration of the thoughtless speculation taking place in Siem Reap. In 2015, another generation of shops opened in the mall, a new promise of economic vitality.

The fact that Vilailuck International Holdings, a Thai company, owns the Angkor National Museum is not insignificant, given the long-standing conflict between Thailand and Cambodia over the ownership of Angkor. At the time of its greatest expansion, the Khmer kingdom included part

37 Statistics about museum attendance were not available. This estimate is based on the personal experience of the author and the general practice of tour operators in Siem Reap who generally organize guided tours to the museums and theme parks, mainly for groups of Asian tourists.

of modern Siam. Then, between 1794 and 1907, Siem Reap province fell under the authority of a Siamese principality. During that period, King Rama IV ordered the construction of a miniature replica of Angkor Wat, which is still exhibited in the courtyard of Wat Phra Kaew in Bangkok, symbolizing Siamese claims to ownership of Angkor. In postcolonial times, Cambodia and Thailand fought over the ownership of the Preah Vihear temple, located on the frontier between the two countries and a witness to the expansion of the Khmer kingdom over territory encompassing parts of contemporary Thailand and Laos. Maps drawn in colonial times assigned the temple to Cambodia and were approved by decree. However, the Thai army occupied the temple in 1954, calling into question the validity of this previous decision. Cambodia requested the assistance of the International Court of Justice, which, in 1962, confirmed Cambodian ownership of the temple based on the study of colonial maps (Cuassay, 1998). Thai claims lost credibility when Thailand failed to appeal the International Court's decision. Nevertheless, when Cambodia proposed nominating Preah Vihear as a World Heritage Site, the tensions between the two countries resurfaced. In 2003, dissatisfaction grew when a popular Thai singer declared that Angkor belonged to Thailand. Violent manifestations of dissent took place in front of the Thai embassy in Phnom Penh. Military confrontations on the border started in 2008 after the UNESCO listing of Preah Vihear (Croissant and Chambers, 2011). They only stopped in 2013, after the reiteration of the International Court of Justice judgement, which helped to lay the groundwork for cooperation between the two countries under UNESCO supervision.

It is evident that the Build Cooperate and Transfer contract has made it possible to turn a blind eye to the long-term conflict between the two countries. Economic benefits for the Cambodian partners derive from this contract. Although this information is not confirmed by official sources (who, in any case, presumably conceal transactions relating to archaeological items), the Thai company is said to have 'rented out' a collection of 1,300 archaeological items from the Angkor Conservation and the Phnom Penh National Museum. The profit-orientated programme of the museum project is also detectable in the double game adopted by the Cambodian partners, who, despite the BCT contract, had also come to an agreement with a South Korean company, Angkor Treasure. The latter was given rental rights to some of the archaeological items that had also been selected by the Thai company. In order to resolve the issue, the only solution Vilailuck International could find was to reimburse the Korean company in order to be able to exhibit the pieces in the Siem Reap museum (Turnbull, 2008).

Figure 4.15 The Angkor National Museum

Photo by the author, 2009

Although the museum will become Cambodian national property 30 years after it opened, the paradox of having the Angkor National Museum owned by a Thai company illustrates the commercialization of Khmer heritage for the sake of investment-related agreements. Vilailuck International takes advantage of its leading position to adopt an implicit attitude of cultural superiority over Khmer society. For example, the Thai managing director declared that one of the main intentions of the museum would be to 'educate Cambodian people about their own history'. The Thai hold over Khmer heritage creates a subtle form of cultural colonialism further concealed by the employment of a team of Khmer curators and conservators.

The recently opened Angkor Panorama Museum is another case in which the Cambodian government has left the task of constructing a narrative about Khmer history and heritage to foreigners. The fact that North Korea is the owner of this museum generated criticism in the Anglophone press, and underlying tension on the terms of the bilateral agreement, which delayed the opening of the museum until the beginning of 2016. The 24-million-dollar museum, sponsored and built by North Korea in cooperation with the APSARA authority, is located on the main axis of the yet to be constructed

Hotel City. The building evokes the basic features of Khmer architecture as recognized by the APSARA's most recent attempts to regulate construction activity. Sloping roofs echoing the pagodas, low-rise buildings, white plaster walls, and series of columns framing Angkor-style statues are all reminiscent of the clumsy appropriation of the grand hotel model (see Chapter 2).[38]

I visited the Angkor Panorama Museum a few days before its official opening in December 2015. The huge portal was slightly open. The Khmer staff were having a break outside and were surprised to see me there, but kindly invited me to meet the North Korean curators inside, where the last arrangements were being made before the official opening. The curators were kind enough to converse with me and to let me look around the grandiose reproduction of Khmer architecture and Angkor remains created by North Korean artists from the Mansudae art studio, the North Korean art production centre based in Pyongyang (see Chapter 2).

The museum exhibits paintings, sculptures, and models depicting the history of the Khmer kingdom, the construction of the Angkor temples, and daily life in Khmer villages. The chief art work is a 360-degree panoramic cyclorama with 45,000 figures illustrating twelfth-century Angkor history. A team of artists from Mansudae produced every single work exhibited in the museum. They spent about two years working on it in Cambodia, while educating themselves about the country's art and history. The realistic and detailed pictorial style, and the focus on heroic scenes of war, magnificent monuments, and the idyllic representations of Khmer rural villages all echo the traits of the propagandistic work of Mansudae in their own country. They also reflect a widespread style of representation in Southeast Asian museums, in which new paintings attempt to recreate the past through detailed illustrations of war and cruel, murderous scenes which pique the visitor's curiosity. The Angkor National Museum and the Panorama Museum pursue the same objective of making heritage spectacular and history into a tale to be performed for audiences who are looking to be educated and entertained at the same time. What is unusual in the Cambodian case, compared to other Asian countries where global tourism is also leading to the incorporation of culture into leisure entertainment, is that the task of representing national history is left to foreigners, who have the power to express their idealized, simplified, and ideological reconstruction of Khmer heritage.

38 The few buildings eventually built in the Hotel City, despite the long delay of the project, followed the APSARA guidelines. They represent the first stage of an institutionally led discussion of the cultural identity of Cambodia and seek to scale up a small series of architectural forms to the larger dimensions needed by tourist and cultural facilities.

4.8 Thematizing urban heritage for consumption

This picture would not be complete without addressing the conversion of legacy buildings and urban spaces for tourist functions, which also takes place out of the sight of the cultural policies of the Cambodian national government.

Heritage conservation remains a marginal practice in Siem Reap, where significant parts of the urban fabric are being razed to the ground to make space for new developments. Nevertheless, small owners have taken an interest in the conservation of legacy buildings and have opened guesthouses, restaurants, bars, and shops in some of them. The largest number of such projects is located in the Old Market district, originally laid out by the French colonial administration in the 1920s and 1930s. The first map of the district dates back to 1918, showing three blocks of shophouses surrounding the market hall. There was a further project to build three distinct sectors to be separated and delimited by a canal; however, construction was slow and the plans were never completely implemented. Building activity actually continued into the 1990s. After Cambodia regained independence in 1991, the Old Market (as well as the administrative district) was part of the public domain of the state. Plots of land were given to public officials who had helped in the reconstruction of the country.[39]

With the increasing number of tourists, the district has been subject to profound transformation, as its central location made it particularly attractive for tourism-related activities. Conversion for tourist use started in 1999, when a British expatriate opened the first guesthouse in one of the shophouses bordering the market hall. Other foreigners followed this example, renting several shophouses from Khmer owners in which they opened restaurants, bars, tourist accommodation, and shops.

Tourist activities gradually spread from a road familiarly called Pub Street (for obvious reasons) to the rest of the neighbourhood. In 2001-2002, seeing the popularity of the district among foreign expatriates, Khmer owners started to build new shophouses on available plots which copied the style of the colonial ones, with their neoclassical decorations, covered galleries with arches, and yellow-gold plastering. While some kept their shops, which turned out to be very profitable, the majority moved to live in quieter and cheaper areas of the city while benefiting from increasing rental income. Some of the tiny alleys to the rear of the shophouses, originally used for

39 Personal communication with several developers of tourist activities in the Old Market area, December 2009.

family activities, have been converted into bustling tourist areas which evoke the narrow streets and high density of historic European cities.

As a consequence of these functional conversions, the traditional combination of a family's residence and commercial activity in the shophouse has been largely abandoned, and commercial activity has been expanded into the upper floors. The majority of foreign tenants and a small number of Khmer owners and renters are transforming the architecture and interior space of the shophouses. Owners and tenants do not consider the buildings as valuable heritage to be preserved carefully in their physical form. Rather, they see the shophouses as malleable objects for the expression of their own aesthetic tastes.

The priority of the criterion of personal taste was expressed by one of the French tenants, who explained: 'It is difficult for me to imagine how contemporary Khmer architecture should draw on the past. Apart from colonial buildings which were built by foreigners and from the architectural production during the short period of the Sangkum, I could not find any example of recent Khmer architecture I could draw on. Moreover, as a foreigner, I do not feel responsible for providing an answer to the question of how Khmer architecture should develop. For this reason, I prefer that the design should reflect my own tastes'.[40] He copied features from a bar he particularly liked in Bangkok to design the interior of his café, and brought furniture for it from Thailand.

This French tenant's attitude is shared by many others who, because of lack of interest in Khmer architecture, or desire to implement their own ideas, design heterogeneous interiors that draw on a great variety of sources. The typology of the shophouse makes this possible, since it can be treated as a single built unit or combined with others in order to increase its dimensions, and walls can be removed to change the layout of the rooms. The ceilings are high enough for mezzanines to be added. Several tenants have combined two or more shophouses, taking down the walls between them to create larger rooms. Many owners believe that the district will be indefinitely profitable and experience endless growth, so the asking prices for property in the area have exponentially increased and many insufficiently profitable commercial activities have had to give way to new ones which try their luck in a highly competitive environment.[41]

Some owners and tenants appreciate the qualities of the shophouses and preserve some architectural elements and spatial forms. For instance,

40 Personal communication with a shophouse tenant, December 2009.

41 For instance, the owner demanded US$1.3 million for 2000 square metres on Pub Street in December 2015: personal communication with estate agent working in Siem Reap, December 2015.

the woodwork of the roof is left visible in the large restaurant hall of the Grand Café, which occupies five shophouse units (Figure 4.16). Others dislike the architecture, but see the shophouses as attractive spaces for developing a new architectural identity: 'Shophouses were nothing more than boxes originally', said the developer of seven tourist activities in the area of the Old Market. 'The buildings lacked interest, and it was necessary to add new styles to them that would correspond to a particular place'.[42] 'Place-making' is essential to the developers' approach. Starting from similar architectural units, they have individualized the shophouses' commercial activity thematically. Sometimes they look back nostalgically to colonial times; in other cases, 'Khmer identity' is staged through evocative pictures of Apsara dancers, wooden mouldings, and hand-woven fabrics.

Nevertheless, as in the case of hotel design, allusions to features of local culture appear to be no more legitimate in the Old Market district than those which reproduce an 'elsewhere'. Local heritage is only one of the possibilities available to the developers. For instance, the Miss Wong bar invites tourists in for 'a sip of the old Shanghai' and is advertised as the 'most atmospheric and most seductive bar in Siem Reap' with its 'cherry-red lanterns suspended from the doorway'.[43] Spatial arrangements have similar characteristics to theme parks, as they develop particular ideas, concepts, or identities in the limited space of one or a few units. The juxtaposition of all these microcosms resembles the theme parks' succession of reproduced spatial or cultural realities.

Customers are attracted by the light-hearted re-creations of specific places, where they can enjoy a particular atmosphere and also socialize with specific groups of people. Unlike many other urban spaces, which attract either locals or tourists, the Old Market is a site of great social mixing, in which different populations cross each other's paths and sometimes meet, as in the cafés that both the rising Khmer middle class and the tourists have come to appreciate. There are restaurants and cafés which mainly attract tourists in couples, others for single travellers and expatriates looking for a cool place to use their laptops; there are gay and lesbian bars, noisy bars where young tourists in tank tops and flip-flops come to have a few drinks and flirt, and cosy shops selling locally made crafts. It is not surprising that unwary tourists get drugged in some of the bars playing loud music until the middle of the night, attracting young Khmer women in very tight dresses and huge quantities of make-up in search of a Western fiancé. The

42 Personal communication with tenant of seven shophouses at the Old Market, December 2009.
43 http://www.misswong.net (accessed 27 March 2016).

Old Market district also anchors the expatriate community to a space where, like in a village square, they can easily find their friends and acquaintances, have access to Western goods such as ice cream, and enjoy activities such as concerts that, at least initially, were unavailable in the rest of the town.

Nevertheless, the provincial hospital and the few shops run by Khmer families, mainly targeting Khmer customers, have resisted. They sell medicines, books, and electrical goods, and seem to bear witness to a bygone era when the district provided ordinary, everyday services to a local population. In this process of commercial and tourism-orientated conversion, the market hall has also stayed put, but the food stalls that once occupied the central and inner sections have given way to a profusion of souvenir sellers.

It is only now that the APSARA authority, in collaboration with the French-sponsored Mission du Patrimoine established at the Cambodian Ministry of Culture, has come to see this district as an urban heritage to be conserved. To do this, they have tried to implement the measures for heritage conservation proposed by the master plan for Siem Reap. Heritage trails have been marked on maps that the tourist can follow in order to learn about the history of the district. Basic traffic regulation has helped the tourists to walk around more safely and reduced illegal parking. Ideas about conservation, however, are not implemented by architectural and urban regulation, or through pilot restoration projects, since APSARA has little power over private property. Its department of Development of Urban Heritage has built two covered wooden bridges over the Siem Reap River, with benches where tourists can sit and rest. A new complex of bars and shops was built entirely of wood at a time when deforestation has become disastrous for Cambodia. Near this complex, the Hard Rock Café has opened in a newly built colonial-style building (Figure 4.17). It faces the decrepit Martini, the oldest nightclub of Siem Reap, where, in 2005, young people used to alternate dancing to rock music and traditional Khmer melodies. Burnt down in a recent fire of unknown origin, the Martini was to open again in 2016 and continue to challenge the chief symbol of tourism globalization, the Hard Rock Café. These recent projects on the doorstep of the Old Market show how the heritage of wooden and colonial architecture has been instrumentalized to fabricate artificial reproductions of the past. This newly branded tourist complex seems to be a dissonant anachronism, deaf to the environmental concerns faced by the country. The Hard Rock Café, in a fake colonial building, has been built where a real colonial building once stood. These reproductions are simply the material embodiment of images and narratives. The legitimacy granted by heritage masks the economic and political conflict, serious environmental concerns, unequal power struggles, and social injustices which underlie contemporary Cambodian society.

Figure 4.16 Grand Café: plan of the first floor, façade, and cross-section

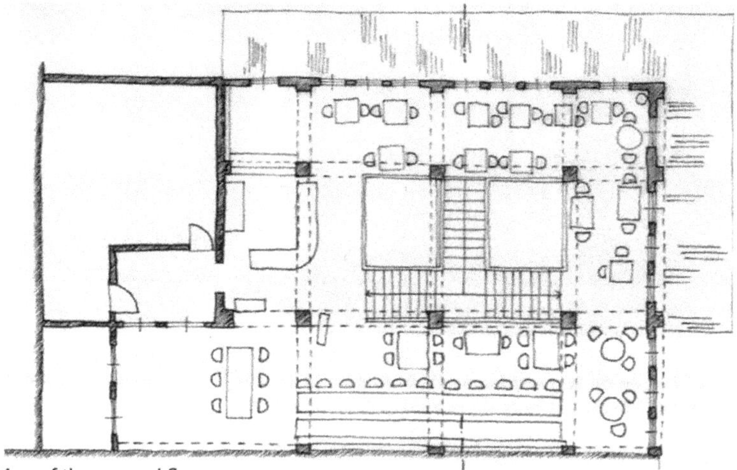

Map of the ground floor

Façade

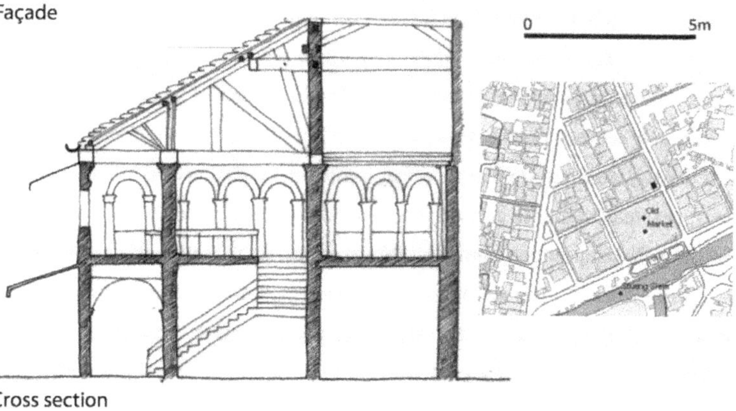

Cross section

Drawings by the author, 2009

Figure 4.17 The Hard Rock Café

Photo by the author, 2015

4.9 Models and imitative trends: Towards a contemporary Cambodian architecture?

One of the guesthouse owners in the Taphul neighbourhood once said to me, 'If I had to rebuild my guesthouse today, I would not do it as I did. Instead I would do what my neighbour did: I would build small wooden bungalows'.[44] His guesthouse was a concrete building, which he had chosen from a catalogue with the assistance of a builder. The guesthouse that now appealed to him was a nearby wooden house, which a Swiss tenant had surrounded with several new houses constructed out of straw. The appeal of this model made me realize the power of emulation in establishing new architectural trends in Siem Reap. Foreign informants working for NGOs, companies, and estate agents generally criticize the widespread tendency to imitate neighbours and acquaintances. They perceive this as evidence of a lack of ideas and of business acumen. Although I would not deny that imitation has had a negative impact on Siem Reap's urbanization processes (see Chapter 3), it also has potential for the evolution of contemporary architectural design in Cambodia.

Immediately after the listing of Angkor as a UNESCO World Heritage Site, the first hotels to be opened in Siem Reap were extremely simple concrete constructions, a single wing subdivided into several rooms. A

44 Personal interview with guesthouse's owners, 2008.

few years later, the model of the Grand Hotel was reproduced so many times that it lost the distinctiveness that this type of building requires if it is to preserve its elite status. Since the beginning of the 2000s, the influence of building catalogues and design magazines was visible not only in the urban landscape, but also in the discourse of owners who were fascinated by villas and shophouses featuring stylized classical decorations.

However, when I came back to Siem Reap in 2015, after a two years' absence, I realized that owners' and developers' openness to architectural influences had been transformed in a very short time. Since architecture has been seen as a field of production through which claims about Cambodia's advancement could be expressed and encouraged, certain models and styles have been rapidly absorbed as markers of progress. In a country where education in design and planning is still in its infancy, foreign architects and projects have been sources of inspiration. Influences from neighbouring Southeast Asian countries have reached Cambodia through individual architects, catalogues, magazines, and television programmes. Architectural design in the sphere of tourism has especially been receptive to foreign influences, which have begun to affect other areas of urban production only in recent years.

Several imitative trends have marked the urban transition of Siem Reap. They have gradually reduced the homogenizing force of the generic speculative architecture produced during the first years of tourism development. One of these trends is the conservation or construction of wooden houses. Several hotels combine traditional wooden architecture with the global model of the bungalow and randomly incorporate fragments of Angkor sculpture and decoration. Today, the scarcity of wood is pushing architects and developers to use concrete and brick to build new houses or restore inherited wooden ones. The Swiss developers of the Sala Lodges Hotel have transferred eleven wooden houses from different parts of Cambodia to Siem Reap, in order to create an 'idyllic village', which 'contribute[s] to the preservation of an architectural heritage, which is threatened with extinction' (Figure 4.18).[45] Here, the imprint of colonial narratives suffuses the idealization of Cambodian rural life, reproduced in the comfortable environment of a luxurious hotel. Following this trend, restaurants and hotels which recreate village environments are mushrooming in Siem Reap, attesting to the pervasive influence of nostalgia and the values assigned to traditional architecture.

45 http://www.salalodges.com/ .

Figure 4.18 Sala Lodge Hotel

Photo by the author, 2015

Figure 4.19 Extension of the Somadevi Hotel by ASMA Architecture

Photo by the author, 2015

Another emerging imitative trend is the reproduction of colonial architecture and atmospheres. The Victoria Hotel and the conversion of the Old Market area for tourism have certainly functioned as models for this trend. Following their example, neo-colonial shophouses have mushroomed along Siem Reap's riverbanks. Developers imagine these buildings as sites of consumption that reflect new criteria of architectural taste; they are aesthetic reproductions of a bygone style, but do not foster or express a critical attitude to the colonial past. They evoke JICA's guidelines for the development of downtown Siem Reap. JICA saw colonial architecture as a model for sustainable development because of its compactness, and imagined Siem Reap's urban centre as a pleasant environment for leisure activities, which would reproduce this model. In echoing JICA's guidelines, privately sponsored projects show that the lack of formal implementation of master plans does not preclude other subtler and more indirect pathways of influence for foreign-sponsored intervention in the sphere of architecture.

Wooden and colonial architecture has been introduced into Siem Reap's urban landscapes thanks to these multiple intersecting sources of influence. However, these attempts to find roots in Cambodia's architectural past encounter difficulties, since architects and developers inevitably either essentialize the past or empty architectural language of its cultural and historical meaning. ASMA Architects is the first firm to respond to these difficulties and to the desire for innovation in Cambodian architectural design. The daughter and son of Ros Borath, both trained at the Architectural School of Paris-Belleville, established ASMA in 2002, employing Cambodian and French architects. ASMA has benefited from the longstanding cultural and professional exchanges between planners from the two countries. Lisa Ros defines her work as 'modernist architecture in the 20s meaning of the term' (Sullivan, 2016). Her idea of modernism has its roots in Khmer architecture from the 1950s and 1960s, combining references to international architecture, Angkor urbanism, and local construction techniques using natural ventilation. ASMA's architects have worked on ways to adapt buildings to a tropical climate by drawing on the spatial organization of the ancient Khmer capitals, in particular their extensive use of water features. ASMA's clients are generally wealthy developers who target the tourist market. Buildings designed for tourists, which function as models, are thus newly produced in Siem Reap's urban environment. Emulation among developers has helped to increase the number of ASMA's commissions. Its buildings have become increasingly visible in the urban landscape: among the most recent is the new wing of the Somadevi Hotel, one of the grand hotels along Sivatha Road (see Chapter 3). The drastic contrast in style between the massive older building and the ASMA-designed one shows that imitative trends have produced rapid changes in the developers' perceptions of architectural quality, in the space of only a few years (Figure 4.19). As the number of buildings designed by ASMA increases, other projects imitate their architectural language and combine it with influences drawn from Thai catalogues of buildings featuring villas with minimalist decorations, flat roofs, large glass surfaces, and white outer walls. These combinations constitute a pervasive trend, with a simplified architectural language which has loosened its link with the past and affirms its modernity.

While urban planning and regulations have left unresolved the question of how to build the contemporary city in Siem Reap, the rapid transformation of the meanings and representations associated with the architectural fabric suggests that these architectural projects are forming the embryo of a new contemporary city, a city that will gradually reduce and possibly even erase the negative impact of early speculative and unreflective urbanism.

Conclusion

The dialectical relation between international heritage recognition and urban development has been at the heart of this book, in which I have explored the ways in which the UNESCO World Heritage label engenders and triggers urbanization on the margins of the Angkor archaeological park. The following pages suggest three research trajectories that have proved useful for Siem Reap-Angkor, and which could be expanded to the analysis of heritage politics in other countries and sites where tourism has become one of the main engines of local and national economies.

Heritage space and non-heritage space: A heuristic model

The territorial system established as a consequence of international heritage recognition is based on the interconnection of two components, namely the heritage space and the non-heritage space. I have analysed this system through the lens of 'human territoriality', defined as control over 'objects, people, and relationships' within a delimited region called a 'territory' (Sack, 1983, p. 56; see Chapter 1). The implementation of territoriality in Siem Reap-Angkor has produced an ambivalent and contradictory process.

Firstly, the bureaucracy of heritage management has become increasingly complex as APSARA departments have increased in number, their relations with national and local authorities have developed, and additional regulations for the archaeological park of Angkor have been established. For instance, tourists now have to comply with a dress code meant to respect the sacred values of Angkor (Plush, 2016). More and more red pillars mark the boundaries of zones 1 and 2, even in remote villages that no one would suspect are protected. Small protective boundaries surround some minor temples in the Siem Reap region, constructing an artificial separation of contemporary pagodas and ancient remains. Approximately, one hundred families formerly living in the precincts of the archaeological park have been relocated to the Run Ta Ek land reserve outside zone 2, with the aim of preventing further construction in the archaeological park. These are among many examples of recent attempts to define acceptable behaviour and to regulate access and occupation of land within the boundaries of the park. They have aimed at reinforcing the territoriality of the archaeological parks and thus the separation of the heritage and non-heritage spaces.

At the same time, breaches in the regulatory machine have undermined the enforcement of human territoriality. Developments have encroached on the archaeological park. A Circular from the Royal Government of Cambodia (No. 01/SR, 6 May, 2003) stated that

> in the Angkor region, the anarchical activities have risen again by group of people that bring concern on the protecting and developing actions that disturb the stability of Siem Reap/Angkor region. The anarchical activities are: looting and vandalism of cultural properties, cutting trees for appropriation of land, appropriating land for title deed, for buying and selling land, setting up shops in the forbidden places, and building various constructions in the Angkor Park which is prohibited and protected by law [sic].

The Circular was issued a few months before Angkor was moved from the World Heritage in Danger list to the World Heritage List, in 2004. This was a crucial period for Cambodia: the government had to show proof of its commitment to heritage conservation (see Chapter 1) in order for Angkor to be given the UNESCO label. In spite of the fact that the Circular has in principle been in force for over ten years, an estate agent told me at the end of 2015 that 'it is now possible to buy land in the "APSARA zones"!' Some of his acquaintances had bought land 'just in front of Angkor Wat' to plant mangos. Moreover, journalists from the *Phnom Penh Post* claimed that 'in the months leading up to Cambodian national elections on July 28, authorities in the Angkor archaeological park allowed dozens of land owners to build new houses and develop plots of land inside highly protected land of the world heritage site' (Bopha and Marks, 2013). Are the new owners of mango plantations waiting for similar loosening of institutional control to undertake development projects? The administrative requirements for obtaining a land title in the Angkor park are clear in principle, but confused in practice. While APSARA is, by law, the only legitimate authority which can deliver titles in zones 1 and 2,[1] it is not uncommon for local authorities (*sangkaet*) to deliver 'soft titles' (see Chapter 3),[2] which would not be officially recognized in case of dispute, but allow people – at least for a certain period – to occupy land, and eventually to build on it.

This means that not only in Siem Reap (see Chapter 3), but also in the archaeological park, regulations are used as a 'false front' and people flirt with transgressing the law up to the limits of acceptable behaviour. The

1 Interview with Cambodian lawyers, 2015.

2 Interview with estate agent, 2015.

overall conceptual framework that I have proposed here, based on the contrast between a heritage and a non-heritage space, is intended as a heuristic model. This model can be used to ask how far a system of control of heritage sites will guarantee the enforcement of territoriality, and what are its effects. The model is also aimed at analysing the specific ways in which the heritage and non-heritage spaces interact, the relations of complementarity and dependence that they develop, and the tactics that are played out to the advantage of particular interests and private profit.

Angkor is undoubtedly a singular case study for various reasons, including the large number of archaeological remains spread over a vast territory, its iconic status in the field of international heritage conservation, and its major role in the economic development of Cambodia. All these factors have contributed to exacerbating the separation between the archaeological park and the town, and to endanger the preservation of the archaeological park.

In spite of the singular nature of Angkor, the proposed model may be used to analyse the consequences of heritage recognition in other countries where tourism plays an important part in the national economy and where national regulations are weak enough to allow intense and uncontrolled development to take place in the vicinity of heritage sites. The Buddhist sanctuary of Borobudur in central Java may be taken as a comparison. Valued and preserved as a monument from colonial to postcolonial times, it has been isolated from its rural surroundings with the relocation of villages which were previously close to the temples. Similarly, villages near the Buddhist complex of Pagan in Burma have also been relocated in order to make room for the establishment of an archaeological zone, and the proximity of Wat Phu temple to Champassak town in Laos has resulted in urban encroachment in the years since the temple's UNESCO World Heritage listing in 2001.

In some of these cases, attempts have been made to overcome the territorial dichotomy based on the existence of related heritage and non-heritage spaces. One such attempt is the implementation of the notion of cultural landscape. Cultural landscapes include larger areas within the heritage space, and, in so doing, move beyond the focus on monuments and buildings and possibly broaden the scope of heritage to cover a greater variety of spaces and legacies. The rise of the notion of cultural landscape is symptomatic of the reform of international attitudes to heritage to include an increasing number of objects and cultural expressions. This expansion might in the end result in the elimination of selection as an intrinsic process of heritage recognition: everything might then be seen as heritage ('le tout patrimoine', Neyret, 2004).

However, the case of Angkor has shown that the notion of cultural landscape does not remove the contrast between heritage and non-heritage, since it only pushes the protective boundaries further away. It also sheds more light on the resistance to the implementation of this notion in Cambodia. A 'retraction' of the heritage system, back to conservation of only the historic monuments within the perimeter of the archaeological parks, did, in fact, follow the attempts by the international consulting team for the ZEMP (Zoning and Environmental Management Plan) to re-list Angkor as a cultural landscape. In 2016, a project for the relocation of the villages on the edge of the Phnom Kulen mountains and their sanctuaries, which will soon be nominated by Cambodia as UNESCO World Heritage sites, has revived this resistance. Further comparative research could examine whether heritage bureaucracies and regulatory systems have been remodelled in order to ensure the protection of heritage on the territorial level, or whether development pressures are resulting in the use of new tactics and the search for spaces in which to concentrate the externalities of tourism development, either within, or on the margins of cultural landscapes.

The trajectories of the 'coloniality of power'

The heritage system based on the notion of the historic monument has been handed down from colonial times and has survived down to the reform of international attitudes to heritage (see Chapter 1). Colonial influences permeate not only heritage management, but also contemporary representations of Cambodian society, traditions, and places (see Chapter 4). Taken together, these legacies can be better understood through the notion of the 'coloniality of power' (Quijano, 1991). Even after the fall of colonial regimes, cultures and imaginations have continued to be colonized by forms of influence more subtle than the exercise of political and economic power. For instance, the belief that European knowledge is superior to others, and even that it constitutes a universal model, is a prime expression of coloniality.

In contemporary Cambodia, locally formed perceptions of heritage and cultural identities have been largely overlooked compared to imported notions, narratives, and images. There have been few attempts to merge local understandings and international heritage frameworks. The 'docility' of the Cambodian government in complying with the requirements of the World Heritage Committee (see Chapter 1) reflects a desire to reach international standards through the appropriation of the Committee's language and codes. It also reveals how troubled the reconstruction of national cultural identity can be in a post-conflict and post-genocide country. As Winter has perceptively remarked, 'the desire to re-establish the "authentic", the "traditional" or even the "pure" has been paralleled by a willingness to open up, and to absorb the foreign' (2007, p. 139).

The reproduction of the past in contemporary architecture is a manifestation of the same unease and ambivalence. The folklorization of national heritage and history is not exclusive to Cambodia, but constructs nostalgic representations of the 'traditional past' by other modernizing postcolonial societies too. In Cambodia, the emergence of cultural elites and civil society associations, as well as the close connection between heritage and international tourism, makes the influence of an inherited sense of exoticism and stereotyped representations of culture even stronger. Quijano defines 'decolonization' as the recovering of people's capacity to determine their individual and collective choices (1991, p. 19). This capacity still seems to be a distant prospect for Cambodia, where the production of heritage and of the contemporary city takes place in a vortex of multiple foreign influences surrounding the still empty space of self-awareness and accomplishment.

Nevertheless, the balance of power does change, and the influence of French colonial legacies has started to give way to that of other powers from Southeast and East Asia. We have seen how French assistance in the field of urban planning has been rejected, while Japanese assistance (JICA) has concomitantly increased its ascendancy in Siem Reap through the implementation of a number of sector projects (see Chapter 2). Moreover, infrastructure projects scheduled in the JICA master plan have been taken over by other donors and consultant teams including the Korean International Cooperation Agency (KOICA) and the Asian Development Bank. The synergy between Asian consultants and donors creates a reconfigured system of influences. It has its roots in the functionalist, technocratic approach to the city developed by the Japanese, who see the efficiency of the urban infrastructure as one of the main criteria for evaluating the success of planning. Property developers obviously endorse this approach because land values increase in the areas where infrastructure is available. 'Developers who can get future transportation master plans have the impression of having found a goldmine', one estate agent told me.[3]

The presence of East Asian donors in urban planning is paralleled by the increasing influence of Asian sponsors in the museum field. All the museums opened in Siem Reap in postcolonial times have been funded, and are at present run, by Asian investors and institutions (see Chapters 2

3 Ibid.

and 4). Museums authorize bilateral and multilateral agreements; they are, primarily, tools of international cultural diplomacy. The task of producing and presenting a discourse on Cambodian history is left in the hands of foreign experts, scholars, and artists, who are supposed to transfer their competence and skills to Cambodian staff. Once the contract between the Cambodian government and the foreign counterparts expires, the museums will become Cambodian property. Coloniality will be fully implemented once both the foreign-educated staff and the cultural facilities are identified as 'Cambodian'.

The overview given here leads to the conclusion that cultural representations, expert knowledge, donors' philosophies, and political priorities are together shaping a new coloniality of power that is shifting the locus of foreign influence from Europe to Asia. The willingness of Cambodian parties to let this new form of coloniality take root is certainly due in part to the anxiety of self-determination, but also to the political and economic advantages of signing cooperation agreements. Siem Reap-Angkor becomes a site of the convergence of influences of diverse origins. Far from committing to a decolonization process as conceptualized by Quijano, Cambodian institutions have embraced a new set of rationalities and narratives which reshuffle the ways in which global power hierarchies are reflected.

The town, forgotten and yet central

In a place where decision-making and the production of space are shaped by a web of foreign influences, the role of local residents in the making and management of their city is worth exploring. Cambodians traditionally had the power and capacity to build their own houses in the villages that preceded the town and were further absorbed by urban development. After the listing of Angkor as a UNESCO World Heritage Site in 1992, the establishment of a complex administrative structure for the Siem Reap-Angkor region, and the increasing power of the developers, ordinary residents' stewardship has gradually been reduced. The reorganization of the administrative and economic structure of the city following international heritage recognition has led to a profound crisis which has made it impossible to reproduce 'social formations' on the basis of 'pre-existing systems of social relations' (Gilmore, 2008, drawing on Hall and Schwartz, 1988, p. 96). Tourism has paradoxically transformed Siem Reap into a forgotten place, as its residents have been 'deprived of leadership and stewardship by the actions and attitudes of people both present in and absent from these environments' (Markusen,

2004, p. 2303). Siem Reap has also become marginal because the traditions and cultural expressions located or occurring there are overshadowed by the national and international celebration of the heritage space. Furthermore, heritage recognition has produced a number of forms of disconnection of the inhabitants from the heritage site to which they were previously tied by cultural, social, and religious practices.

Disconnection, marginalization, and oblivion have also contributed to define the way Siem Reap has been perceived and shaped by developers, architects, and builders. Significantly, these groups have revived the past through replicas and reconstructions, rather than through heritage conservation. The historical fabric is overlooked while layers of recent buildings, which gradually erase its traditions, incorporate reminders of the past. In this light, the non-heritage space appears as a forgotten place,[4] but also as a very central space in the production of new values, which become visible thanks to the convergence of funding, experts, and ideas. The establishment of an urban municipality in Siem Reap in 2008 illustrates the significance of this process of convergence, which has created 'the town' as a distinct administrative entity where there was once only an agglomeration of villages, communes, and districts. The administrative recognition of Siem Reap is emblematic of the power of current dynamics to reintegrate the previously marginal into new forms of urban centrality. Beyond the economically central position that it has acquired in the years following World Heritage recognition, the recent production of Siem Reap's architectural space shows some signs of emancipation from foreign models. In the near future, its continued reshaping may help to fill the still empty space of Cambodian society's self-determination.

4 The notion of forgotten place has been given diverse meanings in the academic literature, but the common denominator is the exclusion of the city from various kinds of production (artistic, economic, discursive, associative, etc.) which are essential to its continuing vitality.

Bibliography

Agence Française de Développement. 2009. *Road Works for the Development and Beautification Around Siem Reap River Banks*. E-publication: http://afd.dgmarket.com/tenders/np-notice.do?noticeId=4500670. Accessed 1 August 2016.

Akagawa, Natsuko and Tiamsoon Sirisrisak. 2008. 'Cultural Landscapes in Asia and the Pacific: Implications of the World Heritage Convention', in *International Journal of Heritage Studies*, 14: 2, pp. 176-191.

Anton-Clavé, Salvador. 2007. *The Global Theme Park Industry*. Wallingford/Oxford: CABI International.

Ap, John. 2008. 'An Assessment of Theme Park Development in China', in Lew, Alan A. (ed.), *Tourism in China*. London/New York: Routledge, pp. 195-216.

APUR. 1997. *Phnom Penh, développement urbain et patrimoine*. Paris: Atelier Parisien d'Urbanisme.

—. 2003. *Phnom Penh à l'aube du XXIe siècle*. Paris: Atelier Parisien d'Urbanisme.

Armstrong, J.-D. 1977. *Revolutionary Diplomacy. Chinese Foreign Diplomacy and the United Front Doctrine*. Berkeley/Los Angeles, CA/London: University of California Press.

ARTE-BCEOM, Royaume du Cambodge, Conseil Supérieur de la Culture Nationale, APSARA. 1995. *Plan d'Urbanisme de Référence et projets prioritaires. Rapport Définitif*, vol. 1.

—. 1995. *Plan d'Urbanisme de Référence et projets prioritaires. Projet Cité Hôtelière*, vol. 2.

—. 1995. *Plan d'Urbanisme de Référence et projets prioritaires. Annexes*, vol. 3.

Ascher, François, Jean-Louis Cohen, and Jean-Claude Hauvuy. 1987. *Luxe, habitat, confort: les références hôtelières*. Unpublished Research Report ARDU. Paris: IPRAUS Documentation Centre.

Ashworth, Gregory J. and J.E. Tunbridge. 1990. *The Tourist Historic City*. London/New York: Belhaven Press.

Asian Development Bank. 2004. *Enhancing the Fight Against Poverty in Asia and the Pacific. The Poverty Reduction Strategy of the Asian Development Bank*. E-publication: http://www.adb.org/documents/enhancing-fight-against-poverty-asia-and-pacific-poverty-reduction-strategy-asian. Accessed 29 July 2016.

—. 2011. *ADB Country Partnership Strategy. Cambodia 2011-2013*. E-publication: http://www.adb.org/documents/cambodia-country-partnership-strategy-2011-2013. Accessed 29 July 2016.

Askew, Marc. 2010. 'The Magic List of Global Status: UNESCO, World Heritage and the Agendas of States', in Labadi, Sophia and Colin Long (eds), *Heritage and Globalisation*. London/New York: Routledge, pp. 19-44.

Baille, Britt. 2007. 'Conservation of the Sacred at Angkor Wat: Further Reflections on Living Heritage', in *Conservation and Management of Archaeological Sites*, vol. 8, pp. 123-131.

Baird, Ian G. 2013. '« Indigenous Peoples » and Land: Comparing Communal Land Titling and Its Implications in Cambodia and Laos', in *Asia Pacific Viewpoint*, 54:3, pp. 269-281.

—. 2017. 'Resistance and Contingent Contestations to Large-Scale Land Concessions in Southern Laos and Northeastern Cambodia', in *Land*, 6:16, pp. 1-19.

Baromey Neth. 2011. 'Angkor as World Heritage Site and the Development of Tourism. A Study of Tourist Revenue in the Accommodation Sector in Siem Reap-Angkor', in Hauser-Schäublin, Brigitta (ed.). *World Heritage. Angkor and Beyond. Circumstances and Implications of UNESCO Listings in Cambodia*. Göttingen: Göttingen Studies in Cultural Property, vol. 2, pp. 147-166.

Baudrillard, Jean. 1981. *For a Critique of the Political Economy of the Sign*. New York: Telos Press Ltd.

Bayart, Jean-François. 2004. *Libéralisation économique et violence politique au Cambodge.* Les rapports du FASOPO. E-publication: http://spire.sciencespo.fr/hdl:/2441/f5vtl-5h9a73d5ls97563l15ao. Accessed 3 July 2015.

Becker, Elizabeth. 1986. *When the War was Over: Cambodia and the Khmer Rouge Revolution.* New York: Public Affairs.

Beng Hong Socheat, Khemro and Geoffrey Payne. 2004. 'Improving Tenure Security for the Urban Poor in Phnom Penh, Cambodia: an Analytical Case Study', in *Habitat International,* 28, pp. 181-201.

Benjamin, Walter. 2007. *L'Oeuvre d'art à l'époque de la reproductibilité technique.* Paris: Allia [1st edition 1955].

Berliner, David. 2010. 'Perdre l'esprit du lieu. Les politiques de l'UNESCO à Luang Prabang (Laos)', in *Terrain,* numéro spécial *Transmettre,* 55, pp. 90-105.

Berliner, David and Chiara Bortolotto. 2013. 'Le monde selon l'UNESCO. Introduction', in *Gradhiva,* 18, pp. 1-17.

Blaise, Séverine. 2006. 'De l'aide à la coopération économique: pour un réexamen de la politique japonaise', in *Revue Tiers Monde,* 2:186, pp. 307-328.

Bloembergen, Marieke and Martijn Heickhoff. 2009. 'Conserving the Past, Mobilising the Indonesian Future: Archaeological Sites, Regime Change and Heritage Politics in Indonesia in the 1950s', in *Journal of the Humanities and Social Sciences of Southeast Asia,* 167:4, pp. 405-436.

Blot, Julie. 2013. *Les déguerpissements à Phnom Penh (Cambodge). Déplacement forcé et relocalisation contrainte des citadins pauvres.* PhD Thesis, Université Paris IV Sorbonne.

—, and Amandine Spire. 2014. 'Déguerpissements et conflits autour des légitimités citadines dans les villes du Sud', in *L'Espace politique,* 22:1. E-publication: https://espacepolitique.revues.org/2893. Accessed 15 May 2017.

Bopha, Phorn and Simon Marks. 2013. 'Illegal Construction Rampant in Angkor Heritage Site', in *The Cambodia Daily,* 21 September. E-publication: https://www.cambodiadaily.com/archives/illegal-construction-rampant-in-angkor-heritage-site-42860/. Accessed 18 August 2016.

Bowles, Paul. 1949. *The Sheltering Sky.* London: Penguin Books.

Brannen, Mary Y. 1992. '"Bwana Mickey": Constructing Cultural Consumption at Tokyo Disneyland', in Tobin, Joseph J. (ed.), *Re-made in Japan: Everyday Life and Consumer Taste in a Changing Society.* New Haven, CT/London: Yale University Press, pp. 216-234.

Brickell, Katherine. 2013. '« The Whole World is Watching »: Intimate Geopolitics of Forced Eviction and Women's Activism in Cambodia', in *Annals of the Association of American Geographers,* 104:6, pp. 1256-1272.

Brumann, Christoph and Camille Joseph. 2013. 'Comment le patrimoine mondial de l'UNESCO devient immatériel', in *Gradhiva,* numéro spécial *Le monde selon l'UNESCO,* 2:18, pp. 22-49.

Brundtland Commission Report. 1987. *Our Common Future. The World Commission on Environment and Development.* Oxford: Oxford University Press.

Buciek, K. and K. Juul. 2008. '"We Are Here, Yet We Are Not Here". The Heritage of Excluded Groups', in Graham, Brian and Peter Howard (eds), *The Ashgate Research Companion to Heritage and Identity.* Aldershot: Aldgate, pp. 105-124.

Bui To Uyen. 2012. *L'intégration du développement durable dans les projets de quartier. Le cas de la ville d'Hanoi.* PhD Thesis, Université Toulouse 2 Le Mirail.

Bunnell, Tim and Anant Maringanti. 2010. 'Practising Urban and Regional Research beyond Metrocentricity', in *International Journal of Urban and Regional Research,* 34:2, pp. 415-420.

Burgess, Rod. 2000. 'The Compact City Debate: A Global Perspective', in Jenks, Mike and Rod Burgess (eds), *Compact Cities. Sustainable Urban Forms for Developing Countries.* London/New York: Spon Press, pp. 9-24.

Butland, Rowena. 2009. *Scaling Angkor: Perception of Scale in the Interpretation and Management of Cultural Heritage*. PhD Thesis, The University of Sydney, Australia.
Byrne, Denis. 2014. *Counterheritage. Critical Perspectives on Heritage Conservation in Asia.* London/New York: Routledge.

Calvino, Italo. 1993. *Il barone rampante.* Milano: Palomar and Mondadori.
de Carné, Louis. 1995. *Travels on the Mekong: Cambodia, Laos, and Yunnan: The Political and Trade Report of the Mekong Exploration Commission, June 1866-June 1868.* Bangkok: White Lotus Press.
Carrier, Adeline. 2007. *Les 'lois de la possession' à Phnom Penh: conversion des droits d'usage résidentiel issus du contexte socialiste de réappropriation urbaine (1979-1989) en droits de propriété.* PhD Thesis, Université de Paris 8.
—. 2008. 'Le cadastre et sa pratique: problématique foncière actuelle et études urbaines', in *Bulletin de l'AEFEK* No. 14. E-publication: http://aefek.free.fr/pageLibre000108eb.html. Accessed 1 August 2016.
—. 2009. 'Propriété versus possession. L'urbanisation différenciée de Phnom Penh au regard de la réforme foncière (1863-1953)', in *Péninsule,* No. 59, pp. 92-142.
de Certeau, Michel. 1990. *L'invention du quotidien. 1. Arts de faire.* Paris: Gallimard [1st edition 1980].
de Cesari, Chiara. 2010. 'Creative Heritage: Palestinian Heritage NGOs and Defiant Arts of Government', in *American Anthropologist,* 112:4, pp. 625-637.
de Cesari, Chiara and Michael Herzfeld. 2015. 'Urban Heritage and Social Movements', in Meskell, Lynn (ed.), *Global Heritage: A Reader.* Malden/Oxford/Chichester: Wiley Blackwell.
de Cesari, Chiara and Ann Rigney. 2014. 'Introduction', in De Cesari, Chiara and Ann Rigney (eds), *Transnational Memory. Circulation, Articulation, Scales.* Berlin/Boston, MA: De Gruyter, pp. 1-25.
Chaboreth, Ek and Sok Hach. 2008. *Aid Effectiveness in Cambodia.* Wolfensohn Center for Development at Brookings. E-publication: http://www.brookings.edu/~/media/research/files/papers/2008/12/cambodia-aid-chanboreth/12_cambodia_aid_chanboreth.pdf. Accessed 3 July 2015.
Chandler, David. 2008. *A History of Cambodia.* Boulder, CO: Westview Press [1st edition 1992].
Chapagain, Neel Kamal and Kapila D. Silva. 2013. *Asian Heritage Management.* London/New York: Routledge.
Chapman, William. 1998. '"The Best Laid Schemes": Land Use Planning and Historic Preservation in Cambodia', in *Pacific Rim Law & Policy Association,* 7:3, pp. 529-554.
—. 2013. *A Heritage of Ruins: the Ancient Sites of Southeast Asia and their Conservation.* Honolulu, HI: University of Hawai'i Press.
Chastel, André. 1990. 'L'invention de l'inventaire', in *Revue de l'Art,* 87:1, pp. 5-11.
Cheang Sokha. 2008. 'Siem Reap Port Rehab Plows Ahead', in *The Phnom Penh Post,* 25 January. E-publication: http://www.phnompenhpost.com/siem-reap-insider/siem-reap-port-rehab-plows-ahead. Accessed 29 July 2016.
Cheeang, Vannarith. 2008. 'The Political Economy of Tourism in Cambodia', in *Asia Pacific Journal of Tourism Research,* 13:3, pp. 281-297.
Chen, Xiangming and Ahmed Kanna (eds). 2012. *Rethinking Global Urbanism: Comparative Insights from Secondary Cities.* London/New York: Routledge.
Chhay, Channyda and Shaun Turton. 2015. 'Gov't Takes Angkor Ticketing Back from Powerful Sokimex', *The Phnom Penh Post,* 7 November. E-publication: http://www.phnompenhpost.com/post-weekend/govt-takes-angkor-ticketing-back-powerful-sokimex. Accessed 7 November 2015.
Choay, Françoise. 1969. *The Modern City: Planning in the 19th Century.* New York: George Braziller.
—. 2007. *L'allégorie du patrimoine.* Paris: Seuil [1st edition 1992].

Chon, Kaye S. (ed.). 2000. *Tourism in Southeast Asia: A New Direction*. New York: Haworth Hospitality Press.

Clavé, Salvador Anton. 2007. *The Global Theme Park Industry*. Oxford/Cambridge: CAB Publications.

Clément, Pierre. 1996. *Préparation au lancement des travaux d'infrastructure de la Cité Hôtelière*. Unpublished report.

—. 1996. *Rapport d'évaluation. Appui à la prise en compte de la biodiversité dans la préservation, la restauration et la valorisation de la région d'Angkor*. Unpublished Report. Fonds Français pour l'Environnement Mondial.

—. 2001. 'Les leçons de Hanoi', in Clément, Pierre and Nathalie Lancret (eds), *Hanoï, le cycle des métamorphoses*. Paris: Editions Recherche/IPRAUS, pp. 9-16.

Clément-Charpentier, Sophie. 2008. 'Mort et renaissance d'une capitale', in *Géographie et cultures*, 65, pp. 91-110.

Clément-Charpentier, Sophie and Pierre Clément. 1990. *L'habitation lao*. Paris: SELAF-Peeters.

Clerc, Valérie and Virginie Rachmuhl. 2004. 'Les marchés fonciers et immobiliers des quartiers informels à Phnom Penh, Cambodge', in *Coopérer aujourd'hui*, GRET, 50. E-publication: Les marchés fonciers et immobiliers des quartiers informels à Phnom Penh, Cambodge. Accessed 21 August 2017.

Clerc, Valérie. 2010. 'Du formel à l'informel dans la fabrique de la ville. Politiques foncières et marchés immobiliers à Phnom Penh', in *Espaces et Sociétés*, 3:143, pp. 63-79.

Clymer, Kenton J. 2004. The United States and Cambodia, 1969-2000: A Troubled Relationship. New York: Routledge.

Cochrane, Janet (ed.). 2007. *Asian Tourism: Growth and Change*. Oxford: Elsevier.

Cody, Jeff. 2003. 'Modernité et post-modernité ou comment dépasser la nostalgie. Les hôtels Mandarin Oriental et Peninsula à Hong Kong', in Sanjuan, Thierry (ed.), *Les grands hôtels en Asie. Modernité, dynamiques urbaines et sociabilité*. Paris: Publications de la Sorbonne, pp. 141-166.

Craig, David and Doug Porter. 2006. *Development Beyond Neoliberalism? Governance, Poverty Reduction and Political Economy*. London/New York: Routledge.

Croissant, Aurel and Paul W. Chambers. 2011. 'A Contested Site of Memory: The Preah Vihear Temple', in Anheier, Helmut and Raj Isar Yudhishthir (eds), *Cultures and Globalization: Heritage, Memory & Identity*. Los Angeles, CA/New Delhi [etc.]: Sage, pp. 148-156.

Cuasay, Peter. 1998. 'Borders on the Fantastic: Mimesis, Violence and the Landscape at the Temple of Preah Vihear', in *Modern Asian Studies*, 32:4, pp. 849-890.

Dagens, Bruno. 1995. *Angkor: Heart of an Asian Empire*. London: Thames & Hudson.

—. 2008. 'Angkor, instrument politique: avant, avec et après le protectorat', in Tertrais, Hugues (ed.), *Angkor VIIIe-XXIe siècle. Mémoire et identité khmère*. Paris: Autrement, pp. 94-107.

Dahles, Heidi. 2001. *Tourism, Heritage and National Culture in Java. Dilemmas of a Local Community*. Richmond: Curzon Press.

Darré, Jean-Pierre, 1996. *L'invention des pratiques dans l'agriculture. Vulgarisation et production locale des connaissances*. Paris: Karthala.

Dartigues, Laurent. 2001. 'La notion d'arène. Intérêts pour la recherche en anthropologie politique'. E-publication: https://halshs.archives-ouvertes.fr/halshs-00634920/document. Accessed 19 September 2016.

Dauphin-Meunier, Achille. 1965. *Le Cambodge de Sihanouk ou la difficulté d'être neutre*. Rennes: Nouvelles éditions latines.

Dearborn, Lynne M. and John C. Stallmeyer. 2010. *Inconvenient Heritage: Erasure and Global Tourism in Luang Prabang.* Walnut Creek, CA: Left Coast Press.

Deberny-Peignot. 1931. *60 aspects de l'Exposition Coloniale.* Paris: Editions Arts et Métiers Graphiques.

DED and District Master Plan Team. 2007. *Technical Report on the Final Land-Use Plan for Siem Reap District.* Unpublished report.

de Lajonquière, Etienne L. 1904. 'Les monuments du Cambodge', in *La revue d'Indochine.* Hanoi: Imprimerie Typo-Lithographique F.-H. Schneider.

Delaney, David. 2005. *Territory. A Short Introduction.* Malden/Oxford/Victoria: Blackwell Publishing.

—. 2009. 'Territory and Territoriality', in Kitchen, Rob and Nigel Thrift (eds), *International Encyclopedia of Human Geography,* 11, pp. 196-208.

Delaporte, Louis. 1880. *Voyage au Cambodge. L'architecture khmère.* Paris: Delgrave.

Delaporte, Louis and Francis Garnier. 1998. *A Pictorial Journey on the Old Mekong.* Bangkok: White Lotus.

Demay, Aline. 2011. *Tourisme et Colonisation en Indochine (1898-1939).* PhD Thesis, Université de Paris 1.

Détente Consultants, Score Tourisme, GIE, Villes Nouvelles. 1995. *Mission d'étude tourisme Angkor/Siem Reap – Rapport Tourisme. Main report.*

—. 1995. *Mission d'étude tourisme Angkor/Siem Reap. Annexes.*

De Vienne, Marie-Sybille. 2008. 'Le Cambodge entre intégration et désintégration', in Alain Forest (ed.), *Cambodge contemporain.* Paris: Les Indes Savantes, pp. 257-290.

De Vienne, Marie-Sybille and Jacques Népote. 1993. *Cambodge, laboratoire d'une crise.* Paris: CHEAM – La Documentation française.

DFDL Mekong. 2007. *Cambodia Legal & Investment Guide.* Phnom Penh: Mekong Law Group and DFDL Mekong Legal & Tax Advisers.

Di Giovine, Michael A. 2009. *The Heritage-scape. UNESCO, World Heritage, and Tourism.* Lanham, MD: Lexington Books.

Donovan, Dolores. 1993. 'Cambodia: Building a Legal System from Scratch', in *The International Lawyer,* 27:2, pp. 445-454.

D'Orléans, Ferdinand, Duc de Montpensier. 1910. *La ville au bois dormant. De Saigon à Angkor en automobile.* Paris: Librairie Plon.

Dumarçay, Jacques. 1973. *Charpentes et tuiles khmères.* Paris: École Française d'Extrême Orient.

Dwyer, Michael B. 2015. 'The Formalization Fix? Land Titling and Land Concessions in Cambodia. CDE Policy Brief, No. 4.

Ear, Sophal. 2006. *The Political Economy of Aid, Governance, and Policy-Making: Cambodia in Global, National, and Sectoral Perspectives.* PhD Thesis, University of California (Berkeley).

Economic Institute of Cambodia. 2008. *Cambodia Economic Watch.* E-publication: http://siteresources.worldbank.org/INTCAMBODIA/Resources/Economic-Watch-October-2008.pdf. Accessed 28 September 2015.

—. 2009. 'The Political Economy of Aid and Regime Legitimacy in Cambodia', in Ojendal, Joakim and Mona Lilja (eds). 2009. *Beyond Democracy in Cambodia. Political Reconstruction in a Post-Conflict Society.* Copenhagen: NIAS. pp. 151-188.

Edensor, Tim. 1998. *Tourists at the Taj: Performance and Meaning at a Symbolic Site.* London/New York: Routledge.

Edwards, Penny. 2007. *Cambodge: The Cultivation of a Nation, 1860-1945.* Honolulu, HI: Hawai'i University Press.

Esposito, Adele. 2012. 'Siem Reap: processus et enjeux de la fabrication d'une ville touristique', in *Péninsule*, 1: 64, pp. 155-178.

—. 2014. 'Planning Urban Development from an Outsider's Perspective: Siem Reap, the Backdrop of Evolving Urban Representations', in *Antropologia*, Special number edited by Vignato, Silvia and Matteo C. Alcano. *Southeast Asia: Subjects and Places*, 1:1, pp. 143-154.

Esposito, Adele and Inès Gaulis. 2010. 'The Cultural Heritages of Asia and Europe. Global Challenges and Local Initiatives'. E-publication: http://iias.asia/event/cultural-heritages-asia-and-europe-global-challenges-and-local-initiatives. Accessed 25 September 2016.

Esposito, Adele and Sylvia Nam. 2008. *Siem Reap. Urban Development in the Shadow of Angkor.* Los Angeles, CA: Getty Foundation.

Evans, Damian, Christophe Pottier, Roland Fletcher, et al. 2007. 'A Comprehensive Archaeological Map of the World's Largest Preindustrial Settlement', in *Proceedings of the National Academy of Sciences*, 104:36, pp. 14277-14282.

Fauveaud, Gabriel. 2011. 'Retour sur le drame de l'Ile des Diamants: l'investissement immobilier des grands projets urbains à Phnom Penh', in *EchoGeo 'Sur le Vif'*. E-publication: http://echogeo.revues.org/12367. Accessed 15 May 2017.

—, Gabriel. 2014a. 'Mutations of Real Estate Actors' Strategies and Modes of Capital Appropriation in Contemporary Phnom Penh', in *Urban Studies*, 51:16, pp. 3479-3494.

—. 2014b. 'Phnom Penh ou l'ordre métropolitain: polices, pouvoirs, et territoires' in EchoGéo, 28. E-publication: https://echogeo.revues.org/13807. Accessed 15 May 2017.

—. 2015a. *La production des espaces urbains à Phnom Penh. Pour une géographie sociale de l'immobilier.* Paris: Publications de la Sorbonne.

—. 2015b. 'Le borey, une nouvelle référence résidentielle pour Phnom Penh?', in Franck, Manuelle and Thierry Sanjuan (eds), *Territoires de l'urbain en Asie. Une nouvelle modernité?* Paris: CNRS Editions, pp. 261-280.

Ferguson, France. 1992. *Solitude and the Sublime: Romanticism and the Aesthetics of Individuation.* New York/London: Routledge.

Fiévé, Nicolas. 2003. 'Pouvoir politique, modernité architecturale et paysage urbain dans le Japon de l'ère Meiji. L'hôtel Impérial de Tôkyô', in Sanjuan, Thierry (ed.), *Les grands hôtels en Asie. Modernité, dynamiques urbaines et sociabilité.* Paris: Publications de la Sorbonne, pp. 13-54.

Fletcher, Roland. 2012. 'Low-Density, Agrarian-Based Urbanism: Scale, Power, and Ecology', in Smith, Michael (ed.), *The Comparative Archaeology of Complex Societies.* New York: Cambridge University Press, pp. 285-320.

Foley, Jennifer L. 2006. *"Discovering" Cambodia: Views of Angkor in French Colonial Cambodia (1863-1954).* PhD Thesis, Cornell University.

Fontaine, Antoine. 2008. 'L'élaboration du droit contemporain', in Forest, Alain (ed.), *Cambodge contemporain.* Paris: Les Indes Savantes-IRASEC, pp. 445-474.

Forest, Alain. 2008. "Pour comprendre l'histoire du Cambodge", in Forest, Alain (ed.), *Cambodge contemporain.* Paris: Les Indes Savantes-IRASEC, pp. 17-140.

Formoso, Bernard and Emiko Stock. 2016. 'La société civile cambodgienne: ruptures, incertitudes et ingérences étrangères' in Formoso, Bernard (ed.). *Sociétés civiles d'Asie du Sud-est continentale. Entre pilotage d'Etat et initiatives citoyennes.* Lyon: ENS Editions, pp. 105-150.

Fournereau, Lucien and Jaques Porchet. 1890. *Les ruines d'Angkor: étude artistique et historique sur les monuments khmers du Cambodge siamois.* Paris: Leroux.

Franck, Manuelle, Charles Goldblum, and Christian Taillard (eds). 2012. *Territoires de l'urbain en Asie du Sud-Est. Métropolisations en mode mineur.* Paris: CNRS Editions.

Fraoua, Ridha. 1992. *Proposition d'inscription du parc archéologique d'Angkor et des sites associés de Roluos et Banteay Srei sur la liste du patrimoine mondial.* Unpublished report.

Frey, Bruno S., Paolo Pamini, and Lasse Steiner. 2013. 'Explaining the World Heritage List: An Empirical Study', in *International Review of Economics*, 60:1, pp. 1-19.

Garnier, Francis. 1985. *Voyage d'exploration en Indochine.* Paris: La Découverte Illustrée [1st edition 1873].

Gaucher, Jacques. 2004. 'Angkor Thom, une utopie réalisée? Structuration de l'espace et modèle indien d'urbanisme', in *Les arts asiatiques, Cahiers de l'EFEO*, 59, pp. 58-86.

Gaulis, Inès. 2007. *Les leçons d'Angkor: dix ans de coopération internationale dans la région de Siem Reap-Angkor.* Unpublished research report.

Gauthier, André. 1933. *Le tourisme en Indochine. Itinéraires.* Paris: Publications de l'Agence Economique d'Indochine.

Gautier, Théophile. 1856. 'Tableaux, études et croquis de voyage', in *L'Artiste*, 28 December, p. 33.

Gebert, Rita, Ten Samrach, Solveig Buhl, and Martin Orth. 2007. *Mission Report. Ex Ante Poverty Impact Assessment for Regional Economic Development: Green Belt Siem Reap Province.* E-publication: http://www.oecd.org/dac/povertyreduction/38609100.pdf. Accessed 25 September 2016.

Geertz, Clifford. 1960. 'The Javanese Kijaji: The Changing Role of a Cultural Broker', in *Comparative Studies in Society and History*, 2:2, pp. 228-249.

—. 1983. *Savoir local, savoir global: les lieux du savoir.* Paris, PUF.

Gibert, Marie. 2014. *Les ruelles de Hô Chi Minh Ville, Viêt Nam. Trame viaire et recomposition des espaces publics.* PhD Thesis, Université de Paris 1.

Giebelhausen, Michaela. 2011. 'Museum Architecture: A Brief History', in Macdonald, Sharon (ed.), *A Companion to Museum Studies.* Malden/Oxford/Chichester: Blackwell Publishing, pp. 223-244.

Gillespie, Josephine. 2009. 'Protecting World Heritage: Regulating Ownership and Land Use at Angkor Archaeological Park, Cambodia', in *International Journal of Heritage Studies*, 15:4, pp. 338-354.

—. 2012. 'Buffering for Conservation at Angkor: Questioning the Spatial Regulation of a World Heritage Property', in *International Journal of Heritage Studies*, 18:2, pp. 194-208.

Gillman, Derek. 2010. *The Idea of Cultural Heritage.* New York: Cambridge University Press.

Gilpin, William. 1794. *Three Essays: On Picturesque Beauty; on Picturesque Travel; and on Sketching Landscape: To which is added a poem, on Landscape Painting.* London: R. Blamire.

GIZ. 2013. *Internal Paper 45. Update. Facts and Figures: Outreach and Impact of RED activities and Status of Indicator Achievement.* October 2013. Regional Economic Development Program (RED). Green Belt Siem Reap.

—. 2015. *Internal Paper 113. First Semi-Annual Progress Report 01/2015-06/2015. Regional Economic Development Program (REDIII).* August 2015.

Goldblum, Charles and Annik Osmont. 2008. 'Gouvernance urbaine et coopération internationale', in Bellina, Séverine et al. (eds), *La gouvernance démocratique. Un nouveau paradigme pour le développement.* Paris: Karthala, pp. 297-311.

—, Charles. 2012. 'Phnom Penh ou la métropolisation dépendante: entre processus d'urbanisation et stratégie d'aménagement', in Franck, Manuelle, Goldblum, Charles and Christian Taillard (eds), *Territoires de l'urbain en Asie du Sud-Est. Métropolisations en mode mineur.* Paris: CNRS Editions, pp. 25-74.

Gorer, Geoffrey. 1936. *Bali and Angkor. A 1930s Pleasure Trip Looking at Life and Death.* Singapore/Oxford/New York: Oxford University Press.

Gottman, Jean. 1973. *The Significance of Territory*. Charlottesville, VA: University Press of Virginia.
Graham, Brian, G.J. Ashworth, and J.E. Tunbridge. 2000. *A Geography of Heritage: Power, Culture, and Economy*. London: Arnold.
Grant Ross, Helen and Darryl L. Collins. 2006. *Building Cambodia: 'New Khmer Architecture' 1953-1970*. Bangkok: Key Publisher Company Limited.
Green, Maia. 2011. 'Circulating Compassion. Accounting of Some Categorical Practices in International Development', in Mosse, David (ed.), *Adventures in Aidland. The Anthropology of Professionals in International Development*. New York/Oxford: Berghahn, pp. 33-56.
Grosby, Steven. 1995. 'Territoriality: the Transcendental, Primordial Feature of Modern Societies', in *Nations and Nationalism*, 1:2, pp. 143-162.
Groslier, Bernard Philippe. 1958. *Angkor et le Cambodge au XVIe siècle d'après les sources portugaises et espagnoles*. Paris: PUF.
Groupe 8, with APSARA. 1999. *Assistance pour l'établissement de documents d'urbanisme réglementaire de Siem Reap Angkor. Rapport final*. Unpublished report.
Guanghua, Wan and Sebastian Iva. 2011. *Poverty in Asia and the Pacific. An Update*. ADB Economics Working Paper Series, No. 267. E-publication: https://www.adb.org/sites/default/files/publication/29051/economics-wp267.pdf. Accessed 25 September 2016.

Hall, Colin Michael and Stephen Page. 2000. *Tourism in South and Southeast Asia: Issues and Cases*. Oxford/Boston, MA: Butterworth Heinemann.
Hall, Melanie (ed.). 2011. *Towards World Heritage: International Origins of the Preservation Movement, 1870-1930*. Farnham: Ashgate.
Hamel, Bernard. 1965. 'Siem Reap Beneath the Towers of Angkor', in *Kambuja*, 8, pp. 59-67.
Hannerz, Ulf. 1992. *Cultural Complexity: Studies in the Social Organization of Meaning*. New York: Columbia University Press.
Hap, Phalthy. 2010. *The Implementation of Cambodia's Law on Land Tenure*. PhD Dissertation, Nagoya University.
Harrison, David and Michael Hitchcock (eds). 2005. *The Politics of World Heritage. Negotiating Tourism and Conservation*. Clevedon/Buffalo, NY/Toronto: Channel View Publication.
Harrison, Rodney. 2013. *Heritage. Critical Approaches*. London/New York: Routledge.
Hartshorne, Richard. 1939. 'The Nature of Geography. A Critical Survey of Current Thought in the Light of the Past', in *Annals of the Association of American Geography*, 29, pp. 173-644.
Hauser-Schäublin, Brigitta (ed.). 2012. *World Heritage. Angkor and Beyond. Circumstances and Implications of UNESCO Listing in Cambodia*. Göttingen: Göttingen Studies in Cultural Properties, vol. 2. E-publication: http://unesdoc.unesco.org/images/0021/002166/216667e.pdf. Accessed 25 September 2016.
Heder, Steve and Judy Ledgerwood. 1995. 'Politics of Violence: An Introduction', in Heder, Steve and Judy Ledgerwood (eds), *Propaganda, Politics, and Violence in Cambodia. Democratic Transition under United Nations Peace-Keeping*. Armonk, NY/London: M.E. Sharpe/East Gate Books.
Heikkila, Eric and Philippe Peycam. 2010. 'Economic Development in the Shadow of Angkor Wat: Meaning, Legitimation and Myth', in *Journal of Planning, Education and Research*, 29:3, pp. 294-309.
Heliot, Rebecca. 2015. 'Building Upon a Successful Past – What Could the Future Hold for Public Housing in Cambodia?', in *The Phnom Penh Post*, 28 May. E-publication: http://www.phnompenhpost.com/real-estate/building-upon-successful-past-what-could-future-hold-public-housing-cambodia. Accessed 11 August 2016.
Herzfeld, Michael. 2006. 'Spatial Cleansing. Monumental Vacuity and the Idea of the West', in *Journal of Material Culture*, 11:1-2, pp. 127-149.

—. 2016. *Siege of the Spirits. Community and Polity in Bangkok.* Chicago, IL: University of Chicago Press.

Hetreau-Pottier, Aline. 2008. 'The Urban Value of Siem Reap in the Shadow of Angkor', in Esposito, Adele and Sylvia Nam (eds), *Siem Reap. Urban Development in the Shadow of Angkor.* Los Angeles, CA: Getty Foundation, pp. 1-14.

—. 2008. « Siem Reap : dix ans de bouleversements à l'ombre d'Angkor », in Tertrais, Hugues (ed.), *Angkor VIIIe-XXIe siècle, Mémoire et identité khmères.* Paris: Ed. Autrement, pp. 182-204.

—. 2011. 'Patrimoine versus tourisme: enjeux et réalités de Siem Reap dans la vitrine d'Angkor', in Lancret, Nathalie (ed.) *Observatoire. Mutations architecturale et urbaine à la proximité d'un lieu patrimonial: approche comparative en Asie du Sud-Est,* 2, pp. 14-15.

Hevia, James L. 2002. 'World Heritage, National Culture and the Restoration of Chengde', in *Positions: East Asia Cultures Critique,* 9, pp. 219-243.

Hinton, Alexander L. 2005. *Why Did They Kill? Cambodia in the Shadow of Genocide.* Berkeley, CA: University of California Press.

Hitchcock, Michael, Nick Stanley, and King Chung Siu. 2005. 'The South-east Asian "Living Museum" and Its Antecedents', in Corsane, Gerard (ed.), *Heritage, Museums, and Galleries: An Introductory Reader.* Abingdon: Routledge, pp. 291-307.

Hitchcock, Michael, Victor T. King, and Michael Parnwell (eds). 2009. *Tourism in Southeast Asia. Challenges and New Directions.* Copenhagen: NIAS Press.

—. 2010. *Heritage Tourism in Southeast Asia.* Copenhagen: NIAS Press.

Hofstad, Hege. 2012. 'Compact City Development: High Ideals and Emerging Practices', in *European Journal of Spatial Development,* 49, pp. 1-23.

Hoggett, Paul (ed.). 1997. *Contested Communities. Experiences, Struggles, Policies.* Bristol: Policy Press.

Hollinshead, Keith. 2009. 'The "Worldmaking" Prodigy of Tourism: The Reach and Power of Tourism in the Dynamics of Change and Transformation', in *Tourism Analysis,* 14:1, pp. 139-152.

Hugues, Caroline. 2003. *The Political Economy of Cambodia's Transition 1991-2001.* London/New York: Routledge.

—. 2008. 'Cambodia in 2007: Development and Dispossession', in *Asian Survey,* 48:1, pp. 69-74.

—. 2009. *Dependent Communities. Aid and Politics in Cambodia and East Timor.* Ithaca, NY: Cornell University.

Hugues, Caroline and Kheang Un (eds). 2011. *Cambodia's Economic Transformations.* Copenhagen: NIAS Press.

Huy, Pan. 2003. 'La maison cambodgienne: choix du terrain, prescriptions et typologie', in *Péninsule,* 47, pp. 47-92.

Huybrechts, Eric and Frédéric Mauret. 2011. 'Phnom Penh (Cambodge): le renouveau de la planification urbaine', in *Urbanisme,* 379, pp. 32-36.

ICC Angkor and UNESCO. 2001. *Report of the ICC's Eleventh Technical Committee.*

—. 2002. *Report of the Tenth Plenary Session of the ICC.*

—. 2005. *Report of the ICC's Thirteenth Plenary Session.*

ICEA. 2005. *Etude de faisabilité d'un projet de développement urbain à Siem Reap Angkor. Rapport de phase 2. Version définitive.* Unpublished report.

ICOMOS. 2011. 'The Paris Declaration on Heritage as a Driver of Development', adopted during the 17th ICOMOS General Assembly, UNESCO Headquarters, 1 December. E-publication: http://www.icomos.org/Paris2011/GA2011_Declaration_de_Paris_EN_20120109.pdf. Accessed 29 July 2016.

Inskeep, Edward and Mark Kallenberger. 1992. *An Integrated Approach to Resort Development: Six Case Studies.* Madrid: World Tourism Organization.

IRIN. 2013. 'Ethnic Vietnamese in Cambodia Face Discrimination'. E-publication: http://www.irinnews.org/report/98786/ethnic-vietnamese-in-cambodia-face-discrimination. Accessed 25 September 2016.

Jenkins, Gwynn. 2008. *Contested Space: Cultural Heritage and Identity Reconstructions: Conservation Strategies within a Developing Asian City.* Vienna: Lit.

Jenks, Mike and Rod Burgess (eds). 2000. *Compact Cities. Sustainable Urban Forms for Developing Countries.* London/New York: Spon Press.

Jennings, Eric T. 2003. 'From Indochine to Indochic: The Lang Bian/Dalat Palace Hotel and French Colonial Leisure, Power and Culture', in *Modern Asian Studies*, 37, pp. 159-194.

JICA. 2002. *The Kingdom of Cambodia: From Reconstruction to Sustainable Development.* JICA Country Study for Japan's ODA. Tokyo: JICA.

—. 2005, *JICA Data Book on Siem Reap.* Unpublished report.

—. 2006. *The Study on Integrated Master Plan for Sustainable Development of Siem Reap/Angkor Town in the Kingdom of Cambodia*, 3 vols. Unpublished report.

—. 2010. *The Follow-up Study on Integrated Master Plan for Sustainable Development of Siem Reap City in the Kingdom of Cambodia. Final Report.* Unpublished report.

JICA (Economic Infrastructure Department). 2013. *Urban Growth for Inclusive and Dynamic Development.* E-publication: http://www.jica.go.jp/activities/issues/urban/ku57pq0000162yt1-att/toshi_en.pdf. Accessed 25 September 2016.

Johnson, Andrew. 2011. 'Re-centering the City: Spirits, Local Wisdom, and Urban Design at the Three Kings Monument of Chiang Mai', in *Journal of Southeast Asian Studies*, 42:3, pp. 511-531.

Johnston, Ron J. 1995. 'Territoriality and the State', in Benko, Georges B. and Ulf Strohmayer. *Geography, History and Social Sciences*, 27. Dordrecht/Boston, MA/London: Kluwer: Springer, pp. 213-225.

Jones, Michael. 2003. 'The Concept of Cultural Landscape: Discourse and Narratives', in Palang, Hannes and Gary Fry (eds), *Landscape Interfaces. Cultural Heritage in Changing Landscapes.* Dordrecht: Kluwer Academic Publishers, pp. 21-52.

Judd, Dennis R. 1999. 'Constructing the Tourist Bubble', in Judd, Dennis R. and Susan S. Fainstein (eds), *The Tourist City.* New Haven, CT: Yale University Press, pp. 35-53.

Judd, Dennis R. and Susan S. Fainstein (eds). 1999. *The Tourist City.* New Haven, CT: Yale University Press.

Kanki, Kiyoko, Laretna T. Adishakti, and Tintin Fatimah (eds). 2015. *Borobudur as Cultural Landscape. Local Communities' Initiatives for the Evolutive Conservation of Pusaka Saujana Borobudur.* Kyoto/Melbourne: Kyoto University Press and Trans Pacific Press.

Kant, Emmanuel. 2011. *Observations on the Feeling of the Beautiful and Sublime and other writings*, edited by Patrick Frierson and Paul Guyer. Cambridge: Cambridge University Press [1st edition 1764].

Kasfir, Nelson. 1976. *The Shrinking Political Arena.* Berkeley, CA: University of California Press.

Keating, Neal B. 2013. 'Kuy alterities: The struggle to conceptualise and claim Indigenous land rights in neoliberal Cambodia', in *Asia Pacific Viewpoint*, 54:3, pp. 309-322.

Kii, Masanobu and Kenji Doi. 2005. 'Multiagent Land-Use and Transport Model for the Policy Evaluation of a Compact City', in *Environment and Planning B: Planning and Design*, 32:4, pp. 485-504.

Kimsong, Kay and Matt Reed. 2001. 'Construction Permits Cited in APSARA Firing', in *The Cambodia Daily*, 9 June. E-publication: https://www.cambodiadaily.com/archives/construction-permits-cited-in-apsara-firing-23276/. Accessed 25 July 2016.

King, Anthony. 1995. *The Bungalow. The Production of a Global Culture.* New York/Oxford: Oxford University Press [first edition 1986].

King, Dwight. 2000. 'Corruption in Indonesia: A Curable Cancer?', in *Journal of International Affairs*, 53:2, pp. 603-624.

King, Kenneth and Simon McGrath. 2004. *Knowledge for Development? Comparing British, Japanese, Swedish and World Bank Aid.* London and New York: Zed Books.

King, Victor T. (ed.). 2016. *UNESCO in Southeast Asia. World Heritage Sites in Comparative Perspective.* Copenhagen: NIAS Press.

Kirshenblatt-Gimblett, Barbara. 2002. 'Intangible Heritage as Metacultural Production', in *Museum International*, 56: 1-2, pp. 52-65.

Krätke, Stefan. 2007. 'The Metropolization of the European Union and Regional System', in GaWC Research Bulletin, No. 193. E-publication: http://www.lboro.ac.uk/gawc/rb/rb193.html. Accessed 20 June 2016.

Kreps, Christina. 2003. *Liberating Culture: Cross-Cultural Perspectives on Museums, Curation and Heritage Preservation.* London/New York: Routledge.

Krippendorf, Jost and J.B. Perrin. 1969. 'Cambodge. Restauration des temples khmers. Incidences touristiques, économiques et techniques, No. 1638'. E-publication: http://aefek.free.fr/iso_album/krippendorf.pdf. Accessed 25 September 2016.

Kurfürst, Sandra. 2012. *Redefining Public Space in Hanoi. Places, Practices, and Meaning.* Berlin/Münster/Vienna [etc.]: LIT Verlag.

Kusno, Abidin. 2010. *The Appearances of Memory: Mnemonic Practices of Architecture and Urban Form in Indonesia.* Durham, NC: Duke University Press.

Lamprakos, Michele. 2014. 'The Idea of the Historic City', in *Change Over Time*, special issue *Conserving the City*, 4.1, pp. 8-39.

Land, Anthony and Peter Morgan. 2008. *Technical Cooperation for Capacity Development. Making the System Work Better. Final Report.* Cambodian Rehabilitation and Development Board – Council for the Development of Cambodia.

Lasansky, Medina and Brian McLaren (eds). 2004. *Architecture and Tourism: Perception, Performance, and Place.* Oxford/New York/Berg: Bloomsbury Publishing.

Lee, Jungchan and Kiyo Kurisu. 2015. 'Development of the Compact City Index and Its Application to Japanese Cities', in *Urban Studies*, 52:6, pp. 1054-1070.

Leiper, Neil. 1998. 'Cambodian Tourism: Potential, Problems and Illusions', in *Pacific Tourism Review*, 1:4, pp. 285-297.

Leisch, Harald. 2002. 'Gated Communities in Indonesia', in *Cities*, 19:5, pp. 341-350.

Leroy, Stéphane. 2000. 'Sémantiques de la métropolisation', in *L'Espace Géographique*, 1, pp. 78-86.

Lesmaitre, Anne and Sébastien Cavalier. 2012. 'Analyses and Management Prospects of the International Angkor Programme', in *Museum International. Angkor, a Living Museum*, 54:1-2, pp. 117-125.

Levy, Albert. 2008. 'Sémiotique de l'architecture: Contribution à une Etude du Projet Architectural', in *Actes Sémiotiques*, No. 111. E-publication: http://epublications.unilim.fr/revues/as/2993#tocfrom1n1. Accessed 25 February 2016.

Lewis, David J. and David Mosse (eds). 2006. *Development Brokers and Translators: the Ethnography of Aid and Agency.* Bloomfield, NJ: Kumarian Press.

Linz, Juan and Alfred Stepan. 1996. 'Toward Consolidated Democracies', *in Journal of Democracy*, 7:2, pp. 14-33.

Lloyd Rivera, Georgina. 2009. *The Safeguarding of Intangible Cultural Heritage: Law and Policy – A Case Study of Angkor.* PhD Thesis, University of Sydney.

Löfgren, Orvar. 2001. 'Know Your Country. A Comparative Perspective on Tourism and Nation Building in Sweden', in Baranowski, Shelley and Ellen Furlough (eds), *Being Elsewhere. Tourism, Consumer Culture, and Identity in Modern Europe and North America.* Ann Arbor, MI: The University of Michigan Press, pp. 137-154.

Logan, William S. 2001. 'Globalizing Heritage: World Heritage as a Manifestation of Modernism, and Challenges from the Periphery', in Jones, David (ed.), *Twentieth Century Heritage: Our Recent Cultural Legacy: Proceedings of the Australia ICOMOS National Conference 2001.* Adelaide: University of Adelaide and Australia ICOMOS, pp. 51-57.

Logan, William S. (ed.). 2002. *The Disappearing Asian City: Protecting Asia's Urban Heritage in a Globalizing World.* Oxford/New York: Oxford University Press.

Lombard, Denys. 1970. 'Pour une histoire des villes du Sud-Est asiatique', in *Annales ESC*, 25: 4, pp. 842-856.

Long, Norman. 1989. 'Theoretical reflections on actor, structure and interface', in Long, Norman (ed.), *Encounters at the Interface. A Perspective on Social Discontinuities in Rural Development.* Wageningen: Wageningen University, pp. 221-244.

—. 2001. *Development Sociology: Actor Perspectives.* London/New York: Routledge.

Loo Lee, Sim. 1996. 'Urban Conservation Policy and the Preservation of Historical and Cultural Heritage', in *Cities*, 13:6, pp. 399-409.

Loti, Pierre. 1996. *A Pilgrimage to Angkor.* Chiang Mai: Silkworm Books.

Lowenthal, David. 2015. *The Past is a Foreign Country.* Cambridge: Cambridge University Press [1st edition 1985].

Luco, Fabienne. 2008. '"Manger le territoire": pratiques anciennes et actuelles d'accès à la terre au Cambodge', in Forest, Alain (ed.), *Cambodge contemporain.* Paris: Les Indes Savantes, pp. 419-444.

—. 2016. *Les habitants d'Angkor. Une lecture dans l'espace et dans le temps, des inscriptions sociales de populations villageoises, installées dans un territoire ancien.* PhD Thesis, EHESS.

MacCannell, Dean. 1973. 'Staged Authenticity: Arrangements of Social Space in Tourist Settings', in *American Journal of Sociology*, 79:3, pp. 589-603.

—. 1976. *The Tourist: A New Theory of the Leisure Class.* New York: Schocken Books.

Malo, Henri. 1906. 'L'exposition coloniale de Marseille', in *Le Monde illustré*, 2545, 6 January, pp. 7-8.

Mangin, France. 2006. *Le patrimoine indochinois. Hanoï et autres sites.* Paris: Editions Recherche IPRAUS.

Marchal, Henri. 1928. *Guide archéologique aux temples d'Angkor: Angkor Wat, Angkor Thom et les monuments du petit et du grand circuit.* Paris/Brussels: G. Van Oest.

Markusen, Ann. 2004. 'The Work of Forgetting and Remembering Places', in *Urban Studies*, 41:12, pp. 2303-2313.

Mauret, Frédéric. 1996. *Identification et protection du patrimoine architectural et urbain de la ville de Siem Reap.* Unpublished report.

McDowell, Sara. 2008. 'Heritage, Memory, and Identity', in Graham, Brian and Peter Howard (eds). *The Routledge Research Companion to Heritage and Identity.* London/New York: Routledge, pp. 37-54.

Menzel, Jörg. 2012. *Cambodian Law: Some Comparative and International Perspectives.* Cambodia: Konrad-Adenauer-Stiftung.

Meskell, Lynn. 2015. 'Transacting UNESCO World Heritage: Gifts and Exchanges on a Global Stage', in *Social Anthropology*, 23: 1, pp. 3-21.

Miles, Suzanna W. 1957. 'Maya Settlement Patterns: A Problem for Ethnology and Archaeology', in *Southwestern Journal of Anthropology*, 13, pp. 239-248.

Milne, Sarah. 2013. 'Under the leopard's skin: Land commodification and the dilemmas of Indigenous communal title in upland Cambodia', in *Asia Pacific Viewpoint*, 54: 3, pp. 323-339.

Ministère de l'Information. 1963. *L'oeuvre du Sangkum Reastr Niyum, Bilan de Juin à Décembre 1962 présenté au XIVᵉ congrès international de 1963*. Unpublished report.

Mitchell, Timothy. 2002. *Rule of Experts: Egypt, Techno-Politics, Modernity*. Berkeley, CA: University of California Press.

Miura, Keiko. 2004. *Contested Heritage. The People of Angkor*. PhD Thesis, SOAS.

—. 2005. 'Conservation of a "Living Heritage Site". A Contradiction in Terms? A Case Study of Angkor World Heritage Site', in *Conservation and Management of Archaeological Sites*, 7, pp. 3-18.

—. 2010. 'World Heritage Sites in Southeast Asia: Angkor and Beyond', in Hitchcock, Michael, Victor T. King, and Michael Parnwell (eds), *Heritage Tourism in Southeast Asia*. Copenhagen: NIAS Press, pp. 103-129.

—. 2011. 'World Heritage Making in Angkor: Global, Regional, National and Local Actors, Interplays and Implications', in Hauser-Schäublin, Brigitta (ed.), *World Heritage. Angkor and Beyond. Circumstances and Implications of UNESCO Listing in Cambodia*. Göttingen: Göttingen Studies in Cultural Properties, vol. 2, pp. 9-32.

Molyvann, Vann H.E. 1991. *Parcs archéologiques d'Angkor*. Unpublished report.

—. 2003. *Modern Khmer Cities*. Phnom Penh: Reyum Publishing.

—. 2012. 'Management of the Angkor Site: National Emblem and World Heritage Site', in *Museum International. Angkor, a Living Museum*, 54:1-2, pp. 110-116.

Morton, Patricia. 2003. *Hybrid Modernities. Architecture and Representation at the 1931 Colonial Exhibition*. Cambridge, MA: Massachusetts Institute of Technology Press.

Mosse, David (ed.). 2011. *Adventures in Aidland: The Anthropology of Professionals in International Development*. New York: Berghahn Books.

Mouhot, Henri. 1989. *Voyage dans les royaumes de Siam, de Cambodge, et de Laos*. Genève: Editions Olizane [first edition 1863, in the magazine *Le Tour du monde*].

Nagaoka, Masanori. 2014. '"European" and "Asian" Approaches to Cultural Landscapes Management at Borobudur, Indonesia in the 1970s', in *International Journal of Heritage Studies*, 21:3, pp. 232-249.

Nam, Sylvia. 2011. 'Phnom Penh: From the Politics of Ruin to the Possibilities of Return', in *TDSR*, 23:1, pp. 55-68. E-publication: http://iaste.berkeley.edu/iaste/wp-content/uploads/2012/07/23.1-Fall-11-Nam.pdf. Accessed 25 September 2016.

Neef, Andreas, Siphat Touch, and Jammere Chiengthong. 2013. 'The Politics and Ethnics of Land Concessions in Rural Cambodia', in *Journal of Agricultural and Environmental Ethics*, 26, pp. 1085-1103.

Négri, Vincent. 2014. 'L'évolution des politiques d'inventaire au miroir du droit européen', in *L'inventaire général du patrimoine culturel: bilan d'une decentralisation,* special number of *L'Observatoire, la Revue des politiques culturelles*, 45, Winter 2014-2015, pp. 56-59.

Népote, Jacques. 2006. 'Understanding the Cambodian Dwelling: Space and Gender in Traditional Homes', in Tainturier, François (ed.), *Wooden Architecture of Cambodia. A Disappearing Heritage*. Phnom Penh: Center for Khmer Studies, pp. 108-123.

Neuman, Michael. 2015. 'The Compact City Fallacy', in *Journal of Planning, Education, and Research*, 25:1, pp. 11-26.

Neyret, Régis. 2004. 'Du monument isolé au "tout patrimoine"', in *Géocarrefour*, 79 :3, pp. 231-237.

Nielsen, Bjarke and Frédéric E. Illouz. 2013. 'L'UNESCO et le culturellement correct', in Berliner, David and Chiara Bortolotto (eds), *Le monde selon l'UNESCO*, special issue of *Gradhiva*, 18, pp. 74-97.

Nishigaki, Akira and Yasutami Shimomura. 1996. *The Economics of Development Assistance: Japan's ODA in a Symbiotic World.* Tokyo: LTCB International Library Foundation.

Nissen, Christine J. 2005. *Living Under the Rule of Corruption: An Analysis of Everyday Form of Corrupt Practices in Cambodia.* Center for Social Development. E-publication: http://www.csdcambodia.org/living_under_corruption/living_under_the_rule_corup_eng.pdf. Accessed 21 August 2017.

Norindr, Panivong. 1996. *Phantasmatic Indochina: French Colonial Ideology in Architecture, Film, and Literature.* Durham, NC/London: Duke University Press.

Nozeroy, Noël. 1907. 'L'exposition coloniale de Nogent sur Marne', in *Le Monde illustré*, 2616, 18 May, pp. 338-339.

Nyìri, Pál. 2009. 'Between Encouragement and Control: Tourism, Modernity, and Discipline in China', in Winter, Tim, Teo, Peggy and T.C. Chang (eds), *Asia on Tour. Exploring the Rise of Asian Tourism.* London/New York: Routledge, pp. 153-169.

OECD. 2014. 'Structural Policy Country Notes. Cambodia', in *Economic Outlook for Southeast Asia, China, and India 2014: Beyond the Middle-Income Trap.* E-publication: http://www.oecd-ilibrary.org/development/economic-outlook-for-southeast-asia-china-and-india-2014_saeo-2014-en. Accessed 30 July 2016.

Ojendal, Joakim and Mona Lilja (eds). 2009. *Beyond Democracy in Cambodia. Political Reconstruction in a Post-Conflict Society.* Copenhagen: NIAS.

Olivier de Sardan, Jean-Pierre. 2005. *Anthropology and Development. Understanding Contemporary Social Change.* London: Zed Books.

Olivier de Sardan, Jean-Pierre and Thomas Bierschenk. 1993. 'Les courtiers locaux du développement', in *Bulletin de l'APAD*, 5, pp. 71-76.

Olivieri, Claude, Jonathan Jourde, and Olivier Sudrie. 2009. *L'assistance technique française. Le cas du Cambodge.* Assessment report.

Ollier, Leakthina Chau-Pech and Tim Winter (eds). 2006. *Expressions of Cambodia: The Politics of Tradition, Identity, and Change.* London/New York: Routledge.

Olszewski, Peter. 2010. 'Museum Fails to Attract the Temple Tourists', in *The Phnom Penh Post*, 14 May. E-publication: http://www.phnompenhpost.com/siem-reap-insider/museum-fails-attract-temple-tourists. Accessed 15 September 2015.

O'Naghten, Hedwige M. 2000. *Les temples du Cambodge. Architecture et espace sacré.* Paris: Geuthner.

Ong, Aihwa. 2006. *Neoliberalism as Exception: Mutations in Citizenship and Sovereignty.* Durham, NC: Duke University Press.

O'Shaughnessy, John and Nicholas J. O'Shaughnessy. 2003. *The Marketing Power of Emotion.* Oxford: Oxford University Press.

Paasi, Anssi. 2003. 'Territory' in Agnew, John, Mitchell, Katharyne and Gerard Toal (eds), *A Companion to Political Geography.* Blackwell: Oxford, pp. 109-122.

Paling, Willem. 2012. 'Planning a Future for Phnom Penh: Mega Projects, Aid Dependence and Disjointed Governance', in *Urban Studies*, 49:13, pp. 2889-2912.

Pak, Kimchoeun, Vuthy Horng, Netra Eng et al. 2007. *Working Paper 34: Critical Literature Review on Accountability and Neo-Patrimonialism: Theoretical Discussions and the Case of Cambodia.* Phnom Penh: Cambodia Development Resource Institute.

Peleggi, Maurizio. 2002. *Lords of Things. The Fashioning of the Siamese Monarchy's Modern Image.* Honolulu, HI: University of Hawai'i Press.

—. 2005. 'Consuming Colonial Nostalgia: The Monumentalisation of Historic Hotels in Urban South-East Asia', in *Asia Pacific Viewpoint*, 46:3, pp. 255-265.

Pelliot, Paul. 1951. *Mémoires sur les coutumes du Cambodge de Tcheou Ta-Kouan. Version nouvelle d'un commentaire inachevé.* Paris: Adrien Maisonneuve.

Peng, Hor, Kong Phallack, and Jörg Menzel (eds). 2012. *Introduction to Cambodian Law.* Konrad Adenauer Stiftung. E-publication: http://www.khmerlex.com/Site/images/library_file/14-kas_31083-1522-2-30.pdf#page=482. Accessed 31 July 2016.

Penny, Dan, Christophe Pottier, Matti Kummu, et al. 2005. 'Hydrological History of the West Baray, Angkor, Revealed through Palynological Analysis of Sediments from the West Mebon', in *BEFEO*, 92, pp. 497-521.

Percival, Tom and Paul Waley. 2012. 'Articulating Intra-Asian Urbanism: The Production of Satellite Cities in Phnom Penh', in *Urban Studies*, 49:13, pp. 2873-2888.

Peycam, Philippe. 2010. 'Sketching an Institutional History of Academic Knowledge Production in Cambodia (1863-2009) – Part 1', in *Sojourn: Journal of Social Issues in Southeast Asia*, 25:2, pp. 153-177.

Phorn, Bopha. 2013. 'After Land Swap, Siem Reap Government Moves Again', in *The Cambodia Daily*, 6 September. E-publication: https://www.cambodiadaily.com/archives/after-land-swap-siem-reap-government-moves-again-41819/. Accessed 24 September 2015.

Picard, Michel. 1995. 'Cultural Heritage and Tourist Capital: Cultural Tourism in Bali', in Lanfant, Marie-Françoise, Allcock, John, and Edward Bruner (eds), *International Tourism: Identity and Change.* London/Thousand Oaks, CA: Sage, pp. 44-66.

Picard, Michel and Robert E. Wood. 1997. *Tourism, Ethnicity, and the State in Asian and Pacific Societies.* Honolulu, HI: Hawai'i University Press.

Placenter Ltd and Sawac. 2004. *Chong Kneas Port Development and Environmental Improvement.* Unpublished Report.

Pleşu, Andrei. 2007. *Pittoresque et mélancolie. Une analyse du sentiment de la nature dans la culture européenne.* Paris: Somogy.

Plush, Hazel. 2016. 'Angkor Wat Enforces Strict Dress Code After Spate of Nude Photography', in *The Telegraph*, 8 July. E-publication: http://www.telegraph.co.uk/travel/destinations/asia/cambodia/articles/cambodia-angkor-wat-enforces-strict-new-dress-code/. Accessed 18 August 2016.

Pottier, Christophe. 1998. 'Elaboration d'une carte archéologique de la région d'Angkor', in Manguin, Pierre Y. (ed.), *Southeast Asian Archaeology: Proceedings of the 5th International Conference of the European Association of Southeast Asian Archaeologists, Paris, 24th-28th October 1994*, vol. 1. Hull: University of Hull Press, pp. 179-195.

—. 2003. 'Nouvelles recherches sur l'aménagement du territoire angkorien à travers l'histoire', in *Comptes rendus des séances de l'Année – Académie des inscriptions et belles-lettres*, No. 1, 147th year, pp. 427-449.

Prak, Chan Thul. 2005. 'Siem Reap River Residents to be Relocated', in *The Cambodia Daily*, 10 May. E-publication: https://www.cambodiadaily.com/archives/siem-reap-river-residents-to-be-relocated-47589/. Accessed 24 September 2015.

Prak, Vireak. 2006. 'Wooden Houses of the Early Twentieth Century: Settlement Patterns, Social Distinction and Ethnicity', in Tainturier, François (ed.), *Wooden Architecture of Cambodia. A Disappearing Heritage.* Phnom Penh: Center for Khmer Studies, pp. 66-89.

Preuil, Sébastien. 2011. 'Le Tonlé Sap au Cambodge: vers une exploitation touristique à trois voies?', in Boujrouf, Said and Ouidad Tebbaa (eds), *Tourisme et pauvreté.* Paris: Editions des

Archives Contemporaines, pp. 177-188. E-publication: http://www.bibliotheque.auf.org/doc_num.php?explnum_id=858. Accessed 29 July 2016.

—. 2014. *La mise en tourisme du patrimoine khmer de la province de Siem Reap au Cambodge: aide à la lute contre la pauvreté ou facteur de paupérisation?* PhD Thesis, Université Versailles St Quentin en Yvelines.

Prigent, Lionel. 2013. 'L'inscription au patrimoine mondial de l'UNESCO, les promesses d'un label?', in *Revue internationale et stratégique*, 90:2, pp. 127-135.

Prud'homme, Rémy. 1969. *L'économie du Cambodge*. Paris: PUF.

Quaintenne, Rose de. 1909. *Quinze jours au pays des rois khmers*. Saigon: Imprimerie Condurier & Montégout.

Quijano, Aníbal. 1992. 'Colonialidad y Modernidad/Racionalidad', in *Perú Indígena*, 13 :29, pp. 11-20.

Rabé, Paul. 2005. 'Land Sharing in Phnom Penh: An Innovative but Insufficient Instrument of Secure Tenure for the Poor', in Expert Group Meeting on Secure Land Tenure: New Legal Frameworks and Tools UN-ESCAP, Bangkok, Thailand, 8-9 December 2005.

—. 2009. *From 'Squatters' to Citizens? Slum Dwellers, Developers, Land Sharing and Power in Phnom Penh*. PhD Thesis, Faculty of the USC School of Policy, Planning and Development. University of Southern California. E-publication: http://digitallibrary.usc.edu/cdm/ref/collection/p15799coll127/id/287313. Accessed 20 August 2017.

Rabinow, Paul. 1995. *French Modern: Norms and Forms of the Social Environment*. Chicago, IL: Chicago University Press.

Raj Isar, Yudhishthir. 2011. 'UNESCO and Heritage: Global Doctrine, Global Practice', in Raj Isar, Yudhishthir (ed.), *Heritage, Memory & Identity*. London/Thousand Oaks, CA: Sage, pp. 39-52.

Rakic, Tijana and Donna Chambers. 2008. 'World Heritage: Exploring the Tension between the National and the Universal', in *International Journal of Heritage Studies*, 2:3, pp. 145-155.

Rann Reuy. 2009. 'Along Siem Reap River, Families to be Relocated', in *The Phnom Penh Post*, 15 December. E-publication: http://www.phnompenhpost.com/national/along-siem-reap-river-families-be-relocated. Accessed 1 August 2016.

Reiner, Alain. 1982. 'Espace, représentation et sémiotique de l'architecture', in *Espace et représentation, Penser l'espace*. Paris: Editions de la Villette.

Renard, Vincent. 2003. 'Les enjeux urbains des prix fonciers et immobiliers', in Prager, Jean-Claude (ed.), *Ville et économie*. Paris: La Documentation française, pp. 85-108.

Richmond, Oliver P. and Jason Franks. 2007. 'Liberal Hubris? Virtual Peace in Cambodia', in *Security Dialogue*, 38:1, pp. 27-48.

Riegl, Aloïs. 1984. *Le culte moderne des monuments. Sa nature, son origine*. Paris: Seuil [1st edition 1903].

Riman, Josef. 1968. *Cambodge. Mise en valeur des temples khmères*. Report. Paris: ICOMOS Archives, No. 606/BMS.RD/CLT.

Roberts, David. 2008. 'Hybrid Polities and Indigenous Pluralities: Advanced Lessons in Statebuilding from Cambodia'. in *Journal of Intervention and Statebuilding*, 2:1, pp. 63-86.

Robinson, Jennifer. 2006. *Ordinary Cities: Between Modernity and Development*. London: Routledge.

Roberts, David. 2009. 'The superficiality of statebuilding in Cambodia: Patronage and clientelism as enduring forms of politics', in Paris, Roland and Timothy Sisk (eds). *The Dilemmas of Statebuilding: Confronting the Contradictions of Postwar Peace Operations*, London: Routledge, pp. 149-70.

Rondet-Saint, Maurice. 1916. *Choses de l'Indochine contemporaine*. Paris: Librairie Plon.

Ros, Borath and Aline Hetreau-Pottier. 1993. *UNESCO Project. Zoning and Environmental Management Plan for the Angkor Area (ZEMP). Urban Development.* Unpublished report.

Rössler, Mechtild. 2015. 'The Landscape Approach. A Global Context for Sustainability', in Albert, Marie-Thérèse. *Perceptions of Sustainability in Heritage Studies.* Berlin/Boston, MA: Walter de Gruyter, pp. 59-69.

Rossi, Jean-Yves. 1993. *Un cadre juridique pour la gestion du site d'Angkor. Rapport de mission.* Unpublished report.

Rowntree, Lester B. 1996. 'The Cultural Landscape Concept in American Human Geography', in *Concepts in Human Geography*, 70:4, pp. 459-474.

Royal Government of Cambodia. 2010. *National Strategic Development Plan. Update 2009-2013. For Growth, Employment, Equity and Efficiency to Reach Cambodia Millennium Development Goals.*

Ryan, Jason and Sari Silvanto. 2009. 'The World Heritage List: The Making and Management of a Brand', in *Place Branding and Public Democracy*, 5:4, pp. 290-300.

Rykwert, Joseph. 1973. *La maison d'Adam au paradis.* Paris: Seuil.

Sack, Robert. 1983. 'Human Territoriality: A Theory', in *Annals of the Association of American Geographers*, 73:1, pp. 55-74.

Sandhu, Kernial S. and Paul Wheatley (eds). 1983. *Melaka: the Transformation of a Malay Capital, c. 1400-1980.* Kuala Lumpur/New York: Oxford University Press.

Sanjuan, Thierry (ed.). 2003. *Les grands hôtels en Asie. Modernité, dynamiques urbaines et sociabilité.* Paris: Publications de la Sorbonne.

Sassen, Saskia. 2012. 'Novel Spatial Formats for Urban Inclusion. Megaregions and Global Cities'. E-publication: http://www.booksandideas.net/_Sassen-Saskia_.html. Accessed 20 June 2016.

Sato, Jin, Hiroaki Shiga, Takaaki Kobayashi, and Hisahiro Kondoh. 2011. '"Emerging Donors" from a Recipient Perspective: An Institutional Analysis of Foreign Aid in Cambodia', in *World Development*, 39:12, pp. 2091-2104.

Sauer, Carl. 1925. *The Morphology of Landscape.* Berkeley, CA: University of California.

von Schiller, Friedrich. 1801. *On the Sublime* [translated by William F. Wertz]. E-publication: http://philosophyproject.org/wp-content/uploads/2013/04/On-the-Sublime-Schiller.pdf. Accessed 10 August 2016.

Schneider, Alison E. 2011. 'What Shall We Do Without Our Land? Land Grabs and Resistance in Rural Cambodia', Paper presented at the International Conference on Global Land Grabbing, 6-8 April 2011. E-publication: http://citeseerx.ist.psu.edu/viewdoc/download?doi=10.1.1.455.1144&rep=rep1&type=pdf. Accessed 1 August 2016.

Ségalen, Victor. 1986. *Essai sur l'exotisme.* Clément de la Rivière: Fata Morgana [first edition 1976].

Selwyn, Tom (ed.). 1996. *The Tourist Image: Myths and Myth Making in Tourism.* Chichester/New/ York [etc.]: John Wiley & Sons.

Sengupta, Indra. 2015. 'Culture-keeping as State Action: Bureaucrats, Administrators, and Monuments in Colonial India', in *Past and Present*, 226: 10, pp. 153-177.

Sharpley, Richard. 2000. 'Tourism: A Vehicle for Development?', in Sharpley, Richard and David J. Telfer (eds), *Tourism and Development: Concepts and Issues.* Clevedon, NY: Channel Views Publications, pp. 11-34.

Shatkin, Gavin. 1998. '« Fourth World » Cities in the Global Economy: The Case of Phnom Penh, Cambodia', in *International Journal of Urban and Regional Research*, 22:3, pp. 378-393.

Shaw, Brian J. and Gareth Shaw. 1999. '"Sun, Sand and Sales": Enclave Tourism and Local Entrepreneurship in Indonesia', in *Current Issues in Tourism*, 2:1, pp. 68-81.

Silva, Kapila and Neel Kamal Chapagain (eds). 2014. *Asian Heritage Management: Contexts, Concerns, and Prospects.* London/New York: Routledge.

Smith, Dorothy E. (ed.). 2006. *Institutional Ethnography as Practice.* Lanham, MD/Boulder, CO/ New [etc.]: Rowman & Littlefield Publishers, Inc.
Smith, Laurajane. 2006. *Uses of Heritage.* London/New York: Routledge.
Smith, Laurajane and Emma Waterton. 2009. *Heritage, Communities and Archaeology.* London/ New York: Bloomsbury Publishing.
Smith, Melanie. 2007. *Tourism, Culture, and Regeneration.* Wallingford: CAP Publications.
Smith, Valene. 1989. *Hosts and Guests. The Anthropology of Tourism.* Philadelphia, PA: University of Pennsylvania Press.
Söderberg, Marie (ed.). 1996. *The Business of Japanese Foreign Aid: Five Case Studies from Asia.* London/New York: Routledge.
Sokphea, Young. 2015. 'Political Economy of State, Business and Civil Societies Interactions in the Era of Globalization: A Cambodia Perspective'. Paper given at the International Convention of Asia Scholars (ICAS), 8 July.
Sophean, Phuoeng. 1997. 'La maison khmère', in APUR, *Phnom Penh à l'aube du XXIe siècle.* Paris: APUR, pp. 84-91.
Sor, Chandara. 2016a. 'Government Takes Over Reins of Angkor Ticket Sales', in *The Phnom Penh Post,* 5 January. E-publication: http://www.phnompenhpost.com/business/government-takes-over-reins-angkor-ticket-sales. Accessed 7 August 2016.
Sor, Chandara. 2016b. 'Angkor Visitor Numbers flat in 2015', in *The Phnom Penh Post,* 6 January. E-publication: http://www.phnompenhpost.com/business/angkor-visitor-numbers-flat-2015. Accessed 25 April 2017.
Springer, Simon. 2009a. 'Violence, Democracy, and the Neoliberal "Order": The Contestation of Public Space in Posttransitional Cambodia', in *Annals of the Association of American Geographers,* 99:1, pp. 138-162.
—. 2009b. 'Violent Accumulation: A Postanarchist Critique of Property, Dispossession, and the State of Exception in Neoliberalizing Cambodia', in *Annals of the Association of American Geographers,* 103:3, pp. 608-626.
—. 2010. *Cambodia's Neoliberal Order: Violence, Authoritarianism, and the Contestation of Public Space.* London/New York: Routledge.
—. 2011. 'Articulated Neoliberalism: The Specificity of Patronage Kleptocracy, and Violence in Cambodia's Neoliberalization', in *Environment and Planning A,* 43, pp. 2554-2570.
Storey, David. 2001. *Territories. The Claiming of Space.* London/New York: Routledge.
—. 2013. 'Violent Accumulation: A Postanarchist Critique of Property, Disposession, and the State of Exception in Neoliberalizing Cambodia', in *Annals of the Association of American Geographers,* 103:3, pp. 608-626.
Storey, David. 2001. *Territories.* London/New York: Routledge.
Strangio, Sebastian. 2011. 'North Korea's New Friend?', in *The Diplomat,* 14 August. E-publication: http://thediplomat.com/2011/08/north-koreas-new-friend/. Accessed 10 March 2016.
Sullivan, Nicky. 2016. 'Bringing Modernism Back to SR Architecture', in *The Phnom Penh Post,* 17 June. E-publication: http://www.phnompenhpost.com/post-weekend/bringing-modernism-back-sr-architecture. Accessed 11 August 2016.
Sundaram, Ravi. 2010. *Pirate Modernity. Delhi's Media Urbanism.* London/New York: Routledge.

Tainturier, François (ed.). 2006. *Wooden Architecture of Cambodia. A Disappearing Heritage.* Phnom Penh: Center for Khmer Studies.
Tambiah, Stanley J. 2013. 'The Galactic Polity in Southeast Asia', in *HAU: Journal of Ethnographic Theory,* 3:3, pp. 503-534 [1st edition 1976]. E-publication: www.haujournal.org/index.php/hau/ article/...3.../479. Accessed 21 September 2016.

Teo, Peggy, T.C. Chang, and K.C. Ho (eds). 2000. *Interconnected Worlds. Tourism in Southeast Asia*. Oxford: Elsevier.

Teo, Peggy and T.C. Chang. 2009. 'Singapore's Postcolonial Landscape: Boutique Hotels as Agents', in Winter, Tim, Teo, Peggy and T.C. Chang (eds). *Asian on Tour. Exploring the Rise of Asian Tourism*. London/New York: Routledge, pp. 81-96.

Tertrais, Hugues (ed.). 2008. *Angkor VIIIe-XXIe siècle. Mémoire et identité khmères*. Paris: Autrement.

Thongchai, Winichakul. 1994. *Siam Mapped: A History of the Geo-Body of a Nation*. Honolulu, HI: University of Hawai'i Press.

Thoraxy, Hing. 1999. *Investments in Cambodia*. Phnom Penh: Cambodian Institute for Cooperation and Peace.

—. 2006. *The Cambodian Investment Challenges in Global Competitiveness*. Phnom Penh: JICA.

Tik, Kaliyann. 2011. 'Siem Reap River Families Agree to Relocate', in *The Phnom Penh Post*, 24 February. E-publication: http://www.phnompenhpost.com/national/siem-reap-river-families-agree-relocate. Accessed 1 August 2016.

—. 2013. 'River Widening Project to Displace 600 families', *The Phnom Penh Post*, 14 November. E-publication: http://www.phnompenhpost.com/national/river-widening-project-displace-600-families. Accessed 24 September 2015.

—. 2014. 'Work Begins on Mega Resort', in *The Phnom Penh Post*, 1 May. E-publication: http://www.phnompenhpost.com/business/work-begins-mega-resort. Accessed 5 August 2016.

TRACTABEL. 1997. *Plan directeur des transports de la province de Siem Reap, Rapport Final*. European Commission.

Turnbull, Robert. 2008. 'A New Museum Puts a Thai Print on Angkor', in *The New York Times*, 2 July. E-publication: http://www.nytimes.com/2008/07/03/arts/03iht-TURNBULL.1.14161266.html?_r=0. Accessed 4 August 2016.

Turtinen, Jan. 2000. *Globalising Heritage: On UNESCO and the Transnational Construction of a World Heritage*. E-publication: http://www.score.su.se/polopoly_fs/1.26651.1320939806!/200012.pdf. Accessed 25 September 2016.

Tyner, James A., Samuel Henkin, and Savina Sirik. 2014. 'Phnom Penh During the Cambodian Genocide: a Case of Selective Urbicide', in *Environment and Planning A*, 46, pp. 1873-1891.

Un, Kheang. 2011. 'State, Society, and Democratic Consolidation: The Case of Cambodia', in *Pacific Affairs*, 79:2, pp. 225-245.

Un, Kheang, and Sokbunthoeun So. 2011. 'Land Rights in Cambodia: How Neopatrimonial Politics Restricts Land Policy Reforms', in *Pacific Affairs*, 84:2, pp. 289-308.

UNCED. 1993. *Agenda 21*. E-publication: https://sustainabledevelopment.un.org/content/documents/Agenda21.pdf. Accessed 25 September 2016.

UNDP. 2002. *United Trade Conference on Trade and Development*. Unpublished Report.

UNESCO World Heritage Committee. 1991. *Angkor. WHC Nomination Documentation*. File 668.pdf. UNESCO Archives.

—. 1993. *Proceedings of the Intergovernmental Conference on the Safeguarding and the Development of the Historical Area of Angkor* (*Tokyo 12-13 October 1993*). E-publication: http://unesdoc.unesco.org/images/0014/001493/149373mo.pdf. Accessed 21 July 2016.

—. 2004. *Comité du patrimoine mondial. Décisions adoptées lors de sa 28e session du comité du patrimoine mondial* (*Suzhou, 2004*). E-publication: http://whc.unesco.org/archive/2004/whc04-28com-26f.pdf. Accessed 25 September 2016.

—. 2005. *Operational Guidelines for the Implementation of the World Heritage Convention*. WHC 05/2. E-publication: http://whc.unesco.org/archive/opguide05-en.pdf. Accessed 29 July 2016.

—. 2008. *World Heritage and Buffer Zones*. World Heritage Papers No. 25. E-publication: whc.unesco.org/document/101967. Accessed 25 September 2016.
—. 2009. *UNESCO's Work to Protect Cultural and Natural Heritage Worldwide: A Grand Tradition*. E-publication: whc.unesco.org/document/102656. Accessed 25 September 2016.
—. 2013. *CIC pour Angkor. 15 ans de coopération internationale pour la conservation et le développement durable*. E-publication: http://unesdoc.unesco.org/images/0018/001890/189018f.pdf. Accessed 25 September 2016.
Urry, John. 2002. *The Tourist Gaze*. London: Sage [first edition 1990].

Veblen, Thorstein. 1994. *The Theory of the Leisure Class*. New York: Dover Publications Inc. [1st edition 1899].
Viaro, Mario A. 1992. 'Le compartiment chinois est-il chinois?', in *Les Cahiers de la recherche architecturale*, 27-28, pp. 139-150.
Vigers, Dick. 2005. 'A Tale of Two Cities: Angkor and Siem Reap – the Evolution of Competing Sites of Memory', in *Journal of Romance Studies*, 5:1, pp. 91-104.

Wager, Jonathan. 1995a. 'Developing a Strategy for the Angkor World Heritage Site', in *Tourism Management*, 16:7, pp. 515-523.
—. 1995b. 'Environmental Planning for a World Heritage Site: Case Study of Angkor, Cambodia', in *Journal of Environmental Planning and Management*, 38:3, pp. 419-434.
Watanabe, Toshio. 2006. 'How Should Japanese ODA be Viewed? The Importance of Support for Self-Help Efforts', in *Asia-Pacific Review*, 13: 2, pp. 17-26.
Waterton, Emma and Steve Watson. 2013. 'Framing Theory: Towards a Critical Imagination in Heritage Studies', in *International Journal of Heritage Studies*, 19:6, pp. 546-561.
Weber, Max. 1964. *The Theory of Social and Economic Organization*. New York: Free Press of Glencoe/London: Collier-MacMillan [1st edition 1947].
Wheatley, Paul. 1969. 'City as Symbol', an inaugural lecture delivered at University College, London, 1967. First published by H.K. Lewis. E-publication: http://isites.harvard.edu/fs/docs/icb.topic1152255.files/Whealey_1969_City%20as%20Symbol.pdf. Accessed 21 September 2016.
Williamson, John (ed.). 1990. *Latin American Adjustment*. Washington: Institute for International Economics.
Wilk, Richard. 1995. 'Learning to be Local in Belize: Global Systems of Common Difference', in Miller, Daniel (ed.), *Worlds Apart: Modernity Through the Prism of the Local*. New York: Routledge, pp. 110-133.
Wilkins, Emily. 2014. 'Siem Reap Gains its First Asian Traditional Textile Museum', in *The Cambodia Daily*, 10 April. E-publication: https://www.cambodiadaily.com/archives/siem-reap-gains-its-first-asian-tra%C2%ADditional-textile-museum-56340/. Accessed 15 September 2015.
Wilson Gilmore, Ruth. 2008. 'Forgotten Places and the Seeds of Grassroots Planning', in Hale, Charles R. (ed.), *Engaging Contradictions. Theory, Politics, and Methods of Activist Scholarship*. Berkeley/Los Angeles, CA/London: University of California Press, pp. 31-61.
Winter, Tim. 2007. *Post-Conflict Heritage, Postcolonial Tourism. Culture, Politics, and Development at Angkor*. London/New York: Routledge.
—. 2008. 'Postconflict Heritage and Tourism in Cambodia: the Burden of Angkor', in *International Journal of Heritage Studies*, 14, pp. 524-539.
—. 2015. 'Heritage Diplomacy', in *International Journal of Heritage Studies*, 21:10, pp. 1-19.
—. 2016. 'Heritage Diplomacy Along the One Belt One Road', in *IIAS Newsletter*, 74, Summer 2016, pp. 8-10.

Winter, Tim, Teo, Peggy, and T.C. Chang (eds). 2009. *Asia on Tour: Exploring the Rise of Asian Tourism*. London/New York: Routledge.
Winter, Tim and Patrick Daly (eds). 2012. *Routledge Handbook of Heritage in Asia*. London/New York: Routledge.
World Bank, 2010. *Environmental Management Framework. Livelihood Enhancement & Association of the Poor in Siem Reap Project (LEAP)*. E-publication: http://documents.worldbank.org/curated/en/981841468016186598/pdf/E2519oV30P09701IC10EMFoforoLEAP1ENG.pdf. Accessed 30 July 2016.
World Travel & Tourism Council. 2014. *Travel & Tourism. Economic Impact 2014 Cambodia*. E-publication: https://www.wttc.org/-/media/files/reports/economic%20impact%20research/regional%202015/world2015.pdf. Accessed 30 July 2016.

ZEMP Team. 1993. *Zoning and Environmental Management Plan for Angkor*. Discussion Draft.
—. 1994. *Synthesis Report on the Zoning and Environmental Management of Angkor within the Siem Reap Region*. Unpublished report.
Zytnichi, Colette and Habib Kazdaghli (eds). 2009. *Le tourisme dans l'Empire français. Politiques, pratiques, et imaginaires (XIXe-XXe siècle): un outil de domination colonial?* Paris: Société française d'Outre-Mer.

Index

International Institute for Asian Studies

Publications / Asian Cities

Norman Vasu, Yeap Su Yin and Chan Wen Ling (eds): *Immigration in Singapore*
2014, ISBN 978 90 8964 665 1

Gregory Bracken (ed.): *Asian Cities. Colonial to Global*
2015, ISBN 978 90 8964 931 7

Lena Scheen: *Shanghai Literary Imaginings. A City in Transformation*
2015, ISBN 978 90 8964 587 6

Anila Naeem: *Urban Traditions and Historic Environments in Sindh. A Fading Legacy of Shikarpoor, Historic City*
2017, ISBN 978 94 6298 159 1

Siddhartha Sen: *Colonizing, Decolonizing, and Globalizing Kolkata. From a Colonial to a Post-Marxist City*
2017, ISBN 978 94 6298 111 9